Educational Partnerships
SERVING STUDENTS AT RISK

Educational Partnerships
SERVING STUDENTS AT RISK

Marshall Welch • Susan M. Sheridan
University of Utah

Harcourt Brace College Publishers

Fort Worth   Philadelphia   San Diego   New York   Orlando   Austin   San Antonio
Toronto   Montreal   London   Sydney   Tokyo

Publisher	Ted Buchholz
Senior Acquisitions Editor	Jo-Anne Weaver
Project Editor	Erica Lazerow/Krystyn Freidlin
Senior Production Manager	Ken Dunaway
Senior Art Director	David A. Day

Address for Editorial Correspondence
Harcourt Brace College Publishers, 301 Commerce Street, Suite 3700, Fort Worth, TX 76102

Address for Orders
Harcourt Brace & Company, 6277 Sea Harbor Drive, Orlando, FL 32887
1-800-782-4479, or 1-800-433-0001 (in Florida)

ISBN: 0-15-500954-0

Library of Congress Catalogue Number: 94-75545

Printed in the United States of America

4 5 6 7 8 9 0 1 2 3   039   9 8 7 6 5 4 3 2 1

To our lifelong partners. . .
Julie, Justin and Jordan, Steve and Erin.

Preface

This is an exciting time to be an educator. An increasing array of challenges face educators as students with diverse needs continue to enter school. Educators cannot address these challenges alone. The continuing reform dialogue emphasizes a collaborative approach whereby teachers, specialists, and administrators forge partnerships with parents and the community to help students become meaningful members of society. This rhetoric, however, does not typically include a discussion of how these partnerships are formed. Implicit in the dialogue is the assumption that educators have the necessary skills and opportunities to establish and maintain educational partnerships. Reality, however, suggests that most educators enter the profession with few or no skills for working with colleagues or parents. Furthermore, most educators are quickly socialized by the culture and organization of the school to face challenges alone or in isolated settings. We believe that a critical component of professional preparation programs is the inclusion of theoretically based strategies for educational partnerships. Therefore, this textbook has been developed for use in advanced undergraduate, introductory graduate courses or staff development programs for classroom teachers, special educators, school psychologists, school counselors, school social workers, and administrators.

This textbook has been developed to provide theory coupled with practical application to educators who will work with other professionals, parents, and community agencies. We see it as a tool kit. The theoretical components serve as the blueprint, and the various strategies serve as the tools to develop and maintain educational partnerships in the classroom, school, home, and community. Many of the tools and ideas presented in this textbook represent new approaches to meeting the needs of students at risk. We propose some fundamental changes in how things have traditionally been done in the classroom, school, home, and community. We have spotlighted some exemplary programs or projects from across the country to illustrate the ways in which various concepts presented throughout the book have been put into practice. This textbook is based on an ecological perspective, in which the student at risk is at the center of a collaborative process. Partnerships are formed using a variety of human, information, technological, and physical resources in the school, home, and community settings to attain common goals that will empower students to become meaningful members of society.

This textbook is divided into four parts.

Part I - Educational Partnerships: The Foundation for Serving Students At Risk consists of four chapters that present the theoretical base for the book. Chapter 1 introduces the framework of educational partnerships by exploring the historical context and the basic tenets of collaboration. Characteristics of students considered to be at risk are described in Chapter 2. Various theoretical models for collaborative problem solving and decision making are presented in Chapter 3. Also included in this chapter is a comprehensive overview of an ecological approach to collaboration. Effective communication skills and conflict management strategies are discussed in Chapter 4.

Part II - The School: A Spectrum of Educational Partnerships begins in Chapter 5 with an examination of the traditional and evolving components of the school. This chapter explores the culture and organization of the school as well as traditional and reconceptualized roles of educators within the school. Chapter 6 presents various strategies for carrying out traditional and alternative assessment procedures that can be used throughout the development and implementation of educational partnerships. Instructional and behavioral strategies for the classroom are presented in Chapter 7. Each of the strategies discussed is theoretically and empirically based yet practical for use by a single teacher with a diverse group of students. Strategies for developing, implementing, and evaluating school-based partnerships such as teacher assistance teams, team-teaching, or consultation programs are presented in Chapter 8.

Part III - Home and Community: Expanding the Spectrum of Educational Partnerships consists of three chapters. Chapter 9 considers the changing home ecology and family in terms of their traditional and reconceptualized roles in home–school partnerships. Practical strategies for establishing and maintaining home–school partnerships are presented in Chapter 10. Establishing school–community partnerships is explored in Chapter 11.

Part IV - Educational Partnerships: The Future consists of a single, concluding chapter that explores a variety of issues related to educational partnerships.

Each chapter includes an overview of topics, instructional objectives, key vocabulary terms, and case studies that can be used as learning activities. We believe that the information presented in this textbook will provide entry-level skills that can be used to establish educational partnerships to meet the needs of students who are at risk.

About the Authors

Marshall Welch, Ph.D.

Marshall Welch received his Ph.D. in Special Education from Southern Illinois University in 1987. He is an Associate Professor and has been the coordinator of the teacher education program in the Department of Special Education at the University of Utah to prepare specialists in the area of mild to moderate disabilities since 1987. He has been the principal investigator on two previous, federally funded personnel preparation projects, both of which were designed to prepare specialists to work collaboratively with classroom teachers and related service personnel. Dr. Welch has conducted numerous field-based investigations in the areas of collaborative consultation and the use of learning strategies as a team-teaching tool for general and special educators in mainstream settings. Dr. Welch has been instrumental in the development of inter-disciplinary professional development sites for pre-professionals in special education, general education, educational psychology, and educational administration. He serves on the advisory boards of two school districts and the Utah Education Consortium for the development of school sites used for interdisciplinary personnel preparation programs. He is on the editorial review board of *Remedial and Special Education* and *Teacher Education and Special Education*.

Dr. Welch teaches courses on collaboration at the undergraduate and graduate level. He has numerous publications on his research in the area of collaboration in teacher education and teacher inservice. He has also conducted considerable research on the effectiveness of distance education in teacher education and teacher inservice which was acknowledged by an award presented by the American Council of Rural Special Education. Additionally, he has developed and produced several video productions that include video-mediated learning strategy instruction, teacher inservice programs, and teacher education programs. He has approximately 500 clock hours in front of a camera conducting teacher education and inservice presentations. Prior to coming to the University of Utah as coordinator of the teacher education program in the area of mild to moderate disabilities, Dr. Welch was both a secondary education social studies and special education teacher in a resource room for students with learning disabilities. Prior to his years as an educator, Dr. Welch was a professional musician and composer.

His personal interests include hiking and camping in the mountains and deserts of Utah with his family.

Susan M. Sheridan, Ph.D.

Susan M. Sheridan received her Ph.D. in Educational Psychology from the University of Wisconsin-Madison in 1989. There she co-wrote several grants, conducted research, and published many articles on consultation and collaboration with her advisor. Dr. Thomas R. Kratochwill. Specifically, she assisted in the development, coordination, implementation, and supervision of a three-year training grant designed to train school psychologists to serve as consultants to special education teachers of behaviorally disordered children. Likewise, Dr. Sheridan conceptualized a service delivery model designed to engage parents actively in collaborative educational problem solving (i.e., "conjoint behavioral consultation"). Many research projects have been conducted evaluating the effectiveness of this model. She also has an extensive publication list of articles and textbook chapters on the topic of collaborative consultation and home-school partnerships.

Dr. Sheridan is currently an Associate Professor in the Department of Educational Psychology at the University of Utah. Since arriving to Utah in 1989, Dr. Sheridan has had on-going research or has assisted in several projects in various local educational agencies. As a result of her scholarship and research productivity at the University of Utah, Dr. Sheridan was bestowed the 1993 Lightner Witmer award by the Division of School Psychology of the American Psychological Association for early career accomplishments. She has published several chapters and journal articles on the topic of consultation and collaboration, and has presented at several local, state, and national conferences.

Dr. Sheridan is President of the Utah Association of School Psychologists and editor of the state newsletter (The Observer). She has served on the Utah long-range strategic planning in education committee, and is currently the representative of the Utah Association of School Psychologists/ Department of Educational Psychology to the Advisory Board of the Utah Center for Families in Education.

At the national level, Dr. Sheridan chairs the Publications Committee of Division 16 (Division of School Psychology) of the American Psychological Association and has been program chair for Division 16's APA convention for two years. She is an associate editor for a major journal in school psychology *(School Psychology Quarterly)* and serves on the editorial board of three other journals. She is a Nationally Certified School Psychologist and holds Utah state certification in school psychology.

She enjoys golfing, jogging and spending time with her family.

Brief Table of Contents

Table of Contents

Part 1

EDUCATIONAL PARTNERSHIPS: THE FOUNDATION
FOR SERVING STUDENTS AT RISK

Part 2

THE SCHOOL

Chapter 5 • The School

Part 3

HOME AND COMMUNITY

Chapter 9 • The Home

Part 4

EDUCATIONAL PARTNERSHIPS: THE FUTURE

Chapter 12 • Future Issues

Part 1

Educational Partnerships:
The Foundation for Serving
Students At Risk

Chapter 1

Chapter Overview

The Framework for Educational Partnerships

Chapter Objectives

After reading this chapter, the reader should be able to
1. Identify various *legislative and restructuring movements* that have affected traditional educational structures and practices.
2. Define *collaboration* and the *collaborative ethic.*
3. List and explain the *characteristics* of collaboration.
4. Identify the *goals* of collaboration.
5. Describe the *assumptions* of collaboration.
6. Outline the *benefits* of collaboration.
7. Indicate various sources of *resistance* and *barriers* to the establishment of collaborative partnerships in educational settings.
8. State various ways of *overcoming barriers* to collaboration.

The education of all youth is the shared responsibility of classroom teachers, special educators, administrators, related professionals, and parents. When parents and educators pool their knowledge, efforts, and resources, they are able to achieve outcomes they could not achieve alone
(Hudson, Correa, Morsink, & Dykes, 1987, pp. 192–193).

Historical Context for Collaboration

Collaboration represents an important educational framework that is gaining increasing support within applied and scientific communities. It is an integral part of educational restructuring that stems from a combination of legislative and pragmatic emphases. Before delving into the conceptual and philosophical bases of this text, a brief history of collaboration will be reviewed.

Legislation for Services to Students with Disabilities

The Education for All Handicapped Children Act of 1975 (PL 94-142) was instituted to ensure the rights of children with disabling conditions in educational settings. Specifically, there are six basic principles incorporated into the law: (1) the right of access to public education programs; (2) the individualization of services; (3) the provision of educational services in the "least restrictive environment"; (4) the broadening of services to be provided by the schools and a set of procedures for determining how this should be done; (5) the general guidelines for identification of a disability; and (6) the principles of state and local educational agency responsibilities (Walker, 1987). The law explicitly requires a multidisciplinary individual evaluation that is nondiscriminatory, and the development of an *individualized educational program* (IEP).

Public Law 94-142 was modified and renamed The Individuals with Disabilities Education Act of 1990 (IDEA). Inherent in the spirit of IDEA is a philosophy of *normalization* (Gartner & Lipsky, 1987). It is very clear that whenever possible, students with disabilities should be placed in the regular classroom, wherein special services or adaptations should occur. According to the *least restrictive environment* (LRE) criteria, "removal from the regular education environment" is to occur "only when the nature and severity of the handicap is such that education in regular classes with the use of supplementary aids cannot be achieved satisfactorily" [Sec. 612 (5) (B)]. We refer to *educational environment* through this textbook as a setting beyond the traditional mainstream classroom to include the home, playground, lunch room, school bus, and community. Additional legislative and court cases contributing to the collaborative movement in education are reviewed in Chapter 5.

Two specific components of IDEA require collaboration. First, the multidisciplinary team approach of developing a student's IEP reflects the necessity to share expertise, resources, and responsibilities in the delivery of educational services to students with disabilities. Second, it is incumbent upon specialized personnel to provide appropriate and ongoing technical assistance to teachers in classroom settings where students with disabilities have been integrated.

Educational Reform Movement

Legislative mandates have not been the sole impetus for serving students at risk. Much of the attention given students with special needs evolved gradually during the educational reform movement that began in the 1980s. This movement has been described as occurring in three discrete "waves" (Ysseldyke, Algozzine, & Thurlow, 1992). A report by the National Commission on Excellence in Education (1983) entitled, *A Nation at Risk: The Imperative for Educational Reform,* is considered to be the foundation for the first wave of the educational restructuring movement that characterized the 1980s. Additional reports followed (for example, *A Place Called School* by John Goodlad, 1983; and *High School: A Report on American Secondary Education* by Ernest Boyer, 1983), each extolling the need for greater commitment toward excellence in schools. These reports, however, have not specifically addressed the need for change in the education of students considered to be at risk or with disabilities (Welch & Hardman, 1991).

By the mid-1980s, the second wave of educational reform focused on improving the quality of school organizations and teachers. Within this context, the rhetoric for reform first acknowledged the needs of disadvantaged students. Reports such as *Children in Need: Investment Strategies for the Educationally Disadvantaged* (Committee for Economic Development, 1987) and *Time for Results: The Governors' 1991 Report* (National Governors' Association, 1986) urged for the establishment of partnerships consisting of educators, business leaders, and policy leaders to create programs for students at risk. Consequently, the reform movement emphasized restructuring of school organizations. This emphasis often incorporated the practice of *site-based management* in which administrators, teachers, and staff became responsible for implementing change on site. Such an approach requires reconceptualization of traditional roles in the utilization of existing resources (human, technological, informational, financial, and physical) within the school building.

The end of the 1980s saw a shift of focus toward students with special needs, which characterized the third wave of educational reform. The focus included critical issues such as family structure, drug use, and suicide (Office of Educational Research and Improvement, 1988) vocational and post-secondary education (William T. Grant Foundation, 1988) and the dramatic increase of students at risk despite reform efforts (Smith & Lincoln, 1988). Perhaps one of the most influential reports was a call for shared responsibility in meeting the needs of students with learning problems by Assistant Secretary of Education Madeline Will (1986). What distinguished this from other reports was the notion of partnerships.

Reconceptualizing Service Delivery through Educational Partnerships

Within the context of legislated services to students with disabilities and the educational reform movement, we propose throughout this textbook that the challenge of meeting the needs of a diverse student population can best be realized through multidisciplinary educational partnerships. Beyond serving students at risk, such a collaborative approach will, we believe, respond to the needs of teachers, school, and community. It requires a significant paradigm shift that can bring about innovative educational outcomes (Villa, Thousand, Paolucci-Whitcomb, & Nevin, 1990). Administrators, teachers, support personnel and parents are empowered by collaboratively generating innovative solutions to attain mutually shared goals. By sharing responsibility and resources in meeting student needs, professionals also share in the accountability of services. The existing structure of educational service delivery does not, however, foster collaboration. Instead, services are often provided in isolated settings through fragmented agencies that perpetuate barriers between students and professionals.

Under IDEA, students who experience problems in the classroom are often referred for a multidisciplinary psychoeducational assessment. The outcome of this evaluation is often placement in a special education program (that is, classrooms separated from the mainstream general education environment, where students receive individualized instructional services). Unfortunately, too often "special education placement" fails to include "special education services," and specific curricular recommendations to enhance learning are ignored. We believe the emphasis on least restrictive environment (LRE) is to some extent problematic in that it focuses on settings rather than student need. Similarly, the legislative use of categories and labels for purposes of funding services focuses on, and thus perpetuates, differences rather than focusing on meeting students' needs. Within the context of educational reform dialogue, we propose a "MAIN" concept of service delivery, based on the *m*ost *a*ppropriate *i*ntervention according to *n*eed rather than on labels or categories. Teams of professionals working together with parents should first identify what services are needed, then explore ways that the services can be provided. This approach demands collaborative decision making and problem solving to determine who will be responsible for specific services. The nature of the services needed will dictate where the services will be delivered and by whom.

The existence of separate systems implies separate responsibilities for meeting the needs of students with disabilities. It emphasizes a continuum of geographic locations, rather than a needs-driven service-delivery model. Furthermore, it implies a separation of responsibilities rather than joint responsibility. Educational partnerships, on the other hand, connotes shared accountability.

There are additional problems with the traditional refer-test-place process. It is very expensive and time-consuming, requires coordination of efforts from many professionals, and is typically implemented with the sole purpose of determining eligibility for placement (Sheridan & Kratochwill, 1991). A number of studies have demonstrated that current practices are both inconsistent and unreliable (Algozzine & Ysseldyke, 1981; Epps, Ysseldyke, & Algozzine, 1983; Christenson, Ysseldyke, & Algozzine, 1982; Ysseldyke,

Algozzine, & Epps, 1983; Ysseldyke, Algozzine, Richey, & Graden, 1982). And the typical outcome of the referral-assessment process is usually predictable—once referred, there is a high probability that a student will be tested (92 percent nationally) and placed in a special education program (73 percent nationally) (Algozzine, Christenson, & Ysseldyke, 1982). Despite the clear stipulation of the least restrictive setting, 74 percent of special education students are in pull-out or separate programs (Gartner & Lipsky, 1987).

This large percentage of students with disabilities in pull-out or other segregated programs would be less problematic if outcome data were available to support their effectiveness. Unfortunately, "there is no compelling body of evidence that segregated special education programs have significant benefits for students" (Gartner & Lipsky, 1987; p. 375). The research findings actually go in the opposite direction. In a review of fifty recent studies comparing the academic performance of mainstreamed and segregated students with handicapping conditions, Walker (1987) reported that the mean academic performance of the integrated group was in the 80th percentile, while the segregated students scored in the 50th percentile.

An additional problem with the traditional model of service delivery relates to its lack of functional utility. For example, although a multidisciplinary team evaluation is required for determining the need for services, results from traditional assessments (IQ and achievement scores) do little to clarify learning problems, suggest functional or instructional recommendations, provide information on baseline performance, or identify areas of a student's competence. Furthermore, when students are found ineligible for special educational services, "teachers often are left without any useful suggestions, and students often do not receive alternative classroom interventions" (Graden, Casey, & Christenson, 1985; p. 378). Thus, although these students are experiencing problems, their special needs may be left unmet.

These educational practices contribute to the growing number of students at risk (Will, 1986). Further, there are identified segments of student populations whose unique learning needs have not been addressed. These include students from diverse ethnic, cultural, socioeconomic, and racial groups. Likewise, there are thousands of children living in alcoholic families, abusive situations, single-parent households, and impoverished conditions (emotional as well as financial). This state of affairs, coupled with the *Nation at Risk* report (National Commission on Excellence in Education, 1983), calls for major efforts at restructuring traditional educational programs.

Since the 1970s, concepts of normalization (Wolfensberger, 1972), heterogeneous schooling (Villa & Thousand, 1988), and full-inclusion schools (Stainback & Stainback, 1990) have arisen. Strong advocacy groups, legislative mandates, and empirical research have come together in strong support for comprehensive mainstreaming efforts. In response, a "paradigm shift" in education has pointed to a new and different form of service delivery (Villa, Thousand, Paolucci-Whitcomb, & Nevin, 1990). This shift became necessary as educators were exposed to challenges in meeting the needs of diverse groups of learners that rendered their previous view of the world (paradigm) inappropriate.

It seems clear that education and educational personnel are at a turning point. Energies and resources must be redirected to provide appropriate educational services to all students. Interdisciplinary collaboration provides a sound framework for organizing, delivering, and evaluating services, and expanding options for all students within their educational settings.

Collaboration as a Philosophical Foundation

Webster's Eighth Collegiate Dictionary (Webster, 1981) defines *collaborate* as a verb meaning "to labor together; to work jointly with others especially in an intellectual endeavor; to cooperate." Collaboration, then, can be defined as the act of individuals joining together to work on tasks in a cooperative and purposeful manner. Inherent in this definition is the belief that the outcomes of collaborative efforts are better than those attained through individual means. This philosophical position is in radical juxtaposition to current practice and structures of schools where most teachers are isolated from other professionals (Elmore, 1987). As an "ethic" in educational settings, collaboration can be considered a guiding belief or set of values and principles endorsed by all participants in the educational community.[1]

Several definitions of collaboration have been offered in the educational literature. For example, West (1990a) defined educational collaboration as "an interactive planning or problem-solving process involving two or more team members. . . . Team interactions throughout the process are characterized by: mutual respect, trust, and open communication; consideration of each issue or problem from an ecological perspective; consensual decision-making; pooling of personal resources and expertise; and joint ownership of the issue or problem being addressed" (p. 29). According to Friend and Cook (1990), "collaboration is a style for interaction between at least two co-equal parties voluntarily engaged in shared decision making as they work toward a common goal" (p. 72). Olsen (1986) discussed collaboration as "interactive processes based on joint problem solving and a set of commonly held beliefs, norms, and practices" (p. 12). A common thread across definitions includes the notions that collaboration is *interactive* and *dynamic*. It is a *process* among *partners* who share *mutual goals*, and who work together to *make decisions* and *solve identified problems*.

In an attempt to differentiate collaboration from consultation, Pryzwansky (cited in West, 1990b) explained that "collaboration is another type of helping relationship (contrasted with consultation, therapy, education) in which one professional is an active partner with the professional seeking assistance" (p. 1). Similarly, Schaeffer and Bryant (1983) defined collaboration as "shared decision making in governance, planning, delivery, and evaluation of programs. It is a pluralistic form of education where people of dissimilar backgrounds work together with equal status. It may be seen as working *with* rather than *on* a person" (p. 3).

Like the general notion of collaboration, *collaborative consultation* has been defined by several authors. Idol, Paolucci-Whitcomb, and Nevin (1986) defined the concept as "an interactive process which enables people with diverse expertise to generate creative solutions to mutually defined problems. The outcome is enhanced, altered, and different from the original solutions that any team member would produce independently" (p. 1). Subsequently, the definition was expanded to include five basic elements: shared belief system; productive group relations; situational leadership and distributed functions theory of leadership; interactive processes; and mutually owned outcomes (Villa et al., 1990).

We define *collaboration* as a dynamic framework for educational efforts that endorses collegial, interdependent, and co-equal styles of interaction between at least two partners working jointly together to achieve common goals in a decision-making process that is influenced by cultural and systemic factors. Embedded within this definition is the necessity of interdisciplinary partnerships. Consistent with the theme of this textbook, we believe that the optimal condition for collaboration is one in which the participants are partners. A partnership assumes a close, cooperative relationship wherein all parties, including students, have specified and joint rights and responsibilities. In collaborative partnerships, educators pool and share talents, resources, and efforts to achieve a commonly defined mission regarding the education of *all* students. In this framework, all participants in the collaborative process benefit. The beneficiaries of collaborative partnerships are located at various levels and settings: the classroom, school, home, and community.

In educational partnerships, the importance of both process and content expertise cannot be understated. *Process expertise* concerns the skill and ability level of individuals to address issues systematically and efficiently. In other words, one must have competence in knowing how to look at and assess complex problems, analyze environmental factors and conditions surrounding their occurrence, and develop and evaluate interventions intended to solve presenting concerns. It is equally important, however, to have *content expertise*. This refers to one's competence and knowledge related to specific problems or situations in terms of their nature, course, prognosis, and interventions. While each individual in a collaborative relationship may not share equally in process and content expertise, each skill is mutually important to the overall effectiveness of the partnership.

As an overarching philosophical framework for educating all students, collaborative efforts can take many forms and be operationalized in various ways. These forms are known as *structures* or *formats*. For example, among the various collaborative formats are organizational interventions, triadic consultation, intervention or teacher-assistance teams, school-community partnerships and parent-teacher collaboration. An example of one form of a collaborative partnership, a cooperative teaching model, is described in the "spotlight" feature in this chapter. These and other structures for implementing "the collaborative ethic" in school, home, and community settings are described in later chapters of this textbook. Figure 1–1 illustrates a number of methods and services that can be delivered collaboratively within the spectrum of educational partnerships.

Figure 1–1
Spectrum of
Strategies and
Services of
Educational
Partnerships

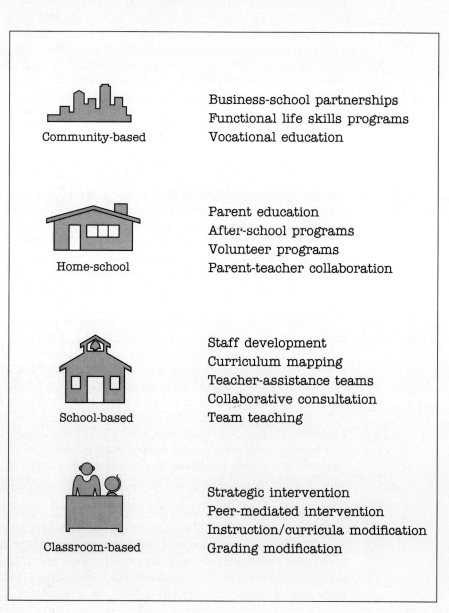

Community-based

Business-school partnerships
Functional life skills programs
Vocational education

Home-school

Parent education
After-school programs
Volunteer programs
Parent-teacher collaboration

School-based

Staff development
Curriculum mapping
Teacher-assistance teams
Collaborative consultation
Team teaching

Classroom-based

Strategic intervention
Peer-mediated intervention
Instruction/curricula modification
Grading modification

In determining the most appropriate collaborative format, one must remember that the contextual characteristics of a situation define and determine the type of collaborative structure selected. In other words, collaboration is situation-specific; the format for collaboration will vary depending on the situational context. Issues can be addressed at various levels (individual, classroom, or entire school) and outcomes can be related to individual students or realized at a broader systems level.

In sum, collaborative partnerships are ongoing, dynamic efforts, not static roles or concrete functions. It is important to recognize that collaboration is not an end, but a means to an end. In other words, educational partnerships are simply mechanisms by which process and content expertise can be merged toward the attainment of goals. They are proactive rather than reactive. The goals of collaborative partnerships include instilling knowledge and skills among professionals to enhance educational experiences for students, solving existing problems, and preventing problematic situations in the future (Curtis & Meyers, 1988; Gallessich, 1985).

Spotlight: Cooperative Teaching Project

The Cooperative Teaching Project (CTP) was a collaborative effort implemented in Hiawatha Elementary School in the Minneapolis Public School District for students in kindergarten through grade 3. The student composition of this school could be considered "high risk"; in kindergarten through grade 3, 44% of the students are minority, 59% are eligible for free or reduced-cost meals, 95% are bused to school, and there is a 42% student turnover rate in one academic year (Self, Benning, Marston, & Magnusson, 1991). The project allowed special education, compensatory education, and regular education teachers to work together on addressing the educational problems of low-achieving students without the fragmentation that typically occurs in traditional service-delivery systems.

As part of the CTP, supplemental small-group reading/readiness instruction was provided daily by special education and compensatory education teachers to students at greatest risk for academic failure. Speech/language clinicians provided 25 minutes of small-group supplemental instruction three days per week to students with limited language skills. Curriculum materials and methods were chosen to support daily reading instruction provided by classroom teachers. All teachers worked collaboratively to maximize student time on task, correct student responses, and generalization of skills. All supplemental groups met in regular classrooms to minimize disruptions and increase academic instructional and engaged time. Students were viewed as full participants in their classrooms because they were not removed for supplementary instruction. continued on following page continued from previous page

The educators were organized into interdisciplinary teams that met regularly in problem-solving groups to share ideas and information. Likewise, they reviewed individual student progress and coordinated instructional plans based on changing student needs. Classroom and supplemental teachers exchanged formal lesson plans, reflecting a shared focus on specific academic objectives. The cooperation of these professionals provided the team members with different viewpoints, knowledge bases, strategies, and skills.

Results of this project are very promising. Students taught with this model made significant academic gains. The majority of students receiving CTP service were able to progress at or above district expectations without being labeled or pulled out for special education. Teacher attitudes toward CTP were positive, and regular education teachers assumed the primary responsibility for instructing at-risk students. Finally, there was a significant increase in cooperative planning between regular and special education staff.

Characteristics of Collaborative Educational Partnerships

There are several characteristics indicative of the collaborative ethic (Gutkin & Curtis, 1990; Zins, Curtis, Graden & Ponti, 1988). A key principle is the *interdisciplinary nature* of collaboration. The unique ecological context of school settings combines professionals from various disciplines and areas of expertise (for example, general and special education teachers, administrators, school psychologists, school counselors, nurses, social workers, custodians, parents, and so forth). The nature of collaboration enables colleagues from these diverse backgrounds to pool their talents and areas of expertise, and work together to provide the best possible education to all students. Within the philosophy of the collaborative ethic, it is both critically important and mutually advantageous to recognize and use the competencies and expertises of professionals across, rather than only within, disciplines.

A second characteristic of collaborative partnerships concerns their overall purpose. In the broadest sense, collaborative efforts strive toward the *attainment of mutually determined goals* regarding educational outcomes for students. The objectives are multiple, and include (1) solving immediate problems; (2) preventing future problems; (3) pooling and sharing of knowledge, skills, resources, and efforts to allow access or development of new, creative alternatives; (4) developing and refining professional skills through the exchange of ideas, knowledge, expertise, and resources; and (5) enhancing educational services to *all* students. Initially, educators often implement procedures in a reactive fashion to solve existing difficulties. However, through the use of a structured consultative format, the sharing of expertise and utilization of new techniques and strategies can promote an increase in participants' knowledge and skills. The professional growth thus afforded to those who work as collaborative partners may well prevent certain future problems or aid in solving them. In sum, collaboration is not only reactive, but also proactive!

A third characteristic of collaborative partnerships is that they endorse both *direct* and *indirect service-delivery approaches*. The exact manner in which services will be delivered is specific to individual situations, and the persons responsible for carrying out services will vary depending on the needs of a given situation. However, not all individuals who contribute to the process will be involved in the actual implementation of services at all times. For example, a school psychologist may work indirectly through a classroom teacher and parent to address difficulties experienced by a student with academic or behavioral difficulties. Although the school psychologist is an active partner throughout the stages of problem solving, interventions may be delivered most effectively in the natural home and classroom settings by the parent and teacher without direct services by the psychologist. On the other hand, several collaborative techniques described in Chapter 8 also involve direct approaches to addressing educational problems. For example, cooperative teaching (Bauwens, Hourcade, & Friend, 1989) may involve the mutual and shared efforts of general and special education teachers in actively providing academic services in the general education classroom.

Another characteristic of educational collaboration calls for *cooperative professional relationships*, rather than independent or isolated efforts. All members of a collaborative partnership share in the ownership of problems and issues. Likewise, they all share responsibility for defining and addressing the task at hand. For example, consider a second-grade girl named Juanita who recently moved to your school from Mexico. She speaks very little English, and Spanish continues to be spoken in her home. Juanita's assigned teacher speaks no Spanish; however, the school librarian and her family have relatives in Mexico, visit the country frequently, and speak Spanish fluently. The collaborative ethic proposes that although not directly responsible for Juanita's education from a traditional perspective, the librarian, and perhaps some of her children who are also enrolled in the school, may be instrumental in providing the needed assistance to Juanita.

The relational status within collaborative partnerships is *coordinate,* meaning that each member has equal opportunity in the decision-making process. This is related to the notion of *parity*, which refers to the equal and complementary status that partners share within a collaborative relationship. This does not imply that all members are identical; indeed, a benefit of this approach is that individuals with diverse backgrounds, skills, and expertises come together to address educational issues. For example, one member may be highly skilled in classroom management, another in *curriculum development* and adaptations. Thus, the strengths and skills of each individual contribute to the overall decision-making efforts, and each member has co-equal status within the collaborative relationship.

A final characteristic of educational collaboration concerns its emphasis on *goal attainment.* Goals can be identified to improve existing programs or address pressing issues. They can focus on strengths of a system and promote prosocial objectives to prevent problems from arising. Or they can focus on deficits and limitations of a system and strive to remediate its flaws. A structured model allows group members to address work-related issues in a systematic and organized manner. Decision-making or problem-solving efforts are directed toward improving the presenting situation for a given student, teacher, classroom, or system. For example, a school counselor may refer a child with low self-esteem to serve as a peer tutor in a special education classroom. In this way the counselor is providing positive experiences for the student, while the special education teacher is getting additional help to meet specific needs of individual students.

In a comprehensive curriculum aimed at the preparation of teachers, support staff, and administrators, there are five additional principles of educational collaboration (West, Idol, & Cannon, 1989). Specifically, these authors emphasized: (1) team ownership of the identified problem, involving both equality and parity (that is, blending of the differing skills, knowledge and beliefs of each member of the team to enhance problem solving); (2) recognition of, and respect for individual differences in the implementation of interventions generated through the problem-solving process; (3) use of situational leadership and a mutually interdependent team structure to achieve goals and maintain positive relationships among team members; (4) conflict resolution based on cooperative goal structures; and (5) effective communication skills to facilitate meaningful interactions in the problem-solving process.

Assumptions of Collaboration

A number of assumptions must be made when promoting a collaborative ethic in educational settings (Curtis & Curtis, 1990; Phillips & McCullough, 1990). A summary of these assumptions is presented in Table 1–1. First, although members of a school community have different backgrounds, interests, and skills, it is assumed that all individuals in a given school community (teachers, administrators, counselors, psychologists, special educators, parents, paraprofessionals) have similar values and goals regarding the education of students. It is critical the educators share the belief that all students in a school are members of a community of learners for whom all personnel are responsible. In other words, everyone in the school community is responsible for *all* students.

Second, collaborative partnerships must be a valued, sanctioned, and supported activity in the school. There must be a belief that pooling the talents and resources of all personnel is mutually advantageous, with a diverse

---

Table 1–1 **Assumptions of Collaborative Ethic**

1. All individuals in a given school community have common values and goals regarding the education of students.
   A. All of the children in a school are members of a community of learners for whom all personnel are responsible.
   B. Everyone in the school is responsible for *all* students.
2. Collaboration is a valued, sanctioned, and supported activity in the school.
   A. Pooling the talents and resources of all personnel is mutually advantageous, with a diverse range of benefits to all.
   B. Student, teacher, or organizational problems merit the expenditure of time, energy, and resources.
   C. Members within the school community must be *proactive* in order to operationalize collaboration, and do more than endorse the ethic in theory only.
3. The correlates of collaboration are important and desirable.
   A. Group morale and cohesion, knowledge of problem-solving and decision-making processes, and skill in using new classroom strategies are important side effects of collaboration.
   B. Positive correlates will likely increase as a function of collaborative efforts.
4. There is a need to structure and organize collaborative efforts.
   A. Collaborative planning and problem solving involves several systematic stages embedded within an ecological problem-solving framework.
   B. Organizational structures must be developed to allow, facilitate, and enhance collaborative interactions.
5. There is joint responsibility for all phases of collaborative problem solving.
   A. All members of a school community share in problem identification and solution.
   B. All members are jointly accountable for services rendered to all students.

---

range of benefits to all. All participants must believe that students, teachers, and the organization merit the expenditure of time, energy, and resources (Phillips & McCullough, 1990). However, members within the school community must be *proactive,* and do more than endorse the ethic in theory only. Administrators, parents, general education teachers, special educators and related service providers must work together to develop organizational structures to allow, facilitate, and enhance collaborative interactions.

Third, the correlates of partnerships are important and desirable (Phillips & McCullough, 1990). For example, staff morale and cohesion, knowledge or skills in problem-solving and decision-making processes, and knowledge and skill in implementing new and varied instructional strategies will increase as a function of collaborative efforts. These are assumed to be valued by members of the school community.

A fourth assumption of educational partnerships relates to the need to structure and organize collaborative efforts. Collaborative planning involves several systematic stages. Various models have been presented in the context of collaboration and consultation. We endorse an ecological approach, which is presented in Chapter 3 and referred to throughout the remainder of the text. Implicit in this assumption is the need for careful situational assessment and analysis, generation of alternative solutions, design and implementation of a chosen strategy, evaluation of programs, adaptation or modification of procedures, and reevaluation of implemented strategies (Gutkin & Curtis, 1990; Zins et al., 1988).

To maximize the benefits of collaborative partnerships in a school, joint responsibility for all stages of collaborative decision making is assumed. All members of a school community share in the ownership of issues within the school community and decisions affecting its consituencies. Likewise, all members are jointly accountable for services rendered to all students.

Activity 1-1

"I think it's great that the disabled kids have allowed their nondisabled peers to come to their school" muses Dr. Hermansen, principal at Eisenhower Jr. High School in Salt Lake City, Utah. But this is a unique school. The entire faculty and staff are perceived as teachers because each experience is viewed as a learning experience. Therefore, the cafeteria supervisor and office secretaries are considered part of the teaching team when students with mental retardation serve as food servers or attendance couriers. Consequently, the students with special needs are seen as meaningful members of the school community by helping out in the lunch room and school office. Adults are not the only teachers at the school. Students with behavior disorders and those receiving counseling for low self-esteem are utilized as peer tutors in special education classrooms. These students serve as valuable human resources to the counselor, special education teacher, and their peers. But the peer tutors are the beneficiaries of collaboration as well. They learn how to behave appropriately as well as get a boost in their own self-image by helping other students.

Envision yourself as a team member at Eisenhower Jr. High School.

1. How are the roles of special educator, school psychologist, classroom teacher, building principal, and school counselor different at Eisenhower than other schools in which "traditional" roles are practiced? How is your specific role the same or different?

2. What is the philosophy of the school? What effect does it appear to have on the school as a whole?

3. In what ways does this school reflect basic tenets of the collaborative ethic?

Benefits of Collaborative Educational Partnerships

There are many potential benefits of a collaborative model of educational service delivery. Several benefits are presented in Table 1–2 and in the following discussion. This discussion is not exhaustive, but provides the reader with an overview of several benefits of collaborative services. It should be recognized that these lists are by no means exhaustive. Indeed, the benefits afforded to each school will be as unique as the situation within which collaborative efforts are attempted.

Collaboration within a school community requires individuals to interact and communicate with each other repeatedly and continuously. The *increased communication among school personnel* is believed to enhance understanding of roles and perspectives, and affect positively the interpersonal relationships between participants involved in collaboration. Furthermore, to the extent that communications are focused on work-related issues, the effective and efficient establishment and coordination of programs and services can be enhanced.

The meaningful involvement of individuals at all levels (administrators, parents, general educators, special educators, and special-service providers) in educational decision making has been shown to *increase ownership and commitment to program goals* (Duke, Showers, & Imber, 1980). Participant investment in the school's goals, objectives, and activities appears to be related to overall effectiveness and productivity.

The pooling of knowledge and skills of a range of professionals with diverse experiences, allows one to *obtain a broader conceptualization of problems.* In essence, the questions asked and solutions generated are broadened and multiplied. Because more facets of an issue can be explored, collaboration can provide an *increased understanding of the complexities of a situation* (Phillips & McCullough, 1990).

Table 1–2   Benefits of Collaboration

1. Increased communication and collaboration among school personnel.
2. Increased ownership and commitment to program goals.
3. Increased understanding of the complexities of a situation.
4. Greater conceptualization of a problem.
5. Increased range of solutions generated.
6. Diversity of expertise and resources available.
7. Superiority of solutions generated.
8. Integrity in program implementation and maintenance.
9. Successful implementation of school innovations and changes.

Along with more comprehensive interpretations of issues, collaboration promotes the generation of an *increased range and number of possible solutions*. Theoretically, the quality of solutions generated will be superior to those generated by any one individual. Likewise, given the assumption that all partners will share in the responsibility of providing the most optimal educational services within any situation, the *range and diversity of expertise and resources available will be greatly enhanced* (Curtis & Curtis, 1990).

Through collaborative partnerships, all participants in the educational community share in the entire range of problem-solving activities. Collaboration extends beyond brainstorming ideas and allocating resources, to monitoring, evaluating, and refining educational programs and services. All members of the school community are accountable for ensuring more quality educational services for all students. Thus, an important benefit to schools is that *school programs and innovations are implemented and maintained with integrity* (Berman & McLaughlin, 1977; Fullan & Pomfret, 1977).

Identifying and Overcoming Barriers to Collaboration

Although the benefits of partnerships appear obvious, several barriers exist to the practice of collaboration by education professionals. These diverse barriers can be grouped into four categories: conceptual, practical, attitudinal, and professional (Phillips & McCullough, 1990).

Conceptual Barriers

Conceptual barriers include the notions that members of the school community (e.g., administrators, teachers, special service staff, parents, and students) have regarding their role and the roles of others. These are typically shaped over several years and reinforced by individuals within and between various education-related professions. Indeed, prior history or experience with an individual in a prescribed role is one of the greatest determinants of how others in that role will be perceived and utilized in the future.

Some examples may help illustrate how conceptual barriers can impede collaborative partnerships in educational settings. Historically, the task of educating students with disabilities has been the "job" of the special educator, not the regular classroom teacher. This is one conceptual barrier. For many years parents were of the belief that school objectives (such as teaching a child to read) were a teacher's responsibility. This is another such barrier. Likewise, teachers generally failed to recognize the importance of parental involvement, and perceived parents as a peripheral or trivial component of the educational process—a third barrier. Such territorial issues, attitudes, and preconceived notions regarding roles and functions are clearly contrary to collaborative efforts that endorse shared and joint responsibility for educating *all* students.

Pragmatic Barriers

Practical and logistical barriers are often considered the most serious. In fact, *lack of time* is typically reported as the most pervasive impediment to implementing consultation and collaboration (Idol-Maestas & Ritter, 1985). Other pragmatic difficulties encountered in work settings include large caseloads, scheduling problems, and competing and overwhelming responsibilities. These barriers are reported by virtually all school personnel, including general education teachers, special educators, school psychologists, and administrators.

Pragmatic barriers are potentially very damaging. Although collaboration may be endorsed in a given school building, it will not be practiced unless adequate time and resources are made available to ensure that structured collaborative efforts are carried out formally and predictably. In other words, school organizational structures must be developed and put into place prior to implementation to facilitate collegial interactions. When the process is compromised due to lack of time, resources, or organizational support, services will likely be inefficient and ineffective.

Attitudinal Barriers

When engaging in any new endeavor, individuals typically hold some expectations regarding the outcome, and sometimes these expectations are unrealistic. In the educational arena, several innovative programs have fallen to the wayside because the expected benefits were not experienced immediately. Such unrealistic expectations can seriously undermine feasible and important change efforts. Another example of an unrealistic expectation is the belief that change should be not only immediate, but flawless, and free from stress and effort. Likewise, fear of the unknown may contribute to a firmly held belief that the "old" way of doing things will suffice in any situation. Yet, conceptual shifts regarding the manner in which educational services are delivered are practically always be incompatible with the "old" ways and require paradigmatic changes in people's decision-making and problem-solving efforts.

From an ecological-systems perspective, it is important to recognize that educational systems (like all systems) are often resistant to change (Fullan, 1985; Skrtic, 1987; Waugh & Punch, 1987). Furthermore, change can be anxiety-producing (Fullan, 1985), and most educators are not adequately prepared for change (Welch & Hardman, 1991). Any meaningful change efforts must therefore go slowly. In the implementation of new structures (such as collaborative partnerships), participants should be encouraged to anticipate flaws and stress so that they will not be unpleasantly surprised. There will be a need to continuously assess problems, analyze conditions, create programs, implement strategies, evaluate outcomes, modify plans, and reevaluate efforts.

In sum, it is imperative to understand that change efforts must be planned carefully, implemented systematically, and analyzed objectively. Furthermore, participants must be realistic in their expectations, and recognize that change takes time. This last point should be emphasized by recognizing, "If there is one factor that is more important than any other in determining the outcome of a change effort, it might well be the need for a carefully developed and detailed plan for change, a plan that extends over a two- to three-year period" (Curtis & Curtis, 1990) (p. 4).

Professional Barriers

A pervasive problem in implementing collaboration in educational settings concerns lack of training or differences in training among various disciplines (Pugach & Allen-Meares, 1985). Complete lack of preservice training may contribute to misdirected, inefficient, or ineffective problem-solving efforts. Differences in training among professionals can result in disproportionate knowledge and experience in problem solving (as a structured and sequential approach), and in the prerequisite skills necessary to engage in collaborative efforts (such as effective communication and conflict management skills). Although school psychologists and special educators sometimes receive preservice training in these critical areas (Phillips & McCullough, 1990), general education teachers typically do not. Unfortunately, philosophical differences and degree of knowledge and skills in problem solving may be directly related to one's ability to participate fully in a collaborative partnership.

Several skills are necessary in the development and implementation of a collaborative approach. For example, the goals, objectives, and components of problem solving (namely, problem definition, situation analysis, brainstorming, evaluation of alternatives, development of an action plan, strategy implementation, and assessment of plan effectiveness) must be understood

**Activity
1-2**

Organize into small groups of three or four with individuals representing different disciplines. On a sheet of paper, develop two columns. Title the columns "Disabling Forces" and "Enabling Forces." Generate a list of potential barriers to collaboration in traditional school settings for the first column. Next think of strengths within the school that can be used to foster and enhance collaborative efforts. List these in the second column.

After both the "disabling" and "enabling" forces have been identified, provide a subjective weight to each one. The weight should correspond to its importance as a disabler or enabler. For your hypothetical school, do the "disablers" outweigh the "enablers," or vice versa?

by participants. Likewise, good interpersonal, communication, and conflict-management skills are important to facilitate positive work relations among partners (Zins et al., 1988). Participants should be familiar with effective interventions for academic, social, and behavioral difficulties; however, all members of a collaborative team are not required to be experts in each of these areas. It is more important that they have skills to access resources or individuals who do possess the necessary expertise in a given situation.

Given the breadth of content and process knowledge required for effective collaboration to be a reality, it is obvious that training efforts must be directed toward preparing all individuals within the school community (including administrators, parents, general education teachers, special educators, and special service providers). Staff-development efforts may take the form of workshops, in-services, or conferences. Equally important, however, is the attention that must be afforded to this critical training issue in preservice preparation programs. Innovative methods for preparing prospective professionals in collaborative interactions include (1) interdisciplinary courses offered for students in all educational disciplines, taught cooperatively by faculty representing all programs (Sheridan & Welch, 1991; Welch, Sheridan, Hart, Fuhriman, Connell, & Stoddart, 1992); (2) requirements that students enroll in courses designed to introduce role and function issues of other educational professionals (Friend & Cook, 1988); (3) competency-based skill training (Kratochwill, Sheridan, Rotto, & Salmon, 1992); and (4) live or videotaped observations, followed by supervised field experience (Kurpius & Lewis, 1988).

Chapter Summary

In this chapter, we explored collaborative partnerships as they apply to work in educational settings. Several definitions of collaboration were presented. The definition endorsed in this text views the collaborative ethic as *a dynamic framework for educational efforts that endorses collegial, interdependent, and co-equal styles of interaction between at least two parties working jointly together to achieve common goals in a decision making process that is influenced by cultural and systemic factors.* Several important concepts are included in this definition. First, it is a *dynamic process* that is flexible and changing to meet the needs of a particular situation. Second, it is a *framework for educational efforts.* It is not a concrete product or role function; rather, it is an overall philosophy of a school community. Third, the nature of the relationship between parties is *collegial, interdependent, and co-equal.* All individuals have equal status in the problem-solving and decision-making relationship, and no one alone can achieve what the partners in collaboration can achieve together. (To coin a cliché, the whole is greater than the sum of its parts!) Finally, the focus of collaboration is on proactive *decision making and problem solving* toward the attainment of *mutually defined goals.*

There are several benefits to a collaborative educational model. With a collaborative approach, there is likely to be increased communication among school personnel. The active involvement of partners at all levels increases ownership and commitment to program goals. Likewise, the participation and observations of several individuals provide educators with a broader understanding of existing problems and issues. At the same time, an increased range of potential solutions is possible. For solutions to be implemented, however, it is desirable that individuals within the school community hold similar goals and values for the education of all students. Collaborative partnerships must be valued and supported at all levels of the educational hierarchy. It is also important that the side effects of collaboration, such as increased morale and cohesion, are desirable to patrons, and that partners share in joint responsibility for all phases of problem solving.

True collaboration may be difficult to achieve in some school communities because of conceptual, attitudinal, practical, organizational, and professional barriers that continue to exist in many settings. It is imperative that organizational structures be developed and all partners be educated in collaborative problem solving in order for the vast benefits to be realized.

Case Study 1–1

Hawthorne Elementary School is a school located in a middle-class suburban district. There is a self-contained classroom for students with behavioral disorders within this school. Ms. Snow, a relatively inexperienced female teacher, is responsible for this group. The majority of students in this classroom are thirteen- and fourteen-year-old boys, several of whom have been receiving special education for a number of years. Several of the students are minorities (that is, Hispanics and African Americans).

This particular class has developed a reputation of being extremely unruly in the classroom, on the playground, in the lunchroom, and anywhere on school grounds. There are four students in the class who are perceived as causing the most problems (Michael, Sam, Jorge, and Carlos). The building administrator, Mr. Ortiz, and several general education teachers have been becoming impatient and anxious. There have been many complaints that these boys are instigating verbal and physical fights on the playground. They also display obscene gestures and make comments to other children to the point of causing complete chaos at times and interfering with the educational process. A particular problem voiced by many teachers is that the four main instigators verbally harass younger female students on the playground until they cry or run into the school building.

Parents of other students in the school are also beginning to complain, as they are hearing stories of problems with this group of students. Some vocal parents are threatening to write letters to the editor of the local newspaper or move their children to private schools. The entire school staff, including other teachers, teacher aides, the principal, and secretarial and paraprofessional staff, are becoming irate and are threatening to seek higher administrative support to expel these students from the school (even though this is strictly against legislative mandates). Likewise, they perceive the teacher as inept, and want her fired. These individuals simply want the students controlled, and believe that it is her job as the BD teacher to do it.

The BD teacher (teacher in the self-contained classroom for behavior-disordered students) describes the situation, and these students, as "hopeless." She uses words such as "brats," "juvenile delinquents," and "hellions" when discussing them. She doesn't feel supported or assisted by other school staff, and does not know where to turn for help. She complains that she is being "dumped on" and that because the others were all trained in general education, they also "just don't understand" special education.

1. Which characteristics of collaboration are violated here?

2. How might collaboration take place in this situation? In other words, what might it "look like"?

3. How would collaboration benefit this situation?

4. What would be some barriers to collaboration in this situation? How might these barriers be overcome?

Key Vocabulary Terms

IDEA
least restrictive environment (LRE)
paradigm
paradigm shift

collaboration
collaborative ethic
process expertise
content expertise

parity
interdependence
site-based management

[1]To our knowledge, the phrase "collaborative ethic" was originally coined by Phillips and McCullough (1990). We have borrowed and used the term because it conveys the philosophy of this text so aptly.

Chapter 2

Chapter Overview

Students At Risk

Chapter Objectives

After reading this chapter, the reader should be able to
1. Describe the student population considered to be at risk.
2. Define *at risk*.
3. Define and differentiate between the terms *handicap* and *disability*.
4. Understand and describe characteristics of disabilities from a cross-categorical perspective that includes mild, moderate, and severe disabilities.
5. List and describe characteristics of learning disabilities, mental retardation, and emotional/behavior disorders.
6. Understand, list, and describe five interrelated factors of socioeconomic status (SES).
7. Understand and describe culture, discontinuities between school and community culture, ethnicity, ethnic groups, racial groups, and cultural pluralism.
8. Understand, list, and describe social and anthropological, communication, and language factors associated with cultural diversity.
9. List and describe an array of physical and mental health issues that place children and youth at risk.
10. Provide a rationale for establishing educational partnerships for serving students at risk.

Introduction:
What Do We Mean When We Say "At Risk"?

The third wave of the educational reform movement of the 1980s was characterized as focusing on the needs of all students, including those considered to be at risk. But what do we mean when we say "at risk"? Efforts to gain an understanding of what it means to be at risk presents a paradoxical challenge for educators (Meier, 1992; Natriello et al., 1990). On one hand, an awareness of factors and characteristics may help establish steps to address an array of problems facing children and youth. Fears and inability to meet the individual needs of students may be due, in part, to a poor knowledge base and lack of skills on the part of educators. On the other hand, there is the risk of clinging to stereotypes that further delineate differences that may, in turn, lead to a self-fulfilling prophecy that can impede progress. Furthermore, there is the danger of inadvertently promoting a pathological perspective in which educators focus on problems or characteristics within the child rather than on how teachers and schools might be organized to deliver educational services (Wehlage & Rutter, 1987). Educators are struggling to cope with this challenge while attempting to understand and define the term *at risk*. We agree with Slavin (1989), who suggested the term is ambiguous and varies in practice. To address this ambiguity, we must first ask, at risk of what? Second, we must ask who is at risk?

At Risk of What?

Many parents and educators use the term "at risk" to describe students who are experiencing academic failure in educational settings (Cooper & Speece, 1990; Reynolds, 1989). Children have also been described as being at risk for referral to special education (Bryan, Bay, Sheldon, & Simon, 1990). Some are referring to students who are at risk of dropping out of school (Wehlage, Rutter, & Turnbaugh 1987). Other discussions have focused on students who are bilingual or speak no English at all (Duran, 1989; Fradd & Weismantel, 1989). Within this context, most discussions on potential school dropouts focus on students from minority or impoverished backgrounds. These students have historically been considered educationally disadvantaged due to social class, race, ethnic origin, poverty, sex, or geographic location and may come to school with attitudes, knowledge, or skills incompatible with learning in American schools (Passow, 1970). Educators must also realize that the environment of Anglo-American schools may be part of the problem. Ecologically speaking, educators are not providing a good "fit" for these diverse groups; and therefore, the problem is not necessarily inherent in individual students. While these students are often at risk of dropping out, it is important to note that U.S. Department of Education's *Twelfth Annual Report to Congress* (1990) estimated that only 53 percent of students with disabilities successfully completed high school. Therefore, the risk of dropping out of school appears to cut across socioeconomic and ethnic boundaries to include students with disabilities.

Educators must be careful not to confine the notion of being at risk as a short-term perception limited to school settings. This approach does not take into account the long-term consequences for students. McCann and Austin (1988) observed that students who are at risk of not achieving educational goals are equally at risk of not becoming productive members of society. Pellicano (1987) suggested that students are at risk of becoming "unproductive, underdeveloped, and noncompetitive; of becoming a domestic 'Third World.' Concomitantly, they place society at risk." (p. 47). The term was used in the landmark report, *A Nation at Risk* (National Commission on Excellence in Education, 1983) suggesting that

> What is at risk is the promise first made on this continent: All, regardless of race class or economic status, are entitled to a fair chance and to the tools for developing their individual powers of mind and spirit to the utmost. This promise means that all children by virtue of their own efforts, competently guided, can hope to attain the mature and informed judgment needed to secure gainful employment and to manage their own lives, thereby serving not only their own interests but also the progress of society itself (p. 8).

We take a broad, life-span perspective on this issue. We believe that the failure and frustration experienced in school during the earlier phases of an individual's life are potentially symptomatic precursors to similar experiences throughout youth and adult life. Students who, for whatever reason, fail to master basic skills in school are less empowered to become independent and contributing members of the community. To focus solely on school-based needs without consideration of lifelong skills and outcomes is shortsighted. So, who are these students who are at risk?

Who Is At Risk?

Pallas, Natriello, and McDill (1989) characterized students at risk as having (1) minority/racial/ethnic group identity; (2) poverty in the household; (3) a single parent; and (4) a poorly educated parent or guardian. Other factors are often associated with being at risk as well. Some include children coming from families with limited proficiency in speaking or understanding English, children who do not regularly attend or participate in school, students who are not achieving or who exhibit disruptive and delinquent behavior, students who abuse chemical substances, teenage girls who are pregnant or unwed mothers, and students considering suicide (Lombardi, Odell, & Novotny, 1990; Morsink & Lenk, 1992). These characteristics have traditionally not included students with disabilities (Lipsky & Gartner, 1989). It is important to understand, however, that disabling conditions know no bounds and cut across ethnic and socioeconomic groups.

At Risk and Disabled

Hardman et al. (1992) described students at risk as being vulnerable to failure and requiring specialized support in school but not identified as disabled. Research, however, indicates that it is often difficult to distinguish students who are low-achievers from those with mild disabling conditions such as learning disabilities or emotional and behavioral disorders (Aksamit, 1990; Ysseldyke, Algozzine, & Thurlow, 1992). Consequently, a significant number of children experiencing academic difficulty are being referred and subsequently identified as eligible for special education (Zins et al., 1988). In a comprehensive study conducted by Phi Delta Kappa (PDK) International (Frymier, 1989; Frymier & Gansneder, 1989), *at risk* was defined as students who are likely to fail in either school or life. The results of their study suggested that considerable overlap exists between students who are receiving special education services and those who are not yet considered to be eligible. In essence, the results of the PDK study suggested that administrators and teachers consider students with disabilities as being at risk for failure in school and in life.

Furthermore, children who come from disadvantaged families and environments are more likely to be referred to special education (Aksamit, 1990; Algozzine & Ysseldyke, 1983). More students with disabilities are likely to come from low-income, single-parent families with limited educational experiences than students who are not disabled (Wetzel, 1987). "More minority children continue to be served in special education than would be expected from the percentage of minority students in the general school population" (USDOE, 1990, p. 7).

> The Iowa Department of Education (1989) broadly defined students at risk as (as cited in Wood, 1992): Any identified student who is at risk of not meeting the goals of the educational program established by the district, not completing a high school education, or not becoming a productive worker. These students may include, but are not limited to, dropouts, potential dropouts, teenage parents, substance users and abusers, low academic achievers, abused and homeless children, youth offenders, economically deprived, minority students, culturally isolated, those with sudden negative changes in performance due to environmental or physical traumas, and those with language barriers, gender barriers, and disabilities (p. 2).

We agree with the notion that educators must look beyond social and ethnic variables to consider a combination and interaction of individual and environmental characteristics (Natriello et al., 1990; Stodolsky & Lesser, 1967). Consequently, educators can no longer merely look to home environments or sociocultural factors as precursors to academic failure. There may be, in fact, environmental factors at several levels within the school setting that contribute to the risk of failure in school and in life. An ecological approach considers the interactions of student and environmental variables that create a need for more and different educational settings more closely matched to individual needs of students (Natriello et al., 1990).

Operational Definition of "At Risk"

We believe students who, due to a variety of factors, are denied equal opportunities and experiences or encounter significant difficulties in a variety of settings are *at risk* of becoming less empowered and autonomous *throughout life*. We conceptualize and define students at risk as

> any child or youth who, due to disabling, cultural, economic, or medical conditions, is (a) denied or has minimum equal opportunities and resources in a variety of settings and (b) is in jeopardy of failing to become a successful and meaningful member of his or her community (i.e., home, school, and business).

Children and Youth with Disabilities

The *Thirteenth Annual Report to Congress* revealed there were nearly 4.5 million school children with disabilities during the 1989-1990 school year (USDOE, 1991). This constitutes nearly 10% of the student population. The *Americans with Disabilities Act* (ADA) defined *disability* as a physical or mental impairment that substantially limits one or more major life activities. The term *handicap* is derived from a time when people with disabilities begged in the street with "cap in hand" to survive. Today *handicapped* is defined as a socially or environmentally imposed limitation that impedes an individual's ability to function (Hardman et al., 1993b). For example, an individual who relies on a Seeing Eye dog is disabled due to a loss of sight. That same individual may be handicapped when attempting to use an elevator that does not have floor buttons identified in braille.

The field of special education has a long legal history (described in Chapter 5) that culminated with three major legislative acts designed to serve individuals with disabilities. Section 504 of the Rehabilitation Act of 1973 (Public Law 93-112) mandates that "no otherwise qualified handicapped individual in the United States . . . shall, solely by reason of his handicap, be excluded from participation in, be denied the benefits of, or be subjected to discrimination under any program or activity receiving Federal financial assistance." This legislation paved the way for the *Individuals with Disabilities Education Act (IDEA)* (Public Law 101-476) which was originally signed into law as Education of the Handicapped Act (Public Law 94-142) in 1975. This law requires a free and appropriate public education for all children. It also dictates specific procedures for ensuring education to students with disabilities that will be described later in Chapter 5. The Americans with Disabilities Act (ADA)

**Activity
2–1**

Consider each of the following scenarios and decide if the individual described is "disabled" or "handicapped."

A. Rose is eighteen years old and has Down's syndrome. She has a job at a fast-food restaurant near her independent group home, from where she takes the bus to and from work.

B. Sherrie is in junior high school and has a profound hearing loss. She is proficient at reading lips. Her math teacher has a tendency to "talk to the chalkboard" as he lectures and computes problems. The desks are arranged in rows, and she sits in the front, so she is unable to attend to comments or questions from her classmates.

C. Sue is a bright young lady who does not know how to take effective notes. The exam questions in her history class come from lectures. She is failing her class due to poor exam grades.

D. Ed is in junior high and wears a prosthetic device after losing one leg to cancer. He is getting above-average grades in his PE class.

E. David has average intelligence but has difficulty paying attention in class. He often interrupts the teacher with comments and disrupts peers while they work on individual assignments. David goes home and plays video games by the hour and will watch a movie on his VCR two or three times in one sitting.

F. Louise displays autistic behavior in which she often rocks in her seat, flips her hands, and utters incoherent phrases aloud. When frustrated, she will occasionally hit her forehead with her fists until restrained. While she has difficulty engaging in social conversation, Louise understands verbal directions and attends mainstream food-preparation and ceramics classes at her high school with a peer tutor.

1. What, if any, factors in each of these scenarios contributes to a disabling condition?

2. What, if any, factors contributes to an individual's ability to be a meaningful and contributing member in his or her social situation?

3. How do environmental variables interact with the individuals' characteristics in a way that may contribute to a disabling condition?

(Public Law 101-336) was signed into law by President George Bush on July 26, 1990. Its intent was to eliminate discrimination toward individuals in the private sector. The ADA definition of *disability* emphasizes the functional needs of an individual rather than characteristics associated with a disability category (Hardman et al., 1993a).

In contrast to ADA, IDEA emphasizes a procedure of identification and classification using ten disabling conditions: mental retardation, hearing impairments including deafness, speech or language impairments, visual impairments including blindness, serious emotional disturbance, orthopedic impairments, autism, traumatic brain injury, other health impairments, and specific learning disabilities (PL 101-476, 1990, sec. 1401, 1, A). This process does not, however, require separate, categorical service-delivery programs. Instead, an intervention blueprint for service delivery known as an *individualized education program (IEP)* is designed, based on the specific needs, rather than the category of disability, of the student. The IEP is described in greater detail in later chapters.

Traditionally, discrete categories of disabilities have been used to describe the characteristics of exceptional students. The evolution of the categorical approach can be traced to a medical perspective used to learn more about individuals with psychiatric disorders or brain injuries. As evident by the language used, disabilities were "diagnosed" and individuals were "prescribed" a "treatment" by a physician (Smith, 1983). Categorical labels have a practical purpose only to the extent that they facilitate communication when discussing individuals with disabling conditions. For example, a global reference to "a child with a disability" is too broad for useful purposes compared to discussing "a child with a visual impairment." Categorical labels have predominately been used for determining the number and type of disabilities for funding purposes.

Despite these practical applications of categorical labels, some educators would argue that they create stigma and perpetuate differences (Reynolds, 1991). Others insist labels have little or no relevance to the development and implementation of service delivery (Ysseldyke, Algozzine, & Thurlow, 1992). It has also been suggested that the nebulous nature of definitions makes it impossible to clearly delineate one disability from another.

In contrast to the traditional emphasis on disability labels, a *cross-categorical perspective* focuses on the severity of a student's learning and/or behavior problem. It also considers interactions between disabling condition and environmental factors. The characteristics and definition of severity that have been adapted from Hardman et al. (1993b) are presented in Table 2–1. Regardless of whether traditional categorical labels or cross-categorical descriptions are used, students who are identified as having a disability are eligible to receive support from special education services. These services can be delivered in mainstream as well as special settings and are described in detail in Chapter 5.

Educators must have a fundamental knowledge base regarding the characteristics, and thus the categories, of disabling conditions. It is important, however, that educators understand that educational services are delivered not according to category but according to individual need. Furthermore, educators must realize that with the appropriate strategies, resources, and support, most students with disabilities, including those with multiple or profound conditions,

Table 2–1   Characteristics of Severity Associated with Disabling Conditions

Dimensions of Disabling Conditions	Mild	Moderate	Severe
Intelligence	LD/BD—IQ ranges from low average to above average. Mental retardation—IQ of 70 or below.	Two to three standard deviations below average achievement	Three standard deviations below average on norm-referenced assessment instruments.
Achievement	LD/BD—significant discrepancies between ability and academic achievement. Mental retardation—usually performs two standard deviations below normal levels of achievement on norm-referenced achievement tests.	Two to three standard deviations below average achievement.	Three standard deviations below average on norm-referenced assessment instruments.
Adaptive behavior	LD—not usually considered. BD—difficulty in establishing and maintaining relationships and social interactions. Mental retardation—reduced ability in personal independence.	Difficulty in establishing relationships and personal independence without the aid of support services.	Significant performance problems in social interactions and independent functioning.
Performance problems in settings	Performance problems are primarily limited to academic settings and tasks.	Performance problems evident in other settings beyond school.	Performance problems evident in all settings and most tasks.

Table 2–1   continued

Dimensions of Disabling Conditions	Mild	Moderate	Severe
Service patterns	Requires minimal or no alternative service delivery. Modest adaptations in instruction, curriculum, and evaluation may be necessary.	Substantially altered support services. Some services are delivered in specialized settings for most of a school day.	Substantially altered service patterns often accompanied by intensive service delivery.
Identification of causality and characteristics	Causality of LD/BD is difficult to identify. Causality of mental retardation is identifiable in some cases. Characteristics of problems are usually identified in school settings.	Causality is identifiable in some cases. Characteristics are often identified before child enters school.	Causality is identifiable in most cases. Characteristics are generally identifiable at birth or following severe trauma.

can be educated with their nondisabled peers in a general classroom setting or neighborhood school for at least part of the school day (Sailor, 1989). Approaches for meeting the educational and social needs of students with disabilities are presented in later chapters.

An overview of the characteristics of disabling conditions follows. The orientation provided here will employ an ecological perspective in which the interaction between student and environment is examined. This approach is designed to inform educators on the factors that may contribute to student difficulties in school settings. We begin by examining disabilities associated with mild learning and behavior problems, which comprise the largest segment of the student population eligible for special education services. According to the National Center for Education Statistics, the most prevalent disabling conditions are learning disabilities, speech impairments, mental retardation, and emotional disturbance (1992a). The majority of speech problems experienced by students are relatively minor and are associated with articulation difficulties that are usually addressed through speech therapy. Furthermore, the vast majority of articulation difficulties do not have the seriously adverse effect on the development of academic or lifelong skills of the student that other disabling conditions might have. Therefore, the focus of our examination will be on the other three prevalent mildly disabling conditions that educators are most likely to deal with. It is important for educators teachers to understand that it is becoming increasingly common to have students with moderate to severe disabilities in the general classroom setting for part of the school day. Consequently, this overview briefly examines disabilities that are more severe and lower in incidence than many milder conditions. It is beyond the scope of this chapter and text to provide a comprehensive overview of all disabling conditions. Educators are urged, therefore, to consult with specialized personnel in the school or other literature to obtain pertinent information about specific disorders.

Students with Mild to Moderate Disabilities

Students with mild to moderate disabilities demonstrate academic and/or interpersonal/social difficulties that often first manifest themselves in academic settings. Consequently, the nature of difficulties experienced by these students generally affect school performance. Usually, the needs of the students can be met within mainstream classroom settings with supplementary support services. While these students may experience difficulty in an academic environment, they generally can adapt to and meet the demands outside school with little or no assistance from support services. Three categories are typically considered as mild to moderate disabilities: learning disabilities, mental retardation, and emotional or behavior disorders.

Learning Disabilities

We begin our overview of the student population with *mild disabilities* by examining the most prevalent yet often misunderstood condition, *learning disabilities*. According to the 1991 Report to Congress, nearly 2 million children, comprising approximately 50 percent of the student population eligible for special education services, are classified as having a learning disability. Due to this prevalence, our discussion on learning disabilities is somewhat more comprehensive than on other disabling conditions.

A learning disability is legally defined in the Individual with Disability Education Act as: those children who have a disorder in one or more of the basic psychological processes involved in understanding or in using language, spoken or written, which may manifest itself in imperfect ability to listen, think, speak, read, write, spell, or do mathematical calculations. Such disorders include such conditions as perceptual disabilities, brain injury, minimal brain dysfunction, dyslexia, and developmental aphasia. Such a term does not include children who have learning problems which are primarily the result of visual, hearing, or motor disabilities, of mental retardation, of emotional disturbance, or of environmental, cultural, or economic disadvantage [Sec. 1401(15)].

The legal definition is exclusionary in nature, meaning that a number of other exacerbating conditions, such as limited intelligence, sensory impairments or cultural deprivation, cannot cause a learning disability. While it is possible that some of these conditions may occur concomitantly, they cannot be the primary cause of a learning disability. It is equally important for educators to understand that a learning disability is a lifelong condition and is not limited to academic problems in school settings. An individual's difficulty associated with reading or writing will follow them throughout school and into the workplace.

Since the passage of the legislative act defining learning disabilities, professionals and advocates have revised the legal definition. Bryan, Bay, Lopez-Reyna, and Donahue (1991) characterized the revised definitions as (1) describing learning disabilities as a generic group of heterogenous problems, (2) linking learning disabilities to dysfunction of the central nervous system, and (3) including social skill deficits as a characteristic (p. 115). Academically speaking, a student with a learning disability is characterized as having average or above-average intelligence but below-average scores on standardized, norm-referenced achievement tests. Ysseldyke et al. (1992) argue, however, that legal and professional definitions do not provide a criteria for determining severe discrepancies. They maintain that definitions of learning disabilities do not clearly distinguish students with learning disabilities from low-achieving students. Glenn (1988) suggested that minority students are often considered "slow," requiring compensatory education, while the label "learning disability" is applied to white children. The criteria for identifying a learning disability varies widely from state to state, district to district, and school to school. The nebulous nature of defining a learning disability may account for the discrepant prevalence figures reported by individual states. It may also explain the dramatic increase and preponderance of students with "learning disabilities."

Kavale and Forness (1985) listed a number of possible causes for learning disabilities. These causes can, for the most part, be categorized into two theoretical groups: perceptual-motor and language (Bender, 1992). *Perceptual-motor theorists* believe that perceptual problems are the result of dysfunction in the central nervous system. *Language theorists* attribute difficulties to significant delays and deficits in language development. There are two important points for educators to understand with regard to causality: (1) all of the research done on causality is theoretical to date, and (2) causality is generally difficult to identify.

A learning disability can be conceptualized as a psychological processing deficit (Bryan et al., 1991). In other words, the condition impedes an individual's ability to convert visual and/or auditory stimuli for efficient completion of tasks. A variety or combination of factors may be the cause of such a condition, including deficits in perception, discrimination, attention, memory, and language.

A *perceptual deficit* involves difficulty or an inability to discern related parts of a stimulus from a pattern. For example, a student may perceive a letter in the alphabet as a series of unrelated lines rather than as its meaningful whole (Hardman et al., 1993b). On a more abstract or complex level, a student with a learning disability may not perceive the relationship of one concept to another. This makes it difficult for students to understand cause-and-effect relationships or to compare and contrast one thing to another. For example, when given a list that includes apples, orange, pears, carrots, celery, and potatoes, a student with a learning disability may perceive the list as "things to eat" rather than fruits and vegetables.

Individuals with learning disabilities often exhibit *discrimination deficits* that impair their ability to distinguish one stimulus from another (Bender, 1992). A common example of a visual discrimination deficit is the confusion between the lowercase letters of "b" and "d." Auditory discrimination deficits are exemplified by difficulty in distinguishing sounds such as the difference between the letters "v" and "f." Developmentally, many children initially experience these types of discrimination difficulties. Students with learning disabilities, however, continue to experience them, with resultant problems in reading, spelling, and oral language.

Attention deficits are manifested by a general inability to stay with or concentrate on a task or activity (Mercer, 1991). Individuals with learning disabilities often focus on irrelevant rather than important stimuli. For example, students with spelling or handwriting problems may concentrate on the appearance of their notes at the expense of understanding the concept presented during a lecture. Occasionally, students simply fail to heed what they perceive as trivial pieces of information, such as operational signs of a simple arithmetic problem; consequently, they may perform multiplication rather than addition. Students may also be distracted by other persons or activities around them.

Deficits associated with perception and attention are likely to influence an individual's ability to retain and recall information. A *memory deficit*, however, is a psychological condition that inhibits an individual's ability to encode information that will be retrieved for use at a later time. Students with learning disabilities can experience a host of memory problems, ranging from long- and short-term memory to various sensory input modes. For example, a student may readily recall what is seen but experience difficulty remembering what is heard. These difficulties may be associated with inefficient encoding processes or strategies. Individuals with learning disabilities may attempt to recall the spelling of a multi-syllable word letter by letter rather than by grouping the syllables.

**Activity
2–2**

Matt is a bright seventh grader with a learning disability that interferes with his reading and ability to express himself in writing. He has difficulty sounding out words as he attempts to spell or read. His history teacher requires students to take turns reading aloud. Matt stammers when he reads aloud as he attempts to use a phonetic approach of decoding words. Matt has described his difficulty as "sounds blur together." At times, he concentrates so intensely on words as he spells or reads that he has difficulty grasping concepts. Matt has learned to compensate by simply remembering what he hears and therefore does not attempt to write down information. The teacher also publicly displays exceptional essays written by students on the bulletin board. Matt copes with these situations by displaying an air of indifference. He "forgets" to bring his book or "loses" his written assignment. His teacher describes Matt as having a "bad attitude" and "not trying hard enough." Matt often feels persecuted and will make comments such as, "My teacher hates me." He makes such rationalizations after receiving poor grades on written exams and assignments despite the fact he can often verbally define and describe complex concepts. Matt's teacher will not consider giving Matt an oral test because he feels "that wouldn't be fair to the rest of the class."

1. What types of processing deficits does Matt appear to exhibit?

2. What instructional activities appear to "tap into" Matt's disabilities, and what effect do they have on his academic behaviors and attitude?

Individuals with *language deficits* are often less skilled in phonological, semantic, and syntactic tasks (Donahue, 1987). This often results in problems associated with production and comprehension of oral and/or written language. In addition to academic difficulties, language deficits can contribute to problematic social skills. For example, an individual with a language disability often does not understand nor perceive the nuance in puns or the tone of voice in sarcasm. Consequently, this individual is at risk of social alienation that can impair interactions at work or in interpersonal relationships.

As a result of any combination of these deficits, a learning disability usually manifests itself in a school setting when a student exhibits a significant discrepancy between ability and performance in one or more of the following areas: (1) oral expression, (2) listening comprehension, (3) written expression, (4) basic reading skill, (5) reading comprehension, (6) mathematical calculation, and (7) mathematical reasoning (Hardman et al., 1993b). Therefore, it is important that educators understand the ecological relationship between academic tasks in an educational setting and a student's ability and performance. Many classroom activities "tap into" a student's learning disability, creating frustration on the part of both teacher and student. For example, it is often difficult for teachers to understand why students are experiencing difficulties, because a learning disability is not visually discernable like other disabling conditions. It is highly unlikely that a teacher would expect a visually impaired child to use a textbook, yet a student with a reading disability is often expected to read "just like everybody else." Consequently, a lack of teacher awareness or understanding of the nature and characteristics of learning disabilities may create undue stress for both the teacher and student.

Despite cognitive understanding of a concept, language deficits often interfere with an individual's ability to express ideas or information in oral or written form. Consequently, a teacher may erroneously conclude that a student with a learning disability has not mastered the concept when, in fact, the student merely was not able to demonstrate understanding. Poor written expression can be exacerbated by poor spelling due to perceptual and discrimination deficits. Similarly, word recognition during reading may be hampered, resulting in poor reading comprehension. Even if students are not impeded by difficulties associated with perception and discrimination, attention and/or memory deficits can interfere with successful completion of tasks.

Mental Retardation

As the prevalence of learning disabilities increases, the number of children identified as having *mental retardation* declines. According to the 1991 *Report to Congress,* approximately 11 percent of the student population receiving special education services was identified as having mental retardation. This represents a 37 percent decline in prevalence of mental retardation (USDOE, 1990). The decrease in numbers has been partially attributed to three factors (Henley, Ramsey, & Algozzine, 1993). First, Polloway and Smith (1983) speculated that students who might have been identified as mentally retarded in the 1960s and 1970s are more likely to be classified as having a learning disability since the passage of federal legislation in the mid-1970s. This might be due in part to a less stigmatizing label and the fact that the category didn't "exist" prior to federal legislation. Second, the intelligence score (IQ) criteria for determining eligibility score was lowered from 85 to 70. Third, the inclusion of adaptive behavior in the definition of mental retardation may have influenced identification procedures.

Intelligence is one key factor in defining and conceptualizing mental retardation. While many professionals debate what intelligence is and how it is measured, it is generally agreed that mild mental retardation is characterized by an IQ score of 70 or below on standardized tests. *Adaptive behavior* refers to an individual's ability to meet social standards for personal independence and appropriate interactions in his or her environment (Drew, Logan, & Hardman, 1988). An individual with mental retardation has deficient adaptive behavior skills, such as responding to social cues when interacting with others, using personal hygiene habits and dressing appropriately, and understanding and communicating ideas with other people.

A landmark study by Mercer (1973) exemplifies the importance of employing an ecologically based approach of analyzing the interaction of student and environmental characteristics when assessing adaptive behavior. Mercer found a preponderance of Hispanic and African-American children were classified as mentally retarded and placed in special education classrooms. She used the term "six-hour retarded child" to describe these children, as school personnel appeared to use school-based rather than out-of-school behaviors to assess student performance. In other words, many students from ethnically and culturally divergent settings were mislabeled because they appeared to be mentally retarded in an academic setting, though not in other environments. Reschly (1988) reported the results of a national survey that indicated that African-American children are still identified as mentally retarded more than any other ethnic group. Reschly (1988) acknowledged the challenges associated with assessing adaptive behavior and therefore advocated that both in-school and out-of-school behavior be considered, as each have distinct patterns and components. Educators are still grappling with this important yet somewhat abstract concept.

Causes of Mental Retardation.   Several causes of mental retardation have been identified (Drew et al., 1988; Hardman et al., 1993b; Henley et al., 1993) and are summarized here. It is important to understand, however, that most students with mild mental retardation do not typically demonstrate overt, organic causal factors. *Genetic factors* are often a cause of mental retardation. Down's syndrome is one of the most common conditions resulting from a chromosomal imbalance of three number-21 chromosomes. The Fragile X, or Martin-Bell, syndrome usually afflicts males more than females due to a "break" in an X chromosome. *Infection* during pregnancy and infancy can also result in mental retardation. A protozoan infection of a pregnant woman can cause toxoplasmosis, while cytomegalic inclusion disease is caused by viral infection. Encephalitis can cause damage to the central nervous system that may result in mental retardation. Ingested *toxins* can also cause varying forms of mental retardation. A common and growing condition is fetal alcohol syndrome, caused by the consumption of alcohol by a pregnant woman. Other events during gestation or birth can result in mental retardation, too, including physical accidents prior to or during birth. Precipitous (rapid births) or a lack of oxygen (anoxia) are examples of trauma. *Metabolic problems* can also cause forms of mental retardation such as phenylketonuria (PKU). A baby with PKU is unable to metabolize or process phenylalanine, a substance (amino acid) found in food and milk. This condition creates an accumulation of poisonous substances that, if untreated, can cause varying degrees of mental retardation.

Characteristics of Mental Retardation.   As with other disabilities, the characteristics of mental retardation vary in terms of severity and condition. Characteristics have been summarized here, however, into four broad dimensions that may help educators understand the disability (Drew et al.,

**Activity
2–3**

Denise is a sixteen-year-old girl from a poor farming family. Her mother worked throughout pregnancy as a part-time painter to help the family financially. After Denise was born, the family noticed significant developmental delays in learning how to walk and talk. Once Denise did learn to walk, she exhibited a slightly stooped posture and dragging of one foot. As Denise entered school, she experienced difficulty mastering fundamental academic tasks such as counting and letter recognition. She spoke in simple three- to four-word sentences. Denise experienced difficulty in completing simple tasks that involved step-by-step procedures at home and in settings such as the school cafeteria. When she learned how to count, she had difficulty transferring the skill to everyday routines. Testing by a school psychologist revealed she had an IQ of 65. Despite her academic difficulties, Denise received a certificate of completion at high school. She now lives in a group home and takes the bus to and from her job at a motel where she is employed as a maid.

1. What causal factors appear to have contributed to Denise's disability?

2. What characteristics of mental retardation does Denise demonstrate?

3. Despite her mental retardation, how has Denise demonstrated that she is an independent and meaningful member of society?

1988). These interrelated dimensions are cognition, academic achievement, speech and language, and social/adaptive behavior.

Cognition can be thought of as the process of thinking and remembering and problem solving. Lower intelligence, which is part of the definition of mental retardation, will impair cognition to a degree. Cognition involves the retrieval of information and the use of skills, experience-based knowledge, and resources to complete a task. An individual with mental retardation typically demonstrates difficulty in cognition when confronted with a new situation or task. Cognitive deficits will therefore limit academic achievement.

The degree of severity in mental retardation includes mild, moderate, and severe/profound. A student with mild mental retardation is likely to experience lower *academic achievement* in areas such as reading, spelling, and math as compared to their peers. This is not to suggest, however, that students with mild mental retardation are incapable of learning basic, fundamental skills in academic areas. These students can often develop a functional vocabulary through recognition of basic survival words (such as "danger" and "exit") as well as basic operations in arithmetic. The difficulty these students often experience is independent application of these skills in novel or "real-life" situations. Therefore, the focus is not to perform well on a standardized test, but in authentic situations. On the other hand, individuals with moderate to severe mental retardation have significantly lower cognitive and academic abilities and thus require significant support and adaptations. For example, students with moderate degrees of mental retardation will experience considerable difficulty writing or spelling their name and other personal information such as a phone number, birthdate, or address. They may also have difficulty in social interactions. However, with appropriate support, many of these individuals can adapt and become meaningful members of the community.

Delayed *speech and language development* is a characteristic of mental retardation. The degree of severity is quite broad, ranging from fairly normalized speech and language patterns to no speech at all. Speech problems often manifest themselves in difficulty with articulation and production, such as stuttering. Sometimes voice quality, such as volume, tone, and inflection, is diminished. The ability to understand and express abstract ideas is often minimized due to language problems associated with semantics, vocabulary, and syntax. This, in turn, is related to cognitive deficits. Consequently, language may need to be simplified to some extent when interacting with a student who has a form of mental retardation.

The quality of interactions with other individuals and their environment is related to *social and adaptive behaviors*. These behaviors were addressed in our discussion on the definition of mental retardation.

Serious Emotional Disorders

In terms of prevalence, *serious emotional disorders* rank fourth behind learning disabilities, speech disorders, and mental retardation (Ysseldyke et al., 1992). It has been estimated that 2 percent of the student population exhibit severe behavior disorders such as schizophrenia or autism, while 7 percent to 10 percent have less severe behavior problems that still warrant some type of intervention (Coleman, 1992). By 1990, 9 percent of the students of students eligible for special education services were classified as having a behavior disorder (USOE, 1991). This category is unique with respect to the various terms or names, such as *behavior disorders, emotionally disturbed, emotional behavior disorders,* used to describe the condition. Further exacerbating the confusion is the fact the condition can range from rather mild behavior problems such as noncompliance to a teacher's request to more severe actions such as physical aggression toward others or self-injurious behaviors. A review of the term and definition was initiated by the Secretary of Education in 1992 as a move toward revising the term to *emotional or behavioral disorder* and broadening the definition (Huefner, 1993). Therefore, we will refer to the condition in our discussion as an emotional or behavior disorder. The current IDEA definition of a serious emotional disorder describes a condition

> exhibiting one or more of the following characteristics over a long period of time and to a marked degree, which adversely affects educational performance: an inability to learn which cannot be explained by intellectual, sensory, or health factors; an inability to

Activity 2–4

Bruce is a ninth grader with normal intelligence and highly successful, professional parents who have high aspirations for their only son. Throughout elementary school, Bruce demonstrated average academic skills and was relatively shy. After entering junior high school, he began experiencing stomachaches and often missed school. Physical examinations did not reveal any medical problems. By the time Bruce was in ninth grade, he simply stopped going to school. He usually walked home after his parents had left for work. Bruce has no friends and retreats to his bedroom upon returning home. Due to his poor attendance record, he is in danger of repeating his entire ninth-grade year.

Norman is a junior in high school and comes from a home with a single parent, the result of a lengthy divorce procedure. His grades are below average. He often verbally lashes out at his teachers, whom he describes as "jerks." He will sit in most of his classes but refuses to do any work he deems as a "stupid waste of time." When approached or reprimanded, Norman has been known to throw his books at his teachers, resulting in suspension from school. Consequently, many teachers are content to allow Norman to sit quietly as he carves on his desk or draws tattoos on his arms. Norman, however, does enjoy his art and music classes, where he completes all assignments, actively participates, and is mild-mannered. His art and music teachers often express surprise when they hear other teachers describe Norman's behavior during informal discussions in the teachers' lounge.

1. How can the behaviors of Bruce and Norman be characterized in terms of chronicity, frequency, and severity?

2. Which two broad categories of emotional or behavior disorders do Bruce and Norman appear to represent?

3. Do their behaviors appear to constitute what might be classified as an emotional or behavior disorder?

build or maintain satisfactory relationships with peers and teachers; inappropriate types of behavior or feelings under normal circumstances; a general pervasive mood of unhappiness or depression; or a tendency to develop physical symptoms or fears associated with personal or school problems (U.S. Department of Health, Education, and Welfare, 1977, p.42478).

An individual with an emotional or behavior disorder can be characterized as someone with persistent and consistent severe behaviors that interfere with productive learning processes despite receiving the supportive educational services and counseling assistance available to all students. Consequently, the individual is unable to achieve adequate academic progress and satisfactory interpersonal relationships for reasons that cannot be attributed to primarily physical, sensory, or intellectual deficits (Algozzine, Schmid, & Conners, 1978; Henley, Ramsey, & Algozzine, 1993). Emotional or behavior disorders can be broadly characterized into two behavioral categories: internalizing and externalizing (Coleman, 1992). *Internalizing behaviors* are generally manifested by introverted and socially withdrawn behaviors. Examples of internalizing behaviors include being shy, fearful, or somatic. While every individual may demonstrate these behaviors from time to time, a disabling degree of internalizing behavior disorder interferes with an individual's ability to be a meaningful member of a group. *Externalizing behaviors* are typically exhibited by aggression, disobedience, temper tantrums, and overactivity. Both types of behaviors can be attributed to environmental and biological factors (Coleman, 1992).

Internalizing and externalizing behaviors must be examined within the context of three dimensions: chronicity, frequency, and severity (Coleman, 1992). While considering *chronicity*, educators must determine a pattern of behavior over a specific period of time. Behaviors may persist or be exhibited for a short amount of time. Similarly, the *frequency* of behaviors may occur often or sporadically. Finally, the *severity* of the problematic behavior must be determined. A verbal outburst when losing a game on the playground or classroom is significantly different than physically threatening another individual.

While it is not possible to characterize all students with emotional or behavior disorders, a general pattern has emerged over the years. These students generally have low-average intelligence scores (Coleman, 1992). Consequently, those with behavior problems often experience academic difficulty in school. It is difficult to attribute these learning problems to inadequately developed cognitive and academic skills or merely to emotional problems (Henley et al, 1993). A preponderance of students classified as having an emotional or behavior disorder are males from low socioeconomic backgrounds (Coleman, 1992; Hardman et al, 1993b). Juvenile delinquents are frequently associated with this population. It is, however, often difficult to determine if the individual is in trouble with the law due to a disabling condition or other factors, such as neglect, abuse, or less than favorable living environments, that may have contributed to the deviant behavior.

A number of models—biophysical, psychodynamic, behavioral, and ecological—have been developed to help educators understand emotional or behavior disorders as well as to plan and manage interventions. The theoretical framework of causal factors and interventions have been adapted from the literature and are summarized in Table 2–2. It is important to understand that educators rarely know exact causes of emotional or behavior disorders. In actuality, a variety of biological, psychological, and social/environmental factors are likely to influence a student's behavior (Wicks-Nelson & Israel, 1984).

Table 2–2   **Theoretical Models of Causality and Intervention of Behavior Disorders**

Theoretical Model	Causal Factors	Interventions
Biophysical	Behavior disorders are a result of organic and/or genetic factors.	Medication and nutrition therapy are provided. Teacher's role is that of a liaison to educational/medical specialists in daily monitoring of prescribed intervention.
Behavioral	Behavior disorders are learned, maladaptive responses to environmental factors.	Environments and behaviors are modified to promote the learning of appropriate behaviors.
Ecological	Deviant behavior is a result of the interaction of an individual with others in the environment. Sociocultural variables within an environment will have an impact on an individual's behavior.	Community-based social services are provided to influence families and the community.
Humanistic	Behavior disorders are attributed to poor self-esteem.	Humanistic education is provided, emphasizing positive and nurturing educational experiences and life-space interviewing.
Psychodynamic	Unconscious drives and internal personal conflicts influence behavior.	Psychoanalysis and therapeutic school environments are provided.

Students with Moderate to Severe Disabilities

Students with *moderate disabilities* usually exhibit intellectual/academic and interpersonal characteristics that are two to three standard deviations below average on standardized, norm-referenced tests (Hardman et al., 1993b). A *standard deviation* is a specific unit of measure used to determine differences between what is considered normal and what is not. On the most commonly used intelligence tests, a standard deviation consists of 15 points. Therefore, an individual with a moderate intellectual disability will typically score any-where between thirty to forty-five points lower than average on an IQ test. Problems in learning and behavior are demonstrated in a variety of environ-ments and are not limited to school settings. Typically, the degree of severity and causes of moderate disabilities are more easily identified than mild dis-abling conditions. Furthermore, in contrast to mild disabilities, interventions and service delivery are substantially altered in meeting the needs of students with moderate learning and behavior disorders.

A condition such as *autism* can vary in degree from moderate to severe. The amount and nature of accommodation and support necessary to deliver services can vary across settings. Because of its low prevalence, autism might even be considered a low-incident condition, which will be briefly discussed here. Autism is defined in IDEA as a developmental disability that signifi-cantly affects verbal and nonverbal communication and social interaction. Characteristics are often identified by parents while their child is still an infant. These characteristics include: (1) impaired or delayed language (no expressive language, repeating back what has been said to them, sponta-neous spoken phrases that are irrelevant to conversation), (2) self-stimulation (spinning objects, hand flipping, rocking), (3) resistance to change in routines and exhibition of ritualistic behaviors (arranging objects in the bedroom in a specific order), and (4) sometimes low intellectual functioning. Medical treat-ment through the use of medication and behavior-management techniques have generally been effective interventions with students who have autism. Therefore, they may be integrated into their neighborhood school and even mainstream classroom settings for part of the school day when adequate and appropriate support services are available.

Almost every aspect of life is affected for students with *severe disabilities*. Intervention is often focused on functional needs such as self-care, mobility, and communication. Consequently, the significant degree of need requires the support and services of persons from a variety of professions, such as medicine, social services, rehabilitation (Hardman et al., 1993b).

Traumatic brain injury (TBI) might be categorized as a severe disabil-ity, although the degree of severity may wane to a certain extent following treatment. The causes of TBI can vary throughout the life span. For exam-ple, it may occur due to birth trauma or child abuse in a youngster, to sport-related accidents during childhood and adolescence, to work-related or car accidents during adulthood. The single most prevalent cause of TBI is car accidents that typically occur during the teenage years (Gross, Wolf, Kunitz, & Jane, 1985). TBI can have a profound impact on a number or combination of functions (Hardman et al., 1993b). These include: (1) gross and fine motor functions, (2) memory and cognition, and (3) behavior. Problems in any of these areas will affect a student's academic performance to some degree. The treatment of TBI typically involves an array of profes-sionals. The most obvious would be physicians. Social workers, counselors, and psychologists also play a critical role with the individual and family to deal with the emotional trauma that typically occurs after an injury of this kind. Throughout recovery, physical, occupational, and speech therapists may be utilized.

Historically, the need for multidisciplinary support meant services were delivered in special, and often segregated, settings. Current efforts toward social inclusion have brought students with severe disabilities back into the mainstream school for all or some of their day. With appropriate and available support services, many students with severe disabilities can meaningfully interact with their nondisabled peers in mainstream classrooms.

Typically, students with severe disabilities often have multiple conditions that influence their functioning (Hardman et al, 1993b). This can involve a combination of sensory impairments that effect seeing, hearing, or talking, as well as physical conditions such as cerebral palsy that may impede mobility. Intellectual and cognitive ability may also be affected by mental retardation or severe traumatic brain injury. While mild mental retardation is associated with mild to moderate disabilities, more severe degrees are characteristic of profound disabilities.

It is important that educators understand that even students with moderate to severe disabilities can, with the appropriate support services, attend their neighborhood school as well as mainstream classrooms for at least part of the school day (Sailor, 1989). The primary objective of integration is to promote socialization between students with disabilities and their nondisabled peers. While it is unrealistic for such students to have the same expectations and goals as nondisabled students, they can nevertheless be meaningful members of normalized settings when educational partnerships between specialists, classroom teachers, parents, and students are forged.

A junior high cooking class serves as an appropriate setting for students with moderate to severe disabilities to learn and interact with their nondisabled peers while they develop functional life skills.

Spotlight: The CONCEPTS Project

The Collaborative Organization of Networks: Community, Educators, Parents, The Work place, and Students (CONCEPTS) project was implemented by the Saline Area Schools in southeastern Michigan in 1987 (Kaskinen-Chapman, 1992). By 1989, ten students with intensive needs left a special school and returned to their neighborhood schools. Of these students, three had severe multiple impairments, three were classified as moderately mentally retarded, one as mildly mentally retarded, two had autism, and one had physical disabilities. Each of these students spent part of the school day in mainstream classrooms with nondisabled peers for academic and social activities. The project required significant restructuring of service-delivery programs to enable classroom teachers to work with specialists. The project implemented comprehensive and ongoing staff development to provide teachers with the necessary skills to meet the needs of the children with disabilities. Nine of the ten students mastered more than 60 percent of their objectives listed on their individual education programs. Teacher and student attitudes toward children with disabilities improved significantly over a three-year period.

Low-Incidence Disabilities

We define *low-incidence disabilities* as any condition that represents 2 percent or less of the student population. According to figures presented in the 1991 *Report to Congress,* this segment of the student population is comprised of individuals with multiple disabilities, a combination of visual and hearing impairments, hearing impairments, orthopedic impairments, visual impairments, and other health problems. An individual with *multiple disabilities* exhibits a combination of any disabling condition that typically includes some form of mental retardation (Hardman et al., 1993b). There are, however, some students who have more than one disabling condition, such as a combination of *visual and hearing impairments,* but mental retardation is not a primary symptom. An individual may experience a total loss of sight or sound, yet impairment might be considered partial, meaning the individual's inability to see or hear is only partially disabling. *Visual impairments,* for example, can be accommodated through a variety of academic interventions such as providing readers, braillers, or a partner to simply describe what a teacher or student writes on the board. Textbooks can be readily recorded for students with visual impairments. Similarly, a student may dictate written assignments or use a device such as a brailler or typewriter. Students with *hearing impairments* will usually encounter significant language delays and difficulties. Many students with hearing impairments can function in a mainstream setting when certain accommodations are made. For example, a student's desk can be strategically placed so that the student can read the lips of the teacher. Similarly, the desks of other students can be arranged in a circle so that the student can read the lips of peers as they speak in class.

Orthopedic impairments are characterized by some type of physical disorder that minimizes an individual's movement. These physical disorders may be the result of traumatic brain injury, spinal cord injury, amputations, and muscular dystrophy (Hardman et al., 1993). Orthopedic impairments are generally identified by a physician early in a child's life. The degree of severity can range from mild, requiring little or no specialized support services (physical therapy), to severe, requiring services from a variety of medical, psychological, and vocational specialists.

Some students may exhibit *other health impairments* that result in "limited strength, vitality or alertness, due to chronic or acute health problems such as a heart condition, tuberculosis, rheumatic fever, nephritis, asthma, sickle cell anemia, hemophilia, epilepsy, lead poisoning, leukemia, or diabetes which adversely affect . . . educational performance" (23 Code of Federal Regulations, Section 300.5[7]). Perhaps the most recent and controversial health problem facing educators is *acquired immune deficiency syndrome* (AIDS). Children may be exposed to the *human immunodeficiency virus* (HIV) through tainted blood transfusions, or direct transmission from their mothers during pregnancy who have acquired the virus through sexual activity or intravenous drug use. The virus attacks the immune system, resulting in the condition known as AIDS.

It is important for educators to understand that students with low-incidence disabling conditions cannot, by virtue of their disability, be excluded from meaningful interaction with their nondisabled peers. Even students with multiple impairments can and should be integrated into mainstream settings for parts of the school day, provided that specialized support is readily available.

Disadvantaged Children and Youth

Many children and youth are at a disadvantage in the pursuit of a meaningful and independent life due to a number of potential obstacles. Some of these students come from impoverished homes, while others are from ethnic and cultural minorities. It is critically important to clarify that these students are not deficient nor disabled. However, like their peers with disabilities, students from poverty or culturally divergent backgrounds are potentially at a disadvantage in meeting expected norms and values of a school dominated by Anglo-American culture and standards that may be contrary to their own. Using the socially defined context of *handicap* described earlier, it might be feasible to consider students from impoverished or culturally diverse environments as "handicapped" due to socially imposed conditions or standards. To illustrate this point, consider Cuban's (1989) suggestion that students from diverse ethnic, cultural, and economic backgrounds are at risk for failure because they do not meet the imposed norms and expectations of the school environment. Title I of the Elementary and Secondary Education Act of 1965, later superseded by Chapter I with the enactment of the Education Consolidation and Improvement Act of 1981, was established to overcome educational deprivation associated with poverty and race (Natriello et al., 1990). Title I and Chapter I programs are described later in Chapter 5.

We advocate an ecological analysis of the interaction between student and environmental characteristics. It is important to identify factors within the environment that may come into conflict with characteristics of students who come from diverse cultural and ethnic backgrounds. Consequently, adjustments in attitudes, behaviors, and tasks can be made within the educational setting that will not only accommodate diversity, but embrace it. This is a significant shift from a pathological perspective of "diagnosing" a problem within a child that must be ameliorated by a specialist or special program. We begin our look at disadvantaged children and youth by providing a conceptual foundation of what is meant by poverty and cultural/ethnic diversity.

Poverty

The U.S. Department of Commerce Census (NCES, 1992b) reported that 13.5 percent of the entire American population lives below the poverty level. In 1990 a total of 19.9 percent of all children lived in poverty (NCES, 1992a). Of that total, 15.1 percent were white, 44.2 percent black, and 37.7 percent Hispanic (NCES, 1992a). Children and youth coming from economically disadvantaged environments often require support services to compensate for the effects poverty has had on their learning (Kennedy, Jung, & Orland, 1986). Childhood disease, child abuse, inadequate prenatal care, and general family conflict are highly correlated with poverty (Fleischner & Van Acker, 1990).

Socioeconomic status (SES) delineates social class, which in turn is associated with poverty level. SES and class are determined by five interrelated factors: income, wealth, occupation, education, and power (Gollnick & Chinn, 1990). *Income* is the amount of money earned and brought into the family during a year, while *wealth* is defined by a family's net worth through assets such as savings accounts or ownership of stock and property. Low income is likely to result in an inability to purchase important items such as proper clothing and foods that maintain good health. Moreover, when poor health occurs, low income minimizes medical treatment in the form of doctor

Spotlight: There Are No Children Here

Alex Kotlowitz (1991) tells a compelling story of two boys named Lafeyette and Pharoah growing up amid poverty, crime, gangs, drugs, and the welfare system in Chicago's public housing program. The book, *There Are No Children Here*, describes everyday occurrences in their lives that include dodging gunfire exchanged by gangs in the courtyard and witnessing open drug transactions. The boys' single mother, LaJoe, is unemployed and on welfare but manages to pay $80 a month for burial insurance for her children. While the schoolchildren test below grade level, the school is free of graffiti and violence. The principal implemented PROJECT AFRICA, in which funds are raised to send students to Africa for the summer. Cultural artifacts are prominently displayed throughout the school, celebrating the students' heritage. The story, however, paints a vivid picture of how childhood is stolen from children who are coping day to day with their poverty.

examinations and medications. Therefore, income and wealth can have an indirect effect on a student's academic achievement.

Occupation is often thought of it terms of either white-collar or blue-collar jobs. White-collar jobs are conceptualized as higher-paying, sometimes professional jobs, requiring a greater emphasis on mental labor. Blue-collar jobs tend to involve manual labor. Higher-paying occupations requiring primarily mental labor create a sense of prestige, which in turn often influences the behavior received from others. Similarly, blue-collar jobs often command lower wages or income, which may result in less prestige.

The amount of *education* is highly correlated with occupations, income, and wealth. Typically, families from higher SES groups have greater chances of completing high school and college, higher education that empowers an individual to obtain a better job. *Power* is thought of as one's influence on society and organizations. Individuals with power are able to control resources that can influence their own destiny and that of others. The cyclical effect of the interrelated nature of these factors on academic achievement should be clear.

Wood (1988) suggested that students coming from stressful environments due to low socioeconomic factors are "tough and tenacious in confronting the challenges life presents to them" (p. 5). He goes on to remind educators that "if their responses are less than fully competent, or even maladaptive, this is the result of faulty knowledge rather than lack of effort" (p.5). Consequently, educators must be mindful of the fact that students at risk due to disadvantages are often coping with circumstances that may hamper their ability or willingness to learn in a school setting. Success for children of poverty is based on teachers' understanding of the students' life out of school and an ability to adapt academic activities to the students' needs (Henley et al.,

1993). It is difficult for a student to learn when hungry. Awareness of how socioeconomic factors affect student behavior and attitude may minimize the possibility of educational chauvinism.

In keeping with this discussion on adaptive behavior, it is important to bear in mind that children of poverty often come to school with skills that enable them to cope and survive in a world outside of school. These survival skills, however, often clash with acceptable adaptive behaviors of a school setting. Aggressive children who have learned to fend for themselves or seek peer affiliation to promote self-esteem and confidence will undoubtedly be "at risk" for failure in a school environment that promotes and rewards individual efforts in passive activities such as reading and writing (Henley et al., 1993).

Cultural and Ethnic Diversity

Culture is defined as a set of variables that include attitudes, values, norms, beliefs, and customs that are transmitted to group members, creating a sense of identity as well as a pattern of behavior (Gollnick & Chinn, 1990). Culture influences how an individual thinks and feels. Pai (1990) quoted Kluckhohn (1968), who suggested, "Culture is like a map. A map isn't just the territory but an abstract description of trends toward uniformity in the words, deeds, and artifacts of a human group. If a map is accurate and you can read it, you won't get lost: if you know a culture, you will know your way around in the life of a society" (Kluckhohn, 1968, p. 35).

There are several micro-cultures within the United States, each with its own subset of cultural variables. Micro-cultures can be characterized in terms of geographic region, religious affiliation, age, gender, class, organizations, ethnicity, and class. *Culture conflict* occurs when variables of one microculture clash with those of another. The clash between cultures can place students at risk for failure and frustration. The values and beliefs of a divergent culture may radically differ from those of Western-Anglo and school culture. For example, Correa (1989) pointed out that the American school system is based on democratic principles that urge individuals and families to participate in decision making. This participation includes the right to question authority, which conflicts with the value of respect and acquiescence to authority held by traditional Hispanic and Asian cultures. As just alluded to, the family is highly revered in Asian culture. Children are socialized to think of the family first. American schools often transmit the contradictory value of "being your own person" and becoming self-sufficient. Pai (1990) cites Spindler's (1963, pp. 134-136) characterization of Anglo-American culture grouped into five general categories: Puritan morality, work-success ethic, individualism, achievement orientation, and future-time orientation. Characteristics of each category are described in Table 2–3.

Cultural patterns within a school may also conflict with the background and experience of students coming from divergent cultures. Hernandez

Table 2–3   Characteristics of Anglo-American Culture

Puritan morality	Emphasis on thriftiness, self-denial, duty, delayed gratification, and sexual restraint.
Work-success ethic	Belief that hard work will result in success, coupled with the perception that unsuccessful individuals are lazy, stupid, or both.
Individualism	Focus on self-reliance, originality, and "putting yourself first."
Achievement orientation	Assumption that one should not be satisfied with a given position in life and that an individual must strive to achieve higher goals and status.
Future-time orientation	The practice and belief that an individual must work hard and save today to ensure a better future.

(1989) identified four discontinuities between school and community that may affect student-teacher interactions in a classroom setting: tempo, management, organization of students, and participation. *Tempo* refers to how quickly students and teachers interact. The pace of verbal and nonverbal interaction may vary depending on the student's cultural background. Differences in communication style are examined in later discussions. The manner in which teachers monitor/control behavior as well has how attention is focused characterizes *management. Organization of students* refers to the manner in which students are grouped for academic and social tasks. Whole-class, small-group, or one-on-one interactions are examples of different classroom organization strategies. Certain cultural traits will affect the effectiveness of student grouping. Frequency of volunteering, responding, and interrupting speakers constitutes *participation*. Teachers have cultural expectations of student behaviors in each of these areas. Students from divergent cultures may behave in ways that deviate from these expectations. Consequently, the educational process is one of *enculturation*, in which students learn their own culture, and *acculturation*, as students attempt to understand and cope with a new and alien culture (Pai, 1990). Therefore, some learning and behavioral difficulties experienced by students may be a result of differences between cultural expectations of school and divergent cultural variables of the home and community (Pai, 1990).

Ethnicity is defined as an identification with others who have the same ancestral background (Gollnick & Chinn, 1990). Ethnicity is composed of complex, interrelated factors rather than a single trait or static category (Pai, 1990). Individuals from a specific *ethnic group* share a variety of cultural traits such as language, history, values, and customs that originate from another nation. These traits define the group and set them apart from other groups. Ethnicity is not limited to non-white groups. Cultural groups such as the Irish, Poles, Italians, and Jews exhibit unique traits (Pai, 1990). Groups can also be

Despite the potential for learning and behavior problems when cultural, ethnic, or socio-economic differences clash with the culture of Anglo-American schools, students can benefit from interaction with peers from diverse backgrounds.

distinguished by physical characteristics of race. *Racial groups* are often characterized by skin color, texture of hair, and the shape of facial features such as the eyes and nose. Ethnic and racial groups hold cultural variables that may be similar or divergent from Anglo, middle-class culture.

Data from the 1990 census suggest Caucasians continue to decline in numbers while Hispanic and Asian groups extend further into the mainstream of American culture. The percent of white Americans dropped from 83.1 percent in 1980 to 80.3 percent in 1990. Black Americans remain the second largest ethnic group, constituting 12.1 percent of the population, followed by Hispanics (9 percent) and Asians (2.9 percent). Despite the changing demographics of American society, the cultural variables of the Anglo-American middle class continue to dominate school settings.

Conflict is inevitable when students from different cultures and ethnic groups do not share the same values, beliefs, and behaviors as teachers (Pai, 1990). Some explanations for academic difficulties experienced by children from low SES groups and different cultures have been categorized by Ornstein and Levine (1989) and are summarized in Table 2–4.

Table 2–4   Factors Related to Poor Academic Achievement of Students from Low SES Backgrounds

Differences in teacher/student backgrounds

> Middle-class teachers experience difficulty understanding the experiences and cultural base of low SES students.
>
> Differences in dialect and language impede effective student-teacher communication.

Teacher perceptions of student inadaquacy

> Teachers may perceive students from low SES groups as incapable of learning, which may lead to a self-fulfilling prophecy for students.

Low standards of performance

> Teachers may perceive students from low SES groups as incapable of learning, which may lead to reduced expectations of student performance and workloads.

Ineffective instructional grouping

> Students may be grouped into homogeneous groups of low-achievers, creating a stigmatizing effect and minimal learning expectations.

Difficulty of teaching conditions

> Student frustration may be manifested in behavior problems, creating an environment difficult to manage and work in.

Differences between parental and school norms

> Belief systems and values from the home may be significantly divergent from the belief system and values of the school.

Lack of previous success in school

> A history of failure and frustration in school may be internalized by students, creating a perception of inadequacy that reduces motivation.

Negative peer pressure

> Disillusionment is a defense mechanism of rejecting school norms that is transmitted to peers.

Inappropriate curriculum and instruction

> Students from low SES backgrounds often lack the vocabulary and knowledge/experience base to meaningfully interact with curriculum.

Delivery-of-service problems

> Inefficient instructional delivery techniques may be employed, which ultimately contribute to further frustration and failure.

Source: Adapted from A. C. Ornstein and D. U. Levine, 1989, "Social class, race, and school achievement: Problem and prospects," *Journal of Teacher Education, 40* (5), pp. 17–23.

Gay (1981) suggested that while cultural conflict in the classroom cannot be entirely eliminated, factors contributing to potential conflict can be identified and managed. Educators who effectively work and interact with or in different cultures are *multicultural* (Gollnick & Chinn, 1990). Research suggests that teachers who examine their own cultural beliefs in consort with developing a knowledge base of other cultures and gaining skills for adapting instruction become multicultural. Thus, they are more effective in meeting the needs of students with cultural differences (Burstein & Cabello, 1989). A multicultural educator facilitates *cultural pluralism*, an ideal that encourages diversity as something that ultimately enriches society and embodies the ideology of democracy (Pai, 1990).

A multicultural awareness begins by understanding the relationships of various cultural variables between a dominant and nondominant culture. Teachers can enhance their multicultural awareness in three ways (Hernandez, 1989). First, they can become aware of their own culture as an individual and as a teacher. Second, teachers can develop an awareness of their students' as individuals and members of a diverse culture. Third, it is important to understand the sociocultural factors that influence teaching and learning. It is important to note that no single set of characteristics can be ascribed to members of a cultural or ethnic group (Ortiz, 1987). There is always the danger of applying and perpetuating stereotypes when attempting to understand various ethnic or cultural groups. In reviewing the literature, we have identified a number of cultural variables and consolidated them into three broad categories: social and anthropological factors, communication, and language.

Social and Anthropological Factors.   Social factors are comprised of cultural variables such as roles, values, and beliefs that influence the way an individual or institution behaves. Dissonance is encountered when social factors of one group conflict with those of another. Consequently, the quality of student performance or interaction between individuals is affected by the degree of understanding and accommodation afforded by one cultural group to another.

Time is an interesting cultural trait. Anglo-American culture perceives time as a commodity and values punctuality. However, Hispanic and some Native American cultures view time in a flexible rather than static manner. As a result, students and their parents from these cultures may often be perceived as "irresponsible" for being chronically late for meetings or in turning in work (Morrow, 1987; Pai, 1990).

Students from Asian backgrounds often approach problems indirectly as not to offend others (Pai, 1990). As a result, these individuals may appear docile when they are restraining strong feelings out of respect to authority figures. Roles of individuals from Asian cultures are often defined by age, sex, and status (Yacobacci-Tam, 1987). While Anglo-American culture in the schools encourages students to "become their own person," students of Asian culture are expected to subjugate personal desires and concerns in favor of family needs (Morrow, 1987). Finally, pride and shame can have a profound impact on behavior. Failure may be perceived as bringing dishonor to a family (Morrow, 1987; Yacobacci-Tam, 1987).

Communication.   Communication of messages can be conveyed verbally and nonverbally. In this context, we are looking at the social or pragmatic aspects of expressing and understanding information rather than the technical mechanics or process of written and spoken language. Groups and individuals within groups have distinct verbal and nonverbal communication patterns that are used in specific social situations (Pai, 1990). These patterns can have a positive or negative effect on perceptions and interactions between other individuals or groups (Hernandez, 1989). For example, a person exhibiting a southern accent and the use of certain expressions or euphemisms may be perceived as a "hillbilly," which in turn may affect interpersonal interactions and expectations. Conversely, an individual with an upright posture and a slight British accent may be perceived as an "intellectual" or perhaps a "snob."

Anglo-American communication styles are typically reflected in school culture and can be broadly characterized (Pai, 1990). Thoughts and feelings are communicated through direct expression and reciprocal dialogue. During this exchange, individuals are expected to maintain eye contact while taking turns listening and talking. Children are urged to distinguish facts from feelings through analytical and objective thinking. Consequently, children are assessed according to their ability to succinctly articulate information and ideas in standard written or spoken English.

Henley et al. (1993) cite a number of landmark studies that revealed communication of poor, African-American children is different from the white, middle-class English often used in school settings. While the communication and language is not deficient, the differences create a cultural clash when students use dialect and speech accepted by peers and family outside school with teachers. Pai (1990) reported African-American children and youth often come from cultural backgrounds in which communication is conveyed in an indirect, storytelling style with little eye contact. Similarly, students from Asian and Appalachian cultures often use indirect or circular storytelling to express information (Morrow, 1987). Hispanic children and youth do not often initiate conversation and are frequently more concerned with social/interpersonal relationships and opinions rather than facts (Pai, 1990). These behaviors often conflict with Anglo-American educators' penchant for direct, succinct answers.

Nonverbal communication involves meaning associated with physical behaviors. In Anglo-American culture, eye contact is considered to be an appropriate behavior of acknowledging the person speaking. Eye contact, however, is perceived as rude or disrespectful in Asian or some Native American cultures. Body language such as gestures, posture, and positioning of hands and arms can convey unintended aggressive or submissive messages. Pai (1990) suggested that body movements, posture, and gestures of African-American children and youth are often misinterpreted as expressions of resistance and challenge to authority.

Language.   While there is a degree of overlap, we differentiate *language* from *communication*. We considered the *social* aspects of expressing and understanding information in our discussion of communication. Language is characterized by phonology/ articulation, semantics/morphology, and syntax. The phonological characteristics of Spanish may result in articulation errors made by *limited English proficiency* (LEP) students. For example, Ortiz and Yates (1988) cited studies reporting that Spanish speakers learning to speak English often experience difficulty in discriminating and pronouncing "ch" and "sh." Walker (1987) reported that students who are Native Americans often experience difficulty with proper verb tense (for example, "winned" for "won"). These kinds of differences will contribute to linguistic confusion and frustration on the part of LEP students.

The Bilingual Education Act of 1968, under Title VII, was reauthorized in 1984 to provide federal funds for developing and implementing educational programs to meet the needs of LEP students (Hernandez, 1989), defined by the act as "those not born in the United States; those whose native language is not English; those from environments in which English is not the dominant language; and American Indian and Alaskan natives who come from environments in which a non-English language has significantly influenced their proficiency in English" (Hernandez, 1989, p. 83).

Obviously, students who either speak English as a second language or not at all are likely to experience difficulty in English-speaking school settings. However, educators often have difficulty distinguishing between academic problems due to linguistic differences and those due to disabling conditions (Ortiz & Garcia, 1988). For example, an inordinate number of Hispanic students are erroneously referred for special education services as their academic difficulties are not a result of a disabling condition (Baca & Almanza, 1991; Benavides, 1988; Ortiz & Polyzoi, 1988; Ortiz & Yates, 1988). To minimize the possibility of inappropriate referrals, Benavides (1983) identified a number of high-risk predictors to be used to assess LEP students prior special education referral. The *Prereferral Screening Instrument* (PSI) (Benavides, 1988) can be used to gather information on the general background of the student as well as a history of school experiences and programs, an achievement-behavioral profile, and results from previous tests and screening procedures. Interpretation of the collected data on the PSI can assist educators in appropriate instructional decision making for meeting the academic needs of LEP students.

There are three basic goals of bilingual education for LEP students (*Basic Principles for the Education of Language-Minority Students,* 1982; Hernandez, 1989). Students are to (1) become proficient in speaking and understanding English, (2) achieve academically in all content areas, and (3) experience positive personal growth. They may receive special language education in regular classroom settings as well as *English-as-a-second-language* (ESL) programs (Hernandez, 1989; Plata, 1990). Services in ESL classrooms are usually delivered by bilingual teachers. It is important to realize, however, that bilingual teachers will not always be readily accessible to teachers in general classrooms. There are some basic steps a teacher can follow in preparing and teaching a bilingual lesson that are presented later in Chapter 7.

Physical and Mental Health Issues

Disabling, cultural, and socioeconomic factors are not the only variables that may potentially contribute to risk of failing to become meaningful and contributing members of society. A growing number of physical and mental health issues must also be considered. While educators can do little to stem causation of these issues, they must be cognizant of their impact on student performance and esteem in school settings.

The problems associated with *teenage pregnancy* are issues educators must also face. Sadker and Sadker (1991) provided a compilation of alarming statistics. It has been estimated that approximately 1 million teenage pregnancies occur each year. Teenage pregnancy is the cause of 40 percent of the dropout rate for girls. Teenage pregnancy minimizes the lifelong potential of many women while increasing their need for medical social services. Consequently, teenage mothers and their children are more likely to suffer from poverty and health problems.

A concomitant concern of teenage pregnancy is drug and alcohol consumption of pregnant mothers resulting in utero exposure of infants. *Fetal alcohol syndrome* often results in microcephaly as well as other physical deformities, developmental delays, and mild forms of mental retardation. "Crack babies" are born addicted to cocaine, with low birthweight, physical and neurological trauma, and significant developmental delays. While many of these infants eventually catch up physically with their peers, many others exhibit significant language, attentional, and behavior problems by the age of three years (Viadero, 1990; Ysseldyke, Algozzine, & Thurlow, 1992).

Many students are engaged in *substance abuse* that includes consumption of alcohol, marijuana, cocaine, and common chemicals such as paint thinner, glue or over-the-counter medications like cough syrup. The U.S. Department of Education reported that 44.1 percent of all high school seniors had used some type of drug illegally (NCES, 1992b). Alcohol is the most widely used drug, as 91 percent of high school seniors reported using alcohol while 33 percent reported having five or more drinks on one occasion at least once within two weeks (National Institute on Drug Abuse, 1990). The number of students abusing chemical substances is alarming. It should not be surprising that substance abuse is highly correlated with poor school performance (Sadker & Sadker, 1991).

Child abuse and neglect includes physical mistreatment, sexual molestation and exploitation, emotional traumatization, and disregard (Sadker & Sadker, 1991). While over a million cases of child abuse and neglect are reported each year, it is estimated that at least 2 million cases are never reported (Medden & Rosen, 1986). Abuse and neglect can have profound impact on the behavior and mental health of children and youth. Mental health problems are typically manifested by depression and suicide. Strather (1986) reported a number of disturbing statistics regarding suicide. Youth suicide has increased by 300 percent in the past thirty years. Dysfunctional families, chemical dependency and child abuse are highly correlated with teen suicide.

Classroom teachers often can do little or nothing about these deleterious conditions and factors that affect a student's life. The primary role and responsibility of the teacher is to provide an exemplary experience and environment while a student with these special needs is in his or her care. A secondary role is to communicate and work with other professionals such as social workers, counselors, and school psychologists who can and do provide appropriate support services. Teachers should also understand that they are required to report any known or suspected cases of child abuse to appropriate officials. These reports can be made anonymously; educators should refer to rules and procedures outlined by their district and state. Finally, through a strong partnership, teachers may utilize the expertise of these colleagues to address their own emotional or professional needs and concerns while working with children and youth who have extraordinary physical and emotional needs.

Conclusion: The Need for Educational Partnerships

The increasing number of children and youth with various educational, social, and medical problems putting them at risk in school and life seriously strains special education as a resource (Ysseldyke, Algozzine, & Thurlow, 1992). It is clear that no single agency can meet this challenge alone. Consequently, it is necessary to forge partnerships with a variety of services from education, social, and medical agencies to take a proactive approach of meeting the needs of students who are at risk (Bucci & Reitzammer, 1992; Greer, 1990). A consortium of eleven government, health, and social agencies drafted a public statement entitled *New Partnerships* (1989, pp. 12–17) outlining specific educational goals directly related to Public Law 100-485 (The Family Support Act of 1988). These goals include

[Forging] critical connections between school and support services.

[Expanding] the range and capacity of education programs for learners who are at risk.

[Making] the right match between people, their needs, and the programs designed to help them.

[Reducing] the future number of at risk learners by developing innovative and prevention approaches.

[Beginning] a more comprehensive and effective system for all youth and adults at risk.

The remainder of this text will examine traditional and reconceptualized roles and responsibilities of educators, as well as the organizational structure of the school, home, and community as the foundation of establishing educational partnerships to meet the needs of students who are at risk. This text will also provide a number of strategies to meet the needs of students at risk that can be implemented through educational partnerships consisting of professionals and parents at various levels that include classroom settings, the school, the home, and the community.

Chapter Summary

The term *at risk* has acquired many meanings. Students considered to be at risk encompass a broad span of the entire student population. We view the context of this discussion as potentially symptomatic precursors to difficulties throughout life. Therefore, we define children and youth who are at risk as those who, due to disabling, cultural, economic or medical conditions, are (1) denied or have minimum equal opportunities and resources in a variety of settings and (2) are in jeopardy of failing to become successful and meaningful members of their community. This includes students with disabilities and those who are culturally and ethnically divergent. This means that all educators have a responsibility of meeting the needs of nearly 4.5 million school children with disabilities.

There are ten categories for disabilities; however, the categories have limited use for determining services for students. A cross-categorical approach clusters students into three groups according to degree of need in various settings: mild, moderate, and severe. The highest prevalence of disabling conditions falls within the mild cluster, in which difficulties are usually related to academic difficulties. Students with speech problems, learning disabilities, mental retardation, and emotional-behavioral disorders represent this group. Students with moderate disabilities usually exhibit intellectual/academic and interpersonal characteristics that are significantly below normal ability in a variety of environments other than just school settings. Students with severe disabilities need significant assistance in functional skills in most settings.

In addition to disabling conditions, educators must meet the diverse needs of disadvantaged children and youth. Nearly 20 percent of all children live in poverty. Factors such as income, wealth, parents' occupation and education, and power can have a significant impact on students' physical and mental health, which ultimately affects their learning experiences and prospects for a bright future. Students coming from diverse cultural and ethnic backgrounds may experience difficulty in school due to a mismatch of their background and the dominant Anglo-American culture of schools. Consequently, educators must be sensitive to cultural traits such as values and norms as well as language and communication differences in order to promote meaningful educational experiences.

Physical and mental health issues also contribute to risk of failing to become meaningful and contributing members of society. A growing number of physical and mental health problems such HIV, AIDS, teenage pregnancy, substance abuse, physical abuse, and neglect can have a detrimental impact on students' academic performance.

The overwhelming challenges facing educators in their goal of meeting the needs of a diverse student population make it necessary to forge educational partnerships to provide appropriate services. Furthermore, collaboration among professionals provides technical and emotional support for colleagues in and out of school settings.

Case Study 2–1

Peter is a seventh grader with mental retardation who recently moved to Valley View Junior High School. The multidisciplinary team—consisting of the school principal, school psychologist, special education teacher, a general education teacher, and Peter's parents—met to discuss his individual education plan (IEP). The team concluded that Peter needed to learn some functional life skills, such as coin identification, reading "survival" words for everyday routine, basic arithemetic operations, and appropriate social skills. As the team explored where Peter would receive his educational program, everyone on the team, with the exception of Peter's parents, assumed he would spend most of his school day in a segregated special education setting for students with mental retardation. His parents indicated that Peter was taught functional skills in some of his mainstream classes, but more importantly, he developed social skills by interacting with his nondisabled peers. When Peter's parents objected to the team's proposal for placement in a segregated setting, the principal responded by saying, "Well, Peter is eligible to receive special education support, and that's where we deliver those services for students with mental retardation."

1. Does this school appear to be using a categorical approach to service delivery, and if so, is it necessary or appropriate?

2. Does having a disabling condition mean services must be provided in special settings?

3. Are the terms "eligibility" and "placement" synonyms? How does this team (excepting Peter's parents) appear to be using these terms?

**Case Study
2–2**

Masa is a bright, well-liked seventh-grade boy who recently moved to the United States with his family from Japan. Both of his parents are well-educated professionals in the computer industry. Despite taking formal, grammatically based English courses in Japan, Masa often experiences difficulty understanding what his junior high school teachers say in class due to the fluency of their speech and to cultural euphemisms with which he is unfamiliar. His written work displays many fragmented sentences and minor errors in grammar. Consequently, his grades are often at a "C" level or below. Masa's history teacher contacted his parents by phone to discuss the situation. The very next day, a gift of a potted plant from Masa's parents was delivered to the history teacher. The teacher politely refused the gift and privately told colleagues in the teacher lounge that he didn't want it to appear that he was being bribed in any way by accepting the plant. Masa usually diverts his eyes when teachers call on him in class or attempt to discuss his difficulties with him after class. This behavior has been interpreted by some of his teachers as conveying poor self-esteem. Consequently, his teachers have referred him for testing to determine eligibility for special education to "deal with his emotional and academic problems."

1. To what extent does socioeconomic status appear contribute to Masa's difficulties in school?

2. What cultural factors appear to contribute to Masa's situation?

3. To what extent do Masa's teachers understand cultural factors that may affect their relationship with Masa and his parents?

4. How appropriate is the referral to special education? What, if anything, should be done differently in this situation?

Key Vocabulary Terms

at risk
handicapped
disability
Americans with Disabilities
  Act (ADA)
Individual with Disabilities
  Education Act (IDEA)
cross-categorical perspective
learning disabilities
mental retardation
serious emotional disorders
adaptive behavior
internalizing behaviors

externalizing behaviors
perceptual deficits
discrimination deficits
attentional deficits
memory deficits
language deficits
autism
traumatic brain injury
culture
ethnicity
ethnic group
racial group
multicultural

cultural pluralism
limited English proficiency
  (LEP)
mild disabilities
moderate disabilities
severe disabilities
income
wealth
occupation
English-as-a-second-language
  (ESL)
Individualized Education
  Program (IEP)

Chapter 3

Chapter Overview

Consultation-Based Approaches to Collaboration

Chapter Objectives

Upon completing this chapter, the reader should be able to
1. Define consultation.
2. Discuss the theoretical background, procedural objectives, and strengths and weaknesses of mental health, organizational development, and behavioral consultation.
3. Explore various aspects of the consultation relationship.
4. Identify competencies important for effective consultation.
5. Outline the stages of an ecological, collaborative model of consultation.
6. Specify the goals and objectives of each stage of the collaborative process.
7. Develop a complete action plan, with details regarding implementation and evaluation of an intervention program.

Evident from our discussion in Chapter 2 is the fact that schools are comprised of students from various racial, ethnic, socioeconomic, and intellectual domains. To meet the increasing demands on educators to provide appropriate educational opportunities for all these students, many have advocated alternative educational delivery systems (Graden, Zins & Curtis, 1988). Interest in alternative systems has mounted particularly in the past two decades, as educators have become disenchanted with current efforts to meet the unique demands of diverse groups of students. For example, since the inception of Public Law 94-142 (1975), students experiencing learning or behavioral problems have been referred to a multidisciplinary team to undergo extensive psychological, intellectual, and academic testing. This refer-test-place process has been the subject of much scrutiny and debate, with mounting evidence pointing to its lack of reliability, efficiency, and functional utility (Algozzine & Ysseldyke, 1981; Christenson, Ysseldyke, & Algozzine, 1982; Ysseldyke, Algozzine, & Epps, 1983; Ysseldyke, Algozzine, Richey, & Graden, 1982). Furthermore, when students are found ineligible for special educational services, teachers often are left without any useful suggestions, and students tend not to receive alternative classroom interventions (Graden, Casey, & Christenson, 1985). Thus, although these students are experiencing problems, their special needs may be left unmet.

Based on these and other problems, it seems clear that all stakeholders in educational communities (including parents, administrators, school psychologists, counselors, social workers, and special and regular educators) must redirect their collective energies and resources to provide appropriate educational services to *all* students in the least restrictive setting. The notion of *least restrictive environment* means that, according to law, all students, including those with disabilities, must be educated in the regular education classroom to the greatest extent appropriate. The effectiveness of alternative systems to meet this goal is dependent largely upon the collaborative efforts of educators, parents, and community-based resources.

As suggested in Chapter 1, collaboration serves as a conceptual umbrella for several forms of partnerships. Consultation represents one type of collaboration, and serves as a framework for providing alternative educational services in school settings. It provides an empirically sound approach for organizing, delivering, and evaluating services, and expanding options for all students within their educational settings (Sheridan & Kratochwill, 1991).

The purposes of this chapter are to (1) define consultation, (2) describe three theoretical approaches to its practice, (3) explore important aspects of consultation relationships, (4) present a number of competencies important for effective collaboration, and (5) outline stages and considerations of an ecological consultation approach.

Definition of Consultation

Consultation has been defined by several authors in various ways. We conceptualize consultation in a manner similar to Curtis and Meyers (1988), who defined it as "a collaborative problem solving process in which two or more persons (consultant[s] and consultee[s]) engage in efforts to benefit one or more other persons (client[s]) for whom they bear some level of responsibility, within a context of reciprocal interactions" (p. 36). It is an indirect form of service delivery through which students' needs are clarified and appropriate strategies for intervention are developed, implemented, and evaluated (Sheridan & Kratochwill, 1991).

While the participants in consultation include consultant (e.g., school psychologist, special educator), consultee (e.g., classroom teacher, parent), and client (e.g., student), it is important to recognize that the roles are not static. According to Curtis and Meyers (1988), "*a unique feature of the above definition is the potential for consultant and consultee to shift roles.* While the consultant (e.g., school psychologist) generally tries to help the consultee (e.g., teacher), there are times in the relationship when the teacher possesses the expertise needed to help the school psychologist . . . *both* participants in the consultation relationship share power and influence in a process that is characterized as a reciprocal interaction" (p. 37, original emphasis).

Implicit in the definition of consultation is the requirement that the person(s) serving as consultant bring to the relationship some type of expertise. Some have argued that the consultant should be an expert in the *content* of a case (Gallesich, 1985). From this perspective the consultant should be knowledgeable about the problem and effective methods for addressing it. Others have argued that the consultant should be an expert primarily in the *problem-solving process* (Gutkin & Curtis, 1990), whether or not he or she had any experience with the specific problem. We believe that a balance of both content and process expertise is necessary to serve in the consultant role effectively. Although relevant information and technical expertise are critical to problem solution, their effectiveness will be minimized if conveyed in the context of ineffective communication or haphazard progression through the necessary stages of problem solving. Likewise, while skillful questioning and appropriate interpersonal skills are important to facilitate the problem-solving process, these qualities are insufficient in addressing serious and often intractable learning or social/emotional difficulties.

Research has suggested that consultation is an effective form of intervention in applied settings (Mannino & Shore, 1975; Medway & Updyke, 1985). Mannino and Shore (1975) found that 69 percent of the studies reviewed showed positive change at the consultee, client, or system level. Medway (1979) noted that 76 percent of the investigations reported at least one or more positive effects from consultation interventions. Consultation is also considered a highly desirable role by educators, including teachers, special educators, school counselors, and school psychologists. Several approaches to consultation have been described as appropriate in educational settings. We now review various models.

Models of Consultation

A detailed discussion of the several models of consultation in the psychological and educational literature is beyond the scope of this chapter. Interested readers are referred to West and Idol (1987) for a review; they identified ten distinct models that differed in terms of theoretical underpinnings, procedural details, responsibilities of participants, and goals of consultation. Despite such differences, however, several commonalities are shared among consultation-based service-delivery models (Gallesich, 1985; Gutkin & Curtis, 1990). In this chapter, we focus on those commonalities in describing mental health, organizational development, and behavioral consultation. Each of these models has contributed to current conceptualizations and practices of school consultation. We then offer an integrated model of consultation that (1) adopts important aspects of each approach, and (2) incorporates ecological principles to be implemented in collaborative educational partnerships.

Mental Health Consultation

According to Mannino and Shore (1986), references to *mental health consultation* (MHC) in educational settings date back to 1886. Gerald Caplan is most often associated with mental health consultation as currently conceptualized (Caplan, 1970), and it is on Caplan's articulation of the model that we now focus.

Caplan (1970) defines consultation as "a process of interaction between two professional persons—the consultant, who is a specialist, and the consultee, who invokes the consultant's help in regard to a current work problem with which he is having some difficulty and which he has decided is within the other's area of specialized competence" (p. 19). Within mental health conceptualizations, consultation is not considered a new or special profession. Rather, it is a method of communication and special way in which existing professionals may operate. The "twin goals" of MHC are to help consultees improve their ability to handle or understand current work difficulties, and to increase their ability to master future similar problems. You will notice that both of these goals focus on the consultee. Improvement in the client (student) is considered a side effect (albeit a desirable side effect) of MHC.

Mental health consultation is founded in psychodynamic tradition. From this perspective, the behaviors of a consultee are considered to reflect emotional instability. In consultation, the consultant attempts to discern patterns wherein the consultee transfers emotional reactions onto seemingly unrelated situations. For example, as an obese child, a consultee may have experienced ridicule and sarcasm from her "popular" peers. In her professional functioning as a teacher, she may seek consultation to deal with a group of attractive and well-liked students whom she characterizes as "mean, insensitive, and self-centered."

According to Caplan, there are four directions that mental health consultation can take. *Client-centered* consultation focuses on problems exhibited by a student, with attention to interventions that can be delivered by the consultee. This includes most student-focused cases addressed throughout this text. An example is a teacher and school counselor working together to develop a program to increase the attendance rate of a middle school student. *Consultee-centered* consultation (which appears to be the cornerstone of MHC) involves providing support to the adults in the child's life (for example, teachers and parents). The emphasis is on removing intrapsychic barriers that hinder the consultee's ability to work with the child. An example is a teacher who has difficulties interacting with an obese youngster because of unresolved problems resulting from having been overweight as a child herself. *Program-centered administrative* consultation is concerned with improving services or programs affecting an entire system. For example, a team of teachers, special staff, and administrator in a high school may work with a consultant on developing and implementing a comprehensive drug awareness program. Finally, *consultee-centered administrative* consultation attempts to remedy issues specific to administrative practices. An ineffective vice-principal in a high school, for example, may be the focus of consultation aimed at improving her behavior management skills.

Advocates of MHC have described at least four areas of deficit that can contribute to consultee difficulites. These include lack of (1) information, (2) skill, (3) self-confidence, and (4) objectivity. When *lack of information* is a concern, consultees demonstrate limited knowledge regarding a specific area. For example, a teacher might have an extensive background in mathematics instruction but have little information regarding effective social skills development and training. When *lack of skill* is an issue, a teacher might have a great deal of information or knowledge but demonstrate ineffective ability to perform. An example would be a new teacher who has absorbed a wealth of information from basic teacher training coursework but has had little experience integrating and applying this knowledge in actual classroom settings. *Lack of self-confidence* refers to a consultee's doubts about his or her knowledge or skills. Despite having obtained a great deal of information and experience, personal uncertainties may hinder his or her ability to apply these effectively. Finally, *lack of objectivity* is considered to be particularly detrimental to a consultee's ability to function effectively, as it involves allowing subjective feelings (which stem from unresolved childhood conflicts) to cloud one's judgment and cause one to behave less professionally than would otherwise be the case. It is the consultant's task to identify and direct intervention efforts toward the source of the consultee's problem (for example, provide information, teach skills, enhance self-confidence, or increase objectivity).

Although Caplanian MHC has been instrumental in theoretically advancing the field of consultation, it is plagued with several practical and empirical problems. First, there are no procedural guidelines available for practitioners who wish to utilize MHC in their settings. Second, the ethical integrity of providing therapeutic-like services to teachers and other consultees in the professional school environment has been questioned. Third, the various concepts that serve as important components of the model (for example, lack of objectivity) are very difficult to define, observe, and measure objectively. Thus, several conceptual aspects of the approach remain untested.

Organizational Development Consultation

Whereas MHC is concerned primarily with specific difficulties experienced by individual consultees, *organizational development (OD) consultation* addresses problems manifested by the organization, or system. Rather than focusing on issues *within* the environment (such as, individual consultee or client problems), OD targets the entire ecology of the environment as the level of change. OD in school settings can be defined as "a planned and sustained effort at school self-study and improvement, focusing explicitly on change in both formal and informal norms, structures, and procedures, using behavioral science concepts and experiential learning" (Schmuck, 1990; p. 899). A central tenet of OD is that participants are actively involved in the assessment, diagnosis, and transformation of their own organization. Its primary goal is to help schools become "self-renewing and self-correcting human systems . . . [it] enables the school to monitor and respond to its environment, and to find, maintain, and use the human resources, ideas, and energy needed to respond to that environment" (Schmuck, 1990, p. 900). For example, comprehensive educational restructuring may be warranted in a school, with the implementation of site-based decision making the result.

Organizational consultation is based on theory and research in industrial/organizational psychology. The principles of group dynamics and social psychology are used to understand organizational problems and to assist members of the organization make needed changes at a schoolwide (that is, "systems") level.

Human-systems theory provides the philosophical framework for OD consultation. There are many assumptions of human-systems theory, but two of its driving principles are especially relevant:

1. There is a natural tendency toward differentiation and specialization in organizations, which typically results in a variety of structures or subsystems. For example, several subsystems can be identified in schools. These can be delineated by professional roles and identities (such as special education teachers, regular education teachers, school psychologists, counselors, social workers, nurses, administrators, custodians, secretaries,

parents, and students). Or, they can be defined departmentally (such as math, language, science, and social studies).

2. The subsystems of an organization are interrelated, interdependent, and reciprocal. This means that change in one part of a system causes change in other parts of a system. For example, an experienced and influential secretary in a school may retire after eighteen years of service. This change in staff will not only have a direct influence on the administrator and other office staff, but may also cause changes in the relationships between parents and the school or between teachers and the administrator.

Maher and Bennett (1984) present five organizational domains in schools that can be conceptualized as subsystems in an educational setting. These include *human resources* (teachers, paraprofessionals, janitors, secretaries, administrators, specialists), *technological resources* (computers, curricula, audiovisual equipment, school buses), *informational resources* (rules and regulations, inservice/staff development, operational manuals), *financial resources* (discretionary funds, grants, state and federal flow-through monies), and *physical resources* (classrooms, playgrounds, library, media centers). Any and all of these can be used alone or in combination to address needs and maximize attainment of educational goals.

Throughout this text, we conceptualize a student-centered ecological approach to collaboration that encompasses each of the five organizational domains. A conceptual model depicting these important considerations is presented in Figure 3–1. The paradigm is comprised of three ecological settings (i.e., home, school, community) and the five domains of resources (i.e., human, technological, informational, financial, physical). Collaborative problem solving involves accessing and utilizing resources from any combination of these settings and domains.

According to Schmuck, the primary goal of OD in schools is "to help schools become self-renewing and self-correcting human systems" (p. 900). There are three keys to school organizational change: (1) clarity and authenticity in communication; (2) collaboration founded on respect, mutual freedom, and shared control; and (3) commitment to the organization improvement process. The primary concerns, or targets, of OD include systems issues such as increasing communication, establishing clear organizational goals, integrating personal and organizational objectives, developing a climate of trust in decision making, enhancing problem solving, working with conflicts, and improving group procedures (Schmuck & Runkel, 1988).

Consultants engaged in organizational development in school settings focus on the formalized interaction patterns of professionals in the educational environment and the clients whom they serve (that is, parents and students) (Henning-Stout, 1993). Thus, they are often concerned with behaviors, feelings, statements and relationships among students, teachers, administrators and parents. For example, they might be concerned with negative communications and poor relationships between the school staff and a vocal

Figure 3–1
Conceptual
Model of
Student-
Centered
Ecological
Approach to
Collaboration

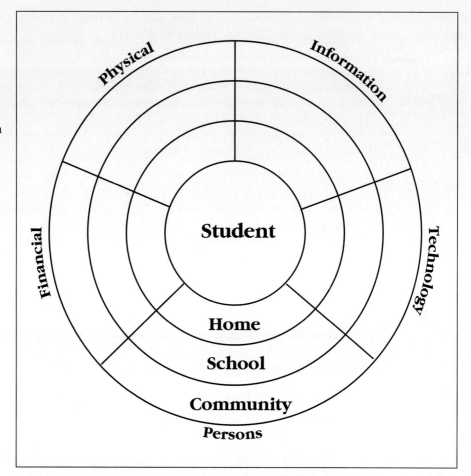

parent group. Building a positive work relationship between the groups would be a likely focus of OD consultation. The practices of an OD consultant include extensive assessment procedures (such as record reviews, interviews, and surveys), and interventions such as laboratory training, survey feedback, and process consultation.

Laboratory training is a very broad concept, with several techniques (for example, sensitivity groups, T-group training, and retreats). It is an educational process for learning about human interactions through experiencing such interactions. It is assumed that involvement and experience in such groups will help participants learn about human interactions, with this knowledge generalizing back to the work setting. *Survey feedback* is a method of using assessment data collected through questionnaires, interviews, and observations as part of the intervention. In the example provided earlier, an OD consultant might survey the parent group and school staff to assess their respective perceptions of the school's goals, programs, and overall effectiveness. Feedback

Activity 3–1

An elementary school in a rural community has experienced an increased problem with fighting on the playground during afternoon recess. In analyzing the problem, it was observed that a small group of fifth-grade boys were the primary instigators of the fights, with third- and fourth-grade boys being the recipients of their aggressive overtures. The problems typically occurred on the outskirts of the school property, where few adults were available to monitor students. A team of educators in the school decided that a structured recess program was needed to alleviate the problem on the playground.

Form small groups of 3 or 4 students, and identify human, technological, informational, financial, and physical resources necessary and available for a structured recess program for implementation in this school.

from the survey could be provided to the groups to inform them of the mutuality of perspectives and objectives. The consultant and group members would discuss the data, collaboratively interpret its meaning, and plan strategies for solving the identified problems.

Process consultation is seen as the primary tool of the OD consultant. It is an insight-oriented technique wherein the consultant brings to the attention of the client (or client system) certain individual, interpersonal, and intergroup processes that the client may not have attended to previously. In the case of the school staff and parent group, an OD consultant might provide observations on the ineffective communication patterns among the groups, the different expectations they appear to have of each other, and the vies for control apparent between the PTA president and school principal.

There are many strengths of OD consultation. First, its general goals, objectives and theoretical framework are very appealing for work in school settings. Second, its potential breadth and depth are extensive; a diverse range of problems can be addressed profitably from an organizational perspective. Third, it is typically planned and carried out in a systematic manner. Finally, it provides an inherent, built-in system of self-study that is grounded in behavioral science. However, some problems with OD have also been identified. Perhaps the most important weakness of the model is that there is little empirical support that its focus on changing organizational processes and enhancing interpersonal relationships among members produces improved educational experiences for students. Likewise, the transfer of skills from laboratory training or workshops to educational and instructional practices is assumed but not certain. Finally, the maintenance of system changes after terminating OD consultation is questionable. In theory, the process should help schools become "self-renewing and self-correcting," but little research has been conducted on whether such long-term changes are actually attained.

Behavioral Consultation

Behavioral consultation (BC) is an indirect form of service delivery that involves the problem-solving efforts between a mental health specialist (the consultant) and one or more persons (the consultees) who are responsible for providing some form of psychological or educational assistance to another (the client) (Bergan & Kratochwill, 1990). It typically involves clarifying and specifying client problems, devising and implementing a behavior change plan, monitoring and evaluating plan effectiveness, and establishing strategies for maintenance and generalization of behaviors.

BC relies heavily on behavioral analysis as its theoretical base. As such, it is concerned primarily with identifying reinforcement contingencies that maintain behavior. Recently, broad ecological and social-learning factors have been recognized as important determinants of behavior. Thus, the focus of contemporary behavioral consultation tends to be the interaction between persons, environments, and behaviors (Martens & Witt, 1988). This approach "recognizes the ecological complexity of behavioral intervention and acknowledges the active roles the consultee and the child play in mediating their own and one another's behaviors" (Henning-Stout, 1993, p. 23).

The goals of BC incorporate client, consultee, and organizational change. Change in client (student) behavior is generally perceived as the ultimate concern for consultants operating within this orientation. Changes may be desired in a variety of social, emotional, or educational domains. For example, a parent may desire change in her son's oppositional behaviors, or a teacher may perceive a need to address a student's difficulty with multiplication problems. BC can help effect these changes in a structured, effective manner. Changes may also be preventive in nature (Kratochwill & Bergan, 1990). For example, behavioral consultation between a teacher and school psychologist geared toward helping a child complete his work or increase accuracy may be instrumental in preventing academic failure. Goals associated with consultee change might include modification of knowledge or skills that could be used immediately and in the future to prevent problems from occurring. Finally, goals of BC may also focus on producing change in the organization (school) where the client and consultee function to produce changes at a macro level, such as developing an attendance program in an inner city high school.

The seminal work of Bergan, Kratochwill, and their associates (Bergan, 1977; Bergan & Kratochwill, 1990; Kratochwill & Bergan, 1990) provides a structure and operational format to guide a consultant's practice. Behavioral consultants use a problem-solving approach to treat academic and social difficulties. Specifically, the process of BC occurs in four general stages, which are implemented through a series of three standardized interviews (see Kratochwill & Bergan, 1990). The stages, and their respective interviews, allow one to move from problem specification and analysis to plan development, implementation, and evaluation. The emphasis is on conducting a functional analysis of presenting problems by determining conditions or events in the environment that promote or maintain certain behaviors. Many authors have offered variations on the BC model that follow the same general procedures but emphasize different aspects of practice. For example, Idol, Paolucci-Whitcomb and Nevin (1987) promoted a model they called *collaborative consultation* that followed the basic problem-solving stages but emphasized the interpersonal aspects of collaboration (the process) over technical issues surrounding problem solution (the content).

To master the consultation approach offered later in this chapter, it is important for readers to understand the traditional BC stages. We will now briefly describe the objectives and procedures of each stage. Examples of the objectives and questions of each interview are presented in Table 3–1. For a more comprehensive review, readers are referred to the guide provided by Kratochwill and Bergan (1990).

The *problem identification* stage of behavioral consultation is designed to specify the problems presented during consultation. The steps in the process eventually result in the (a) identification of a specific target problem; (b) designation of the goal or goals to be achieved through consultation; (c) measurement of current client performance/baseline data collection; and (d) assessment of the discrepancy between current and desired client performance. The problem-identification process is initiated by means of a Problem Identification Interview (PII) with the major objectives of goal specification, assessment, and various procedural considerations.

The *problem analysis* stage of behavioral consultation is conducted when data collected during problem identification indicate the existence of a target problem(s). Problem analysis occurs in two broad phases. The first phase involves analyzing the factors that might lead to problem solution (the analysis phase); the second involves the development of plans to remediate the problem (the plan design-phase).

Problem analysis is implemented through a standardized Problem Analysis Interview (PAI). In this interview, the consultant and consultee determine whether the problem is severe enough to warrant attention in consultation. Conditions and/or skills are discussed that might influence the child's behavior. A plan is then designed by the consultant and consultee(s) to attempt problem solution. Specific objectives of this interview include problem validation, problem analysis, plan design, and procedural goals.

The third stage in consultative problem solving is *treatment implementation*. During this stage of consultation, the plan designed in problem analysis is put into operation. The function of consultation during treatment implementation is to maximize the likelihood that the plan will produce desired outcomes. Although there is no formal interview during treatment implementation, there are several types of interactions that can occur between the consultant and consultee(s), including direct observations or brief contacts to monitor implementation, training sessions to develop skills in the treatment agents, and assisting in plan revision.

Table 3–1   Objectives and Example Questions of Behavioral Consultation Stages

Problem Identification Interview (PII)

Objectives

Define the problem(s) in behavioral terms.

Identify important environmental conditions that impact the behavior.

Provide a tentative strength of the behavior.

Discuss and reach agreement on a goal for behavior change.

Establish a procedure for collection of baseline data.

Example Interview Questions

BEHAVIOR SPECIFICATION (Give me some examples of your concerns. Which of these behaviors is most problematic?)

BEHAVIOR SETTING (Where does the child display this behavior? Give me some examples of where this occurs. Which of the settings is most problematic?)

IDENTIFY ANTECEDENTS (What typically happens before the behavior occurs?)

SEQUENTIAL CONDITIONS ANALYSIS (What else is typically happening in the classroom/playground/home when the behavior occurs?)

IDENTIFY CONSEQUENT CONDITIONS (What typically happens after the behavior occurs?)

BEHAVIOR STRENGTH (How often does this behavior occur? How long does it last?)

GOAL OF CONSULTATION (What would be an acceptable level of this behavior?)

DISCUSS DATA COLLECTION PROCEDURES (What would be a simple way for you to keep track of the behavior?)

Problem Analysis Interview (PAI)

Objectives

Evaluate and obtain agreement on the baseline data.

Conduct an ecological analysis of the behavior.

Design an intervention plan including specification of conditions to be changed and the practical guidelines regarding treatment implementation.

Reaffirm record-keeping procedures.

Example Interview Questions

GENERAL STATEMENT RE: DATA AND PROBLEM (Were you able to keep a record of the behavior?)

BEHAVIOR STRENGTH (According to the data...)

ANTECEDENT CONDITIONS (What did you notice before the problem occurred? What things may have led up to its occurrence?)

CONSEQUENT CONDITIONS (What typically happened after the occurrence of the behavior? What types of things did you notice afterwards?)

SEQUENTIAL CONDITIONS (What else was happening in the classroom/playground/ home when the behavior occurred? What time of day or day of week seemed most problematic? What patterns did you notice?)

ESTABLISHING A PLAN (What can be done to reach our goal?)

Table 3–1   continued

CONTINUE DATA-RECORDING PROCEDURES (Can we continue the same recording procedure as before?)

Treatment Implementation
Objectives
Monitor implementation of the intervention.
Provide training to treatment agent, if necessary.
Determine need for immediate revisions in plan.
Continue data-collection procedures.

Treatment Evaluation Interview (TEI)
Objectives
Evaluate treatment data, and determine if the goals of consultation have been met.
Evaluate the effectiveness of the treatment plan.
Discuss strategies and tactics regarding the continuation, modification, or termination of the treatment plan.
Discuss strategies for maintenance and generalization of treatment gains.
Example Interview Questions
EVALUATE GENERAL PROCEDURES AND OUTCOME (How did things go with the plan?)
QUESTIONS ABOUT GOAL ATTAINMENT (Has the goal been met?)
EVALUATE PLAN EFFECTIVENESS (Do you think that the behavior program was responsible for the change in behavior?)
EVALUATE EXTERNAL VALIDITY OF PLAN (Do you think this plan would work with another child with similar difficulties?)
CONDUCT POST-IMPLEMENTATION PLANNING (Should we leave the plan in effect for a while longer?)
PROCEDURES FOR GENERALIZATION/MAINTENANCE (How can we encourage the child to display these behavior changes in other problem settings? What procedures should we use to make sure that the behavior change continues over time?)
QUESTIONS ABOUT PLAN MODIFICATION (How can we modify the procedures so that the plan is more effective?)
FOLLOW-UP ASSESSMENT (How can we monitor the child's progress to ensure that these positive changes continue?)

After a treatment plan has been in effect for an adequate amount of time, the *treatment evaluation* stage of behavioral consultation is undertaken to determine whether the goals of consultation have been attained, whether the plan has been effective, and if the treatment is acceptable to the consultee(s) and client. Treatment evaluation may indicate that consultation should be continued, terminated, or that a post-implementation treatment plan should be put into effect. Treatment evaluation is initiated through the Treatment Evaluation Interview (TEI). In this interview, the consultant and consultee(s) determine whether goal attainment has been achieved. The need for further problem identification or analysis is discussed, and post-implementation plans are established to reduce the likelihood of problem recurrence.

A strength of behavioral consultation is the procedural detail that has been provided for its implementation (see Kratochwill & Bergan, 1990). It has been acknowledged for its attention to detail and its utilization of a systematic data base for identifying problems and evaluating outcomes. It is expressly intended to use a set of principles to maximize the successful resolution of existing problems. The standardized nature and practice of BC also lends itself very nicely to research and training. In fact, there is now a great deal of empirical support for behavioral consultation, particularly for use in school settings (see Kratochwill, Sheridan, & Van Someren, 1988). In a meta-analysis of consultation-outcome research, more empirical support was available for behavioral consultation than for the other models (Medway & Updyke, 1985). Several recent case studies and small-case experimental designs have also illustrated the effectiveness of behavioral consultation in effecting client change (Pray, Kramer, & Lindskog, 1986; Sheridan, 1992; Sheridan, Kratochwill, & Elliott, 1990).

However, behavioral consultation is not without its weaknesses. One criticism is that it is quite narrow in its conceptualization of effectiveness. Traditionally, the only proof of success in BC is evidence that the client met the objectives specified at the beginning of consultation. The consultees' satisfaction with consultation, and the degree to which they feel more capable of handling similar problems in the future, are not considered sufficient variables on which to assess consultation outcome.

As a result, BC has been criticized for espousing an overly narrow behavioral scope that limits the range and type of target behaviors identified. Relatedly, it encourages consultants and teachers to analyze a given problem molecularly, without addressing the broader contexts within which it occurs (Martens & Witt, 1988). By focusing too narrowly on a specific target behavior, BC may encourage educators to "lose the forest for the trees."

Consultation Relationships

By definition, consultation is an interpersonal endeavor. It involves human interaction among individuals in a dynamic, ongoing relationship. Thus, considerations central to the nature of the consultative relationship warrant attention. Among these are coordinate power status, a consultee's right to reject suggestions, active involvement of the consultee, and voluntary interactions (Gutkin & Curtis, 1990).

Spotlight: Project RE-AIM

Relevant Educational Assessment and Interventions Model, RE-AIM, was a federally funded continuing-education program designed for support-services personnel (i.e., school psycholgists, school social workers, and special education consultants) in the state of Iowa (Grimes & Reschly, 1986; Reschly & Grimes, 1991). The general goal of the project was to provide statewide training to related service personnel in the areas of consultation, functional assessment, and decision making. Three continuing education modules were developed, based on a consultation service-delivery model: behavioral consultation, curriculum based assessment, and referral question consultative decision making. The common elements among these modules included: (1) interviews with referral agents (usually teachers); (2) the use of data in the natural setting (direct observations or permanent products) to define problems, establish target behaviors, monitor interventions, and evaluate outcomes; (4) emphasis on interventions in natural settings; and (4) decreased emphasis on special education eligibility determination.

Behavioral consultation (Bergan & Kratochwill, 1990) was used as the cornerstone of the model. Systematic, highly structured procedures were taught to help participants move effectively through the stages of problem identification, problem analysis, treatment implementation, and treatment evaluation. Beyond consultation skills, behavioral assessment and decision making were addressed to complete formal training prior to its implementation in school settings.

In an evaluation of Project RE-AIM, Reschly and Grimes (1991) reported that participants in training improved in their ability to demonstrate important objectives in behavioral consultation interviews. When local educational agencies made a commitment to the model, case completion was much higher than in agencies without clear expectations. Following completion of the four-stage behavioral consultation problem solving process, 90 percent of consultees (most of whom were teachers) rated the problem behavior as improved. Likewise, consultees had very favorable ratings of consultation.

Positive results attained in Project RE-AIM have made the development of the Iowa Renewed Service Delivery System (RSDS) possible. As of this writing, approximately 90 percent of the educational agencies in Iowa have adopted the RSDS model. The competencies required in consultation-based decision making are deemed essential to produce more effective services for children and youth.

Coordinate Power Status

A key aspect of the consultant-consultee relationship is that it is coordinate in nature. In other words, the consultant and consultee(s) have co-equal status, or *parity*, in making decisions (West, 1990). It is important to recognize that a *coordinate power status* in decision-making does not presume complete equality in expertise. It is assumed that each participant brings to consultation different, complementary areas of expertise, each of which contributes uniquely to the process. This is contrasted to a hierarchical relationship, wherein open communication is restricted and the consultant dominates and controls decision making. There have been several studies suggesting that consultees prefer collaborative approaches to consultation (Babcock & Pryzwansky, 1983; Pryzwansky & White, 1983; Wenger, 1979).

An interesting line of research by William Erchul and his colleagues (Erchul, 1987; Erchul & Chewning, 1990; Erchul, Hughes, Meyers, Hickman, & Braden, 1992) investigated various interpersonal processes in consultation. These researchers suggest that effective consultation takes place in a *cooperative* relationship, wherein consultants generally take a leadership role and consultees follow that lead. They also believe that consultation is more effective when both consultants and consultees accept unique, albeit different, roles (rather than competing for control, for example). According to Erchul (1992), *"Teamwork* subsumes cooperation and implies further that who leads and who follows may change over the course of the consulting relationship" (p. 365, italics added). We recognize the necessity of a leadership role in collaborative interactions, particularly when decision making or problem solving is the primary objective. We further endorse Erchul's (1992) suggestion that consultation be considered cooperative and implemented constructively within a "teamwork" modality.

Consultee's Right to Reject Suggestions

When consultees are afforded equal status in consultative decision making, by definition they have the prerogative to reject consultants' recommendations. Acceptance of the consultee's right to reject suggestions may help preclude power struggles between the consultant and consultee. Consultees may reject suggestions for a number of reasons, and consultants must remain flexible and cognizant of those factors which affect the acceptability of an intervention. *Treatment acceptability* is defined as "judgments by lay persons, clients, and others of whether treatment procedures are appropriate, fair, and reasonable for the problem client" (Kazdin, 1981, p. 493). It is safe to say that unless a consultee finds a treatment acceptable in terms of his or her time, resources, and other practical and theoretical aspects, it is likely that it will not be implemented (or it will be implemented incorrectly) (Witt, Martens & Elliott, 1984). The theoretical orientation of the consultee, the time and/or resources required to implement the intervention, and the perceived effectiveness of the plan are factors that might contribute to the degree to which a consultee finds a treatment desirable (Witt et al., 1984). In consultation, then, consultants and consultees should work together to develop a plan that is acceptable both in terms of (1) objective criteria (that is, there is sound empirical support for its effectiveness); and (2) subjective criteria (meaning, it is acceptable to the consultee) (Gutkin & Curtis, 1990).

Active Involvement of the Consultee

The *active involvement* of the consultee is generally seen as an important ingredient of consultative interactions. This is based on the belief that active participation in the identification and analysis of a problem will increase "ownership" for its solution; and when a consultee "owns" a treatment plan, it is assumed that it will be implemented with integrity (that is, correctly; as intended). It has been demonstrated that consultee implementation of interventions developed in consultation is related directly to the degree of consultee involvement in problem solving (Reinking, Livesay, & Kohl, 1978).

Teachers generally believe that it is important to be involved in developing programs for students experiencing difficulties (Gutkin, 1986). However, many are not trained in consultation and may not know the most efficacious way to fulfill this role (Kratochwill & Van Someren, 1985). There is now some support that increasing a consultee's level of *self-efficacy* (meaning the individual's belief in his or her own ability to can effectively handle difficult situations) may contribute to active participation by the consultee in consultation (Brown & Schulte, 1987; Gutkin & Hickman, 1988). In a reciprocal manner, active involvement in consultation may also increase a consultee's self-efficacy (Ponti & Curtis, 1984).

Voluntary Nature

Another central aspect of the consultation relationship is that participants are involved *voluntarily*. In other words, no one is "forced" to participate. In ideal circumstances, a consultee voluntarily approaches a consultant to request assistance with a particular problem or concern. This suggests that the consultee recognizes the existence of a problem that warrants attention and is willing to exert time and energy to remedy the situation. In other situations, however, consultation may be suggested by a third party (such as a school administrator or supervisor). As long as the consultant and consultee provide consent for their involvement in the process, consultative interactions can be productive regardless of how consultation was initiated. When consultation is not initiated spontaneously by the consultee, good interpersonal skills (such as warmth, empathy, and active listening) can increase his or her consensual agreement to consultation.

Competencies Important for Effective Consultation

A number of professional and interpersonal competencies are considered prerequisite for effective consultation to occur. These include self-awareness, good interpersonal and communication skills, knowledge of intervention technology (*content expertise*), effective problem-solving skills (*process expertise*), an understanding of organizations and organizational functioning, and an awareness of

Collaborative consultation is a dynamic problem solving process involving individuals with diverse backgrounds and expertise.

and sensitivity to cultural, racial, ethnic and gender issues (Zins & Ponti, 1990). Although the integration of these competencies cannot guarantee an effective outcome in consultation, they contribute to the overall likelihood that the consultation process will proceed in a positive and productive manner. Of particular importance is the recognition that while each of these competencies appear necessary, none is sufficient to ensure consultation effectiveness. For example, a combination of content expertise (knowledge about effective interventions, learning difficulties, social-emotional problems), process expertise (understanding the components of problem solving), and good interpersonal skills are all deemed necessary to the overall outcomes of consultation interactions.

West and Cannon (1988) identified several essential consultation competencies for individuals involved in collaborative interactions. Using a Delphi technique, an expert panel identified forty-seven such competencies in eight categories. The competencies receiving the highest ratings included skills in the following:

1. *Interactive communication*—communicating clearly in oral and written form; using active, ongoing listening and responding skills, interviewing effectively; giving and soliciting continuous feedback.

2. *Collaborative problem solving*—integrating solutions into a plan of action, using observation and interviewing skills to increase objectivity and mutuality throughout problem solving, and remaining available throughout implementation.

3. *Personal characteristics*—being caring, respectful, empathic, and open in consultation interactions; and demonstrating a willingness to learn from others throughout the consultation process.

4. *Evaluation of consultation effectiveness*—using continuous evaluative feedback, and evaluating the impact of several variables on desired consultation outcomes.

The essential competencies identified in this study have been used as the basis for a comprehensive curriculum to train all individuals involved in collaborative problem solving (West, Idol, & Cannon, 1989).

An Ecological Approach to Consultation

Consultation practice and research requires the recognition that children, families, teachers, classrooms and schools are complex systems. The integration of several sources of information is necessary to measure different problem domains, broaden the scope of potential issues to be addressed in consultation, and expand the understanding of a particular child or system problem. It is with these goals in mind that we now turn to an ecological approach to collaborative decision making. The basic model will be presented in the remainder of this chapter; opportunities for application will be presented throughout the remainder of the text.

There are four basic stages in the collaborative process. The stages, and their component sub-stages, are presented in Table 3–2. Our ecological approach to consultation, developed for use in educational partnerships, is derived primarily from the behavioral consultation model described by Bergan and Kratochwill (1990), with some important relationship considerations from mental health consultation and systemic considerations from organizational development. A collaborative process worksheet is presented in Figure 3–2. It should be emphasized that these stages outline the general process that is followed by dyads or teams of individuals in collaborative interactions. They act only as a guide for decision making, and are not meant to dictate rigidly the collaborative process. This is important to note, because there is always a risk for practitioners entering a consultative interaction to adhere rigidly to a linear format. Structured worksheets may create or perpetuate the notion that the process must strictly follow a chronological order of steps. Researchers have discovered, however, that although each of the stages appears important to the outcome of a case (Fuchs & Fuchs, 1989), they need not be followed in an orderly and sequential manner (Tindal, Parker, & Hasbrouck, 1992). There is often overlap between the stages, and it may be necessary to reconsider issues addressed earlier in the process. On the other hand, a benefit of a sequential problem-solving process is that the structure often helps keep participants on task and minimizes digression.

One case study will be presented in the following sections to illustrate important objectives of each of the stages in the collaborative process. The

| Table 3–2 | **Stages of the Collaborative Process** |

Situational Definition
  A. Identify component parts.
  B. Prioritize component parts.
  C. Provide an operational definition, focusing on one component part.
  D. Identify tentative antecedents and consequences.
  E. Determine data collection procedures.
Ecological Analysis
  A. Conduct a conditions and/or skills analysis:
    1. Antecedents
    2. Consequences
    3. Situational
  B. Identify setting, participants, and strength.
  C. Identify existing procedures or previous intervention attempts.
  D. State short-term and/or long-term goals.
Plan Development and Implementation
  A. Brainstorm alternative solutions.
  B. Identify chosen alternative.
  C. Identify resources necessary and available to contribute to solution.
  D. Specify implementation steps, timelines, and responsibilities.
Plan Evaluation
  A. Specify how, when, and by whom the plan will be monitored.
  B. Specify how, when, and by whom progress will be evaluated.
  C. Determine next steps (future actions on unaddressed problems, follow-up, etc.).

student in this case (Kerry) is a second-grade student referred for consultation by her teacher for distractable and inattentive behaviors.

Stage 1: Situational Definition

Perhaps the most important stage of the entire collaborative process is defining the presenting situation. This requires specific and precise clarification of the issue to be addressed. Early consultation research by Bergan and his associates (Bergan & Tombari, 1975, 1976) has suggested that once a problem is identified accurately, a solution almost always follows. However, if problems are defined incompletely or incorrectly, problem solving will likely be ineffective or terminated prematurely. Given the importance of this stage, educational partners should take care to ensure that adequate time and energies are expended in efforts to identify and clarify the issues to be addressed in the collaborative process.

The ecological context and way that a situation is defined will determine the direction of future steps. An issue can be defined at one of several levels.

Figure 3–2
Collaborative Process Worksheet

IV. Plan Evaluation			
A. Review steps, with desired and obtained outcomes, and determine necessary revisions and responsibilities:			
Program Steps	Desired Outcomes	Obtained Outcomes	Revisions/Responsibilities
1.			
2.			
3.			
4.			
5.			
6.			
B. Specify follow-up procedures:			

Figure 3–2
continued

B. Setting: Discuss various problem settings, but prioritize only one.

C. Participants (e.g., who is involved?):

D. Strength (e.g., how frequent, intense, severe?):

E. Existing procedures or previous intervention attempts:

F. Short-term and/or long-term goals:

III. Plan Development and Implementation

A. Brainstorm alternative solutions:

Alternative Solutions   Possible Consequences

B. Identify chosen alternative:

Figure 3–2
continued

C. Develop management plan:

1. Specify resources needed and determine availability:

Necessary Resources	Available?	
	Yes	No
Physical:		
Technological:		
Information:		
Financial:		
Human:		

2. Complete management plan matrix:

Program Steps	Who	What	When	Where	Desired Outcome
1.					
2.					
3.					
4.					
5.					
6.					

Figure 3–2
(Continued)

IV. Plan Evaluation

A. Review steps, with desired and obtained outcomes, and determine necessary revisions and responsibilities:

Program Steps	Desired Outcomes	Obtained Outcomes	Revisions/Responsibilities
1.			
2.			
3.			
4.			
5.			
6.			

B. Specify follow-up procedures:

For example, it can be defined as a district or school issue, a classroom problem, or a difficulty within an individual teacher, child, or family. It should be recognized that the higher the level targeted, the broader the impact. For example, if a student is referred for behavioral problems, the issue can be defined as his or her lack of self-control (student-level) or the teacher's lack of behavior management skills (teacher-level). If it is determined through observation and consultation that the entire class is unruly, consultation may revolve around helping the teacher develop and use more effective disciplinary tactics at the classroom level. When it is appropriate, one can easily see the potential benefits of approaching issues at a broad rather than narrow level.

Oftentimes issues referred for consultation are complex and multifaceted. Therefore, it is important to define and prioritize the component parts. This process of analyzing parts of a complex issue will make problem solving and decision making more manageable. For example, Kerry's teacher referred her to the school psychologist, describing her as "highly distractible and inattentive." While this teacher may know exactly what she means, other members of the partnership may conceptualize these types of problems differently. The target issue can be clarified by eliciting specific examples of her concerns. Taken a step further, she may state that Kerry looks out the window, walks around the room, does not complete assignments in class, and fails to turn in homework on time. Any one of these behaviors can be selected as the focus of consultation. By narrowing in on a specific target, (such as "out of seat" or "fails to turn in homework"), the assessment and consultation process is made simpler and more manageable. A number of factors should be considered when selecting a target on which to focus in consultation. Table 3–3 lists

Table 3–3 **Philosophical Considerations for Selecting Targets of Consultation**

1. Behaviors should be changed that are physically dangerous to the client or to others.

2. Behavior is abnormal if it is aversive to others, especially by virtue of its deviance from the norm or unpredictability.

3. Select a behavior to maximize the flexibility of the client's repertoire and the long-term individual or social good.

4. Behavior to be changed should be stated in positive or constructionist terms.

5. Optimal, not average, levels of performance should be sought.

6. Select for modification only those behaviors that the environment will continue to maintain.

7. Target behaviors should be selected that fall within the parameters of the consultant's repertoire.

some common considerations. For purposes of illustration, let us assume that "out of seat behaviors" is selected for consultation.

When determining the focus of collaborative decision making, it is important to ensure that individuals involved in the task have a clear and precise definition of the presenting issue. Thus, regardless of the level at which issues are defined, it is important to operationally define that which is to be targeted for intervention. *Operational definitions* specify problems or behaviors in terms that are observable, concrete, specific, and objective. For example, a principal may want to define a problem as Paul's "aggression." However, this may be conceptualized in many different ways, leading to an unclear understanding of the specific concern. A better definition might be "use of physical force (i.e., kicking, hitting, striking out at peers) when engaged in group activities on the playground." In the case of Kerry, "out of seat behavior" can be operationally defined as "Kerry is in a place other than her assigned desk or workplace (e.g., bookshelf, pencil sharpener, hallway, window) without adult permission during academic or instructional time."

When specifying the target in collaborative interactions, it is important to define the situation in such a way that something can be done about it. This emphasizes the importance of considering environmental events that can be targeted and altered, rather than internal conditions that are largely outside the realm of educational interventions. For example, a problem may be defined as a student having a learning disability, an alcoholic parent, or an organic disorder. Focusing solely on the educational label, the family dysfunction, or the internal medical problem allows educators little control over its remediation. In other words, educators can do little to "fix" a problem when it is defined in these terms. However, if a situation is defined in terms of its behavioral manifestations (for example, Kerry is out of her seat five times per hour), or in terms of instructional or environmental conditions (for example, Kerry has failed to master simple multiplication facts; or Kerry is out of seat primarily during indepedent math assignments), educators are more likely to have some control over its treatment.

After defining a specific component of a discrete problem, collaborators will attempt to identify environmental conditions that may be contributing to its occurrence. This includes a tentative articulation of antecedents and consequences (events that precede and follow the situation). Because careful observations and baseline data collection will not have occurred yet in most cases, this discussion will be speculative and confirmed or disconfirmed during the next stage (ecological analysis).

One likely outcome of Stage 1 is the need for more information. Data collection is necessary to determine the actual severity of a situation, environmental factors affecting its occurrence, and other ecological considerations. It is thus likely that a great deal of time will be spent in the early parts of Stage 1 identifying and defining the situation. Efforts should then shift to developing a method for data collection. This empirical approach to decision making is critically important in analyzing the situation accurately, designing an

Activity 3–2

An extremely important component of consultation is defining target behaviors in specific and concrete terms, known as *operational definitions*. Develop operational definitions for the following general problems. Remember that the definitions should be clear, observable, and objective.

1. Lily is "hyperactive" during afternoon recess.

2. Bob is a "slow learner."

3. Carol "lacks social skills."

4. Steven is "immature."

intervention based on the data, and evaluating the effectiveness of the collaborative process.

Stage 2: Ecological Analysis

Once an issue is accurately identified and relevant information is obtained through interviews, observations, and other assessment techniques (see Chapter 6), the various components that may be contributing to the situation are analyzed. The goals of an *ecological analysis* are to (1) examine salient ecological conditions surrounding and potentially contributing to the situation; (2) determine its topographical features (what it "looks like", how strong it is, how often it occurs); and (3) explore resources that may assist in interventions.

Oftentimes the environmental conditions surrounding a problem contribute so greatly to its prevalence that they are thought to have a controlling influence. When identifying the "real problem" (Zins, Curtis, Graden & Ponti, 1988), ecological, or *contextual, factors* must be considered. This means that rather than focusing solely on topographical features of a problem (e.g., what it looks like, how often it occurs), one must analyze contextual variables within the environment in which it occurs (for example, conditions that may reinforce its occurrence, time of day a problem occurs, persons involved across situations, curricular or instructional practices). In the case of Kerry, it may be observed that she has great difficulty attending to seatwork when desks are arranged in groups of four, but demonstrates little difficulty when they are in rows or when an individualized study carrel is provided. Here, the physical layout of the classroom is an important factor to consider when assessing Kerry's "attentional problems."

One way to examine environmental events is by exploring antecedent, consequent, and sequential conditions. *Antecedent conditions* are events that precede the occurrence of a problematic situation. For example, in the case of Kerry, her teacher may be asked to identify events that typically happen before Kerry gets out of her seat inappropriately. The teacher may be able to identify a common stimulus, such as the provision of instructions to take out math workbooks and begin working independently on worksheets. *Consequent conditions* are environmental events that follow a specific situation. In response to a question about what generally happens after Kerry leaves her seat, her teacher may recall that Kerry's classmates often talk to her as she walks around the room. This information is important, because these environmental conditions (antecedents and consequences) can be altered in an intervention designed to decrease Kerry's distractibility and increase her on-task behaviors. *Sequential conditions* are common patterns across problematic occasions, such as time of day or day of week (Kratochwill & Bergan, 1990). For example, Kerry's teacher may recognize that her out of seat behavior is generally worse in the afternoon immediately following recess, at which time math instruction is provided. Other existing conditions to examine include rules in effect, structure of the setting, and difficulty level of assignments. For example, it would be important to uncover the expectations (implicit and explicit) placed on Kerry for staying in her seat and finishing her work.

By exploring events in this way, some practical and effective methods of altering the environment to increase Kerry's on-task behaviors become obvious. For example, antecedent conditions can be altered by changing the way in which instructions are given; consequent conditions can be modified by employing a group contingency in the classroom to decrease inappropriate talking during independent seatwork time; and sequential conditions can be manipulated by changing the workbook instructional time to the morning hours.

Conditions analyses are important to explore when the target of consultation is behavioral in nature (e.g., inattention, fighting, skipping school). However, in some situations it will be important to conduct a *skills analysis* along with or in place of a conditions analysis. Skills analyses allow educators to explore the skill level of an individual or group of individuals when the concern is one of ability. For example, skills analyses are appropriate to determine the level of a student's academic or social skills. They are conducted by (1) identifying the target skill that should be present; (2) breaking the skill down into its component parts; (3) assessing the target student's ability to perform each component subskill; (4) determining the uppermost level at which the target student can perform to mastery; and (5) developing an intervention for the student, starting at the point at which he or she demonstrates mastery.

Taking the example of Kerry, it may be questioned during the ecological analysis whether Kerry has adequate math skills to complete the assigned work. A simple assumption on the part of the teacher is usually inadequate to make this determination. For example, a perusal of one of Kerry's sample math worksheets may reveal that she makes several errors on problems that require addition with carrying. A formal skills analysis may demonstrate that while Kerry is able to add single digits and double digits that do not require carry-over, she does not know the rules for carrying numbers. Thus, training in this skill would become part of the intervention.

A few additional considerations are necessary before moving to the next stage (plan development). First, it is important to specify clearly the goals for consultation to ensure that the expectations are clear and appropriate. Goal specification provides clear direction to the process, and allows partners an objective manner for measuring attainment of consultation objectives. For example, in the case of Kerry, the teacher and consultant might determine that Kerry is out of her seat approximately five times during each math period, with each instance lasting approximately five minutes. An acceptable level of "out of seat behavior" might be twice per period, each lasting no more than three minutes.

Finally, all existing resources that can be used in an intervention program should be identified (Zins & Ponti, 1990). All organizational subsystems should be considered. This includes the human, informational, technological, physical, and financial resources available to a consultation team (see section on organizational development earlier in this chapter). In the case of Kerry, human resources might include peer tutors, parent volunteers, special educators, custodial staff, community service-providers, and Kerry herself. Informational resources could include training or inservice by the school psychologist on matters regarding classroom management of children with attentional difficulties. Technological resources may include beeper tapes to cue Kerry to return to her seat, record forms for keeping track of her behavior, or the classroom computer to serve as a reinforcer. Physical resources would be the classroom setting itself, as well as other settings that might be used by Kerry's teacher, such as the library or media center. The importance of establishing collaborative partnerships with all relevant persons is highlighted especially at this point. The active involvement of teachers, administrators, school psychologists, counselors, parents and students will help identify a wide range of possible resources to be utilized in the development and implementation of a comprehensive program.

Stage 3: Plan Development and Implementation

By this point in collaborative decision making, partners have identified and defined a target; established goals for consultation; explored and analyzed important ecological and skill factors contributing to problem occurrence; and pinpointed resources that can be included in a treatment program. All of this information must now be integrated and utilized in the development of a feasible, effective plan.

There are three steps to plan development. To develop a meaningful intervention, partners in consultation must (1) brainstorm alternative solutions; (2) identify a chosen alternative; and (3) develop a management plan (that is, specify implementation steps, timelines and responsibilities). Like-wise, individuals within the process must be careful to remain open and flex-ible rather than committed to a personal agenda. Considering a range of possible options is important, and brainstorming will allow for a number of diverse alternatives to be explored.

Brainstorming is defined as "a group problem-solving technique that involves the spontaneous contribution of ideas from all members of the group" (West et al., 1989, p. 206). By definition, brainstorming takes place in a group and relies on contributions from all members. This process takes advantage of the diverse expertise of all partners involved in consultative decision making. Input from each member is critical, so it is very important that each feels that his or her views are valued. Interpersonal skills of active listening, nonjudgmental responding, and reframing can facilitate the brain-storming process (see Chapter 4).

There are certain "rules" to increase the effectiveness of brainstorming. First, it is desirable to set a time limit on brainstorming (say, five minutes) to impose structure and move the process along. Second, it is important to think creatively and generate as many ideas for solutions as possible. This will allow several diverse alternatives to be considered. Third, all qualitative judgments of alternatives should be withheld until the next step of plan development. Rather than engaging in lengthy discussion about the feasibil-ity or desirability of each option, it is preferable to use brainstorming time simply to get ideas on the table. This encourages rapid and creative think-ing, facilitates the generation of many suggestions, and allows participants to feel uninhibited to state ideas openly. Fourth, all ideas should be recorded quickly and accurately. A recorder should be identified prior to brainstorm-ing; however, this person should be encouraged to remain an active partici-pant in the generation of alternatives. Fifth, the situational leader should use active listening and reframing when necessary to manage conflict and ensure accurate recording of ideas.

After the formal brainstorming process is completed, each of the alterna-tives is examined. A major question to address is the likelihood of each alter-native to be successful in resolving the target issue. This determination should be research-based, and the pooled expertise of various members in the collab-orative partnership will maximize the probability that information on treatment effectiveness is readily available. Important points to consider in the evalua-tion of intervention alternatives include cost, time, and skills required for implementation. It is likely that some options will be practically or logistically impossible; these can be deleted prior to discussion. Likewise, the possible consequences on faculty, students, and others not directly involved in the pro-gram must be discussed. Other factors that may affect acceptability of an inter-vention include theoretical orientation of treatment agents (those responsible for implementation of the program), complexity of the plan, number of per-sons required to participate and severity of the problem (Witt et al., 1984).

Table 3–4   **Criteria for Judging the Adequacy of an Action Plan**

1. Does the plan appear feasible to the persons responsible for implementing it? Are the treatment agents committed to this plan?

2. Have roles been clarified with each person involved in the plan?

3. Have timelines been established clearly, including beginning dates and dates for review?

4. Are the material and human resources required for implementation easily accessible?

5. Do the potential benefits outweigh the costs (including time, money, materials, human energy, unnecessary side effects, risks)?

6. Have the data collection systems been considered adequately?

7. Does the plan allow for modifications?

Source: Adapted with modification from *Collaboration in the Schools: An Inservice and Preservice Curriculum for Teachers, Support Staff, and Administrators. Instructor's Manual* (p. 218) by J. F. West, L. Idol and G. Cannon, 1989, Austin, TX: Pro Ed. Copyright 1989 by Pro-Ed, Inc. Adapted by permission.

The final step prior to implementing a program is to clarify implementation procedure(s) and develop a *management plan*—a written document that specifies all components of the intervention in concrete and explicit terms. Management plans should include information on *what* will be done, *who* is responsible, *when* and *where* the program will be implemented, and *how* the details will be executed. Thus, it should address the following: (1) the actual activities that will take place; (2) how the plan will be orchestrated or implemented (if extra resources are necessary, their attainment should also be determined); (3) who will be responsible for carrying out and monitoring each activity; (4) when the plan is to be in effect, or when the activity is to be done (how often, for how long, what time); and (5) where the plan will be implemented (classroom, lunchroom, home). A management plan is developed as part of the collaborative process. The collaborative process worksheet (Figure 3–2) includes the procedural details for developing and initiating an effective management plan. West et al. (1989) offered specific criteria for judging the adequacy of a management plan, which are presented in Table 3–4. Finally, procedures to continue data collection should be determined and the details of evaluation (how and when progress will be measured) should be delineated.

All of the preceding steps, if carried out adequately and successfully, should facilitate the implementation stage of collaborative problem-solving. It is particularly important that a clear, specific, complete *management plan* be developed and followed by all individuals involved in the process.

To maximize the success of the program, Zins et al. (1988) suggest two issues worthy of consideration. First, close follow-up by an individual involved in the development of the plan is helpful to provide technical and personal support. In general, this will take the form of an informal meeting to assess how program implementation is progressing. Second, ensuring the integrity of the intervention is of utmost importance. *Treatment integrity* is concerned with the match between how a program was developed, and how it is implemented in practice. Important questions regarding treatment integrity include, "Is the plan being implemented as intended?" and "Is everyone following through on their responsibilities?" If a treatment is being implemented incorrectly, the potential effectiveness of the intervention is in jeopardy. Observations and informal interviews can serve as vehicles by which to assess treatment integrity.

There are several reasons why a plan may be implemented incorrectly. They may stem from lack of clear communication, knowledge, skills, or resources. For example, a counselor may have misunderstood his or her responsibilities in the program. In this case, clarification of the roles of each participant is vital. Alternatively, a teacher may not have the knowledge or skills for implementing a necessary component of the program in the classroom. Procedures for training in the necessary skills (e.g., providing reading materials, modeling, co-teaching) would be appropriate here. Whenever skills training is required to ensure integrity of the procedures, care should be taken to maintain a collegial and cooperative relationship rather than one characterized by dominance and superiority.

Stage 4: Plan Evaluation

After a plan has been in effect for a sufficient amount of time, its effectiveness is evaluated. The timing and details of evaluation should be determined in the planning stage and included in the action plan. For example, it may be decided to evaluate how the plan is working after two weeks of implementation. Progress may be measured by keeping a frequency count of a behavior both prior to and during the treatment implementation stage. Because the goals for consultation were determined during the initial stage, it will be possible to evaluate the degree to which the consultation goals are being attained.

Ideally, plan evaluations should be data-based. Data collection procedures can be as simple as keeping a log of work samples (permanent products) or as demanding as having a teacher, student, or parent keep daily frequency counts of a target behavior. Because data will be collected during all stages, the data can be graphed and analyzed to determine the effectiveness of an intervention objectively. Decision-making rules for analyzing data trends are presented in Table 3–5 (adapted from West et al., 1989).

In evaluating the effectiveness of a plan, there are several directions that a consultation team might take. The decision will rest largely on the outcome

Table 3–5   **Decision-Making Rules for Analyzing Data Trends**

- Stable data trends mean that the beneficial or detrimental factors are clear. If the factors are detrimental, a program change can be made; if they are beneficial, this can be a clear indicator that the behavior is maintaining.

- A deteriorating trend indicates that the behavior is getting worse and that a program change is warranted.

- A decreasing trend means that the behavior is improving on its own and an intervention is not warranted. It is implied that adequate assessment of the behavior has not occurred, and something is occurring during the measurement that is positively influencing the behavior.

- A variable trend indicates that the occurrence of the behavior is so variable that a stable and clear pattern does not emerge. Two possible solutions are to

  1. extend the length of measurement time until some data stability is achieved, and

  2. determine the sources of the extreme negative and positive points on the data trend.

- A variable-stable trend indicates that the data trend has been extended long enough to achieve some stability; now a decision can be made regarding possible program change.

- An increasing-decreasing trend means that at first the behavior gets worse, followed by a period of improvement. As long as the behavior continues to improve, a program change should not be made.

- A decreasing-increasing trend means the opposite of the trend described above. The behavior is initially improving, followed by a period of deterioration. The latter shows a strong case for a program change. Caution should be exercised in taking measurements for a very short period of time; the result could be a faulty decision based on the first half of the data trend.

- An unstable trend is variable and has no discernible pattern. A program change cannot be made under the conditions being measured. The solutions may be to

  1. continue collecting data until stability is achieved,

  2. determine if the wrong behavior is being measured, or

  3. determine if there are reliability problems in how the behavior is being measured.

Source: Adapted with modification from *Collaboration in the Schools: An Inservice and Preservice Curriculum for Teachers, Support Staff, and Administrators. Instructor's Manual* (p. 218) by J. F. West, L. Idol and G. Cannon, 1989, Austin, TX: Pro Ed. Copyright 1989 by Pro-Ed, Inc. Adapted by permission.

of the intervention. If the plan appeared to be ineffective or only partially effective at resolving the situation, previous phases of the collaborative process should be reviewed. It might be determined that the situation was incorrectly or inadequately defined. In this case, it is desirable to recycle to the identification stage, redefine the target of consultation, and proceed through the stages once again. On the other hand, various contextual determinants may have been overlooked, requiring a reconsideration of the ecological analysis and subsequent stages. It also might be decided that revisions in the existing plan are necessary or that an alternative strategy needs to be tried altogether.

In some cases, the plan will be effective and the goals of consultation will have been met. Under these optimal conditions, it may be decided to phase out the plan. When discussing termination of a program, it is important to discuss ways to maintain and generalize the gains procured through the intervention. *Maintenance* refers to the demonstration of treatment effects over time (Barrios & Hartmann, 1988). For example, if a student continues to demonstrate increased on-task behaviors three months after the program is terminated, it might be concluded that the treatment gains are "maintained over time." *Generalization* is the demonstration of treatment gains with persons, places or behaviors that were not targeted in the original treatment (Barrios & Hartmann, 1988). For example, treatment plans to increase on-task behaviors are generally implemented initially in the classroom setting. If a target student shows increased on-task behaviors in the library, "generalization across settings" is

Activity 3–3

Teams vary greatly in their approach to problems and the steps they take to resolve issues. If you are currently working in a school setting, observe an ongoing team meeting. If you do not have access to a formalized team, observe fellow students engaged in a role-play. Use the collaborative process worksheet to identify how many of the steps are followed by the team. Generate overall impressions of the team by considering the following questions:

1. What is the situation being addressed by the team?

2. Is there an identified leader?

3. Are all persons involved in the situation present?

4. How do individual team members contribute to the overall purpose of the meeting?

5. Is any type of format followed, or do team members discuss issues in an unfocused manner?

6. Are various perspectives and resources considered?

7. Are roles and responsibilities clearly articulated?

suggested. Unfortunately, maintenance and generalization do not typically occur spontaneously. In fact, unless specific details for maintenance and generalization are included in the structured collaborative process, the likelihood of observing such effects is minimal (Stokes & Baer, 1977).

Along with considering procedures to maximize maintenance and generalization of intervention effects, a specific *follow-up plan* should be determined to assess the degree to which the gains made during the implementation stage have maintained. If regression is seen, suggestions for re-implementation of the plan may be appropriate. Or strategies for modifying the procedures may be appropriate.

Oftentimes, issues that are brought to consultation are very complex. As discussed earlier, it is appropriate to break a situation down into component parts. The way a target is operationally defined, then, is often only part of the "big picture." Once progress is seen in one area, it is appropriate to address the next component part. At times the effects of an intervention are seen on not only the target issue, but also on related parts (that is, generalization across behaviors is demonstrated). However, it is more likely that specific attention will need to be directed toward other components of the overall situation. Thus, recycling through the entire consultation process (beginning with situational definition) will provide necessary attention to the additional components.

Chapter Summary

Consultation is becoming increasingly recognized as the foundation by which to provide a number of alternative services in the schools. Several models of consultation have been described in the educational literature (cf. West & Idol, 1987). Most approaches share the common characteristics of indirect service delivery, voluntary and coordinate relationships, and dual goals of prevention and remediation. Three consultation models (mental health, organizational development, and behavioral) have provided the impetus for our articulation of an ecological approach to consultation. As described in this chapter, consultation is one important form of a collaborative educational partnership implemented in school settings.

There are four stages in our ecological approach to consultation. The first, situational definition, is implemented to define the target of consultation and determine procedures for collecting baseline information. The importance of defining the issue of concern cannot be overstated, and operational definitions should be clear, concrete, observable and specific. Tentative conditions surrounding the situation will also be explored; however, specific antecedents and consequences cannot be confirmed or disconfirmed until careful observations are conducted.

The second stage of consultation, ecological analysis, is conducted to ascertain the specific environmental conditions that occur in conjunction with the situation. Antecedent conditions are events that precede the occurrence of a problematic situation, and consequent conditions are those that follow it. Likewise, sequential conditions should be identified, which include common patterns such as typical time of day or day of the week that an issue arises. By pinpointing these ecological events, it is possible to develop a good hunch about why a problem situation exists, and to modify the environment to control its occurrence. If the conditions are identified accurately and modified appropriately, the chances for problem resolution are greatly improved.

During the third stage, a plan is developed and implemented to address the issues identified and analyzed. Brainstorming is an important process that involves the spontaneous contribution of group members regarding possible treatment plan options. Finally, during plan evaluation, the program steps and outcomes are reviewed to determine the effectiveness of the program and determine the need for continuation, revision, or termination. Although this stage is critical to the overall outcome of team practices, it is often disregarded in practice.

The four stages of our ecological approach to consultation and collaboration can be implemented in dyads (such as a teacher and special educator or a parent and school psychologist) or in larger teams of professionals. The stages are presented in a highly structured and linear fashion to help participants remain focused and attain the primary objectives of consultation. However, it is important to recognize that in practice, there is often overlap in the fluid progression of consultation steps. When practitioners understand the objectives of each stage and recognize when those objectives are met, the benefits of collaborative problem solving will be maximized.

Case Study 3–1

Sara M. is a six-year-old, first-grade student with average to above-average intellectual abilities. She has a younger brother, and lives in the country with her mother. Sara's teacher is very concerned with her extreme shyness, and reported that Sara has not said a single word since the beginning of the school year. She rarely participates in activities with other children in the classroom or on the playground, preferring to wander or sit alone. When she does participate with others, the activities tend to be short-lived, and Sara does not speak. Other children have begun to accept Sara's lack of talking, and phrase their questions so that she can point, nod, shake her head, or use other nonverbal gestures. When a verbal response is required, other students typically respond for Sara. However, the other children are beginning to leave Sara out of games because of her lack of responsiveness. Sara's academic progress may also be hindered, in that she fails to ask or respond to questions, read orally, or volunteer for projects.

Sara's teacher expressed her concerns with Mrs. M., who stated that Sara has adequate language abilities, and speaks freely at home. However, similar behaviors were reported to occur when the family goes out in public (for example, to the store). She cannot understand why Sara refuses to talk in public. Mrs. M. agreed to assist school personnel in implementing procedures to encourage Sara to speak at school.

1. How might a team of professionals define the problematic situation?

2. Who should be involved in the collaborative process in this case?

3. What ecological conditions seem important to Sara's lack of speech? What antecedent, consequent, and sequential conditions should be explored?

4. What resources should be considered to address the issue?

5. What are some possible plans that could be tried to meet the consultation goals?

6. How might progress toward the consultation goals be measured in this case? In other words, how might the effectiveness of a plan be determined?

Key Vocabulary Terms

least restrictive environment (LRE)	treatment acceptability	antecedent conditions
consultation	active involvement	consequent conditions
mental health consultation (MHC)	self-efficacy	sequential conditions
organizational development (OD) consultation	voluntary nature	skills analysis
	content expertise	brainstorming
lack of objectivity	process expertise	management plan
human-systems theory	contextual variables	treatment integrity
behavioral consultation (BC)	operational definition	maintenance
situational definition	ecological analysis	generalization
coordinate power status (parity)	conditions analysis	follow-up plan

Chapter 4

Chapter Overview

Effective Communication and Interpersonal Skills in Collaborative Partnerships

Chapter Objectives

Upon completing this chapter, the reader should be able to:

1. Discuss the importance of effective communication and interpersonal skills in collaborative partnerships.
2. Identify skills that have been identified as important in collaboration.
3. Describe the components of active listening.
4. Discuss the uses and limitations of open and closed questions.
5. List and define the five relationship building skills.
6. Discuss various communication phases that relationships undergo.
7. Identify specific skills that are important in each of the stages of the collaborative process.
8. Define conflict.
9. Identify several sources of conflict.
10. Generate a list of strategies to manage conflict.

Introduction

In Chapter 3, the importance of a structured approach to collaboration was emphasized. However, the integrity and effectiveness of the ecological consultation model will be compromised if communication and interpersonal skills are not integrated with technical expertise (Sheridan, Salmon, Kratochwill, & Rotto, 1992). Personal characteristics and professional competencies influence consultative relationships and the outcomes of collaborative interactions (Kirby, 1985). An individual's skill and expertise, personality factors and self-awareness, and attitudes and expectations are all important variables in the collaborative process (Fine, Grantham & Wright, 1979). Attention to basic communication and interpersonal factors is important to facilitate effective interactions.

Collaboration is a dynamic process between persons; thus, participants must be flexible and open in order to respond effectively. Establishment and maintenance of a positive collaborative relationship among participants in partnerships often determines whether interactions will continue and establishes the degree of commitment among individuals (Brammer & Shostrom, 1982). Approaching the partnership as an open and supportive relationship comprised of individuals who are prepared to actively listen and to offer information, skills, and resources allows members to strive toward positive resolution of identified problems (Fine et al., 1979).

This chapter explores the communication skills necessary for establishing effective interpersonal relationships within educational partnerships. Establishing an effective relationship provides the impetus for more direct strategies. Several communication skills essential to building and maintaining productive partnerships will be discussed. Following a detailed analysis of developmental stages and selected skills for each stage of collaboration, conflict and conflict management will be discussed as well.

Effective Collaboration Skills

The attitudes and skills of all participants in the collaborative partnership are important in determining the quality of problem-solving efforts. A balance of interpersonal and technical competence is critical to maximize effective work relations. We begin by examining the specific qualities and behaviors present in effective consultants and helpers.

Several researchers have identified personal qualities necessary for an effective consultant. Conoley (1981) suggested that the consultant must be friendly, open, supportive, nonthreatening, and good with groups to promote positive collaborative interactions. Cormier and Cormier (1985) proposed additional qualities as characteristic of effective helpers, including intellectual competence, energy, flexibility, support, goodwill, and self-awareness. West

Table 4–1 **Essential Consultation Skills**	
Skill	**Examples**
I. Interactive communication	A. Communicate clearly and effectively in oral and written form.
	B. Interview effectively to elicit information, share information, explore problems, set goals and objectives.
II. Equity issues, values, and beliefs	A. Facilitate equal learning opportunities by showing respect for individual differences.
	B. Advocate for services that accommodate the educational, social, and vocational needs of all students.
III. Personal characteristics	A. Exhibit the ability to be caring, respectful, empathic, congruent, and open.
	B. Demonstrate willingness to learn from others throughout the process.
IV. Collaborative problem solving	A. Integrate solutions into a flexible, feasible, and easily implemented plan of action.
	B. Utilize observation, feedback, and interviewing skills to increase objectively and mutuality.
V. Evaluation of effectiveness	A. Evaluate the impact of input, process and outcome variables on desired outcomes.
	B. Utilize continuous evaluative feedback to maintain, revise, or terminate activities.

and Cannon (1988) surveyed one hundred "experts" in consultation to identify essential consultation competencies for regular and special educators. Using a Delphi technique, they identified forty-seven competencies in eight categories as essential to the consultation process. The skills that received the highest ratings from the majority of panel members are presented in Table 4–1. These competency areas were further operationalized in a training package for use by professionals engaged in educational collaboration.

Communication Skills

Effective communication is essential at every stage of the collaborative process. It is important for developing a positive relationship and for movement towards problem management (Cormier & Cormier, 1985; Egan, 1986;

Fine, 1990; Johnson & Johnson, 1991). Important to effective communication are skills at sending and receiving information, active listening, questioning, and relationship building.

Sending and Receiving Information

The first component of effective communication is sending a message. The main objective is to ensure that the message is understood accurately by its receivers. There are three considerations to sending a message: phrase the message so that it can be comprehended correctly, have credibility as a sender, and ask for feedback regarding how the message affected the receiver (Johnson & Johnson, 1991). Suggestions for enhancing your ability to send information effectively are presented in Table 4–2.

Sending information represents only half of the essential components of effective communication. Receiving the information is the second half. To be a good receiver of messages, listeners must (1) demonstrate that they sincerely *want* to understand the ideas and feelings being conveyed, and (2) interpret the sender's ideas and feelings correctly (Johnson & Johnson, 1991). The importance of conveying a desire to understand the sender's message cannot be overstated. In fact, a major barrier to effective communication occurs when listeners evaluate or judge information as it is being communicated, rather than hearing it at face value. Statements such as, "I don't believe you," "That's a dumb idea," and "That will never work," impede the free flow of information and inhibit communication. When receiving messages, skills such as paraphrasing content, describing perceptions, and negotiating the

Table 4–2   Suggestions for Sending Messages

1. Clearly own your messages by using first-person singular pronouns ("I", "my").

2. Make your messages clear, complete and specific.

3. Make your verbal and nonverbal messages congruent.

4. Be redundant (i.e., say the same thing in different ways to ensure that the point is clear).

5. Ask for feedback concerning the way your messages are being received.

6. Make the message appropriate to the receiver's frame of reference (e.g., is the listener an expert or a novice? a child or an adult?).

7. Describe your feelings by name ("I feel sad"), action ("I feel like crying"), or figure of speech ("I feel down in the dumps").

8. Describe the others' behavior without evaluating or interpreting.

Source: Adapted from D. W. Johnson, and F. P. Johnson (1991). *Joining together: Group therapy and group skills.* 4th ed. Englewood Cliffs, NJ: Prentice-Hall.

meaning of a message are important (Johnson & Johnson, 1991). These are explored further in our discussion of listening skills.

Active Listening

Listening refers to "the ability of helpers to capture and understand the messages transmitted by clients; verbal or nonverbal, vague or clear" (Egan, 1986; p. 71). The main goal of listening is *understanding*. There are at least three components of total or complete listening. These include listening to and understanding (1) nonverbal behavior, (2) verbal messages, and (3) the person (Egan, 1986). Nonverbal behavior plays an important role in communication with others. Although the spoken word is generally emphasized, it has been estimated that 65 percent or more of the meaning of a message is conveyed by nonverbal behavior (Cormier & Cormier, 1985). Facial expressions, bodily motions, voice quality, and autonomic physiological responses are more than a channel of communication. They also serve to confirm or repeat what is being said verbally, deny or confuse what is being said verbally, strengthen or emphasize what is being said, and control or regulate what is happening within a conversation (Egan, 1986).

Reading nonverbal behavior involves discovering the meaning of what is being said verbally and nonverbally, without overinterpreting, or reading

Nonverbal behaviors such as body language, posture, facial expressions, and gestures can express positive and negative feelings.

more from the behavior than is actually intended. Since the same nonverbal behavior might mean different things to different people and at different times, the key is to understanding its role in communication is to consider the *context*. In other words, it is important to consider the entire message that is being conveyed, as well as the situation in which it is being communicated. Moreover, individual differences will likely dictate partially the meaning of the unspoken message. For example, some Indian cultures do not reinforce eye contact in conversation. Thus, if working with a parent or student from these ethnic groups, it is inappropriate to interpret lack of eye contact as a lack of interest in the subject matter or as a deficiency in social skills. The point is that participants in collaborative partnerships must remain aware of nonverbal behavior without distorting the meaning or problem situation (Egan, 1986). To repeat, the most important function of listening is understanding, not "dissecting" the speaker (Egan, 1986; p. 82).

Important subskills of effective listening are clarifying, attending, paraphrasing and summarizing. An easy way to remember these skills is with the acronym *CAPS*.

Clarifying.   Persons engaged in collaborative partnerships must effectively listen to and understand verbal messages. The content of verbal messages may include experiences (events and occurrences that happen to an individual), behaviors (actions of self or others), or affect (feelings and emotions that accompany either experiences or behavior) (Egan, 1986; Ivey, 1988). When attempting to understand a problem situation, one can request *clarification* on any of these levels (experiences, behaviors, or feelings).

Questioning is an important tool to increase clarification in communication. *Questions* are statements that elicit additional information and guide the process of communication. Effective questioning skills provide a systematic framework for directing an interaction. Although they are central to assessing and analyzing situations in collaboration, they must be used carefully. The main function of questions is to obtain information that will facilitate understanding of a problem or situation. When used inappropriately, the individual receiving questions may feel as though he or she is being interrogated, controlled, or put on the spot. These can all cause defensive and otherwise negative feelings and reactions. In general, questions can be one of two types: open or closed.

Open questions, or *providing an open invitation to talk,* are designed to elicit more than a single word or yes-no response from an individual. They provide limited structure and allow the individual to express pertinent concerns and feelings (Ivey, 1988). For example, an open question might be, "Describe the typical lunchtime routine." Comparatively, a closed question might be phrased "Do you supervise the students during lunch?" Open invitations to talk typically begin with "What," "How," or "Describe." They are extremely useful in a number of situations. First, they help begin an interview. An example of a question used in this case might be, "How have things been since the last time we talked?" Second, they encourage an individual to elaborate on a specific point. For example, one might say, "Tell me more about that." Third, they help elicit examples of specific behaviors and allow a better understanding of what is being described. "What do you do when Lisa tantrums?" is an example of a question used for this purpose. Finally, questions are important in the assessment and analysis of problems. Information on *what* the issue is, *who* is involved, *why, when,* and *where* problems occur, and *how* others respond are essential in ecological analysis. These key words refer to the function that the question serves, not necessarily the word with which the question begins. A general framework for diagnosis and question asking is provided in Table 4–3.

One advantage of the use of open-ended questions is their ability to elicit essential information. They allow one to obtain information regarding an individual's perceptions, attitudes, and experiences. Likewise, they contribute to the determination of an overt definition of the situation. As such, open questions should be used carefully and selectively to initiate conversation and encourage elaboration on specific points.

Closed questions are questions that can be answered in a few words or sentences (Ivey, 1988). They are useful for focusing a discussion and obtaining specific information. Oftentimes, closed questions begin, with "Is," "Are," or "Do." Examples of closed questions include, "Is Paul always off-task?" "Do you allow Pam to go outside for the afternoon recess?" "What score did Julie receive on her spelling test?" It should be realized that when closed questions are used, the burden of questioning remains on the speaker. Although closed questions can be appropriate in interviews or meetings, they are often perceived as being directive and limiting. In essence, they serve to request specific validation of points rather than broad observations or perceptions.

Table 4–3 Framework for Diagnosis and Question Asking

Type of Question	Examples

Who?	Who is the client?
	   What are personal background factors?
	   Who else is involved?

What?	What is the problem? What are the specific details of the situation?
When?	When does the problem occur? What immediately precedes and follows the situation?
Where?	Where does the problem occur? What environments and situations are involved?
How?	How does the individual react? How do others react to the individual?
Why?	Why does the problem occur? What function does the behavior serve?

There are several potential problems in the use of questions (Ivey, 1988). First, the use of too many questions may be perceived as "grilling," and can make an individual defensive. Multiple questions, often with slightly different purposes, may confuse the individual. Some questions may be used in a controlling manner to convince another of a certain point of view. For example, a question such as, "Don't you think that positive reinforcement would be better than time-out?" may lead a person in one biased direction. Although it may be helpful at times to make a statement such as this, it is best not to frame it as a question.

The excessive use of "why" questions can cause another problem in communication. "Why" questions can cause a person to become defensive or uncomfortable. Take the case of a mother and her six-year-old son. After finding mud all over the new white carpet, she approaches her son and asks, "Why did you walk through here with mud on your shoes!?" A likely response is, "I don't know!" or, "I didn't do it!" Neither of these responses, offered largely because of the way the question was asked, facilitates problem solving or problem resolution. In general, it is best to avoid "why" questions.

When consulting or collaborating with an individual from another culture, one must be extremely aware of the use of questions and the manner in which one's questions and questioning style affect that individual. Firing questions rapidly at a person from non-Western groups may be perceived as aversive. When working with a parent, student, or educator from another ethnic group, questions should be used carefully to increase trust and cooperation.

A final consideration in the use of questions is that the person asking the questions generally controls the situation. He or she determines who will talk about what, when the talk will occur, and under what conditions responses will be made. While this can be helpful in discussions that get out of control or off track, it can also be used intrusively or unfairly. All members of collaborative partnerships must help monitor the control and comfort level of discussions, and ensure that it progresses in an equitable and constructive manner (Ivey, 1988).

Attending.   To be accurate and effective, active listening must include *attending* skills—strategies used to orient the questioner toward the other person in order to be both physically and psychologically present (Egan, 1986). Good attending behavior demonstrates respect and indicates that the listener is interested in what is being said (Ivey, 1988). Therefore, an effective listener attends carefully to both the verbal and nonverbal messages being conveyed. Attending contributes to the collaborative process by instilling confidence, establishing a working relationship, and helping individuals identify, clarify, and manage problem situations.

A subset of behaviors and skills have been identified as important to attending (Egan, 1986). These skills can be remembered using the acronym *SHARE*. First, it is important to *sit squarely* (S). This requires the helper(s) to adopt a posture that indicates involvement. Second, *have* (H) an open posture

Activity 4–1

Effective communicators assess the quality of their interaction in each specific case. Participants in collaborative partnerships should periodically examine personal feelings and attitudes. Engage in a conversation with one other individual. For example, you might discuss a television show, a sporting event, or an upcoming exam. During the conversation, try to consciously monitor your attitudes and feelings. Every five minutes or so, stop the conversation and take notes on what you are feeling. Have your partner do the same. Following the interaction, ask yourself the following questions (Egan, 1986). Compare your perceptions to those of your partner.

1. What were my attitudes toward this particular person? How did they affect my interactions with him or her?

2. Did the individual perceive that I was effectively present and working with him or her?

3. Did my nonverbal behaviors accurately reflect my attitudes?

4. Was my attention distracted and if so, how might I have handled these distractions?

to suggest that you are open and nondefensive. An example of an open posture is one in which arms and legs are uncrossed and relaxed, and the listener periodically leans toward the other. Leaning toward another conveys the message that "I am with you and interested in what you are saying"; leaning back suggests, "I am bored and disinterested." Leaning behaviors should be used flexibly and with other nonverbal cues (such as nodding and smiling) to convey an appropriate level of interest.

A third skill of attending is to *acknowledge* (A) what is being communicated. An excellent way to do this is with the use of *minimal encouragements to talk,* or minimal acknowledgments of what is being said, by means of simple repetitions or questions that encourage a person to continue talking, elaborating, and explaining. They function only to acknowledge prior comments and do not occur simultaneously with the person's speaking turn. Examples of minimal encouragements to talk include (1) "Oh?" "So?" "Then?" "And?" (2) the repetition of one or two key words; and (3) "Tell me more." These minimal acknowledgements are powerful and important in the collaborative process. They can be used in combination with or independent of other attending skills (Ivey, 1988) such as eye contact and leaning.

Fourth, it is important to remain *relaxed* (R) while attending. In other words, fidgeting nervously or engaging in distracting behaviors or expressions can create a sense of insecurity in the collaborative relationship. Likewise, it is important to become comfortable with oneself (including verbal and nonverbal behaviors) as a vehicle of communication.

Finally, a fifth subskill of attending is to *engage* (E) using good eye communication. We use the term *eye communication* to convey the idea that speakers do more than see with their eyes—they communicate with them also. Fairly steady eye contact (as opposed to staring) is natural in North American culture. As with leaning, effective eye communication indicates to the other person that "I am with you; I am interested." When combined with skills such as head nods, affirmations, and minimal encouragements to talk, eye contact can support others and let them know that they are being understood.

We caution readers to remember that these guidelines are not "rules" to be followed rigidly or inflexibly, they are meant only to help listeners orient physically to the person sending the message. Indeed, individual differences will play a large part in the degree to which participants engage in these behaviors. While the use of an open posture, leaning, acknolwedgements, eye communication, and the other interpersonal skills enhance communication by reinforcing the ability to attend to and understand a message, they must be natural and comfortable to the listener. If demonstrated in a "forced" manner, they can be more detrimental than facilitative, suggesting to the speaker that "You are not interesting; it is hard work to listen to you."

Paraphrasing.   The term *paraphrasing* can be defined as restating in one's own words the main points of another person's statements. It focuses on relatively small units of information that were discussed and involves little or no inference (Friend & Cook, 1992). Paraphrasing achieves four purposes. First, it helps one convey an understanding of what has been said. If this understanding is complete, the listener can expand or clarify the ideas. Second, by concisely repeating the essence of the message, one crystallizes the information and helps the speaker focus on a particular situation, event, idea, or behavior. Third, the listener can also use paraphrasing to promote decision making. Finally, paraphrasing encourages the speaker to elaborate on key points. Whereas reflection of feeling concentrates on the emotional aspect of the speaker's communication, paraphrasing emphasizes the cognitive or content aspect of the message (Ivey, 1988).

Cormier and Cormier (1985) suggest five steps in paraphrasing. The listener initially attends to and recalls the message by restating it covertly (that is, what has the speaker communicated?). The second step involves identification of the message content. The listener determines the situation, person, object, or idea that has been discussed. Next, the listener must select an appropriate beginning or sentence stem for the actual paraphrase. Examples of sentence stems include, "It seems like . . ." or "You're telling me . . ." Following the selected beginning, the listener translates the key content into his or her own words. The paraphrase must be delivered as a statement and not as a question. Finally, the listener assesses the effectiveness of the paraphrase by listening to and observing the speaker's response. If the paraphrase is accurate, the speaker typically will confirm its accuracy and usefulness either verbally ("That's right!") or nonverbally (head nods).

Summarizing.   The term *summarization* can be defined as a collection of two or more paraphrases or reflections based upon the critical dimensions of the speaker's statements. The summarization should help focus the interview by condensing and clarifying what was said. Another purpose of summarization is to identify a common theme or pattern that may be apparent across several messages. A listener can also use summarization to moderate the pace of an interview or to review progress throughout the interview process. For example, it is a very useful technique to review key points and to make a transition to the next interview topic. It can also serve as a transitional statement by "pulling together" several messages, checking for agreement, and moving on to the next part of the interview. Summarization may represent collective rephrasing of content statements, affective messages, or both (Cormier & Cormier, 1985; Ivey, 1988).

Accurate summarization requires specific skills such as good recall of the speaker's behavior and messages, not only within an interview but at other times. Summarization involves five steps:

1. The listener attends to and recalls the message or series of messages. In other words, what is the speaker telling you, focusing on, or working on? This is a key component of summarization and requires that the helper be aware of a broad range of feelings and behaviors over time.

2. The listener identifies any apparent patterns, themes, or multiple elements of these messages. What messages has the speaker repeated?

3. The listener selects an appropriate beginning, or sentence stem. This should include the personal pronoun "you" or the client's name. An example might be, "To summarize, you believe that Travis's main difficulty is . . ."

4. Using the selected sentence stem, the listener verbalizes the summarization to describe the message theme or to consolidate multiple elements. Consistent with paraphrasing, the summarization is also delivered as a statement.

5. The listener assesses the effectiveness of the summarization by listening for and observing whether the speaker confirms or denies the summary (Cormier & Cormier, 1985; Ivey, 1988).

An example of a summarization statement follows: "You have been explaining Jeff's frequent outbursts in class. This includes yelling obscenities at the other students, interrupting you while you are lecturing, and slamming the top of his desk when angry." Following a summary statement such as this, the interviewer is able to shift to a new objective, such as specifying the target issue. For example, "Which of these seems to be most disturbing?" might be an appropriate subsequent question.

Relationship-Building Skills

Whereas the discrete skills described here are important to establish a climate of support and shared ownership in the collaborative process, they may not

Activity 4–2

In collaborative interactions, the quality of listening behaviors should be monitored. Egan (1986) suggests several self-assessment guidelines to help individuals determine the effectiveness of their use of listening skills. Engage in a lengthy conversation with a friend, spouse or co-worker. Following this conversation, answer the following questions:

1. Was I aware of the individual's nonverbal behaviors, yet careful not to overinterpret specific gestures or facial expressions?

2. Was I actively listening to what he or she was saying in terms of the experiences, behaviors, and feelings discussed?

3. Was I aware of my personal biases and their effect on my ability to listen?

4. Did I understand the other's point of view, even when it differed from my own?

5. Did I listen to my own reactions, as well as those of the other?

6. Are there other factors that distracted my ability to carefully listen and attend? What should I have done to effectively manage these distractions?

be sufficient in strengthening the interpersonal relationships inherent in human interactions. Additional interpersonal skills such as genuineness, reflection, acceptance, concreteness, and empathy are necessary to develop and build upon the relationships present in collaborative teams. These skills can be remembered with the acronym *GRACE*.

Genuineness.   The quality of *genuineness* requires the listener to assume a sincere and nondefensive role. The genuine listener communicates clearly, without a front or facade. He or she is spontaneous, assertive, and consistent within the collaborative process. The genuine listener is not defensive or aggressive and is aware of personal strengths and deficits (Egan, 1986; Small, 1974).

Egan (1986) suggests that a listener is genuine in a relationship when he or she (1) does not overemphasize the consultative ("expert") role and avoids stereotyped role behaviors; (2) is spontaneous, yet controlled, within the relationship; (3) remains open and nondefensive; (4) is consistent and avoids discrepancies; and (5) is willing to share personal feelings and experiences with the speaker when helpful. Genuineness is particularly important in collaborative educational partnerships. We emphasize throughout this text the notion of *shared ownership* for all facets of the collaborative process. The collaborative ethic suggests that all individuals are co-equal in decision-making status. This requires all participants to remain genuine and sincere in their efforts to enhance the educational experience for all students.

Reflection.   An excellent method of furthering a relationship is to let the other person know that his or her feelings are understood. *Reflection of feeling* involves this kind of response to the feelings of the speaker. It helps the other person express a central concern, and it is appropriate at any time, whether the nature of the feeling is positive, negative, or ambivalent. The following guidelines may be helpful when using reflection of feeling (Ivey, 1988):

1. Identify the feeling. Remember that what an individual says is only part of the message being communicated. How it is said is also extremely important.

2. Time your comments. Do not try to respond to every comment by the speaker. Wait until the appropriate time to reflect.

3. Reflect feeling and experiences by restating what the person is experiencing in your own words.

As an example, consider the case of a disgruntled parent who comments that "You school people just don't know how to handle my child!" An astute educator might respond by reflecting the affect of this parent: "You're very concerned about your child and want what is best for her." A statement like this will help the parent feel "heard" and understood, and possibly able to forego some anger and begin constructive collaboration.

Acceptance.   Implicit in *acceptance* is the communication of *respect* and sincere regard. It conveys the belief that there are inherent strengths and capabilities in all members of the educational partnership. This is played out in the speaker's right to choose alternatives and make decisions (Small, 1974). Ultimately, decisions to partake collaboratively in a consultative relationship, implement treatment strategies, and conduct systematic follow-up are made by the speaker. These often depend on a speaker's feelings of self-efficacy and commitment to the partnership and proposed interventions. Acceptance and respect for the speaker enhance feelings of competence and self-efficacy, facilitate open and mutual communication, and minimize feelings of dependence. Thus, it is important to express acceptance, support, and respect, yet still maintain that the responsibility for change exists within the speaker (Hawryluk & Smallwood, 1986).

Concreteness.   The term *concreteness* refers to keeping the listener's and speaker's communications relevant and specific. The listener should carefully guide the communication, and provide direction without going off on tangents or irrelevant discussions (Small, 1974). The concrete listener has the ability to redirect the speaker to relevant issues while maintaining good listening skills, respect, and sensitivity to the speaker's messages. Appropriate use of concreteness is especially conducive to a collaborative style. It is essential in clearly specifying and operationally defining a behavior and the surrounding conditions. Similarly, it helps clarify potentially ambiguous or subjective verbalizations, and enhances communication in the process.

Spotlight: Communication Skills Training for Parents

In the consultation and collaboration literature, most efforts to improve relationships have focused on enhancing the communication skills of professionals. Little or no effort has been directed at assisting nonprofessionals (e.g., parents, paraprofessionals, consultees) in acquiring effective relationship skills. Kohr, Parrish, Neef, Driessen, and Hallinan (1988) described a study in which parents were trained in a number of socially valid communication skills. Specifically, using didactic instruction, discussion, written materials, videotaped modeling, role playing and performance-based feedback, parents were taught the communication skills of preparation (i.e., comes to meeting prepared), complete communication (e.g., provides summary statements, asks for feedback from partner if present), clarification (e.g., asks questions), consensus (e.g., states areas of agreement), identification of issues (e.g., states areas of disagreement), suggestion of options (e.g., states or summarizes options), decision on action to be taken (i.e., requests or provides clarification on plan details), and feedback and acknowledgement (e.g., makes plans for next meeting).

Eight parents were involved in the communication training. During pretraining probes, each parent demonstrated lack of the target communication skills. In all cases, training resulted in marked improvements in parent performance during simulated role-play probes. Furthermore, six parents actually attempted the skills in real school conferences. All of these subjects demonstrated improved communication skills in actual parent-professional conferences. Parents also rated the training program favorably on a measure of training satisfaction, indicating that this approach to communication skills training may be beneficial in educators' interactions with parents.

Often individuals speak of problems with global terms. Consider the secretary who complains that "Mr. Adams simply doesn't understand my needs! We have a real communication problem!" A "communication problem" can be experienced in many ways. To make the discussion more concrete, a listener might say, "Tell me what you mean by 'communication problem.' "

Empathy.   *Empathy* refers to the ability to appreciate and comprehend the consultee's experience and to communicate this perception to him or her. Empathy presupposes mastery of attending and listening skills. Use of empathy allows the listener to put that speaker's situation into perspective through an understanding of that individual's experiences (Small, 1974).

When communicating empathically, a response is made after listening for both the process and the content of that speaker's message. Additionally, the listener observes the nonverbal behavior to comprehend the full meaning of the message. Finally, the listener reflects the speaker's meaning through non-judgmental feedback that encourages acceptance or clarification of the reflection. The empathic listener is aware that he or she is not an expert regarding the speaker's experiences, and merely strives to develop an understanding of this individual (Egan, 1986; Small, 1974).

Empathy is not always easy to convey. It requires excellent attending and listening skills, a sincere understanding of the affect being expressed by the speaker, and the ability to instill in the speaker a sense that his or her experiences were truly accepted and vicariously experienced by the listener. As an example, imagine a school counselor working with a confused high school student. The adolescent says that she has no "real" friends, gets in fights constantly with her parents, and often feels like giving up. An empathic response might be, "You seem pretty confused about things. It must be frustrating to feel as if no one ever listens to or really understands you."

Developmental Phases of Communication in Relationships

Several researchers in human communication have conceptualized communication within relationships in terms of developmental phases. Three phases are typically described: an entry or initiation phase, a stabilization phase (in which the communicators can achieve varying degrees of personal intimacy), and finally, the termination or exit phase (Beger & Calabrese, 1975; Miller, 1978). The assumptions and characteristics underlying this developmental perspective also seem relevant in collaborative educational partnerships. Throughout the stages of the collaborative process, remember the following assumptions and characteristics. They are likely to apply to the changes occurring within the partnership.

A developmental perspective of relationships assumes that initial encounters are impersonal. In other words, the communicators relate to one another in terms of their social roles (classroom teacher, administrator, special educator, school psychologist or counselor) rather than as individuals (Ms. X and Mr. Y) or partners in the educational process. Uncertainty is high in initial encounters, and the interactants use cautious communication strategies. These strategies are typically conventionally imposed by the social and cultural definitions of their roles and the situation. The relationship goal of the communicators in the initial phase of the interaction is to reduce uncertainty by gaining information about the other. Talk tends to be about superficial topics, and includes a high frequency of questions. Anticipation, prediction, and explanation often help communicators reduce the uncertainty they have about one another (Berger & Calabrese, 1975).

In collaborative partnerships, initial encounters are also likely to be marked by feelings of uncertainty. The strategies employed are likely to help individuals learn about each other, as well as about the specific referral concerns. Open questions and active listening strategies are helpful in this regard, but individuals must also pay attention to how they anticipate interactions with each other. These expectations may not be explicit, but they will likely color the way interactions progress. Think about the expectations you, as a prospective educator, have right now. How might they influence the way you interact with other educators and parents in initial interactions?

As uncertainty is reduced, communicators work toward an agreement on the nature of their relationship. Their goal is to mutually agree on what they expect and need from each other. Once this is achieved, they are in the stabilization phase of the relationship. A relationship can stabilize at different levels of personal intimacy. Interactants may elect to maintain culturally circumscribed roles, or they may opt for more personal relations. Personal relations are marked by a greater reliance on mutually negotiated and idiosyncratic rules in contrast to the social conventions employed in the initial phase (Berger & Calabrese, 1975). The goals of communicators in more personal relations typically center on the exploration of attitudes and basic values. Communicators respond to each other as individuals, rather than undifferentiated role occupants. Miller (1978) describes three different degrees of personal relations: descriptive, predictive, and explanatory. The *descriptive level of personal relations* involves superficial knowledge of the other. With this degree of knowledge, a communicator may simply describe and discriminate his or her partner from others. The *predictive level of personal relation* goes deeper, and involves the possession of information about how the other person believes or behaves. The *explanatory level of personal relations* is the deepest. It occurs when communicators believe they are privy to the other's reasons for behaving or believing in certain ways.

In applying these ideas to collaborative partnerships, several pertinent issues arise. As partners know one another better, they will gradually redefine the relationship. An agreement on what each expects from the other will undoubtedly enhance the collaborative process. Before progressing too far in the collaborative relationship, reflect upon the kind of agreement you anticipate. How personal should you become in a collaborative relationship? What are the risks of stepping out of your conventional role relations, and into more individualized patterns of interaction? What are the benefits? Under what circumstances might more personal interactions be helpful? When might they be a hindrance?

In the final phases of a relationship, communicators decide on the desirability of future interactions. Their goals are to discuss and plan for future encounters or to terminate the current relationship. In collaboration, this phase is likely to be influenced by the outcome of the intervention and the nature of the problem. How comfortable partners feel working together is also extremely important. How do you believe both parties should feel? What kind of relationship would you seek to continue? What kind of relationship would you seek to terminate? What would you do if you were unable to work with a particular individual?

Selected Skills for Stages of Effective Collaboration

In Chapter 3 we presented an ecological model for educational consultation that had four stages: situational definition, ecological analysis, plan development and implementation, and plan evaluation. It is obviously important that effective communication and interpersonal skills be incorporated into the implementation of each stage. In Figure 4–1, we provide a checklist to help participants monitor their own communication skills as they are used in relation to the stages of the collaborative process. We will now discuss specific skills that can be used.

Situational Definition

Oftentimes, meetings held during the identification stage represent the first encounter between participants. Therefore, relationship building is among the primary objectives. Early interactions will thus provide an opportunity to establish rapport, promote positive relationships, and stimulate discussion through mutual participation. In early meetings, active listening and understanding statements are important to help participants feel comfortable and develop trust. Empathy, paraphrasing, and reflection of feelings and statements are helpful to encourage exploration, openness, and mutual commitment.

The goal of the first stage of the collaborative process is to define and clarify the main issue(s) to be addressed in consultation. Therefore, a central outcome is a specific statement of the presenting concern. In collaborative partnerships, it is important to probe sufficiently into the presenting situation and focus attention on the relevant issue rather than on the person experiencing it (such as the teacher or parent). Paraphrasing, summarizing, and restating pertinent information facilitates progress and a collaborative relationship. Feelings of optimism and sincerity should be communicated in a genuine manner. As the relationship progresses, mutual levels of commitment should be conveyed (Dustin & Ehly, 1984).

Throughout the beginning stage of consultation, the following considerations should be explored: Who is the consultee? What are the consultee's role constraints? How are the roles within the collaborative partnership defined? What are expectations for the relationship? How is the situation being defined? What are the barriers, sources of resistance, and other difficulties that might affect the outcome of this case? What roles will be assumed if

Figure 4–1

Checklist of Communication Skills in Collaborative Interactions

This form is meant to be used as a tool to help partners gauge their use of effective communications skills while engaged in the collaborative process. It can also be used to monitor others' behaviors while observing team meetings. When each of the steps of the collaborative process is observed, place a checkmark on the line to the left of the objective at the far left side of the form. Likewise, when an effective communication skill is observed, place a checkmark on the line to the left of the skill at the right side of the form.

Date: Names of Participants:

Stages of the Collaborative Process   **Communication Skills**

Situational Definition   Listening Skills
_____ Identify component parts.
_____ Prioritize component parts.   _____ C—Clarifying
_____ Provide an operational definition.   (open questions)
_____ Identify tentative antecedents and   _____ A—Attending
         consequences.   _____ P—Paraphrasing
_____ Determine data-collection procedures. _____ S— Summarizing

Ecological Analysis   Attending Skills
_____ Identify antecedent conditions.
_____ Identify consequent conditions.   _____ S— Sit squarely
_____ Identify situational conditions.   _____ H—Have an open posture
_____ Identify prerequisite skills.   _____ A—Acknowledge
_____ Identify setting, participants, and strength. _____ R—Relax
_____ Identify existing procedures or previous _____ E—Engage using eye
         intervention attempts.   communication
_____ State short-term and/or long-term goals.

                                                   Relationship Building Skills
Plan Development and Implementation
_____ Brainstorm alternative solutions.   _____ G—Genuineness
_____ Identify chosen alternative.   _____ R—Reflection
_____ Identify resources necessary and   _____ A—Acceptance
         available to contribute to solution.   _____ C—Concreteness
_____ Specify implementation steps, timelines, _____ E— Empathy
         and responsibilities.

Plan Evaluation
_____ Specify how, when, and by whom the plan will be monitored.
_____ Specify how, when, and by whom progress will be evaluated.
_____ Determine next steps.

resistance or barriers are encountered? What are the risks inherent in this case? What are the benefits?

Ecological Analysis

Once collaborative partnerships are functioning, the role of communication shifts to that of maintaining an effective relationship. The objectives of the second formal stage of the collaborative process are to (1) determine setting, participants, and strength of a problem; (2) conduct a conditions and/or skills analysis; and (3) identify resources necessary and available to contribute to resolution of the issue. Throughout this stage, effective use of questioning is paramount. Open-ended questions allow participants to obtain a wealth of information about identified problems and factors by which they are influenced. Review Chapter 3 (in particular Table 3–2) to review types of questions that are common during this and other stages.

Along with questioning skills, collaborative partners need effective listening skills during ecological analysis. The breadth of information obtained at this stage can become overwhelming, and participants need skills at deciphering critical messages. Requests for clarification, paraphrasing, and summarization statements are all important at this stage. Likewise, because the information obtained will be used in developing a plan, concreteness is imperative. Empathy and respect must also be demonstrated as issues are explored in depth. Participants must take care not to send through actions or words a message of blame or responsibility for problematic situations while they are being analyzed.

Plan Development and Implementation

During the third stage of the collaborative process, the priorities include exploring and implementing strategies for solving the defined problem. The members of the partnership assist in generating potential change strategies in a genuine and concrete manner. This is generally accomplished through brainstorming, characterized by nonevaluative comments and supportive nonverbal messages. Following brainstorming, partners must collaboratively identify which suggestions will be incorporated into a management plan. Using concreteness, constructive feedback, and genuineness, the team selects a single strategy or alternative strategies for implementation. Active listening for content and affect, paraphrasing certain key statements, and summarizing important information can facilitate clarity in plan development. Empathy and exploration of feelings can be used to identify potential affective barriers such as discouragement or frustration. Patience and flexibility are essential to prevent resistance during plan development.

During plan implementation, support and encouragement of the members charged with implementing various treatment strategies is critical. The individuals actively engaged in plan implementation should feel empowered to complete their functions effectively, yet also feel supported as members of a collaborative network. In other words, feelings of isolation should be monitored and remedied with empathy, genuineness and concrete feedback.

Plan Evaluation

During plan evaluation, members of the educational partnership assess the progress resulting from the implemented strategies. The plan is monitored and evaluated most effectively with persistence and openness. Persistence allows individuals to gain specific information regarding progress to date. Openness and flexibility during collaborative evaluation of outcomes prevent dissatisfaction or frustration on the part of team members. The follow-up evaluation is completed when the partners feel satisfied with the outcomes of the change process (Dustin & Ehly, 1984). Likewise, the following points should be addressed: Is the collaborative process progressing smoothly as a result of the established collegial relationships? What is the effect of, and how sensitive are team members to, reactions regarding treatment implementation?

Also during the plan evaluation stage, closure is established by reviewing both positive and negative outcomes resulting from the implemented change strategies. The consultee provides valuable feedback regarding the activities and utility of the plan, as well as personal reactions and suggestions. It is imperative that various relationship skills be used, including empathy and genuineness. Paraphrasing clarifies the consultee's reactions and feedback. If applicable, team members should express an openness to work with the consultee in the future in a genuine manner. In this way, participants in the collaborative partnership remain cognizant of personal needs and priorities, as well as those of the consultee and client. Feedback should be used to determine whether the consultee's needs have been met (Dustin & Ehly, 1984). When terminating a consultation relationship, team members should consider the following questions in a self-evaluative manner to enhance their efficacy during future relationships: How do members feel about the course and development of this relationship? How does the

Activity 4-3

Get into groups of three. Select as partners individuals whom you do not know well. Assign one person the task of interviewer, one person the task of interviewee, and one person the task of observer. In about ten minutes, the interviewer should try to find out as much about the interviewee as possible, such as his/her early life, school experiences, interests, hobbies, career goals, family, etc. While the interview is taking place, the observer should watch for evidence of the CAPS, SHARE, and GRACE skills. Keep track of these on Figure 4-1, and discuss what was observed after the interview. Take turns alternating these roles.

consultee perceive the progression of the consultative relationship? What phases have evolved through this interpersonal relationship?

The skills suggested here are not limited to the parameters of each identified area. Partners must be aware of the various skills and utilize them flexibly to maximize their effectiveness according to the needs of the situation. For example, skills such as empathy and paraphrasing should be used selectively throughout the collaborative process rather than applied generically within a particular stage.

Understanding and Managing Conflict

Whenever individuals or groups of individuals interact over a period of time, and particularly when the interaction surrounds problems or issues, conflict is inevitable. *Conflict* has been defined in several ways. Webster (1981) defines it as "competitive or opposing action . . . antagonistic state or action (as of divergent ideas, interests or persons)" (p. 235). In the educational literature, Friend and Cook (1992) suggest that "conflict is any situation in which one person (or group) perceives that another person (or group) is interfering with his or her goal attainment" (p. 118). Traditionally, conflict has been perceived in educational settings as a negative and undesirable state of affairs that was to be avoided at all costs. While this may have been relatively easy to do in the segregated and isolated structure of traditional educational environments, the recent emphasis on collaboration, shared ownership, and team decision making suggests that as human interaction increases in schools, so will conflict. Whether conflict arises among teachers and counselors, administrators and staff, special educators and school psychologists, or parents and school personnel, it is important that educators understand the phenomenon, its causes, and ways to manage it constructively and positively.

Sources of Conflict

There are many possible sources of conflict. Friend and Cook (1992) explored three causes of conflicts between individuals in educational settings. *Conflict among individuals with different goals* occurs when participants desire different outcomes but must accept the same outcome. For example, an administrator may wish to curb a problem of overcrowding by redefining the physical boundaries of a school. Parents, on the other hand, may find this option unacceptable and have as a goal remodeling and increasing school staff. *Conflict among individuals with the same goals* represents a situation where professionals have the same goal but unequal access to resources to attain that goal. An example is when physical resources such as computer software or a video camera is available to only one individual in the school setting. Finally, *conflicts within individuals* are present when internal discrepancies are experienced in regard to personal goals. For example, given what she knows about the benefits of parent involvement in education, a school psychologist may have a desire to change her role to allow more contact with parents. On the other hand, this goal may cause stress and anxiety if she has an overwhelming caseload and little support or training for working with parents. Understanding these sources of conflict can help provide a framework for identifying and interpreting it when it arises.

Identifying the specific sources of conflict in school settings is a complex matter. Conflicts that are experienced by individuals in educational partnerships are influenced by organizational variables, interpersonal issues, and personal characteristics. For example, organizational variables such as leadership style, norms for communication, and decision-making practices clearly affect the manner in which conflict will be manifested and resolved. Issues between individuals within educational partnerships can also result in conflictual interactions. Such interpersonal factors include lack of congruence among participants' expectations, role definitions, professional and personal reference points, and theoretical orientations. Finally, personal variables such as "selective perception" and clinging to personal agendas can clearly interfere with the establishment and maintenance of effective partnerships.

Conflict Management

A strength of collaborative groups is that individuals with diverse backgrounds and expertise come together to address issues. As alluded to earlier, because interaction is high, conflict is inevitable. However, conflict is not inherently good or bad. The manner in which conflict is managed determines whether its outcome is constructive or destructive to the group's function.

By their very nature, collaborative groups are comprised of a number of persons with a number of personalities and styles. Each person will have a different method of coping with conflict. There are generally five conflict management styles that vary along the dimensions of cooperativeness and assertiveness (Friend & Cook, 1992; Thomas & Kilman, 1974) or importance of personal goals and relationships (Johnson & Johnson, 1991). Regardless of the dimensions on which you characterize approaches to conflict management, the five styles are similar. They include competitive, avoidance, accommodating, compromising, and collaborative.

Persons who use a *competitive style of conflict management* perceive their own goals as highly important while relationships are low in importance. These people tend to be high in assertiveness but low in cooperativeness. "Sharks" (Johnson & Johnson, 1991) try to overpower others by forcing them to accept a favored solution. Winning is of utmost importance, even at the expense of relationships.

Avoidant styles of conflict management are characterized as uncooperative and unassertive. These people tend to withdraw in the face of conflict, perceiving both their own goals and relationships as low in importance. "Turtles" (Johnson & Johnson, 1991) often feel hopeless and helpless in conflictual situations, yet may maintain a facade that all is well. In groups comprised of avoiders, conflict continues because no one is willing to address and resolve it.

A person with an *accommodating style of conflict management* believes that relationships are more important than personal goals, and thus demonstrates much cooperativeness but little assertiveness. "Teddy bears" (Johnson & Johnson, 1991) may "give in," or avoid conflict in favor of harmony and to preserve relationships.

A *compromising style of conflict management* uses a balance of assertiveness and cooperativeness. "Foxes" (Johnson & Johnson, 1991) assign a moderate degree of importance to relationships and to personal goals. They sacrifice some of their own ideas and solutions and demand that others do the same. The outcome is generally a "common ground" where issues are addressed in the "middle of the road."

Persons with a *collaborative style of conflict management* tend to be both highly assertive and highly cooperative. They greatly value relationships as well as their own goals. "Owls" (Johnson & Johnson, 1991) perceive conflicts as opportunities to seek out better solutions and achieve a better outcome.

We obviously believe that dealing with conflicts collaboratively can be most effective and productive. Several of the benefits of collaboration (to children, teachers, parents and all educational stakeholders) can be achieved in conflictual situations that are addressed with this style. It does, however, require time and training, and may not be the appropriate in all cases. Nevertheless, just as collaboration can be efficacious in addressing a school or student problem, it can also be beneficial in dealing with conflict within and among groups.

Suggestions for Resolving Conflict

Deciding what to do in the face of a conflict can be difficult, particularly if action must occur quickly. In this section, we review briefly several strategies that can maximize the potential for resolving conflicts in a constructive rather than destructive manner. Perhaps most imperative is that individuals in conflictual situations focus on issues, not people. Furthermore, of the vast number of possible issues that can be addressed, it is often helpful to keep the conflict focused on the issues that have the greatest potential to be agreed upon. It is also important that the emotional component of the conflict be monitored and reduced to allow individuals to interact logically. It may be helpful as well to seek assistance from a third party such as a mediator or facilitator. The person playing this role will vary depending on school composition, but that individual should be completely neutral and objective toward the source of the conflict. Finally, it is important to realize that not all conflicts will be resolved in a manner agreeable to all parties. In these situations, one must adapt to the outcome or terminate involvement in the interaction. While this may be difficult to accept psychologically, it does not mean that one has failed. It simply suggests that differences of opinion were of the magnitude that a working relationship could no longer be successful.

Although each conflict will be unique and require strategies specific to the situation, some general suggestions can be made. These include problem solving, using effective communication skills, and negotiating (Friend & Cook, 1991).

Problem Solving.   Friend and Cook (1991) suggest that conflicts can be conceptualized constructively as problems to be solved, and that the stages of the collaborative process such as those outlined in Chapter 3 can facilitate resolution of the conflictual situation. While this can certainly be an effective means of addressing conflict, it can also be costly in terms of time and resources. We recommend that only long-standing and chronic conflicts be subjected to this process, and that short-term or time-limited conflicts be addressed with one or more of the following strategies.

Use Effective Communication Skills.   Virtually any of the communication skills discussed earlier in this chapter can and should be utilized in high-conflict situations. It is essential that lines of communication remain open, and that individuals approach each other with respect and genuineness. Likewise, active listening and open questioning can be beneficial in obtaining information regarding events and feelings. Empathic responding and taking the perspective of the other person can also help address conflicts due to differences in opinion or beliefs. It is particularly important that communications between individuals be concrete and specific, with a high level of correspondence between verbal and nonverbal messages.

Negotiate.   The process of *negotiation* can be defined as one that "begins with each party involved in the conflict asking for more than is reasonable to expect and then, using a series of offers and counteroffers, reaching an agreeable resolution" (Friend & Cook, 1991; p. 126). When negotiation is used as a strategy for conflict resolution, it is important that individuals (1) understand the sources of motivation of all parties, (2) clarify the issues, (3) set expectations, (4) discuss each issue involved in the conflict, (5) make and respond to offers, and (6) monitor the practices for potential ethical problems.

A number of concrete steps can be helpful when preparing to negotiate. Myers and Myers (1985) recommended the following six actions be taken by individuals in anticipation of a negotiation. First, determine your need and

Activity 4–4

Pair off in order to role-play the following scenarios. First, however, identify your primary style of conflict management using the descriptions of Owls, Teddy Bears, Sharks, Foxes, and Turtles. Use negotiation, problem solving, and interpersonal skills during the role-play to address the issues raised in the scenario.

Owl/Shark: You (Owl) are a retail manager and a "Shark" wants to take a day off. That day is projected to be the busiest one of the season and you need that person to work.

Fox/Teddy Bear: Your Fox babysitter asks you (Teddy Bear) for a raise in her hourly wage. You just gave her a raise and cannot afford to pay her any more than you do now.

Shark/Turtle: A friend has invited you (Shark) to go with him to a big playoff game, but you promised your Turtle girlfriend that you would go out to dinner with her parents.

goal for the negotiation interaction. These may be intangible (such as the need to "save face" or obtain satisfaction) or material (such as a raise in salary). Second, establish your own limits of authority. It is important to know these limits and recognize when it will be necessary to check with authority figures. Third, establish your maximum and minimum limits for settlement. In other words, determine a priori the extent to which you will compromise your goals for the sake of the others. Fourth, determine your approach. For

Activity 4–5

Conflict and interpersonal difficulties are normal parts of team processes, yet participants often try to avoid or fail to admit their presence. If you are currently working in a school, observe a meeting between at least two individuals in that setting. If you do not have access to formalized school groups, observe fellow students engaged in a role play. Following the meeting or role play, answer the following questions:

1. Were there any instances of conflict during the session?

    a. If so, what appeared to be the source of conflict (e.g., conflict among individuals with different goals; conflict among individuals with the same goals; conflict within individuals). Specify the circumstances surrounding the conflict that causes you to characterize the conflict in this way.

    b. If not, why? Which interpersonal skills were demonstrated by participants? Did this help alleviate potential conflict?

2. Was conflict managed in this situation? If so, how? Specify the tactics used by participants (e.g., negotiation, problem solving) to address conflict. Were conflict-management attempts successful?

example, will you play "hard ball"? Will your arguments be data-based? This determination will help set the tempo for the negotiations. Relatedly, it is important to anticipate any questions or arguments that may be raised and be ready to address these counterattacks. Fifth, consult with others prior to the negotiation interaction. Test your ideas on someone and obtain some history of similar negotiations. Finally, develop a written agenda or outline to bring with you to keep the discussion focused. Set time limits for each aspect of your argument and explore pros and cons of the plan. Of particular importance is your ability to look at both sides of the situation and remain flexible (rather than rigid) to the greatest extent possible.

"Pause Button" Technique.   At times, conflict in a group causes confusion or discomfort among an individual or several members. This is a common outcome of conflict, but does not imply that the conflict itself is "bad." As reiterated already, the manner in which conflict is handled determines whether it has a constructive or destructive effect on the team. Sometimes, it is necessary to stop the team interaction and address members' confusions, discomfort, or other sources of conflict directly. One method for doing this is the *"pause button" technique,* a process by which an individual or several team members postpone the task-oriented focus of the group to request attention to interpersonal conflict or confusion. During this "time out" or "pause" from the primary goals of the team, individuals express concerns regarding the manner in which the group is processing information. Examples of issues that may be addressed while the "pause button" is on include faulty communication between members, lack of clarity regarding group goals, inefficient use of time, or lack of adherence to the collaborative model.

The procedure for using the this technique is simple, and varies slightly from group to group. In general, when an individual feels that the progress of the group is being hindered due to interpersonal or other reasons, he or she may request that the "pause button" be on. This stops the group and allows that individual to express his or her concerns. The rest of the team members are also given an opportunity to express their feelings. It is important that the pause button be used constructively. Thus, after each individual has an opportunity to state his or her observations (if they so desire), the team should make a plan to address the primary concern raised while the pause button was on. For example, if a team identifies that the special education teacher is particularly silent during a meeting in which her vocal participation is vital, the team may plan to ask for her input at least once every five minutes.

Chapter Summary

As emphasized in Chapter 3, appropriate collaborative skills include the application of a rational plan or model that will limit the interaction among participants to the specific problem or issue being addressed. The model should be used as a guide for choosing strategies to bring about the desired changes. And, consistent with the "collaborative ethic," a philosophy that invites participation and sharing among all members must be promoted in collaborative interactions.

In this chapter, we emphasized the use of good communication and interpersonal skills to strengthen collaborative relationships. It seems obvious that if one fails to integrate clear communication and effective interpersonal skills with technical expertise, collaborative efforts are likely to fail. Specific communication skills of clarifying, attending, paraphrasing, and summarizing are important. Clarification involves requesting information regarding verbal statements, behaviors, or affect. Questions are typically used to clarify messages, and open questions are typically superior to closed questions. Attending includes a subset of behaviors that can be recalled with the acronym "SHARE" (i.e., sit squarely, have an open posture, acknowledge, relax, and engage with good eye communication).

Paraphrasing is defined as restating in one's own words the main points of another person's statements. Summarization is a collection of two or more paraphrases or reflections based on the critical aspects of the speaker's statements. Summarizations are important to review the main points of an interaction, and to move the discussion to a new topic.

Advanced relationship building skills include genuineness, reflection, acceptance, concreteness, and empathy ("GRACE"). It should be reiterated that although these skills are presented in a discrete manner, their use must be appropriate to the context or situation in which they are used. And the only way to become proficient in the use of effective communication and interpersonal skills is through practice!

Conflict is an inevitable part of any group experience, and educational partnerships are no exception. Contrary to some beliefs, conflict is not inherently negative. Rather, the manner in which conflict is managed determines its effects on a team. Methods to manage conflict include problem solving, effective communication skills, negotiation, the "pause button" technique, and other interpersonal and relationship building techniques discussed throughout the chapter.

Case Study 4–1

East Park School is located in a relatively affluent section of town, and few significant problems come to the attention of educators at the school. An exception this year is Martin, a second-grade student who transferred from Fireside Elementary in another district. Martin is a boy of average intelligence who demonstrates no serious behavior or learning problems. However, he demonstrates a great deal of difficulty in completing assignments. When he completes work in the classroom, it is generally sloppy and disorganized. Getting papers home is a nightmare for Martin; he generally loses or misplaces worksheets or school letters somewhere between his classroom and home. Thus, work that goes home for homework is rarely returned. He is described by both his mother and teacher as distractible, inattentive, disorganized, impulsive, and very active. A multidisciplinary team evaluation at his previous school suggested serious attentional problems, warranting a diagnosis of Attention Deficit–Hyperactivity Disorder (ADHD). The school psychologist at Fireside was an expert in the area of interventions for students with ADHD, so she provided several recommendations for serving Martin in the regular classroom with accommodations. This seemed reasonable since he scored within the average range on tests of intelligence and achievement. She also provided a great deal of parent training to help Martin's family learn how to help him behaviorally and at school. However, the school year ended and Martin's family moved before any of the recommendations could be tried at Fireside.

The second-grade team of teachers at East Park are at a loss with Martin. The school psychologist at East Park does not have a strong background in ADHD, nor do any of the other educational staff. In an initial meeting with Martin's parents, his teacher exclaimed that "a boy like Martin should be in special ed!" She went on saying that she "could not deal with his distractions and inability to complete worksheets with so many other children in the classroom!" The administrator suggested that his parents try him on Ritalin, and his parents insisted that "the school *must* make special accommodations for Martin in the regular classroom!" Tempers were flaring!

1. What were some of the sources of conflict in this scenario? What goals did each participant have in this initial meeting?

2. Which characteristics of the "collaborative ethic" are being violated?

3. What communication skills might facilitate resolution of the issues?

4. What might be some ways that Martin's teachers and parents can negotiate?

Key Vocabulary Terms

listening	paraphrasing	relations
CAPS	summarizing	predictive level of personal
clarification	GRACE	relations
open questions	genuineness	explanatory level of personal
closed questions	respect	relations
attending	acceptance	conflict
SHARE	concreteness	conflict among individuals
minimal encouragements to	empathy	with different goals
talk	descriptive level of personal	conflict among individuals

with the same goals
conflicts within individuals
competitive style of conflict
management

avoidant style of conflict
management
accommodating style of
conflict management

compromising style of
conflict management
collaborative style of conflict
management
negotiation

Part 2

The School

Chapter 5

Chapter Overview

The School

Chapter Objectives

After reading this chapter, the reader should be able to:
1. Describe the school culture and the socialization process of educators.
2. Explain the systemic organization of schools.
3. List and describe the roles, components, and characteristics of general education.
4. Discuss Chapter I and Title I programs for disadvantaged students.
5. Discuss special education and the five basic tenets of the Individual with Disabilities Education Act that influence educational service delivery.
6. Discuss bilingual and second-language-acquisition programs.
7. Compare traditional and reconceptualized roles of educators.
8. Describe the paradigm shift of changing schools and the components of the change process.

Introduction

The school is only one of three learning environments described in this text. While educators may play an important function in home and community partnerships, they have key responsibilities within the school setting. These duties, like the collaborative process itself, are largely determined by cultural and systemic factors. Cultural variables such as attitudes, norms, customs, values, and roles have an enormous influence on the ways in which educators behave. Similarly, organizational components of the school may also influence the actions of educators. Consequently, roles of educators are defined by both of these environmental factors. The degree to which educational partnerships are conceptualized and implemented is dependent upon the interaction of cultural and systemic factors. This chapter begins by examining cultural and systemic factors within the school. The reader will also explore the traditional and reconceptualized roles of educators as a foundation for a paradigm shift for establishing and maintaining educational partnerships.

The Culture of Schools

Culture was defined in Chapter 2 as a set of variables that include attitudes, values, norms, beliefs, and customs that are transmitted to group members creating a sense of identity as well as a pattern of behavior (Gollnick & Chinn, 1990). Culture influences how an individual thinks and feels. *School culture* is influenced by cultural variables of the community at large. Typically, it is the values, norms, and beliefs of the Anglo-American culture that have the greatest impact on the school culture. Consequently, as discussed in Chapter 2, students from divergent cultures often experience failure and frustration resulting from a clash between their cultural background and that of the school. Therefore, it is important for educators to understand how the culture of the school affects students and educators. So what is meant by school culture?

A *school culture*, like the culture of other organizations, defines the way things are and the way members should act (Rossman, Corbett, & Firestone, 1988). A school, like society at large, is comprised of norms, shared beliefs, knowledge, values, and attitudes (Hanson, 1990). The school's culture is a pool of information about what is important, how things are done, and who does what (Erickson, 1987). The leadership of an administrator can have a profound impact on the culture of the school. Schein (1985) suggested that leadership, rather than administration and management, influences the culture to meet a specific mission. Administrative management involves overseeing the overall functional operation of the school in terms of personnel, budgets, and compliance with rules and regulations. Leadership, on the other hand, promotes emotional, philosophical, and psychological aspects of being a member of the school community. Feiman-Nemser and Floden (1986) suggested that "teaching cultures are embodied in the work-related beliefs and knowledge teachers share—beliefs about appropriate ways of acting on the job and rewarding aspects of teaching, and knowledge that enables teachers to do their work" (p. 508). These variables are formally and informally transmitted by and to members in a way that prescribes roles and behaviors (Pai, 1990).

A cultural expectation of classroom instruction is clearly illustrated in the following example (Hart, 1990): A classroom teacher organized a cooperative learning activity in which students worked together in completing a project. The role of the teacher was primarily that of a facilitator as she moved about the clusters of verbally interacting students. The building administrator entered the noisy classroom to observe the teacher as part of a district evaluation process. Upon seeing the flurry of activity, the administrator told the teacher she would return another day to conduct the observation when the teacher was "teaching." In this scenario, it is evident that the administrator had a preconceived notion and expectation of instruction as a teacher-led dissemination of information to students sitting in neat rows.

A *role expectation*, as illustrated in this example, is characterized as the assumed behavior of another in performing a specific task (Owens, 1987). This creates the potential for conflict if the administrator perceives the teacher as failing to fulfill cultural expectations of "the right way to teach." *Role conflict* results when two individuals are unable to establish a reciprocal relationship (Owens, 1987).

Culture creates not only a sense of identity, but stability as well (Rossman, Corbett, & Firestone, 1988). The routine established by traditional roles, behaviors, and expectations helps the school run smoothly. *Socialization,* the inductive process of learning roles and cultural variables through experience, begins for teachers and administrators when they are students themselves. Teacher candidates' notions of teaching are defined by their own experiences and are carried throughout their formal professional preparation. Colleges and universities continue the socialization process. Specialized and compartmentalized programs, such as elementary, secondary, and special education, not only provide prospective professionals with skills they will later use, but also instill cultural variables such as expectations of roles and responsibilities. Then the socialization process continues as the novice professional enters the field and "learns the ropes."

For example, a social studies teacher acquires the skills of disseminating information about the U.S. Constitution during preservice training. Perceiving his role as a scholar of the Constitution, he may resent the special educator who suggests that he consider teaching note-taking skills. In this case, the teacher sees his role as teaching content, not skills. In this way, attempts to modify the firmly entrenched culture are generally resisted as they interrupt the status quo. As we will see in our discussion of the organizational structure of schools below, teachers are afforded significant autonomy and are generally isolated in their own classrooms. Teachers' perceptions of their role are inextricably linked with the isolation of managing the dissemination and acquisition of knowledge to students. While conducting an investigation on teacher receptivity to collaboration (Wade, Welch, & Jensen, 1994), many teachers revealed in anecdotal comments that they did not feel obligated to serve on a teacher-assistance team that helps colleagues solve problems. They perceived this role as an extramural activity analogous to sponsoring the cheerleaders or editing the yearbook and indicated they expected to be compensated for their time if they did, in fact, serve on the team. These revealing comments suggest that collaborative problem solving is not generally perceived as part of the teaching culture (what teachers do). Additionally, the comments reveal that the organizational structure of the school schedule does not lend itself to the nontraditional behavior of collaborating with colleagues to solve problems.

Systemic Organization of Schools

We begin our examination of the systemic organization of schools by reviewing the ecological *domains* within the building. As discussed in previous chapters, every ecological system consists of five types of resources: human, technological, informational, physical, and financial. Human resources consist of the various persons that have specific tasks to help the efficient operation of the organization. Technological resources can range from "high tech" items such as computers to "low tech" materials such as chalkboards or grade books. The bell system is another example of a technological resource. These resources can be thought of as the "tools" that are used to help the organization function. Informational resources can be people (that is, consultants) or tangible objects such as regulation manuals. Physical resources are geographic locations within the system. Moneys from taxes or federal funding provide financial resources to pay for personnel, materials, and services. As we will see, the interactions and utilization of components within each domain are largely influenced by cultural and organizational factors. Domains can be used efficiently or inefficiently, depending upon the nature of culture and systemic variables.

Schools are organizational entities designed for imparting academic skills while maintaining an environment in which "learning can occur for a majority of children" (Elias & Clabby, 1984, p. 145). In addition to providing an education for large numbers of students, schools are also expected to furnish daytime custody of children (Elmore, 1987). In order to carry out this charge, schools have traditionally been organized as bureaucracies. A *bureaucracy* in the form of a school incorporates specialized staff to efficiently deliver educational services (Lee, Bryk, & Smith, 1993). Efficiency is realized through specialization of roles and standardization of categorized services to create a routine (Skrtic, 1991). While contemporary American society has entered the technological age, schools, for the large part, remain in the Industrial Age with programs, curricula, and buildings that are essentially the same as they were 100 years ago (Baptiste, 1992).

Cusick (1992) suggested that maintaining the bureaucratic structure of schools has two results. One outcome is student compliance behaviors such as "work quietly," "raise your hand," "line up," and so on. As such, bureaucratic control is translated into curriculum whereby worksheets and easily graded tests are intended to maintain control and order rather than instruct (McNeil, 1986). The second result is that the logistic coordination of the bureaucracy moves students away from academics and into groups that can be easily managed. It has been argued, however, that the bureaucratic organization of schools has led to a breakdown of human commitment, creating transient relationships, a disintegration of common bonds, and a retreat from shared responsibility (Lee, Bryk, & Smith, 1993).

Based on the organizational structure of schools, the traditional role of faculty and staff is twofold: to instruct and to manage students (Cusick, 1992). Students are primarily grouped by age in elementary settings and by academic subject in secondary settings (Cusick, 1992). Consequently, secondary teachers are subject-matter specialists with social ties primarily linked to academic departments rather than to the school at large (Lee, Bryk, & Smith, 1993). Whether in elementary or secondary settings, teaching is generally an autonomous and private activity with little or no interactions with other adult professionals (Cusick, 1992; Elmore, 1987). A curious interaction of cultural norms and systemic organization with regard to teacher isolation was described by Silver (1973). She suggested that teachers have peers but no colleagues (cited in Feiman-Nemser & Floden, 1986). As such, teachers have social interactions in the teachers' lounge or staff meetings, yet cultural norms generally prohibit teachers from discussing work or sharing problems, as asking for assistance might be construed as a sign of weakness. Similarly, the teaching culture discourages teachers from telling a peer to try a new technique. Physical isolation therefore conveys a message that teachers are expected to cope with problems on their own and that they are not allowed to enter antoher teacher's classroom or provide advice unless invited (Feiman-Nemser & Floden, 1986).

Schools have been described as "segmented, egg-crate institutions in which teachers are isolated" (McLaughlin & Yee, 1988, p. 40). Furthermore, the importance of time in the bureaucratic structure of the school is illustrated by the prominence of clocks (Cusick, 1992) and bell systems that regulate the coming and going of students and teachers. Similarly, it is important to understand the impact of other influences on the function and mission of the school. One administrator lamented that many attempts to implement innovative educational programs within a school are thwarted by bus schedules or athletics.

General Education

Goodlad (1984) categorized *general education* into four broad instructional domains: academic, vocational, social/civic/cultural, and personal. Students are expected to master skills that will enable them to meet academic objectives (reading, writing, and arithmetic) in assisting their pursuit of meaningful employment. General education is also expected to transmit norms and values that will help students become good citizens and members of their culture and community. Finally, the educational experience should instill a degree of self-esteem and self-worth in the personal development of each student.

Instruction is primarily devoted to academics using explicit commercially published curricula approved by state and local agencies. A significant amount of classroom time is structured around printed materials or textbooks that may or may not be appropriate for particular students (Devaney & Sykes,

Activity 5–1

Read each of the following scenarios and identify cultural or systemic variables that appear to be contributing to some type of conflict.

1. A classroom teacher believes providing additional time for a student with learning disabilities to complete a written exam would be unfair to other students.

2. A building administrator resents the university for using her best teachers as cooperating supervisors of student teachers because she feels the teachers should be doing the jobs they were hired to do, which is to teach.

3. A classroom teacher is afraid to ask for assistance from the school's teacher-assistance team with a problem for fear he will be perceived as professionally inadequate.

4. A special education teacher laments that she can either provide the services students with special needs require in her resource room or consult with classroom teachers, but she cannot do both.

5. A classroom teacher disapproves of the token economy system for homework completion proposed by the school psychologist because he feels students should be intrinsically rather than extrinsically motivated to complete assignments.

6. Mr. French was a first-year teacher, eager to implement innovative teaching techniques he learned during his preservice preparation. When Mr. French approached Mrs. Billfeld, a veteran teacher of twenty years, she told him, "We've been doing things just fine. Why not just learn the ropes?"

7. A university faculty member serving as a parent volunteer suggested a student-grouping technique to a classroom teacher who dismissed the idea as too theoretical and not practical "in the trenches."

8. The school counselor and junior high English teacher sought permission to implement a cross-curriculum program for building self-esteem with a written language arts program. The administrator indicated that the school counselor could not be released from scheduling duties.

1988). Elmore (1987) described six "basic realities of daily life" in most classrooms and schools (p. 62) that are presented in Table 5–1.

Goodlad (1984) summarized the characteristics of a general education classroom in his landmark study, *A Place Called School*. Classrooms are typically organized for teacher-led, group instruction of twenty to thirty students to maintain an orderly environment (Cusick, 1992, Devaney & Sykes, 1988). Despite the education en masse, individual students generally work and achieve alone in the group setting. Student activity is usually associated with listening to the teacher, doing written assignments, and taking tests or quizzes. Student progress in mastering the curriculum is routinely based on a scope

Table 5–1   The Six Basic Realities of Traditional Classrooms and Schools

1. **School days are divided into discrete units of time allocated to discrete units of subject matter.**
   Content may vary from day to day depending on teacher pacing, school schedules, or unanticipated interruptions.
2. **The dominant pattern for allocating students to teachers is a single teacher working with a group of students in a single classroom for each unit of time.**
   Teachers may be joined temporarily by other adults such as aides or student teachers. Groups of students may work with different, individual teachers throughout the school day.
3. **Teachers' work is defined by the time spent with students.**
   Elementary teachers spend almost the entire day alone with students within a classroom.
   Secondary teachers have preparation periods in which they do not work directly with students.
   Groups of students usually rotate in secondary settings.
4. **Whole-group instruction is the primary instructional format**.
   Teachers often work with the entire class at one time rather than rotate among small clusters of students.
5. **Most instructional activities are teacher-led or teacher-dominated.**
   Students are usually passive recipients of information disseminated by the teacher. Student participation is often limited to listening or following directions at their desks rather than engaging in physical behaviors or interactions with peers.
6. **Knowledge is defined as mastery of discrete pieces of information mediated by the teacher from external sources.**
   Teachers generally assess student understanding and skill acquisition by administering pencil-and-paper tasks that require students to replicate incremental bits of information from an explicit, commercially published curriculum.

Source: Adapted from R.F. Elmore (1987). Reform and the culture of authority in schools. *Educational Administration Quarterly, 23*(4), 60–78.

and sequence of developmental steps that are standardized to grade- and age-level norms. Grades are awarded as part of an accountability system designed to assess not only students, but teachers as well (Devaney & Sykes, 1988).

Although many students benefit from traditional instructional approaches, there are some who fail to meet expected levels of mastery for one reason or another. These students, as discussed in Chapter 2, may come from disadvantaged backgrounds that impede learning. Or they may be culturally different and experience difficulty due to a mismatch of their culture and that of an Anglo-American culture of the school. Also, there are some students who, due to a disabling condition, experience failure and frustration. Such student variability means that some students cannot be accommodated by the bureaucratic structure and routine of the school. This requires the development of specialized programs within the school to provide support services for students who experience difficulty in general education (Skrtic, 1991).

Chapter I/Title I Programs

The Elementary and Secondary Education Act (ESEA) (Public Law 98-10) was passed by Congress in 1965 to provide direct educational assistance to disadvantaged students (Cusick, 1992). In many respects the ESEA was perceived as a solution to the social problem of poverty, as it was President Johnson's first bill in his "War on Poverty" (Natriello, McDill, & Pallas, 1990; Stringfield & Yoder, 1992). The most significant component of the law was under *Title I,* in which federal dollars were distributed directly to school districts to serve impoverished children. This component of the program was renamed *Chapter I* when the law was reauthorized in 1981 as the Education Consolidation and Improvement Act (Public Law 100-297). Over $80 billion have been provided since the bill was enacted (Stringfield & Yoder, 1992). Approximately 5 million children were served in 1990 with a budget of $4.5 billion (Ralph, 1990). The amount of funding is determined by the number of poor families within a school's boundary and on the basis of poor educational performance of individual students on standardized achievement tests (Ralph, 1990).

Chapter I funds are used to create educational support services within the school. It is important to note, however, that federal regulations have never dictated specific instructional interventions to be used. There are five different types of service delivery models (Natriello et al., 1990): pull-out, add-on, in-class programs, replacement programs, and school-wide programs. Special or remedial instruction is provided in a separate setting by a specialist with a salary that may come from Chapter I funds during *pull-out programming.* *Add-on programming* provides instruction before and after school or during the summer. Instructional support delivered directly to students in the mainstream classroom is referred to as *in-class programming.* *Replacement programming* is segregated and self-contained, where instruction in a given subject area is provided. *Schoolwide programs* are provided to schools in which 75 percent of the student population are from low-income families.

Federal dollars have typically been used to fund diagnostic/prescriptive services for low-achieving students in segregated settings (Natriello et al., 1990; Stringfield & Yoder, 1992). Research suggests that students gain minimal instructional time ranging from ten to forty minutes a day (Ralph, 1990; Stringfield & Yoder, 1992). Natriello and colleagues (1992) cited a number of criticisms of pull-out programs. These services often lack a congruency and coordination of instruction between mainstream and Chapter I teachers. As a result, they often supplant rather than supplement instructional time in basic skills. Moreover, teachers' responsibility for students eligible for support services is diminished, and stigmatization for students may occur. Despite these flaws, a number of organizational/leadership themes and instructional/classroom practices have been identified as contributing to successful Chapter I programs (Stringfield & Yoder, 1992) and are presented in Table 5–2.

Table 5–2 Common Organizational/Leadership Themes and Instructional/Classroom Practices of Effective Chapter I Programs

Organizational/Leadership Themes

The goal and belief that every student could learn.
The existence and use of instructional leaders within the school.
The presence of qualified and experienced teachers.
An emphasis on continuing professional staff development.
Teacher accountability for students' learning.
Mandated coordination between Chapter I and classroom teachers.
On going monitoring of the program.
Discontinuance of ineffective methods, materials, and staff.
Parental involvement in student learning.

Instructional/Classroom Practices

Individualized instruction for improving academic skills.
Integration of assessment, planning, instruction, and evaluation procedures.
Lessons designed for success and challenge.
Frequent use of praise and rewards.
Frequent collaboration and communication between Chapter I instructors and classroom teachers.
Implementation of empirically based "best practices."

Source: Adapted from S. Springfield & N. Yoder (1992). Toward a model of elementary grades Chapter 1 effectiveness. In H.C. Waxman, J.W. deFelix, J.E. Anderson, & H.P. Baptiste, Jr., (Eds.), *Students at risk in at-risk schools.* Newbury Park, CA: Corwin Press.

Spotlight: Success for All

An innovative approach to helping students in Chapter I schools entitled Success For All was first implemented in Baltimore during the 1987–88 school year. By 1993 the program had been successfully replicated in seventy schools in sixteen states. A key element of Success For All programs is one-on-one tutoring by certified teachers for twenty minutes to improve reading skills using regular classroom reading materials. In addition to the tutoring sessions, tutors are also utilized during ninety-minute periods to reduce student-teacher ratios for additional instruction. Students are assessed every eight weeks through curriculum-based assessment. Results are used to regroup students who require additional assistance. Another key component of the Success For All program is the family support team. Teachers, social workers, and counselors work with team coordinators to provide parent-education programs and other activities designed to promote active parental involvement in their child's learning. The program has been adapted for use with limited-English-proficiency students in ten schools in six states (Dianda, 1993). The Success For All approach has resulted in substantial positive effects on reading achievement, decreased referrals to special education, and increased student attendance for the children who have been in the program since first grade (Madden et al., 1993).

Bilingual and Second-Language Acquisition Programs

As the number of culturally diverse students who do not speak English as a native language increases, educators are faced with providing bilingual and second-language-acquisition programs in the schools. Federal and state legislation as well as judicial decisions have had a great impact on the development of these programs (Garcia, 1993; 1990). The Bilingual Education Act of 1968 was designed to meet educational needs of limited-English-speaking children from low-income families. Since its initial passage, the law has been reauthorized four times, resulting in over $1 billion for educational programs for language-minority students. A total of twelve states currently mandate special educational services for language-minority students, while twenty-six states have no such legislation of any kind. The U.S. Supreme Court ruled in the case of *Lau v. Nichols* (1974) that limited-English-proficiency students must be provided language-support programs. The Fifth Circuit Court ruled in the case of *Castaneda v. Packard* (1981) that language programs for limited-English-speaking children must (1) be based on sound educational theory; (2) be designed to effectively implement theoretically based instruction; and (3) produce results within a reasonable amount of time.

Types of Programs.   As educators prepare to meet the needs of students who do not speak English as a native language, three important questions must be addressed: (1) What are the native-language and second-language characteristics of the students, families, and community we serve? (2) What model of instruction is desired? (3) What is the nature of staff and resources necessary to implement the desired instruction? (Garcia, 1993, p. 72). These questions reflect the student-centered ecological perspective advocated throughout this textbook. Ramirez and Merino (1990) described four dominant instructional programs for meeting the needs of language-minority children in schools. *Submersion programming* is the placement of *limited-English-proficiency* (LEP) students into mainstream, English-speaking classrooms with no accommodation or provision for teaching English. Some students may spend part of the day submersed in classrooms while receiving special instruction designed to teach *English as a second language* (ESL). ESL programs focus on language acquisition rather than academic subjects. Content is taught in students' native language as they are in the process of learning English in *transitional bilingual education* (TBE). Programs in which all instruction is delivered in English by bilingual teachers who can address questions asked by students in their native language are known as *structured English immersion strategy* (SEIS).

Effective Classrooms and Teachers of LEP Students.   Settings that are effective in meeting the needs of LEP students can be broadly characterized as collaborative learning centers where students work together (Garcia, 1993). Individual seatwork on tasks such as worksheets is minimized. Teachers typically move from one small group to another to assist students as they work on group projects. Essentially, this format creates the need for students to talk with each other in order to clarify objectives and complete tasks. This exchange promotes language acquisition. Large-group instruction is usually devoted to startup activities in the morning. Basic skills and specific content are often organized around thematic units (Moll, 1988; Pease-Alvarez et al., 1991, cited in Garcia, 1993).

Spotlight: The Infusion Project

The University of Florida implemented a teacher training-program known as the INFUSION Project in 1986. Funded by the U.S. Department of Education, the project was designed to recruit teacher candidates interested in meeting the needs of at-risk and disabled limited-English-proficiency students. The project infused bilingual and multicultural content into a core curriculum of special education preparation programs. Networks were also developed to assist teachers in establishing partnerships. Project participants learned a variety of effective practices to meet the instructional needs of this segment of the student population. Perhaps more importantly, all of the participants, both teacher candidates and cooperating supervisors in the school sites and university, realized they were not alone in their efforts. The emotional and technical support afforded by collaboration "developed confidence in their abilities to provide appropriate services to their students" (Fradd et al, 1990, p. 247).

There are a number of characteristics and behaviors of effective teachers who work with language-minority-students (Garcia, 1993). These educators clearly articulate objectives for specific tasks as well as specific student behaviors that are necessary for successfully meeting instructional goals. Similarly, these teachers demonstrate and communicate high expectations of their students and themselves as teachers. As discussed later in Chapter 7, competent teachers effectively use academic learning time to keep students engaged during instruction while monitoring their progress and providing immediate feedback. Finally, effective teachers often alternate between languages to check for understanding and ensure clarity of instructions.

Special Education

Special education is conceptualized as support services for students with disabilities. In order to understand special education programs, educators need to have a fundamental knowledge base of its long legal history, which has a foundation in civil rights cases (Hocutt, Martin, & McKinney, 1991; Rothstein, 1990). The U.S. Supreme Court ruled in the case of *Brown v. Board of Education* (1954) that separate but equal schools and educational opportunities were unconstitutional. It was ruled in the case of *Pennsylvania Association of Retarded Citizens v. Commonwealth of Pennsylvania* (1972) that public schools are preferable over placement in special, segregated schools. Children's right to due process in educational decision making and the right to an appropriate education were determined in *Mills v. Board of Education* (1972). Each of these legal decisions helped lay the groundwork for legislation.

As discussed in Chapter 2, Section 504 of the Rehabilitation Act of 1973 (Public Law 93-112) provides individuals with disabilities basic civil rights that protect them from discrimination. The U.S. Congress passed the Education of All Handicapped Children Act (Public Law 94-142) in 1975 mandating that students with disabilities were entitled to a free and appropriate public education. Ironically, while the intent of the law was to provide protective rights and equal opportunity for students with disabilities to be educated with their peers, the legislation may have inadvertently created a parallel educational system (Walker, 1987). The organization and culture of schools may have been ill-prepared for top-down, legislated change, leading to the undesired result of a separate subculture of special education with its own set of roles, norms, and routines that differentiate itself from general education (Welch, 1989).

Public Law 94-142 was amended in 1986 through the Handicapped Infant and Toddler Program (Public Law 99-457), which mandated services from birth. Public Law 94-142 was once again reauthorized in 1990, and is now known as the Individual with Disabilities Education Act (IDEA) (Public Law 101-476). Special education programming in public schools is operationalized by IDEA, which is comprised of five basic tenets: (1) eligibility and labeling, (2) free and appropriate public education, (3) individualized educational programming, (4) the least restrictive environment, and (5) procedural safeguards.

Eligibility and Labeling.   Historically, students with disabilities have not always received the type of special support services they needed. Consequently, the statute was designed to identify students who merit support services who might otherwise go undetected. A disabling condition must be discernible in order to be eligible for support services. *Eligibility* is determined by a variety of formal and informal assessment procedures. This process typically involves standardized, norm-referenced tests. These include intelligence and psychoeducational achievement tests to determine students' levels of ability and actual performance. The results of the tests are reviewed and interpreted by a multidisciplinary team (see Chapter 8) that determines eligibility according to federal, state, and local guidelines.   The assessment and eligibility process, however, is based on the assumption that the tests are valid and that discrete disabling conditions can, in fact, be identified.

Once eligibility has been determined, a categorical label is applied to the individual. The *labeling* process is used for fiscal management purposes in the allocation of services. State and federal funding for services are limited and require placing a cap on the percentage of students eligible for receiving special education services.   IDEA emphasizes identification and classification, yet intervention programs do require separate, categorical programs. Instead, service delivery is based on student need, not on labels or categories.

Free and Appropriate Public Education.   The basic premise of the law is that students with disabilities must have meaningful access to public education. In the case of *Hendrick Hudson District Board of Education v. Rowley* (1982), the U.S. Supreme Court ruled that an appropriate education consists of "specially designed instruction" and related services that are designed to provide educational benefit. Therefore, a state is not required to provide an ideal education, but merely a beneficial one (Hardman et al., 1993). The dilemma facing educators is that of defining and measuring a beneficial education. Typically, meeting IEP objectives (discussed next) is the criterion by which educators determine the extent of educational benefit.

Individualized Educational Programming.   The *individualized education program* (IEP) is a management plan in which educators and parents identify specific annual goals and instructional objectives based on need. The IEP is intended to serve as an instrument for determining meaningful progress toward those goals (Huefner, 1991). This plan and the goals within it determine the range of services that will be provided. Consequently, a student cannot be placed within a specific instructional setting before the IEP is written. To do so would be analogous to building a house before developing the blueprint.

The IEP is developed by the student's parents and a multidisciplinary team of educators. Its actual components and the process for its development are described in detail in Chapter 8. The IEP drives service delivery, which is typically managed or coordinated by a special education teacher. However, it is important to realize that services are not exclusively provided by a special educator. Many instructional objectives can be met within mainstream settings under the direct supervision of a classroom teacher.

Least Restrictive Environment.   Students with disabilities are to receive their education in the *least restrictive environment* (LRE). This requires that to the maximum extent appropriate, students with disabilities are educated with their nondisabled peers. Removal of a student from a mainstream classroom is to occur only when the nature and severity of the disabling condition is such that instruction in a classroom with supplementary aids or services cannot be achieved satisfactorily. Many teachers, administrators, and parents erroneously assume that by virtue of being eligible for special education services, students with disabilities will receive those services in special, segregated settings. Specialists such as special education teachers, school psychologists, and paraprofessionals can provide a variety of supplementary services to the student and classroom teacher through collaborative consultation and other forms of educational partnerships such as team-teaching. Students with disabilities may receive most or at least part of their education in regular classrooms while receiving special support in other settings.

One special education setting is the *resource room,* where students spend up to half of the academic school day with remaining time in mainstream classroom settings. The National Center for Education Statistics (1992) reported that nearly 39 percent of all students with disabilities received support in resource rooms, with the majority classified as having a learning disability (57.8 percent) followed by behavior disorders (32 percent) and mental retardation (22 percent). This type of service-delivery model is often referred to as pull-out programming because students are "pulled out" from regular classes to receive additional instruction in reading, language, or math. Skrtic (1991) maintained, however, that resource programming both epitomizes yet contradicts the bureaucratic structure of schools. The premise of resource programming is that the responsibility for a student's educational needs is shared by general and special educators in both mainstream and special settings. In his argument, Skrtic suggested that this "contradicts the division of labor because it requires that students' instructional program be rationalized and assigned to more than one professional, which is justified implicitly on the assumption that professionals will work collaboratively to integrate the program" (p. 187). In reality, programming and delivery of services are often the exclusive responsibility of the special educator, with little or no relationship or congruence to instruction provided in mainstream settings (Allington & McGill-Franzen, 1989; Ysseldyke, Algozzine, & Thurlow, 1992).

A *self-contained room* is a special education setting where students receive most, if not all, of their instruction. The rationale for this type of placement is that students require specialized services that cannot be provided in mainstream settings or require a highly structured environment. These students are often not self-sufficient or mobile enough to work independently. Students may, however, leave this setting to join their nondisabled peers in mainstream settings for nonacademic activities such as art, music, or physical education. In these cases, many of the activities or tasks have been modified to some degree to meet their needs. It is important, however, for educators and administrators to understand that even students with significant disabilities can, to some extent, receive academic instruction in mainstream settings. Paraprofessionals or specialized personnel may accompany the student into the classroom and provide assistance as needed.

Procedural Safeguards.   IDEA includes a number of procedures that protect the student and parents. Non-biased assessment procedures must be used to determine a student's eligibility for services. This means that test instruments must be culturally fair and in the student's native language. Parents have the right to receive notice and give consent at various stages of service delivery including assessment for eligibility. This allows parents to fully participate in every aspect of identification, assessment, planning, and evaluation of service delivery. Similarly, parents have the right to an independent educational evaluation of their child as well as access to their child's records. Student records are confidential and are not accessible to unauthorized personnel. Parents are also entitled to full participation in the development of the IEP and placement decisions. When any of these procedural safeguards fail to produce a satisfactory home-school partnership, parents are entitled to an impartial hearing to resolve disputes.

The roles of educators have traditionally been defined by these various programs and systems within schools. With continued emphasis on educational reform to meet the needs of *all* children, these roles and programs are likely to evolve over time.

Traditional and Reconceptualized Roles of Educators

As discussed in previous chapters, one domain of an ecosystem is human resources. The staff of a school is comprised of many individuals, all with their own specific roles. Some roles are firmly entrenched within cultural expectations of the school environment itself and the community outside the walls of the building. Roles of educators are, however, not static and are subject to change as the task of educating students evolves. Here we examine the traditional and reconceptualized roles of administrators, teachers, specialized support personnel, and other staff within the school.

Building Administrators

It is commonly held that the building administrator is (or should be) the instructional leader of a school (Cusick, 1992). This lofty goal is philosophical in nature, as principals are in actuality often relegated to planning, maintaining, and adjusting an operational routine designed to coordinate the activities of teachers, staff, and students (Murphy, 1991).

Traditional Role of Administrator.   Traditionally, the building administrator has had three functional roles: manager, mediator, and leader (Lee, Bryk, & Smith, 1993). As a manager, the administrator must allocate resources and supervise faculty and staff (Castallo, Fletcher, Rossetti, & Sekowski, 1992). As described earlier, schools are organized as routines. Building principals typically "move from activity to activity, person to person, making dozens of minor but needed adjustments in the routine" (Cusick, 1992, p. 99). The administrator is a mediator by serving as a liaison within the school and with the community. Teachers often expect the administrator to take the role of a buffer between themselves and outside influences such as the district administration, parents, and the community (Feiman-Nemser & Floden, 1986). The principal also serves as a mediator when working with parents during the development and implementation of an individual education plan (IEP) for students with disabilities. In this case, the administrator takes on a managerial role as the *local educational agent* (LEA) by signing the IEP as an assurance that resources will be allocated to facilitate the achievement of IEP objectives. Finally, the principal must demonstrate leadership by interpreting and implementing policies and procedures while establishing a philosophically based mission for the operation of the school.

School administrators' primary task is managing various and simultaneous issues via personal interactions that synthesize people and activity into systematic patterns of predictable behavior (Cusick, 1992). In essence, building administrators are often reduced to street-level bureaucrats who creatively manage a barrage of crises resulting from too many activities crammed into limited time and space (Crowson & Porter-Gehrie, 1980, cited in Cusick, 1992).

Activity 5–2

Are you aware of the different personnel typically found in school settings? How accurate are your perceptions and expectations of the various roles and responsibilities of educators within the school? Can you describe the function of specific school personnel? Complete this activity before reading the following section describing the traditional and reconceptualized roles of educators.

Either as a group or as an individual, make a list of the various professionals within a school who can serve as partners in meeting the needs of students at risk. Next to each role title, briefly describe the role and responsibility of each educator. After completing this chapter, review your list and determine the extent to which your initial descriptions were accurate and complete as well as the extent to which they need to be modified.

Reconceptualized Role of Administrator.   The administrator's role is evolving to include a broader leadership role (Hart, 1993). In this way, leadership is reconceptualized from the traditional role of authoritarian manager to that of a facilitator in developing a community of leaders and learners (Barth, 1990; 1988). In so doing, administrators must clearly articulate a goal or vision of what a school and its community members can be. The new administrator also relinquishes some of his or her power to teachers by empowering them to actively participate in school-based decisions. The administrator's role has been expanded beyond the walls of the school to create partnerships with business and the community at large. A school principal may actively seek a business to "adopt" the school in an effort to secure in-kind contributions in the way of supplies, equipment, or monies. Building administrators are now expected to obtain extramural funds or other outside support in the way of computer hardware or audio/visual equipment through grants to supplant the limited funding district and state agencies can provide.

Classroom Teachers

The role of the classroom teacher is associated with educational and organizational goals (Feiman-Nemser & Floden, 1986). Educational goals involve motivating students, establishing personal relationships, and mediating the learning process. On the other hand, teachers are also expected to meet organizational goals of maintaining order in the classroom while facilitating the bureaucratic operation of the school. As the expectations of society's role for education change, so do the roles and responsibilities of classroom teachers.

Traditional Role of Classroom Teacher.   Haberman (1991) described fundamental functions of urban teaching at all grade levels as (1) giving information, (2) asking questions, (3) giving directions, (4) making/assigning/ grading assignments, (5) monitoring seatwork, (6) reviewing assignments, (7) giving/grading tests, (8) settling disputes, (9) punishing noncompliance, and (10) giving grades. In secondary settings, teachers are subject-matter specialists with social ties primarily linked to academic departments rather than to the school at large (Lee, Bryk, & Smith, 1993). Teachers have been historically prepared to dispense a common knowledge base, in both elementary and secondary settings, largely grounded in Anglo-American culture to a presumed homogeneous body of students in terms of ethnicity, race, and ability. In addition to classroom duties, teachers are also expected to carry out other responsibilities in other settings throughout the school day. These might include serving on school committees, monitoring students in the lunchroom or on the playground, and sponsoring extramural activities such as clubs, fine arts organizations, and athletic groups.

Reconceptualized Role of Classroom Teacher.   Murphy (1991) has categorized the redesign of teachers' work into three clusters: expanded

A traditional
feature of the
classroom is
teacher-led
instruction of large
and small groups.

responsibilities, new professional roles, and new career opportunities. With *expanded responsibilities* beyond instruction in the classroom, teachers are becoming less isolated and more involved in schoolwide decision making and activities. Teachers are now serving on committees from which they were once excluded. They participate in school-based management to plan innovative programs. They also serve on principal- and teacher-selection teams as well as committees for performance evaluation.

Among the *new professional roles* for teachers are roles as collaborators, experts, and researchers (Miller, 1988). One example of a new role is that of a mentor for novice teachers or teacher candidates completing field experiences in teacher-education programs. Within the context of this role, many classroom teachers now find themselves with adjunct status from a nearby college or university. Another role involves curriculum development, whereby teachers are released from part or all of their traditional classroom responsibilities to use their own expertise in creating new materials for schoolwide use.

New career opportunities are facilitated by planning, developing, and implementing comprehensive staff-development programs. Here, teachers learn from each other via peer coaching. Through career-ladder programs, they can enhance their own professional skills through active research and implementation of innovative techniques.

Teachers are now combining effective teaching behaviors such as modeling and guided practice with feedback with opportunities for students to take greater responsibility for their learning during individual practice activities. Schon (1988) proposed an approach of reflection-in-action to allow teachers to enhance their instructional practice while taking the role of "builders of repertoire rather than accumulators of procedures and methods" (p. 26). The teacher's role is to facilitate a process by which students begin to develop their base of general knowledge to an extent they can learn independently throughout the lifelong learning process (Resnick & Klopfer, 1989). Teachers provide students with essential learning tools during direct instruction that can be used to construct meaningful educational experiences. In this way, teachers are turning to a constructivist approach in which students are perceived as builders of knowledge structures rather than recipients of fragmented pieces of knowledge and facts. Rather than playing the role of a pedagogical technician disseminating discrete bits of information and skills, teachers are expected to create and adapt existing curriculum and develop innovative instructional procedures that will enable students to take greater responsibility in their own learning. The teacher's role will be to create centers of inquiry using a variety of instructional materials that will meet the needs of all students (see Chapter 7). The new classroom will rely less on textbooks and more on using a variety of information bases to allow students to create their own learning products. Therefore, the process of reflective teaching is the act of constructing, deconstructing, and reconstructing educational practices to solve unexpected problems (Skrtic, 1992). This process also enables teachers to meet the needs of students from culturally divergent backgrounds by creating a goodness of fit between educational experiences and the ethnic and cultural variables each student brings to the classroom.

Rather than a solitary, isolated act on the part of the teacher, reflective teaching lends itself well to establishing partnerships with colleagues within and apart from a teacher's own discipline. Rather than referring students to special education when they experience difficulties, teachers will play a greater role in providing prereferral interventions by collaborating with specialists. Classroom teachers will, in essence, become partners in the teaching and learning process. Specialists will work in tandem with classroom teachers to provide additional strategic interventions to meet the needs of diverse learners.

Teachers are less likely to work exclusively within the confines of their classroom. They will have a variety of interactions with students, teachers from other disciplines, and individuals such as parents and members of the business community outside the school (Lipsky & Gartner, 1992).

Special Educators

The special education teacher is a professional educator who has been specially trained to meet the needs of students with disabilities. The primary role of the special educator is to manage the instructional program outlined on the student's individualized education program (IEP). Coordination and implementation of the IEP requires the special education teacher to work with parents, administrators, teachers, and other specialized service personnel.

Traditional Role of Special Educator.   The traditional role of a special education teacher has been providing direct services to students with disabilities, usually in segregated settings. Special educators have typically conducted assessment, provided instruction, and managed behavior. Assessment has traditionally revolved around referrals and determining eligibility for special education. This process often utilizes standardized, norm-referenced tests as described in Chapter 6. Data gathered during assessment procedures are used to determine eligibility for special education services and to plan instructional services. In coordinating instructional programs on IEPs, special educators have provided direct services in segregated settings to students with special needs. The assumption has been that working with this student population merits special training in specialized instructional techniques (Lipsky & Gartner, 1989). Ysseldyke and Algozzine (1982) listed some of these special interventions including optometric vision training, visual perception training, auditory perception training, perceptual motor training, and psycholinguistic training. Finally, special educators are trained to implement special techniques to manage student behaviors. These strategies are often designed for special settings and may not be feasible for classrooms with large numbers of students.

Reconceptualized Role of Special Educator.   The role of special educators has evolved into one of support to teachers as well as students by providing direct and indirect services in a variety of settings. Direct service delivery will continue to mean providing assessment and one-on-one or small-group instruction to students. The location of direct instructional services, however, may vary. The special educator is likely to expand the assessment process to include an ecological assessment of factors within the learning environment that may be modified. Direct services may also be delivered in the regular classroom, side by side with the classroom teacher. Consequently, many of the specialized interventions listed previously have fallen by the wayside due to a lack of empirical evidence supporting their efficacy and the fact that most have little or no relevance to instruction in mainstream settings (Ysseldyke & Algozzine, 1982). Direct service may also involve team teaching, which is described in Chapter 8. The specialist, or a paraprofessional under the supervision of the specialist, may work with an individual or small groups of students who are eligible for special education services and those who are academically at risk. Still another possibility is for the specialist to work in tandem with a content-area teacher in secondary settings by demonstrating learning strategies such as note taking skills to an entire class during a lecture. This approach minimizes the likelihood of the types of role conflict described above.

A significant shift in roles will include greater emphasis on indirect service delivery. Stainback and Stainback (1992) suggested that special educators will serve as a resource locator. In this role, they can provide indirect services to the student by locating and providing appropriate materials, equipment, or other personnel to meet the needs of both classroom teacher and student in mainstream settings. Additionally, the special educator may demonstrate a specific technique or strategy that a teacher will ultimately learn how to use. Within this context, the special educator's new role may reflect many aspects of a consultant described in Chapters 3 and 8.

In addition to providing direct and indirect services, the special educator's role will include that of coordinator of services. Within the school, the special educator is likely to be seen as a supervisor of paraprofessionals and volunteers who provide direct services to students in mainstream classrooms. Like other educators, special education teachers will continue their outreach to the community. Businesses, mass transit systems, and public service agencies will serve as authentic settings for learning. Two of the several learning environments for students with disabilities may be a fast-food restaurant or the city bus. This type of partnership outside the school requires effective interpersonal and collaborative problem-solving skills. The special educator also serves as a transition agent in helping students with disabilities successfully move from one setting and life experience to another. Special educators from the elementary school will work closer with their counterparts in junior high schools to facilitate the transition for students. They will work collaboratively with guidance counselors to assist students with disabilities prepare for the work force or college.

School Counselors

The school counselor plays a myriad of roles and can make a significant contribution to educational partnerships. It has been suggested, however, that the role of the school counselor has never been completely or satisfactorily defined (Partin, 1993). Teacher perceptions of the roles counselors play are often discrepant from the perceptions of administrators and counselors themselves. Unlike teachers and administrators, who have a primary responsibility for academics, the school counselor has a focus in two key areas: personal development and career/vocational advising. As in the case of other professionals in the school, the role and responsibilities of counselors are evolving.

Traditional Role of School Counselor.   Counselors play two major roles: administrator and therapist (Thompson, 1992). Partin (1993) suggested that counselors spend most of their time as administrators in scheduling, testing, and completing paperwork. Educators and parents often equate the role of the school counselor with conducting vocational assessment and advising students for making decisions regarding careers and college (Vacc, 1981). In reality, however, a typical high school student receives approximately twenty minutes of a counselor's time to plan for a career or college (Tugend, 1984 cited in Thompson, 1992). This is largely due to the enormous case loads of counselors. On the average, the counselor-to-student ratio in high schools is approximately 1 to 425 nationwide and as high as 1 to

1,000 in some urban areas (Thompson, 1992). In addition to vocational and college advising, counselors have traditionally been expected to identify students with special needs and assist in placement decisions for those students, to conduct testing, to conduct individual and group therapy, to provide crisis counseling, and to interface with businesses and colleges (Ehly & Dustin, 1989; Thompson, 1992).

Reconceptualized Role of School Counselor.   Given the special needs of a diverse student population, the counselor's expertise in mental health and personal development is being utilized more and more. Thompson (1992) characterized the reconceptualized role of the school counselor as a professional who facilitates "acquisition and incorporation into one's self-system life adjustment strategies that foster productive, rather than self-defeating behaviors" (pp. 1–2). While individual counseling will remain a key component of service delivery, the new role of the counselor requires less one-on-one intervention in the school and a greater emphasis on coordinating indirect services and special programs for students, parents, and other educators (Gerler, Ceichalsky, & Parker, 1990; Thompson, 1992). Programs for students might focus on human sexuality, chemical abuse, and problem solving. Counselors are beginning to provide one-on-one consultation services with teachers who, in turn, deliver indirect services to students (Dickinson & Bradshaw, 1992). Likewise, counselors are conducting staff development for entire faculties on topics such as interpersonal communication, multicultural education, suicide prevention, behavior management, and substance abuse (Dickinson & Bradshaw, 1992; Gerler, Ceichalsky, & Parker, 1990; Rice & Smith, 1993; Thompson, 1992). Counselors are also working with families by providing after-school parenting classes to address issues ranging from homework completion to preventing child abuse and neglect.

School Psychologists

Unlike the school counselor, who often has a permanent base within a school building, school psychologists usually serve as itinerant personnel working in several schools. The school psychologist, like the school counselor, plays a major role in the personal development and mental health of students. Additionally, the expertise of the school psychologist can be helpful in making critical academic decisions. In the past, the school psychologist has often been isolated from other educators and parents unless serving on a multidisciplinary team to determine a student's eligibility for special services. Today, as their roles change, it is increasingly common to see school psychologists working side by side with teachers and parents.

Traditional Role of School Psychologist.   The role of school psychologists has traditionally been that of a psychometrician. Students are tested by the school psychologist to determine eligibility for special education services (Ysseldyke, Algozzine, & Thurlow, 1992). Consequently, the school psychologist is usually a member of the multidisciplinary team that develops IEPs for students receiving special education services.   In addition to selecting,   administering,   scoring,   and   interpreting   a   battery   of psychoeducational tests, the school psychologist may also provide a variety of services associated with the mental health of students. These may include administering   personality   inventories   and   implementing   psychological interventions and programs to assist the emotional needs of students. School psychologists have traditionally been removed from direct interaction with classroom teachers.

Reconceptualized Role of School Psychologist.   The school psychologist has an important role in creating effective, positive learning environments (Ysseldyke et al., 1992). In this context, the assessment role of the school psychologist is perceived as a means to an end rather than an end itself (Gutkin & Conoley, 1990). Furthermore, assessment activities are evolving to include procedures that are linked directly to effective interventions, such as behavioral, ecological and curriculum based-methods. The traditional direct service model (such as in individual therapy), is recognized as inefficient and costly, and is being replaced with indirect services meant to empower others in the educational community and prevent future   problems.   Thus,   functions   such   as   consultation,   prereferral

The traditional role of a school psychologist as a psychometrician administering tests is evolving to include providing indirect services in a variety of educational settings.

interventions and prevention programming are being incorporated into the daily activities of school psychologists rapidly (Conoley & Gutkin, 1986).

School psychologists will continue to provide some direct mental health services. However, some of the direct services may be delivered in classroom settings to whole classes. For example, a school psychologist may work with a classroom teacher to implement life-skills curricula such as problem solving or social skills programs (Jones, Sheridan, & Binns, 1993). The reconceptualized role of school psychologists also goes beyond the walls of the school. These professionals will continue to provide consultation, counseling and home-school partnership programs with parents. Thus, the emerging role of the school psychologist is that of a partner enabling the implementation of a myriad of effective and necessary educational, social, and behavioral interventions.

Other School Personnel

There are other personnel within the school system who can play meaningful roles as partners in serving students at risk: paraprofessionals, social workers, physical therapists, and speech therapists.

The *paraprofessional* is unique in a number of ways (Pickett, 1991). First, this individual, unlike most of the partners described thus far, typically does not have a baccalaureate degree in the field of education. Instead, paraprofessionals often receive intense training in specific areas in which they will serve and function. Second, there has been a remarkable influx in the number of paraprofessionals involved in educational programs. It has been reported that there were less than 10,000 paraprofessionals in the school in 1965, while this figure rose to nearly 640,000 in 1987 (Pickett, 1991). Third, the vast majority of paraprofessionals are bilingual women from minority groups. Finally, the use of paraprofessionals is a viable means of implementing many of the reconceptualized roles and responsibilities of teachers and specialists. Incorporating the assistance and skills of paraprofessionals enables specialists to consult with classroom teachers.

The paraprofessional's role is primarily one of support, usually to the special education teacher (Jones & Bender, 1993). Paraprofessionals may conduct ongoing observations of student behaviors and collect data to facilitate the development and implementation of instructional and/or behavioral interventions. Once these interventions are in place, they may provide follow-up activities in the form of reinforcement or review. They may also serve as assistants in developing instructional materials. Other roles for the paraprofessional include performing routine administrative duties, serving as a job coach in vocational settings, or working as a "tracker" who monitors students throughout the school day.

The *social worker* is a professional who often serves as a liaison between school and home. This person may work with several agencies within the community, such as mental health services, the justice system, and the welfare/social service office. The social worker may conduct observations or interviews within the home to gain important ecological information that may be useful in understanding a student's needs for planning interventions. These interventions may be directly applied to the student or the family itself. As we will see in our discussion on the changing school later in this chapter, it is likely that the social worker will become more of a fixture within the school building to coordinate home-school programs such as parenting classes after school or in the evening, and perhaps even during the school day. Furthermore, like the school psychologist and counselor, social workers will begin to move into classroom settings to provide mental health services.

The *physical therapist* (PT) usually serves as an important link between the physical/medical and educational needs of students. This typically involves therapy associated with movement and mobility. For example, a student with cerebral palsy may have restricted use of an arm or hand. The P.T. will design and implement a program to increase the functional range and use of those limbs. The PT often interacts with the *adaptive physical educator,* who provides exercise and recreation activities within the school setting.

The *speech therapist* is often an itinerant member of educational partnerships. This means that a speech/language therapist may work in several schools by rotating from setting to setting. This professional usually works one-on-one with a student who has demonstrated a need for assistance in articulation or expressive/receptive language.

The Changing School

Schools are becoming less teacher-centered and more student-centered. Faculty and staff will and must become more interdependent to allow teams of professionals to address an array of challenges facing students at risk (Clark & Meloy, 1989 cited in Murphy, 1991). Roles and responsibilities will blur as tasks and functions become associated with technical competence and expertise rather than artificially delegated assignments (Murphy, 1991). Indeed, an emerging professional culture is breaking down barriers and isolation to promote collegial interactions for solving problems (Elmore, 1987; 1989). The process of change must begin at colleges and universities during the professional preparation programs in a way that will instill the collaborative ethic while reshaping preconceived notions of roles and responsibilities.

The new school will be characterized as a collaborative community in which teachers themselves will be empowered to take more leadership roles. Lieberman, Saxl and Miles (1988) identified a cluster of skills manifested by teacher-leaders that reflect the ecological problem-solving model described in Chapter 3. These clusters include analyzing the organization (understanding the school culture and its needs), dealing with process (the understanding and management of change), using resources (utilizing a variety of assets within the school in the pursuit of goals), managing the work (delegating tasks, monitoring progress, taking responsibility for specific actions), and building skill/confidence in colleagues (providing emotional and technical support through ongoing communication and staff development).

Bucci and Reitzammer (1992) suggested that noneducational services and personnel will become part of the school community. They describe a new school in which professionals from health and social agencies will become partners with educators to provide an array of services to the growing number of students at risk. The schools may serve as human development centers in addition to academic institutions. Teachers' responsibilities will include addressing social and health factors affecting student learning, which will require them to interact with a variety of services and agencies to address these health and social needs. Various agency services (mental health, family counseling, parent education/support groups) will be housed and delivered in the school building.

A Paradigm Shift: Creating Educational Partnerships

Historically, schools have been places of teaching, but not necessarily places of learning. Schooling has been equated with the curriculum delivered by the teacher, student learning has been incidental, and the fault for non-learning has rested with the student. Such teacher-centered, rather than student-centered, schools that narrowly focus on academic achievement have impeded the ability of special students to "fit into" school and have created, in part, the subsequent development of the vast special education system now in place (Roach, 1991, p. 3).

Many, if not most, educators would agree with this depiction of schools. However, it could also be argued that the reconceptualized roles described in this chapter and strategies for educational partnership presented throughout this book are not currently possible to implement (Maeroff, 1993). Many educators will be able to relate to the scenarios presented in Activity 5–1. As the current educational system exists and operates now, students who are at risk often do not receive assistance until they are "eligible." This reflects a reactionary rather than proactive approach to serving the needs of students. The issue of eligibility also perpetuates delineation of roles and responsibilities that do not necessarily facilitate collaboration. On the contrary, current systemic organization of educational systems consist of somewhat arbitrary and artificial barriers that represent fragmented service delivery.

It is critically important for prospective and practicing educators alike to understand that the existing structures of education are systemically organized in a fashion that will not readily accommodate change in roles and responsibilities. The rationale for this lack of accommodation for change is often based on the maxim, "We can't change because this is the way it is and the way we've always done it." We propose that educators must begin to consider an alternative rationale based on a premise that, "We must change *because* this is the way it is and the way we've always done it!" In other words, our traditional view of how things are done in schools seems to create an artificial limitation on what *could* be done. Given the array of challenges facing educators in meeting the needs of a diverse student population, the current operating procedures merit adjustment. In a manner analogous to President Johnson's "War on Poverty," the current crisis in our schools requires an assault on the status quo. Consequently, a significant paradigm shift is necessary. A *paradigm* is defined as a "shared pattern of basic beliefs and assumptions about the nature of the world and how it works" (Skrtic, 1991, p. 5). A paradigm is essentially a perception of reality reflecting the experiences, perceptions, and values of its creators (Code, 1991, cited in Banks, 1993).

Following are classic examples of paradigms within education that have recently been reconsidered. One dominant pattern of education has been the nine-month school year with summer vacations. At one time in our nation's agricultural history, it was important to allow students time away from school to help with family farming. This practice appears to be firmly entrenched despite the fact our society is predominantly urban and nonagricultural in nature. Why do schools continue to operate in this fashion? Parents, educators, and students have come to accept the *only* rationale as, "This is the way we've always done it." Many schools, however, are implementing year-round schools for a number of reasons, usually due to overcrowding of students.

A second dominant paradigm based on the industrial, bureaucratic model of schools is the practice of grade-level curriculum. Educators have used a developmental model that is based on the assumption that students move from one discrete level of skills to another according to maturation. These levels of skill mastery are based on a norm-referenced scope and sequence. The traditional norm, however, has often been Anglo-American, which may or may not reflect the needs and culture of a diverse student population. When students do not master these skill levels, they are either retained in that grade or referred to special education. Some educators, however, have begun to realize that skill levels are not static. Schools are beginning to implement cross-grade grouping of students using outcome-based education. In this approach, it is common to see sixth graders working with fourth and fifth graders in mastering specific concepts such as decimals or fractions. Consequently, teachers are no longer expected to teach "fifth-grade curriculum." Instead, teachers teach specific concepts and skills, a goal that requires greater flexibility and ongoing collaboration with colleagues to coordinate instruction and student placement.

In essence, the structure of the school, the routine of the classroom, and the pattern of educators' roles and responsibilities in serving all students are undergoing change and will continue to do so (Villa, Thousand, Paolucci-Whitcomb, & Nevin, 1990). Traditional conceptualizations of how things are done are in flux.

Resistance to Change

Change and shifts in paradigm are difficult to implement. The resistance to change is largely due to the fact that schools, like other cultures, cling to specific traditions, rituals, and routines in an attempt to maintain an orderly stability. On

Spotlight: These Are Our Kids

"It was a system that was very broken and needed fixing," is how principal Marcie MacDonald describes the changes in Beehive Elementary School. Students from culturally diverse and low-economic backgrounds were continually being referred to and receiving special education assistance that lacked congruence between instruction in mainstream and resource settings. Consequently, the entire service-delivery model of this year-round school was modified. Cross-grade, outcome-based instruction for reading and math was implemented. As a result, the school's daily schedule was standardized so that reading and math were taught at the same time each day throughout grades to accommodate flexible shifting of students from group to group. Direct support services were provided by six paraprofessionals under the supervision of the special education teacher in mainstream classrooms to students with IEPs and those who were at risk for becoming eligible for special education. Students were routinely assessed every three weeks using curriculum-based assessment and criterion-referenced testing. Those requiring additional assistance were regrouped to receive additional instruction while other students moved on to other skills. Intense remediation was provided by paraprofessionals in empty classrooms that were "off-track" during the year-round school schedule. In addition to instructional intervention, the school psychologist provided problem-solving and functional life skills instruction in mainstream classrooms through team teaching. This approach created greater accessibility to specialized support personnel for formal and informal consultation. The regularly scheduled assessment of students also provided teachers a sanctioned period of time for collaboration and communication. The collaborative approach, according to the principal, made teaching a public activity by making the entire school accountable for serving students, which ultimately resulted in shared responsibilities and a work ethic summarized by the school motto, "These Are Our Kids!" (Welch & Egan, 1993).

a human level, we become comfortable with the status quo because it makes our lives easier. On a systemic level, roles and responsibilities have been designed in such a way that we tend to operate according to specific job descriptions in which " 'That's not my job!' is a mantra describing the work ethic of the modern school" (Lee, Bryk, & Smith, 1993, p. 227).

Waugh and Punch (1987) conducted a comprehensive review of teacher receptivity to change and identified a number of general variables. Teachers are usually resistant to change that counters firmly entrenched cultural variables such as beliefs and attitudes toward the role of teaching. Similarly, fears and uncertainties associated with change are likely to impede innovations. These anxieties are often related to a lack of skill, training, or experience. Consequently, the change process must include staff development, discussed in Chapter 8, that will provide ongoing technical and psychological support. Educators will also resist change if the proposed innovation is perceived as impractical. This is usually contingent upon their own context and experience, as teachers will ask, "Will this change the way I normally conduct classroom activities, and will it be compatible with the way I interact with students?". In other words, constituencies will assess the practicality of change in terms of personal cost. Typically, the personal cost appraisal of change is related to time and effort required. As a result, the change process must not be heaped upon other responsibilities. Adequate time must be allotted to free educators from other duties to develop their new skills and complete new tasks. Finally, teachers attempt to determine the degree of support on the part of colleagues and administration. Educators are more likely to "climb on the bandwagon" if they sense a general consensus of support from other teachers and if the administrator clearly articulates the existence of emotional and technical support.

Change Process

Change, however, *can* occur. Unfortunately, most educators respond to change with a knee-jerk reaction rather than in a proactive way due to the fact that professional preparation programs for educators do not include "change education" as part of their curriculum (Welch & Hardman, 1991). Therefore, it is incumbent upon educators, administrators, teachers, and specialists alike to understand that change is a process and not an event (Lezotte, 1989). How, then, can this process be characterized and operationalized? Fullan (1993, 1986) has provided definitive work on the topic of change at the personal and organizational level. The salient features of the change process are summarized in Table 5–3.

Activity 5–3	Now that you have considered the changing school, identify examples from each ecological domain that might be found in evolving schools. Make a list and share your responses with others. Compare and contrast the list you compiled during this activity with the list you made in the previous breakout activity. Has your "paradigm," or conception of cultural and organizational variables of schools, changed?

Table 5–3   Salient Features of the Change Process in Schools

1. Change ALWAYS takes time.
2. Initial stages of change ALWAYS involve anxiety and uncertainty.
3. Ongoing technical assistance and emotional or psychological support is necessary.
4. Change involves incremental acquisition of new skills through practice and feedback.
5. Adoption of innovation occurs during an "Ah-ha" moment of revelation when participants understand why the new way is better than the old way.
6. Organizational conditions must allow and facilitate the change process.
7. Change involves pressure through interaction with peers and leaders.
8. You can't mandate what matters—the more complex the change, the less you can force it.
9. Change is a journey, not a blueprint, complete with uncertainty.
10. Problems are our friends because (a) they are inevitable and (b) learning cannot occur without them.
11. Vision and strategic planning come later and are made up as you go.
12. Decisions cannot be made by isolated individuals, nor through groupthink.
13. Both top-down *and* bottom-up strategies are necessary.
14. Partnerships with the wider environment are important for success.
15. Every person in the school is an agent of change.

Source: Adapted from M. Fullan (1993). *Change forces: Probing the depths of educational reform.* New York: Falmer Press; and M. Fullan (1985) Change processes and strategies at the local level. *Elementary School Journal, 85*(3), 391–421.

We propose that school communities initiate the change process to facilitate educational partnerships by following this maxim: THINK BIG, START SMALL, GO SLOW. Rather than attempt to redesign an entire school, it may be logistically more feasible to concentrate on small-scale pilot projects that can be managed more easily. We provide guidelines for establishing school-wide partnerships such as team teaching or consultant models in Chapter 8. In those guidelines, we recommend, for example, that team teaching be initially implemented at one grade level in elementary settings or in one academic department at the secondary level. In this way, concerted effort and energies can be focused in a way that will better allow for flexibility and change. This approach will allow change agents to identify what worked well and what did not. Adaptations involving a small number of individuals can be accommodated more easily than those involving an entire faculty.

Pilot-level change can best be realized by considering the following guidelines for establishing effective schools that have been adapted from Fullan (1985) and Maeroff (1993):

1. *Develop a plan* that is collaboratively generated by all of the constituencies involved. The plan should closely resemble the action plan described in Chapter 3. It should utilize an ecological perspective by incorporating a vari-

ety of resources (human, technological, information, physical, and financial) in a matrix outlining *who* does *what, where* and *when,* with a specific outcome or product articulated for each step and activity. It is important to understand, however, that these plans are dynamic and will undergo change. Fullan (1993) suggested that plans will evolve over time as people more or less make them up as they go. The outcome and products can serve as an evaluation criterion to determine the extent to which goals are being met.

2. *Clarify and develop roles* of central staff to facilitate the change process and implementation of the action plan.

3. *Provide ongoing technical assistance* to promote and facilitate implementation of innovative practices. Coaching will assist educators as they attempt to implement new skills. Use a collaborative approach in which colleagues can periodically meet to exchange information and questions that will enable them to improve their performance.

4. *Conduct formative and summative evaluation* to determine what is working well and what needs work. Create specific, observable objectives that can be used to monitor the impact of the project. By using ongoing (formative) evaluation throughout implementation, project participants can make appropriate adjustments. Final evaluation (summative) results will help the school community make decisions regarding continued implementation and institutionalization of the innovation, or rejection.

Activity 5–4

Central School District is located in a geographic area with a high unemployment rate due to the closing of a major factory and is facing a critical shortage of classrooms and materials (such as textbooks) due to an influx of students. The voters, however, rejected a bid to raise taxes to pay for portable classrooms and additional materials. Furthermore, there is a shortage of teachers.

Form small groups to serve as a task force charged to address these issues. Use the collaborative process worksheet from Chapter 3 to assist your task force. Consider how a paradigm shift, or restructuring the traditional organization of the school, might be utilized. Once an alternative solution has been selected, create a management plan that includes an evaluation component to facilitate the change process.

Chapter Summary

In some ways, the school is still very much like the one-room schoolhouse of yesterday. Some traditions and techniques die hard. Conversely, schools have evolved into complex organizations with a sophisticated culture and system of operation. The culture of the school defines the way things are done and the way members should act. Attitudes, beliefs, values, and roles are cultural variables that influence behaviors. Roles, however, are changing as the needs of students at risk become more and more of a challenge. This creates a sense of conflict as teachers are expected to change behaviors they have learned through socialization. From an organizational and systemic perspective, schools are structured as bureaucracies. This results in isolated roles and responsibilities whereby educators often do not have the opportunity to interact or work with others in the school. Schools often consist of subsystems to meet the needs of various student subgroups. General education is intended to provide academic, vocational, civic, and personal learning experiences to students clustered in large groups. Chapter I programs and federally funded programs are designed to provide direct educational assistance to disadvantaged students through at least five different types of service delivery models: (1) pull-out, (2) add-on, (3) in-class programs, (4) replacement programs, and (5) schoolwide programs. Bilingual and second-language programs have been developed to assist students who do not speak English as a native language. There are four models typically used in schools: (1) submersion, (2) English as a second language (ESL), (3) transitional bilingual education (TBE), and (4) structured English immersion strategies (SEIS). Special education programs are support services for students with disabilities. Service delivery is dictated by the Individual with Disabilities Education Act (IDEA), which mandates that all students with disabilities are entitled to a free and appropriate public education. Special education programming is comprised by five basic tenets: (1) eligibility and labeling, (2) free and appropriate public education, (3) individualized educational programming, (4) the least restrictive environment, and (5) procedural safeguards.

As schools continue to evolve, educators must be prepared to change, too. Educators face the sometimes daunting challenge of meeting an array of needs of a diverse student population. It is unrealistic, if not unfair, to expect educators to face these challenges alone. Through innovative and creative problem solving, educators can reshape their roles, responsibilities, and the school itself to take a proactive approach in meeting these challenges. As the rhetoric for reform echoes down school hallways, teachers, administrators, and special support personnel must begin to take appropriate steps on their own before steps are taken by legislators and special interest groups in their behalf. Educators must, however, understand that change is a process, requiring a coordinated effort to realize specific student-centered goals. An awareness of the resources within and outside the school will empower educators to effectively develop and implement educational partnerships that will better serve students at risk.

Case Study 5–1

Mrs. Chin is a new, first-year building principal at Mountain Meadow Elementary School. She began the school year's faculty orientation meeting outlining changes she envisioned. Mrs. Chin described a school in which teachers worked together to meet the needs of the large ethnic student population and the significant number of students who were identified as having mild learning problems. In this model, special education teachers would work directly with students and classroom teachers in mainstream settings. Furthermore, teachers would form teams to work on mutually defined goals through brainstorming and implementing action plans. The school counselor and district school psychologist would provide mental health services such as teaching problem-solving and social skills to students in the classroom and parent-education programs in the evening.

Philosophically, the faculty and staff found Mrs. Chin's vision exciting but impractical. Teachers wondered when they would have time to meet as teams and would they be compensated for the additional time and effort. A majority of teachers felt special educators had no business coming into their classrooms telling them what they should do. The special education teachers voiced concern about coordinating their schedules to work in various classroom settings. In fact, two of the four special education teachers believed their role was to provide special services in special settings to "their" students. After all, classroom teachers had not met these students' needs adequately in classrooms. Similarly, the district school psychologist indicated her caseload of conducting psychoeducational assessment would not allow her the opportunity to establish a regular schedule to work in classrooms. The school counselor did not think parents would be interested in coming to school at night.

1. Despite the new principal's enthusiastic and good intentions, what were some cultural and systemic factors she didn't consider?

2. What traditional roles were the faculty and support staff holding on to?

3. What alternative approach and steps might the principal consider for initating change at Mountain Meadow School?

4. How might you use the concepts presented in Table 5–3 to address this situation?

Key Vocabulary Terms

school culture	school-wide programs	submersion programs
role expectation	paradigm	English as a second language
role conflict	special education	(ESL)
socialization	eligibility	transitional bilingual
bureaucracy	labeling	education (TBE)
general education	individual education plan	structured English immersion
Chapter I/Title I	(IEP)	strategy (SEIS)
pull-out programming	least restrictive environment	local educational agent (LEA)
add-on programming	(LRE)	limited English proficiency
in-class programming	resource room	(LEP)
replacement programs	self-contained room	

Chapter 6

Chapter Overview

Traditional and Alternative Assessment Strategies

Chapter Objectives

After reading this chapter, the reader should be able to

1. Provide a rationale for implementing ecological assessment to assist in planning and managing instruction.
2. Differentiate between traditional assessment and ecological assessment procedures.
3. List and describe various ecological assessment techniques.
4. List and describe the relative strengths and weaknesses of specific ecological assessment techniques.
5. Describe explicit, hidden, parallel, community-based, functional, and absent curricula.
6. List and describe procedures for assessing curricula and instructional techniques used in learning environments.
7. List and describe ways to adapt tests and grading procedures.
8. List and describe various techniques for authentic assessment.

Assessing the Instructional Environment

Kratochwill and Sheridan (1990) conceptualized assessment of the instructional environment as a dynamic, ongoing process throughout instructional delivery. Assessment is actually a series of phases that reflect the collaborative process discussed earlier in Chapter 3. The four phases, which are not discrete and may overlap in practice, include problem definition, ecological analysis, plan development and implementation, and plan evaluation. Using this conceptualization as a foundation, it is important for educators to view assessment as part of instructional management rather than an isolated prerequisite.

Assessment is also critical in determining the extent to which instructional services will be delivered in natural settings. This chapter will examine traditional assessment procedures and describe an alternative approach in which various ecological methods can be used to assess how well the learning environment is promoting educational partnerships.

Traditional Approaches

Assessment has traditionally been conceptualized as a process, usually conducted by a school psychologist or a special education teacher, which occurs prior to and after implementing instructional programs (Kratochwill & Sheridan, 1990). Identifying factors that contribute to students' difficulties often involves expensive and time-consuming psycho-educational assessment procedures (Deshler & Schumaker, 1986). Student eligibility for special education services has traditionally been based on results from tests and variables that often have little or no relevance to planning and delivery of instructional services (Epps & Tindal, 1987; Reynolds, 1984; Thurlow & Ysseldyke, 1980). The traditional assessment process is largely confined to a pathological or person-centered approach in which the locus of the problem is within the student (Deno, Mirkin, & Shinn, 1978; Epps & Tindal, 1987). This traditional approach has focused on student variables rather than on environmental or instructional variables (MacMillan, Keogh, & Jones, 1986; Messick, 1984).

An Alternative Approach: Ecological Assessment

While it is true that students may have specific areas of strengths and weaknesses in academic and social skills, an exclusive focus on internal attributions does not take into account the wide range of other complex factors within the instructional environment (Zins et al., 1988). Ysseldyke and Christenson (1987) suggested that "learning and behavior do not occur in a vacuum" (p. 19) and that learning is an interactive process that occurs between the student and the learning environment. Learning is the product of eco-behavioral interaction with environmental factors such as instructional time and activities, teacher behaviors, and active student participation (Delquadri,

Greenwood, Whorton, Carta, & Hall, 1986). Consequently, it is important to utilize an ecological perspective to determine the impact that the instructional environment factors have on student performance (Graden, Casey, & Christenson, 1986). Direct and indirect assessment of the learning environment should produce valuable information that can be used to collaboratively design and implement instructional and behavioral plans that will meet the needs of students who are at risk. Therefore, service delivery to students at risk is based on needs identified during the assessment process rather than on labels or categories.

Ecological assessment is a collaborative effort that assesses student factors but is broader in scope than traditional evaluation procedures. In ecological assessment, students' overt physical behavior (talk-outs, aggression, withdrawal), cognitive/emotional factors (feelings, thoughts), and academic performance (correct responses on math worksheets) are assessed. In addition to student factors, an ecological approach includes examining variables such as teacher behaviors, instructional procedures and materials, peer interactions, and the physical environment of the instructional setting. Schalock (1986) characterized ecological assessment as a process that involves assessing an individual's capabilities in relation to environmental demands. Consequently, a "goodness of fit" between the individual and the environment can be determined. Identified barriers are circumvented through adaptation of environmental variables.

Ecological assessment is collaborative in nature because it requires ongoing communication between professionals. Most of the assessment techniques involve the participation and input of one or more individuals, and a multimethod framework is important. There are four common methods that can be used in any combination: interviews, direct observation, permanent products, and skill probes (Kratochwill & Sheridan, 1990; Lentz, 1988). Additionally, informal methods of examining the curriculum and instructional formats often utilize components from each of the various ecological assessment methods described here.

Interviews

An interview is the systematic exchange of verbal information that incorporates the steps of the problem-solving model and links assessment with intervention (Kratochwill & Sheridan, 1990). Partners systematically collaborate to identify and analyze environmental conditions and/or problems, formulate and implement intervention plans, and evaluate the impact of the intervention plan. Interviews are perhaps the most utilized technique of gathering information within various consultation models. Widely used in clinical and school settings (Gresham & Davis, 1988), they can be effective in other settings as well. Vocational and special education personnel often interview employers in the community to identify the demands of the job setting (McDonnell, Wilcox, & Hardman, 1991). Social workers, school counselors, and school psychologists may interview parents to assess the family and home environment as part of the ecological assessment process.

When conducting interviews, educators must carefully use effective interpersonal communication skills described in Chapter 4. Table 6–1 depicts the objectives of an interview between two educators aimed at identifying and defining the problem (Kratochwill & Bergan, 1990). In this example, an interview protocol was utilized to conduct the meeting in an efficient manner. Like the interview protocol, other tools can be used to verbally gather information from another individual.

Table 6–1 Objectives and Example Questions of Problem-Identification Interview

OPENING SALUTATION
GENERAL STATEMENT
    What seems to be the problem? What is it that you are concerned about?
BEHAVIOR SPECIFICATION
    What does (child's name) do when (s)he's (general problem)?
    Tell me what you mean by _____.
    Give me some examples of what you mean by _____.
    What are some more examples of _____'s _____ behavior?
PRIORITIZE BEHAVIOR
    We've discussed several behvaviors, such as _____. Which of these is most problematic?
SUMMARIZE TARGET BEHAVIOR IN PRECISE, OBSERVABLE TERMS
BEHAVIOR SETTING
    Where does (child's name) display (specific behavior)?
    Give me some examples of where (name) does this, or where (specific behavior) occurs.
    What are some more examples of where (specific behavior) occurs?
PRIORITIZE SETTING
    In which of these settings is (specific behavior) most problematic?
IDENTIFY ANTECEDENTS
    What typically happens before (specific behavior) occurs?
    What things do you notice before (specific behavior) that might be contributing to its occurrence?
IDENTIFY CONSEQUENTS
    What typically happens after (specific behavior)?
    What types of things do you notice after (specific behavior) occurs that might be maintaining its occurrence?
SEQUENTIAL CONDITIONS
    What else is typically happening in the classroom/playground/home when (specific behavior) occurs?
    Provide a sequence of events that outlines what is going on when (child's name) does this.
    What patterns do you notice?

Table 6–1   continued

SUMMARIZE/VALIDATE CONDITIONS SURROUNDING THE BEHAVIOR
BEHAVIOR STRENGTH
    How often does (specific behavior) occur?
    How long does it last?
    How severe is the behavior?
SUMMARIZE/VALIDATE THE SPECIFIC BEHAVIOR AND ITS STRENGTH
GOAL
    What would be an acceptable level of (specific behavior)?
    What would (child's name) have to do to improve their relationships?
CHILD'S STRENGTHS/ASSETS
    What are some of the things that (child's name) is good at?
    What are some of _____'s strengths?
EXISTING PROCEDURES
    What are some programs or procedures that are currently operating in the classroom?
    What procedures do you use now to deal with the problem when it occurs?
SUMMARIZE/VALIDATE BEHAVIOR, STRENGTH, GOAL, ETC.
PROVIDE A RATIONALE FOR DATA COLLECTION
    It would be very helpful to watch (child's name) for a week or so and monitor the
    occurrence of (specific behavior). This will help us key in on some important facts
    that we may have missed, and also help us document the progress that (child's name)
    makes.
DISCUSS DATA-COLLECTION PROCEDURES
    What would be a simple way for you to keep track of (specific behavior)?
SUMMARIZE/VALIDATE DATA-COLLECTION PROCEDURES
DATE TO BEGIN DATA COLLECTION
    When can you begin this?
NEXT APPOINTMENT
CLOSING SALUTATION

Self-reports, like interviews, can be used to gather information regarding overt behavior as well as physiological and cognitive/emotional factors that are verifiable or subjective and unverifiable.

Overt behavior/verifiable—"How many work sheet problems did you complete?"

Physiological/verifiable—"Do your palms sweat when you take tests?"

Cognitive/emotional/unverifiable—"Do you like your teacher?"

A *verbal elicitor* can assist an interviewer in gathering objective information that may reveal pertinent factors about a problem situation (for example, What steps do you follow when you are doing a long-division problem?").

Checklists and *rating scales* are efficient assessment techniques in terms of cost, effort, and time. They are typically used to assess factors that may affect students' social and academic performance. Both often provide comprehensive pictures of problems that can go undetected during interviews and observation (Kratochwill & Sheridan, 1990). While it is possible for a single individual to complete the checklist and rating scales alone, the interactive process of an interview may provide additional insights through clarification questions and paraphrasing.

A checklist and rating scale differ in terms of their response formats. Checklists often employ two types of responses. One is dichotomous: respondents mark either yes or no in response to a specific question. A second response format involves a list of potential responses in which none or any combination may be marked. For example, a checklist on classroom behavior may include items such as talk-outs, out-of-seat movement, aggressive behaviors, inattentiveness, talking to peers. Any or all of these may be endorsed by the respondent.

The Child Behavior Checklist (CBCL) (Achenbach, 1978; Achenbach & Edelbrock, 1979; Edelbrock & Achenbach, 1984a, 1984b) is a well-documented and commonly used device. There are two versions: one for teachers and one for parents. The teacher version consists of items related to a student's performance and behaviors in school settings. The parent version includes items on school performance, social relations, and specific behavior problems.

When integrating students with severe disabilities into mainstream settings, educators can use the Severely Handicapped Integration Checklist (SHIC) (Stainback & Stainback, 1983). The SHIC can be a useful tool to determine to what extent students with severe disabilities are included into various activities of the regular classroom environment. Similarly, another type of checklist, known as an *activities catalogue,* is a useful instructional decision-making tool for planning community-referenced curricula (McDonnell et al., 1991). An activities catalogue consists of three content domains: leisure, personal management, and work. Demands of a criterion environment (e.g., work, school, home) comprise the personal-management domain. Using the activities catalogue, parents, educators, vocational personnel, and employers collaboratively assess students' needs in developing an instructional program.

Rating scales are generally qualitative in nature. They typically require a respondent to rank opinions or types of behaviors within some range of responses. For example, a qualitative range of possible responses may consist of "superior ability" to "average" to "poor/no skill." Qualitative rating scales often employ a weighted value scale (such as 5 = excellent, 4 = good, 3 = average, 2 = marginal, 1 = poor) that can be used to derive a mean score. Quantitative measurements (such as "always," "often," "sometimes," "rarely," and "never") are often included on rating scales to determine frequency of behaviors.

It is important to understand within the context of ecological assessment that checklists and rating scales can be equally useful when examining teacher and student behaviors as well as when assessing the demands of the instructional environment. Individual teachers may wish to use these devices to take inventory of their own teaching behaviors and environmental activities of their classroom. Combining interviews with checklists and rating scales may assist classroom teachers and specialists in developing appropriate intervention plans to meet the unique needs of students at risk. West (1991) developed the Analysis of Classroom and Instructional Demands, referred to as the ACID test, to identify and describe the demands of a classroom. The inventory, which can be completed by a classroom teacher and/or outside observer, rates a student's ability to meet specific expectations of the classroom environment.

The Instructional Priority System (Welch & Link, 1991) is a qualitative rating scale that employs a simple mathematical formula to prioritize students' instructional needs based on the expectations and demands of the instructional environment. Together, teachers, specialists, and students complete the Needs Evaluation and Examination Data (NEED) form by multiplying highly ranked factors considered critical for success with student performance/ability ranking scores. The derived product identifies specific areas of need as the highest instructional priority. The process has been effective in elementary and secondary settings with a variety of student populations.

Direct Observations

Direct observation is used to record events in contrived and/or natural settings as they occur. Observational instruments are usually designed to assess a wide range of behaviors or situations using structured and objective coding systems. Observation can be used to gather data on both inter- and intraindividual analyses. Interindividual analyses is a comparison of one student's performance with others while intraindividual analyses may focus on differences of a student's behavior over time or in other settings (Lentz, 1988). Comparison students are often identified and used during observation procedures. In this way, an observer may use randomly selected students to see if the target student is behaving in a manner that is unique and truly merits special intervention. There is, of course, the possibility that a comparison student also demonstrates the same type of targeted behaviors as the student who is being observed. The use of scan-checking allows an observer to quickly peruse the behavior of the entire class approximately every minute to ascertain how many students are behaving according to teacher norms and expectations (Alessi, 1988).

Formal Observation Instruments.   Several direct observational systems are available to help evaluators obtain comprehensive behavioral and situational data in ecological assessment. For example, the Social Interaction Observation System (Voeltz, Kishi, & Brennan, 1981) can be used to systematically observe students with severe disabilities' behaviors and interactions that are critical for successful integration into mainstream learning environments. The State-Event Classroom Observation System (SECOS) was developed by Saudargas (1983) to record data simultaneously on multiple student and teacher behavior. This tool is particularly useful in quantifying characteristics of teacher-student interactions.

The Code for Instructional Structure and Student Academic Response (CISSAR) employs a procedure for monitoring the subject of instruction, tasks used, structure of lesson, teacher position in the classroom, and teacher behavior (Stanley & Greenwood, 1983). The CISSAR is a reliable and valid instrument that has been effective in assessing response behaviors of minority, disadvantaged students (Stanley & Greenwood, 1981). The Classroom Performance Record (CPR) (McNergney, Medley, & Caldwell; 1988) is a useful observation instrument to collect data on thirteen specific teaching competencies as well as student participation and behavior.

The Instructional Environment Scale (TIES) developed by Ysseldyke and Christenson (1987) represents a combination of many of the assessment procedures described here. The TIES can be used as a checklist during informal interviews between specialists and teachers or during observations to gather information on twelve components of instructional procedures. Teachers may use the instrument to describe the learning environment and identify student strengths and weaknesses that can be used in planning appropriate interventions.

In addition to commercially developed observation instruments, educators can utilize a variety of informal observation procedures. Alessi (1988) has provided an exhaustive review of the literature and presents a succinct description of various direct-observation techniques that are summarized here.

Interval Recording.   The technique of *interval recording* provides a measure of the number of intervals, or time blocks, that the behavior was observed to occur. Therefore, the units of measure are the observation intervals themselves and not merely the behaviors observed. Intervals are defined as time blocks that can range from five to thirty seconds each. For example, Martha was in her seat working independently for five of the fourteen intervals observed. In this case, an observer noted Martha's behavior every thirty seconds, which means the entire observation period was seven minutes long.

Time Sampling.   In *time sampling,* the number of times a specific behavior was observed is recorded. A relatively simple observation technique to monitor student behavior during instructional time is *momentary time sampling* (Wilson, 1987). This procedure can efficiently measure how much time spent in a learning environment is teacher-directed, student seatwork, or noninstructional. To monitor students on-task behavior during seatwork, an observer makes a plus or minus mark on a tally sheet every ten or fifteen seconds for each appropriate, on-task behavior or inappropriate, off-task behavior observed. The duration of the observation time should be fifteen minutes. The total number of pluses is divided by the sum of both pluses and minuses. This result is multiplied by 100 to calculate a percentage rate. Another consideration for time sampling is to have an area on the recording sheet divided into coded boxes representing specific types of behaviors that might be observed. For example, "OS" stands for out-of-seat" and "TO" represents "talk-outs." An observer can now embellish the data by making a slash mark in each box to indicate the type of behavior that was observed. The main difference between interval recording and time sample recording is that with time sampling, one observes a student for a specific moment at specified times to count behaviors, while interval recording requires observation of a student throughout an entire interval of time and the time blocks as used as units of measurements.

Event Recording.   The technique known as *event recording* is a tally of the number of occurrences of a behavior during an observation. For example, Peter correctly completed fifteen multiplication problems from a worksheet containing thirty problems within five minutes. As in momentary time sampling, a rate or frequency of events can be calculated by dividing the number of occurrences by the observation time.

Duration Recording.   In the technique of *duration recording,* the length of time a specific behavior occurred is noted. Using an earlier example, we could say that Martha remained in her seat engaged in individual seatwork (worksheet) for twelve minutes.

Alessi (1988) identified a number of procedural and interpretive cautions that must considered with any type of observational assessment procedure. The presence of an observer may inadvertently influence student or teacher behavior. On the other hand, an observer may be present during a part of the day that is not problematic for the student, so there simply may not be problems to observe. As alluded to before, a comparison student might also demonstrate similar problems, making comparisons difficult. Also, teachers might poorly define problem behaviors. Clear and specific operational definitions will help the observer to accurately and objectively collect and interpret data.

Permanent Products

Permanent products are homework assignments, worksheets, written papers, and any other tangible product of student performance. They are useful alternatives to tests. Formal and informal tests are usually artificial in the respect that students are responding to simulated tasks found in natural settings. Actual student products created in authentic settings are perhaps the most meaningful indicators of student performance as they reflect the demands and expectations of the criterion environment.

Error Analysis.   A useful method of assessing student performance is *error analysis* of student products. Examining and analyzing students' errors on actual samples of classroom work can provide extremely illuminating information. Identifying subtasks that are problematic for students can assist educators in planning appropriate instructional intervention and may, in fact, minimize the necessity for referring the student for specialized services. For example, analysis of math operation errors committed by students with learning disabilities revealed that over 50 percent of the mistakes in long division were due to subtask errors involving subtraction and multiplication (Miller & Milan, 1987). Instructional intervention could easily be provided to these students by the classroom teacher, paraprofessional or student tutor. This instruction would primarily require reviewing basic subtraction and multiplication operations using existing materials and curriculum.

Skill Probes.   The fourth method of assessing students performance is through the use of *skill probes*. Educators can determine students' strengths, weaknesses, and progress by testing their ability to complete specific tasks. A technique requiring individuals to respond to simulated situations found in natural environments is known as an *analogue measure*. The most commonly used method is psychoeducational testing, which is typically a pencil-and-paper response format. Analogue measures may also include audio and video techniques whereby students listen or watch a presentation and are asked to respond in any number of ways (verbally, in writing, by role playing). The use of audio/video analogues can be useful in assessing students' ability in following directions or social skills. Enactment analogues require the student to respond to events, tasks, or persons from natural environments that are simulated in clinical settings. Similarly, role-playing analogues serve as a direct assessment of a simulated task or situation, such as job interviews.

An effective and increasingly used skill-probe analogue assessment procedure is *curriculum-based assessment* (CBA) (Fuchs, Deno, & Mirkin, 1984; McLoughlin & Lewis, 1981; Tucker, 1985), defined as "the practice of obtaining direct and frequent measures of a student's performance on a series of sequentially arranged objectives derived from the curriculum used in the classroom" (Blankenship & Lilly, 1981, p. 81). The steps for this process include

1. listing the skills presented in the material selected,

2. examining the list to see if all major skills are included,

3. determining if the list has skills in logical sequence,

4. writing an objective for each skill,

5. preparing test items for each skill,

6. preparing test materials for student use,

7. planning how the CBA will be administered,

8. administering the CBA immediately prior to instruction,

9. interpreting results to determine which skills have and have not been mastered,

10. conducting instruction based on student need, and

11. readministering the CBA for follow-up evaluation.

Curriculum-based assessment is an efficient procedure that utilizes classroom materials to evaluate student progress.

CBA is an efficient and useful assessment procedure as it incorporates existing classroom materials rather than specialized instruments. Furthermore, the instructional plan of intervention derived from CBA results utilizes materials already used in the classroom. Special or remedial products with which classroom teachers may be unfamiliar or which may be inappropriate for the classroom setting are not required. Bagnato, Neisworth, and Capone (1986) suggested that CBA can also be utilized in early childhood special education as it reflects a "practical developmental orientation—a direct congruence between testing, teaching, and progress evaluation" (p. 97).

Another useful skill probe is *criterion-referenced assessment.* This is an informal procedure that assesses achievement within, rather than between, students. Student progress is measured in terms of individual progress. Consequently, criterion-referenced assessment is an appropriate assessment technique for individualized instruction. Pre-tests are generally used to determine the entry-level skills of a student or group of students on a given task or subject area. Achievement is calculated using ongoing measures or a post-test. The following example illustrates how criterion-referenced assessment often utilizes actual classroom materials, making it a type of curriculum-based assessment.

A sixth-grade teacher distributed a worksheet containing 100 single-digit multiplication problems (for example, 6 × 9, 4 × 3, 7 × 7) each day for one week. Students were instructed to complete as many problems as they could within fifteen minutes. The teacher examined the worksheets and divided the class into three clusters, each with its own goal. A group of more capable

Table 6–2   Awarding Grades According to Students' Performances on Criterion-Referenced Assessments

Baseline Information

Group A—20% of baseline performance (90) = 18 → 90 + 18 = 108 Goal
Group B—20% of baseline performance (70) = 14 → 70 + 14 = 84 Goal
Group C—20% of baseline performance (50) = 10 → 50 + 10 = 60 Goal

Post-Instructional Assessment Results (One Week Later)

Group A (Goal = 108)	*Group B (Goal = 84)*	*Group C (Goal = 60)*
Sue—100/108 = 93% (A−)	Todd—80/84 = 95% (A)	Bill—39/60 = 65% (D)
Bob—96/108 = 88% (B+)	Rick—75/84 = 89% (B+)	Mary—46/60 = 76% (C)
Tom—54/108 = 50% (F)	Dick—54/84 = 64% (D)	Harry—54/60 = 90% (A−)

students had completed an average of ninety problems over the course of the week. Another group was completing an average of seventy problems, while yet another group of students considered to be at risk were completing an average of fifty problems. The clustering did not require placing students into ability groups per se. Instead, students of varying ability worked together to reach their respective group's goal of improving their baseline rate of average problems correctly completed by 20 percent. While the actual number of problems for each group's goal differed, each cluster of students were aiming for the same percentage rate of improvement. As shown in Table 6–2, grades were awarded according to the degree students reached their particular group's goal. It is interesting to note that Tom, Dick, and Harry each completed the same number of multiplication problems. However, using a criterion-referenced approach of assessment, we can see that in terms of intra-individual performance, Harry actually demonstrated greater gains in his performance than either Tom or Dick.

Curricular and Instructional Analysis

Each member of the educational partnership must be aware that an array of curricula exists. Curricular decision making requires educators and parents to determine the extent to which students' needs, readiness, potential, learning rate, and learning style are congruent with the formally approved curriculum (Meier, 1992). When inconsistencies are identified, educators and parents must make curricular adjustments. The learning environment is characterized in part by the curriculum content and instructional procedures. Effective delivery of educational services is largely dependent upon the degree to which educators are aware of the interface and impact of both of these variables on the student. *Curriculum* is defined as the planned content of instruction that allows educational agencies to meet specific objectives. *Instruction* is defined as the specific behaviors and materials educators use to deliver the curriculum. More simply, curriculum may be thought of as **what** is taught while instruction can be characterized as **how** it is taught. Consequently, comprehensive ecological assessment must include analysis of both curriculum and instruction.

Hoover (1987) identified three types of curricula: explicit, hidden, and absent. *Explicit curriculum,* sometimes referred to as *formal curriculum,* is a body of knowledge identified by official agencies that students are expected to acquire (Ellis, Mackey, & Glenn, 1988). The explicit, or formal, curriculum consists of a scope and sequence of goals pertaining to reading, mathematics, social studies, science, and fine arts (Hoover, 1987). A subset of explicit curriculum is the content of instructional materials (that is, topics addressed in textbooks, activities, and homework).

Parallel curriculum consists of the same content found in explicit curriculum but its breadth and level of complexity has been adjusted to meet the needs and abilities of students at risk. The underlying premise is all students essentially learn the same information but not necessarily in the same way. Rather than "watering down" curriculum with fewer or easier lessons, the content of parallel curriculum is enriched with a variety of instructional activities and techniques that accommodate students with special needs (Meier, 1992). Additional time may be provided to complete assignments in small increments, using textbooks at a lower reading level, or using supplementary materials such as magazines (Gloeckler & Simpson, 1988). For example, a component of a fifth-grade social studies core may include a unit on the western migration in the United States during the mid 1800s. A teacher may choose to enrich a reading passage on the Oregon Trail from a district-approved textbook by showing a film and then allow students to draw a map or mural depicting the historical event. In this way, the fundamental integrity of the curriculum is maintained. A teacher can readily assess students' fundamental understanding of the content in a way other than a written test. A detailed description of alternative instructional and evaluative techniques that might be utilized in parallel curricula is provided in Chapter 7.

It is also important to recognize that parallel curricula may enable students to master the *absent curriculum,* which is content that educators do not teach and that students are not explicitly exposed to nor often required to use or develop. This can refer to specific subjects and topics or to less overt content, such as learning strategies, problem-solving techniques, self-management skills, and interpersonal skills. For example, Donald may be experiencing difficulty in a tenth-grade history class because he does not have efficient note-taking skills. Part of the parallel curriculum might include teaching note-taking skills using content from the history class. In Chapter 8, we will discuss how a specialist might teach note-taking skills in the general education setting by team teaching with the history teacher. Both Donald and many other students in the class will benefit from this curricular adaptation.

Functional curriculum is a subset of explicit curriculum traditionally designed for students with special needs. It emphasizes acquisition of competencies that are practical in meeting the demands of the real world (Payne, Polloway, Smith, & Payne, 1981). The basic skills found in functional curricula are essentially no different from academic skills learned by typical students. All students learn how to read and calculate basic operations in math. The difference, however, is that the practical skills enable students at risk to function independently in a variety of environments. As in the example of learning strategies in parallel curriculum, functional curriculum can often be infused within the general curriculum in mainstream classroom settings. While typical students are learning how to make change during an arithmetic lesson, students with special needs may be learning the functional skill of coin identification. Perhaps more importantly is the fact that typical and atypical students are having social as well as academic needs met. Both are learning how to interact with each other. As we will see later in Chapter 7, academically gifted or able students needing instructional enrichment may have their needs met by taking the role of a peer tutor to teach their peer how to identify coins.

Unlike functional curriculum that is delivered in a classroom setting, *community-based curriculum* provides functional skill instruction in authentic settings (McDonnell, Wilcox, & Hardman, 1991). Driver and vocational education are examples of the type of community-based curriculum that is often infused with general education at the secondary level for typical learners. Atypical learners with special needs, on the other hand, often require instruction in the community to facilitate mastery and generalization of very basic skills. For example, a student with developmental disabilities will learn how to use a mass transit system by actually getting on, paying for, riding, and getting off a bus. *Community* is broadly conceptualized to include a variety of settings, such as the workplace, supermarkets, and service centers like the post office.

Specialized curriculum involves distinctive content areas not commonly included in general education that often require special instructional techniques. Topical areas of specialized curricula might include mobility training for students with physical or visual disabilities or communication skills for students with hearing impairments. There may be times, however, when a classroom teacher is asked to help students generalize specific skills from the specialized curriculum to a mainstream setting. For example, a physical therapist may be working with Peter, who has cerebral palsy. Part of the treatment is developing upper extremity gross motor function such as full-motion arm movement. The therapist may ask the classroom teacher if Peter could erase the chalkboard to transfer skills learned during therapy to a normalized setting.

In contrast to explicit curriculum, the *hidden curriculum* consists of a set of expectations, values, attitudes, beliefs, and behaviors that are based on the interactions between students and teachers, students and students, and

Specialized cur-
riculum includes
specific content or
skills, such as the
use of communi-
cation devices that
are not usually
taught in main-
stream classroom
settings.

students and materials (Ellis, Mackey, & Glenn, 1988). Goodlad (1983) suggested that the hidden curriculum is what is actually taught in the classroom
based on teacher interpretation of what he or she has been charged to
implement from the explicit or formal curriculum.

Curriculum Assessment

There is often a mismatch of the curricula taught in the classrooms and what
students are expected or need to master (Komoski, 1990). What state or district agencies mandate is often inconsistent with what is actually taught in
textbooks or by teachers. Consequently, student mastery of the curriculum
may not be what is actually tested using commercially produced tests provided by publishers or standardized instruments. This variation of curricula
may, inadvertently, create environmental situations that promote student frustration and possibly failure.

An ecological approach of assessing curricular continuity involves a procedure known as *curriculum mapping* (English, 1980), in which educational
partnerships—consisting of administrators, curriculum specialists, classroom
teachers, support-service personnel, and often parents—collaboratively determine the degree of congruence among the different types of curricula. Additionally, curriculum mapping is useful for determining to what extent basic
skills and content areas taught in general classroom settings match what is

taught in special instructional support settings. This is especially critical given the apparently discrepant and fragmented instruction that often exists between general and special classroom settings. The lack of coordination between general and special education settings often results in the implementation of unrelated or fragmented activities and differing curricular materials developed from competing theories (Allington & McGill-Franzen, 1989). It is important to note, however, that descrepancies may exist within the framework of general education as well. For example, first-grade teachers may be using a specific curriculum that does not provide the necessary prerequisite skills for curriculum used in later grades. Finally, educators can collaboratively determine if the scope and sequence of a given curriculum is appropriate. For example, the teacher's guide to a commercially published curriculum for fourth-grade math may indicate that lessons on decimals are included in the scope and sequence of the materials. However, upon closer inspection, classroom teachers may realize that the materials include only two teacher-directed lessons accompanied by two, single-page worksheets containing ten problems. The team of teachers may determine that these materials, while approved by the state and district, provide inadequate depth and instruction in the use of decimals. Consequently, the curriculum will require additional activities and lessons.

Curricular Decision Making

It should be apparent that no one setting may be appropriate for meeting all of the curricular needs of students at-risk. Furthermore, it would be unreasonable to expect one individual to deliver the curricula. Consequently, curricular adaptation requires collaboration by educational partners who possess a diverse wealth of knowledge, skill, and experience. In considering the needs of students at risk, an educational partnership consisting of parents, classroom teachers, specialists, administrators, and sometimes the student must meet as a team to collectively design an array of appropriate curricula. The *academic domain* consists of content primarily related to reading, written and spoken language, and arithmetic. The *self-help domain* is characterized by skills that enable an individual to function independently. While we tend to think of students with moderate to severe disabilities needing this type of curriculum, it is important to recognize that all students must develop skills that will allow them to have meaningful and independent lives. Consequently, it may be appropriate to conceptualize the self-help domain as a continuum with very fundamental skills such as dressing and feeding one's self at one end and more complex skills such as maintaining a checking account at the other. Finally, the *social domain* includes areas related to leisure, recreation, and interpersonal skills. As illustrated in the discussion of functional curricula above, students can simultaneously acquire interpersonal social skills while developing skills associated with the functional use of coins.

Table 6–3   Curricular Decision-Making Matrix

	Mainstream Classroom	Special Education Classroom	Home	Community
Academic Goals				
Self-Help Goals				
Social Goals				

The general education classroom is one of an array of settings exist where the acquisition of skills in each of these domains may be appropriate. With this in mind, it is important that all members of the educational partnerships remember and understand the concept of least restrictive environment (LRE) discussed earlier. Classroom teachers must understand that they may be responsible for teaching skills within the social as well as academic domains. At times, the primary curricular objective may be social rather than academic in nature. We believe that the general classroom setting may be the most appropriate setting to address socialization needs, as illustrated in the example of peer tutoring. There will be times, however, when the team determines that a student's needs can best be met in a special setting. Therefore, it is necessary for the members of the team to specify which components of the curriculum can best be delivered in a special setting. The home and community, discussed in later chapters, are two other important settings for consideration. A curricular decision-making matrix such as the one shown in Table 6–3 may

---

Activity 6–1

Using a curricula decision making matrix, form small groups to make curricular goals for Chet, a 10th grade boy who is wheel-chair bound with cerebral palsy. He has normal intelligence but limited fine motor control which makes holding a pencil and tasks involving handwriting virtually impossible. He can maneuver his own wheelchair by hand but has difficulty with some self-care tasks such as buttoning his clothes. His speech is relatively understandable although his articulation is slow and sometime labored. Chet tends to drool slightly. He has aspirations of going on to college and majoring in Chemistry.

1. What academic goals would you include in each setting?

2. What social goals would you include in each setting?

3. What functional, life-skill would you include in each setting?

Figure 6–1
Mediation Assessment Questions

SUBJECT AREA:	WHO	WHAT	WHERE	WHEN	WHY	NOTES
MATERIALS	Who developed the materials? Who uses the materials?	What materials are typically used? What alternative materials are used or are available?	Where are materials stored? Where are materials used?	When are the materials used? - daily? - weekly? - special times?	Why are the materials used?	
TEACHING FORMAT	Who provides the primary instruction?	What is done during teacher-led instruct. - large group? - small group? - individual? - combination?		What time of day does instruction occur? How long?	Why is this format used?	
STUDENT GROUPING	Who determined student grouping?	- large group? - small group? - cooperative group? - ability grouping?	Where do students work/complete task? - individual desks - learning centers - work tables - homework	When do students work in these groups?	Why is/are these grouping formats used?	
EVALUATION	Who conducts evaluation?	What are the evaluation procedures and criteria used?	Where is evaluation data stored/recorded? Where does evaluation occur?	When is evaluation conducted?	Why is this evaluation procedure used?	
FEEDBACK	Who provides feedback? - teacher - aid - tutor - combination	What type of feedback? - # right / wrong - correction provided - one on one - other:	Where is feedback provided? - on student work - folders	When is feedback provided? - daily? - immediately? - self corrections? - following day? - weekly?	Why is feedback provided this way?	
HOMEWORK	Who is assigned homework? Who evaluates homework?	What kind of homework is assigned?		When can students complete homework? - home only? - free time? - study hall?	Why is homework assigned?	

YOUR CLASSROOM IS SPECIAL!
WHAT MAKES IT CLICK???

Knowing your expectations and classroom demands will help me help students make the grade!

How about setting up a 15-minute meeting so you could show me your classroom and tell me about...

 Textbooks and materials

 Instructional methods

 Assignments and exams

 Daily routine

 Grading

I know you're busy...
What's a good day
and time for you?

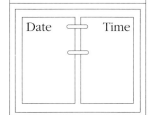

Date   Time

be used by a team of educators and parents to identify specific curricular goals for students with special needs. It is important to note that goals may not be incorporated in each setting listed on the matrix.

Instructional Mediation Assessment

Once curricular content has been identified, ecological assessment must include an examination of the instructional design. The evaluation of how the content is taught is known as *mediation assessment.* Instructional mediation is a process in which information is exchanged to promote learning. The teacher's role in this process is that of a mediator, serving as a bridge between curriculum and student, using tools and methods to facilitate the instructional design. The tools used during instructional mediation include materials, teaching format, student grouping, presentation formats, student behaviors, activities and tasks, duration of activities, and feedback/evaluation procedures. Mediation assessment is an examination of these instructional activities and variables. Results may reveal a mismatch of an instructional variable with student need. For example, mediation assessment might indicate that lecture as a predominant presentation format and cooperative learning for student grouping to complete assignments may be inappropriate for an extremely sociable student with attention deficits. The types of questions educators can ask themselves individually or collaboratively during mediation assessment are presented in Figure 6–1.

An informal inventory such as the one presented in this figure can be completed using a checklist format in a relatively efficient manner by an individual teacher, a team of teachers, or an observer. This information can be kept on file for future reference during collaborative instructional decision making. The information can be readily accessed and used in determining to what extent instructional formats can be adapted if necessary. Strategies for adapting and modifying instruction are examined in detail in Chapter 7.

There are some guidelines to consider when implementing ecological assessment procedures such as mediation assessment (Welch, 1994). Specialists should not expect an open invitation from teachers to "inspect" their classrooms. It is recommended that specialists make the initial request for conducting ecological assessment in person rather than by a memo or note. It is helpful, however, if a written description of the process is provided as an advance organizer to help the teacher prepare for the interview (see Figure 6–2).

Evaluation and Grading

Evaluation and grading students' progress is another aspect of assessment. There is no single effective way to evaluate and grade students. Evaluation procedures should reflect the instructional objective and task. This can be illustrated using the analogy of driver education. A student's ability to correctly indicate the speed in a school zone on a written test employing a multiple-choice response format is not necessarily indicative of his or her driving skill in actual driving situations. Accordingly, students are also expected to demonstrate their knowledge and skill in actual driving. Similarly, if an instructional objective for geography requires a student to correctly name the continents, assessment may simply require a student to verbally recite them. A written test is not necessary. On the other hand, the objective may require students to correctly label each continent on a map. A student with poor handwriting and spelling may meet this objective by pointing to each land mass and orally naming it. In any case, it is incumbent upon all educators to keep the instructional goal and objectives in mind while determining the most appropriate method of assessing student performance.

Test Adaptations

Tests have traditionally been used to evaluate students. There are a number of ways to adapt tests (Vasa, Steckelberg, & Asselin, 1981) to maximize their utility. We have attempted to categorize these adaptations into three general categories: response formats, duration, and frequency.

Response formats can be modified easily to meet the needs of students at risk. Teachers typically use formats such as true-or-false questions and multiple-choice responses for comprehension tests that assess recognition. Unlike recognition formats, short answers and essays require students to recall information. Students with memory deficits or problems in written expression, handwriting, and spelling often experience difficulty demonstrating their knowledge on tests using these types of response formats.

There are other strategies for adapting test-response formats. The use of readers and scribes is one effective method. Students speaking English as a second language or those with mild learning disabilities may need to hear test directions as well as the test items themselves. A reader may need to paraphrase or define specific terms that are unfamiliar to the student. Students who have significant delays associated with written responses may need to dictate their answers to a scribe who records their answers on the exam. Similarly, students may need to simply verbalize what they know using oral tests. This would not require a reader or a scribe, and it allows the teacher to directly assess students' mastery of information.

Tests should be designed in a manner that appropriately measures a student's understanding and ability. Obviously, teachers would not expect a student who does not read English fluently or has a visual impairment to read a written exam. A teacher would more than likely make an appropriate accommodation. However, teachers may unintentionally use test methodologies that tap into disabling conditions and inhibit a student's ability to demonstrate mastery of information. For example, a student with fine motor difficulty that results in labored handwriting cannot realistically be expected to provide a handwritten essay.

Many students have difficulty with the visual presentation of test items. Teachers can make the cosmetic appearance of tests "user friendly" through several simple steps. Minimize the amount of items to avoid a cluttered page, and be sure the items are legible. Wording of test items should also be at an appropriate readability level. Adjust or avoid terms that may be confusing to students. Underline key words or vocabulary words.

Duration of tests is an important factor to consider. Some students may need nothing more than additional time. Reducing the number of items or level of complexity on a test may provide this additional time. Another possible adaption is to simply divide the test into parts to be completed at different times or days.

Frequency of administering tests must also be considered by teachers. Daily or weekly measures provide information on student progress. Waiting until the end of a unit or chapter to assess a student's understanding of concepts may be too late. Instead of using tests as a post hoc activity for determining what a student has learned, tests should be implemented as instructional vehicles for clarifying and establishing academic procedures (Wiggins, 1989). Ideally, teachers should plan instructional activities that follow a teach-test-review-retest format so students have an opportunity to learn from their mistakes.

Before administering any test, the teacher should read the directions and discuss sample items to ensure that students understand what is expected of them. Directions should be kept simple. Reviewing a sample item and procedures for its completion provides a good model for students. It has been argued, however, that the traditional approach of assessing student performance reveals very little regarding the quality and substance of students' achievement (Archbald & Newmann, 1988).

Alternative Assessment Strategies: Authentic Assessment

Authentic assessment is an alternative to the traditional use of tests for assessing student progress. Archbald and Newmann (1988) suggested that authentic assessment is characterized by three features: (1) production of discourse, objects or products, and performances; (2) flexible use of time; and (3) collaboration with others. Meaningful learning activities provide students with the opportunity to develop products (letters, poems, blueprints, a tuned engine, budgets and balanced checkbooks, company reports, musical compositions) that reflect utilitarian as well as aesthetic values that cannot be demonstrated on worksheets or final exams. Most of the output activities just mentioned incorporate products as part of the assessment process. Disciplined inquiry resulting in the development of a product cannot be achieved within rigid time periods. The rationale for authentic assessment is that productive adults usually have flexible time parameters to complete a task. While the real world often involves deadlines, competent adults are allowed flexibility in schedules to meet their objective. Furthermore, adults are usually expected to work with others to accomplish tasks, whereas teachers often require students to work autonomously.

Portfolios.   Like the collective works of a painter or photographer, portfolios require that students compile a sampling of work that represent effort and achievement (Wolf, 1989). The process is accumulative in that progress can be observed by comparing early work to later work over the course of one or several years. The portfolio can be a file or notebook containing teacher summaries and descriptions of accomplishments, samples of writing, journal entries, audio or video recordings of actual performance, and testimonial reviews from experts outside the school attesting to the quality of work (Archbald & Newmann, 1988).

Spotlight: Walden III High School's Rite of Passage Experience

Archbald and Newman (1988) described an authentic assessment procedure known as the Rite of Passage Experience or ROPE. Each senior at Walden III High School in Racine, Wisconsin, is required to demonstrate mastery in fifteen areas of knowledge and competency by completing a portfolio, project, and presentation before a panel of faculty, students, and an adult from the community. Seniors enroll in a ROPE course in which the supervisor helps students select the review panel committee members. The supervisor monitors the completion of the portfolio and projects on a pass/fail basis. The portfolio consists of (1) an introspective and analytical written autobiography, (2) a reflective analysis of work experiences during the senior year, (3) a minimum of two letters of recommendation, (4) a reading record consisting of a bibliography and two book reports, (5) an essay describing the student's own ethical code, (6) an artistic product or written report on art accompanied by a written essay describing artistic criteria for judging a specific type of art, (7) an analytical written report on the influences of mass media, and (8) a written summary and evaluation of coursework and experiments conducted in science. The required project is a research paper exploring an event or theme in American history. Each component from the portfolio and the project must be presented orally and in writing to the review panel. Additionally, seniors are required to demonstrate knowledge and skill in the academic areas of mathematics, American government, geography, and English during oral presentations. Oral presentations are graded using a traditional letter-grade format. Each student committee determines its own criteria for grading. To earn a diploma, each senior must receive a passing grade in a minimum of twelve ROPE areas.

Activity 6–2

Form small groups to collectively address each of the following questions:

1. What products might you include in a portfolio for an elementary or secondary level classroom?

2. What criteria would you use to assess each of these products?

3. In what ways would you record or indicate the student's level of performance that would be meaningful to a college admissions officer or employer who relies of traditional forms of performance measures such as grades and grade-point averages?

4. What are some of the unique (and perhaps) unexpected challenges you encountered as you developed the guidelines for a student portfolio?

5. What are some advantages and disadvantages of the portfolio approach? What issues might parents raise?

IEP Objectives.   Each student eligible for special education support services will have an individualized education program (IEP) comprised of specific objectives. Each objective must describe student behavior, the condition, and the criteria. Awarding grades for achieving IEP objectives can reflect district grading policy (Kinnison, Hayes, & Accord, 1981). For example, an elementary classroom teacher may award a grade for reading fluency to students by calculating the rate of words per minute as they read aloud in class. Liz is a student with a mild learning disability that interferes with word-recognition skills. Consequently, she becomes easily frustrated when reading aloud, resulting in poor fluency. One of her IEP objectives states that Liz is expected to correctly recognize and pronounce (the *behavior*) tenth-grade level vocabulary words on a list taken from her class reader, with no prompts or cues from a teacher or peer, each Friday in her classroom (the *condition*) within sixty seconds and with 80 percent accuracy (the *criteria*). A school district's policy may indicate that an 80 percent response rate constitutes a "B" letter grade. Liz therefore earns a "B" grade.

Contracts.   For students with disabilities, the objectives on an IEP can be readily used as the basis for contracting agreements. Teachers can negotiate a contract with students and/or parents that specify the quality and quantity of work that must be completed in a given period of time to earn a specific grade. Such an approach is usually effective in providing students "due process" in the decision-making process. This often results in a vested interest on the part of the student to follow through on commitments. The process also clearly articulates teacher expectations, reducing the likelihood of ambiguity.

Curriculum-Based Assessment.   Earlier in this chapter, it was suggested that curriculum-based assessment (CBA) could be used for instructional decision making during ecological assessment. CBA can also be used to evaluate student progress. It consists of the direct observation and recording of student performance with materials used in a classroom (Deno, 1987). The assessment process is conducted within one to three minutes, anywhere from one to five times a week (Frisby, 1987). Marston (1989) provided a comprehensive review of studies citing the validity of CBA as a measure of student performance in reading, written expression, and arithmetic. The review concluded that CBA is an accurate and effective means of assessing student performance. The following is an overview of examples in which CBA can be easily incorporated to assess student progress (Fuchs, 1989; Marston, 1989):

1. Count the number of words correctly read from a basal reader or word list within one minute.

2. Count the number of letters correctly formed or words correctly spelled during a three-minute writing task.

3. Count the number of digits correctly written or accurate calculations during a two-minute interval.

4. Assess reading comprehension using the CLOZE method (or fill-in-the-blanks) by counting the number of correct student responses in restoring deleted words found in reading passages.

The cost of constructing CBA instruments is relatively low in terms of time and money, given the materials readily available to teachers. While daily measurement is ideal, it is not always logistically feasible. However, measurements conducted twice weekly provide a teacher at least eight data points, which allows for sufficient time for monitoring and modifying instruction (Fuchs, 1989). The use of instructional assistants, parent volunteers, or even students may enable a teacher to conduct frequent measures. Grades are determined based on the degree to which students demonstrate growth and mastery.

Work-Completion Checklists.   Teachers can check student progress in completing tasks or mastering a sequence of skills on a checklist (Shanks, 1986; Vasa, Steckelberg, & Asselin, 1981). Checklists can be created easily to reflect specific scope and sequence skills in a number of academic domains. For example, a teacher may stipulate that no student moves on to double-digit subtraction involving borrowing until he or she has mastered prerequisite skills such as single-digit subtraction. This approach lends itself well to criterion-referenced assessment by comparing students' pre-instructional level of abilities to post-instruction performance.

Grading

Assessment is the process of measuring student progress, while grades are the units of measure used to report or reflect the level of progress. There are four uses of school grades (Kiraly & Bedell, 1984). The first is as a measure of learning. Grades are used to show levels of accomplishment toward instructional objectives. A second use of grades is communication. Student achievement is communicated to the student, parent, teacher, administrator, and community through grades. Third, grades are used in making educational decisions. They assign students to instructional groups and settings as well as determine advancement or retention. A fourth use of grades is to motivate students. They determine opportunities for further education and financial aid as well as employment.

Grades, however, can also be abused (Kiraly & Bedell, 1984). They can contribute to students' poor self concept as well as produce adverse emotional feelings. They may encourage undesirable behavior such as intense competition, aggression, and dishonesty. Finally, grades may not accurately communicate student progress.

There are several alternative grading strategies available to teachers, each with their own advantages and disadvantages (Hendrix, 1987; Kinnison et al, 1981; Kiraly & Bedell, 1984; Meier, 1992; Shanks, 1986; Vasa, 1981; Vasa, Steckelberg, & Asselin, 1981). Some of these approaches are described here.

Multiple Grades.   Teachers typically give grades for mastery of specific information or content without acknowledging student effort. However, teachers may need to consider awarding more than one grade to reflect the various dimensions of learning and performance (Olson & Platt, 1992). A student with learning disabilities may understand the salient points of a life science class but experience significant frustration in expressing his or her understanding in writing due to handwriting or spelling difficulties. A teacher may choose to award two grades: one for content and one for spelling.

Another technique of awarding multiple grades is to indicate at what grade-level or ability-level a student is performing (Cohen, 1982; Olson & Platt, 1992). Using the previous example of Tom, Dick, and Harry in completing multiplication problems, Table 6–4 illustrates how a teacher might consider awarding multiple grades. Tom turned in an assignment that was far below his capability. Consequently, he earned a letter grade of "F" at an above-average level. Harry has severe learning disabilities yet earned a letter grade of "A" at a below-average level on the same assignment.

Welch and Link (1992) described a method of assessing students' written expression that examines different aspects of paragraph composition. As illustrated in Table 6–5, a point is awarded for the existence of the three basic parts of a paragraph: topic sentence, a minimum of three supporting sentences, and a concluding sentence. Another point is awarded for the correct grammatical form of each of these parts. Finally, a point is awarded if each part functions appropriately. For example, a teacher determines if the

Table 6–4   Example of Awarding Ability-Based Grades

Tom's Grade for Multiplication Unit

Ability	A	B	C	D	Fail
Above Average					X
Average					
Below Average					

Dick's Grade for Multiplication Unit

Ability	A	B	C	D	Fail
Above Average					
Average				X	
Below Average					

Harry's Grade for Multiplication Unit

Ability	A	B	C	D	Fail
Above Average					
Average					
Below Average	X				

topic sentence does, in fact, introduce the topic of the paragraph. The total number of points earned is divided by the total amount of points possible and divided by 100 to derive a percentage score, which in turn can be converted to a letter grade. In this way, the grade reflects various dimensions of paragraph composition, focusing on ideas rather than on spelling and handwriting alone. This type of componential breakdown provides a teacher with important information that can be used during instructional decision making.

Table 6–5   **Multidimensional Grading of Paragraph Composition**

TOPIC: How to have fun without spending money

There are many ways to have fun without spending money. I like to go for walks. And going to the movies. Talking to friends on the phone.

TOPIC SENTENCE
Existence	=	1
Form	=	1
Function	=	1

SUPPORTING SENTENCES (minimum of 3 required)
Existence	=	1 1 1
Form	=	1 0 0
Function	=	1 0 1

CONCLUDING SENTENCE
Existence	=	0
Form	=	0
Function	=	0

TOTAL POINTS EARNED/TOTAL POINTS POSSIBLE $\times$ 100 = % CORRECT

9/15 = 6 $\times$ 100 = 60% of the minimum criterion for acceptable paragraph composition

The scores demonstrate specific areas that require more attention. Perhaps more importantly, the awarding of points for the existence of sentences, regardless of form and function, acknowledges student effort, which may contribute greatly to positive student attitudes toward writing instruction.

Accumulative Point System. Using an accumulative point system, students earn a specific grade by accumulating a number of points per assignment or activity (Wood, 1992). Students have the option of completing a self-chosen number and type of assignments. Teachers essentially present a menu of instructional activities that reflect a range of points that can be earned for successfully completing the assignments within a given period of time. This approach allows teachers to implement a variety of input and output activities that may accommodate specific needs and strengths of students at risk. The accumulative approach of completing tasks also allows students to work at their own pace. Awarding points for completing a variety of assignments provides a nice balance for students who traditionally do poorly on exams. The use of a point system is also fairly easy for teachers, students, and parents to use in monitoring progress. Teachers also have the option of presenting a minimum criteria for earning credit, which is often reported as a passing or failing performance.

Pass/Fail.   In a pass/fail system, students "pass" a course by meeting a minimum set of standards and "fail" when work is deemed as unacceptable. A driver's test is a real-life example of pass/fail grading. Establishing a criteria for a pass/fail system typically involves determining a specific amount of work that must be completed as well as indicators that can be used to assess the level of quality. For example, a junior high teacher may require a minimum of three written reports. Quality indicators may include a minimum of three references following specific bibliography formats and the existence of a thesis statement, correct spelling, use of footnotes, and a conclusion. A passing grade is awarded if a student meets these minimum requirements.

Vasa (1981) identified advantages and disadvantages to the pass/fail system. Students often feel less pressure using this approach, which reduces their anxiety. Teacher expectations are generally clear, which means the student can work toward a very specific goal. Consequently, teachers can evaluate student work in terms of that individual's strengths and weaknesses without comparing the work with other students' products. The process, however, often does not lend itself to providing corrective feedback, nor does it differentiate among students' abilities. Furthermore, some students become less motivated and do less work, knowing they can "get by" with a passing grade.

Activity 6–3	Shelly is a well-liked ninth grader with learning disabilities that affect her spelling and handwriting. She has significant difficulty with phonetic spelling. Shelly receives instructional support on spelling and written reports in a resource-room setting for one 45-minute period per day. She is allowed to type most of her lengthy written assignments on a word processor. She is also allowed to use a spell-check to monitor and correct spelling errors. Shelly is earning average grades in most her classes but she is failing her life science class. Mr. Wolfe, the science teacher, subtracts points for spelling errors on exams that consist of diagrams in which students are expected to correctly spell terms in blanks. Even though Shelly can recall the vocabulary terms, their function, and location on the diagrams, she loses points due to spelling errors. Her handwriting is laborious, which often means she never completes the test diagrams. Consequently, she loses additional points for "incomplete responses" on her exam. Shelly's mother called Mr. Wolfe to ask if he would simply give her credit for her correct responses regardless of the spelling. Mr. Wolfe responded by saying, "Science requires precision. Spelling is part of precision. Excusing Shelly's spelling errors would

**Activity
6–3**
Continued

compromise the integrity of scientific precision. Furthermore, it wouldn't be fair to the rest of the students, and more importantly, it could have stigmatizing effects that would alienate her from the rest of her peers." Shelly's mother indicated to Mr. Wolfe that Shelly comes home from school crying and doesn't even bother studying for tests. Shelly tearfully justifies her behavior by saying, "Why bother? I'm just going to flunk it anyway".

1. As a group, discuss the degree to which Mr. Wolfe's position is legitimate.

2. As a group, discuss the impact of Mr. Wolfe's evaluation process on Shelly's academic growth and self-esteem.

3. Form small groups and collaboratively devise ways the testing procedure might be modified to accommodate Shelly's needs.

4. Form small groups and collaboratively devise an evaluation procedure and grading system that would meet Shelly's needs while addressing the concerns and position of Mr. Wolfe.

Interdisciplinary Ecological Assessment in Educational Partnerships: Conclusions

Most educators would agree that combining any or all of the techniques just described would provide a multidimensional perspective of ecological factors. By the same token, most would agree that such an approach would be, at best, challenging for any one professional to effectively carry out alone. Ecological assessment will, therefore, require a significant shift in traditional role conceptualization. A collaborative interdisciplinary approach of forming educational partnerships to conduct ecological assessment is not only preferred, it is a necessity. The responsibility for assessment has traditionally been delegated to school psychologists or special education teachers. The caseload of itinerant school psychologists and teaching responsibilities of both classroom teachers and specialists are such that comprehensive ecological assessment will be difficult unless a collaborative approach is utilized.

Ecological assessment is a radical departure from traditional assessment procedures. This reconceptualized approach of multidimensional and need-based assessment reflects the collaborative ethic that serves as the foundation of educational partnerships from which this text has evolved. An educational partnership of professionals is a realistic and preferred mechanism of effectively implementing ecological assessments of instructional environments. Utilizing the expertise of available personnel in the school building and/or district, different assessment procedures can be equitably delegated to guidance counselors, social workers, classroom teachers, special education teachers, instructional aides/paraprofessionals, school psychologists, teacher-assistance teams, and even administrators. It is important to consider the relative strengths and weaknesses of each of the techniques described here throughout ecological assessment.

Chapter Summary

Ecological assessment is an ongoing process in which educators examine a variety of components and variables within a learning environment. Traditional assessment procedures typically use a pathological perspective by focusing exclusively on students' deficits. In addition to considering student factors, an ecological approach uses a variety of techniques to identify variables related to physical environment, curriculum, instruction, and the subsystems within the entire learning environment that may impact student performance and service delivery.

Educators can choose from five methods when conducting ecological assessment. An interview is the systematic exchange of verbal information that can be used to plan appropriate instructional and/or behavioral interventions. A verbal elicitor can assist an interviewer when using self-reports, checklists, or rating scales to identify factors that may affect students' social and academic performances. Direct observation is another method that can be used to obtain academic and social data on student performance in a criterion environment. In addition to various commercially available observation instruments, educators can use informal procedures such as interval recording, time sampling, and event recording to examine student performance. A third method is to obtain permanent products such as homework assignments, written work, or completed worksheets. Using error analysis, educators may be able to identify specific subskills that are problematic or deficient and are contributing to poor performance. A fourth method involves skill probes using curriculum-based assessment and criterion-referenced tests. This procedure incorporates materials and tasks from authentic environments to assess students' strengths and weaknesses. Educators may examine curricula and instructional factors that may be contributing to student difficulty, thus requiring some type of adaptation or modification. Curriculum mapping allows educators to determine the appropriateness of materials. Once curricular factors have been identified, decisions regarding specific curricular goals and modifications can be made. Similarly, ecological assessment includes examining instructional format, materials, student grouping, classroom activities, and evaluation procedures to determine if there is a mismatch between student needs and the instructional process.

Evaluation of student progress has typically involved the use of tests. Adaptations of tests may meet the needs of students at risk. Adapting tests may involve changing response formats, as well as the duration and frequency of exams. An alternative to traditional tests is the implementation of authentic assessment procedures such as student portfolios, contracts, curriculum-based assessment, and work completion checklists to earn grades. Grading procedures may also be adapted by providing multiple grades, accumulative points, IEP objectives, and pass/fail criteria.

Educators have begun to acknowledge the important role of the home and family ecology in planning and providing student centered services. Collected information is used in planning and implementing appropriate educational interventions. Alternative methods for evaluating and grading can meet the individual needs of students at risk. Ecological assessment requires an educational partnership in which professionals from varying disciplines and parents collaborate in problem solving and planning need-based interventions.

Case Study 6–1

Ms. Watson, a fifth-grade teacher, was concerned about Bobby's behavior in class. She indicated to Mr. Quann, the special education teacher, that Bobby was "hyperactive" and wondered if he should be referred to special education. When Mr. Quann asked Ms. Watson to describe Bobby's behavior, she said that he was out of his seat, distracting other students to the point that they could not complete their work. This was especially frustrating for Ms. Watson as she was not able to devote full attention to the number of students experiencing difficulty with their own math worksheets because she had to deal with Bobby's behavior. The classroom teacher wasn't sure if there were any specific patterns to Bobby's disruptive behavior when asked by the special education teacher and therefore consented to allow Mr. Quann to make classroom observations.

The special education teacher asked Ms. Watson to describe what she considered to be appropriate classroom behavior. She indicated that students should work quietly at their desk and speak only after raising their hand and being called on. Using momentary time sampling, Mr. Quann made three fifteen-minute observations for three consecutive days. Each observation was made at a different time of the day and subject. Mr. Quann had team-taught with Ms. Watson and so the students were used to seeing him in the classroom. He unobtrusively placed himself in the rear of the classroom to chart Bobby's behavior every ten seconds.

The first observation was made during reading lessons in the morning. Using Ms. Watson's criteria for appropriate behavior, Mr. Quann observed that Bobby was behaving appropriately 93 percent of the time. The second observation was during language arts in which students completed spelling and handwriting lessons. The results of Mr. Quann's momentary time sampling revealed that Bobby was working appropriately at a rate of 85 percent. The final observation was conducted during independent seat-work of math problems on a ditto worksheet. Bobby's behavior was observed as being appropriate only 43 percent of the time. Anecdotal notes confirmed Ms. Watson's observations that Bobby was out of his seat and disturbing students around him.

Mr. Quann asked to see Bobby's math worksheets during his follow-up meeting with Ms. Watson. The worksheets were completed with 100 percent accuracy. Mr. Quann asked Ms. Watson to make a note of when Bobby completed his math worksheets during the practice activities on the following day. At the end of the next school day, Ms. Watson found Mr. Quann in the teachers' lounge and told him that Bobby had completed the math worksheets in less that ten minutes and was the first one to finish.

1. What do the results of the momentary time sampling appear to suggest?

2. What does the additional anecdotal information provided by Ms. Watson in the teachers' lounge appear to suggest with regard to Bobby's behavior during math seatwork activities?

3. What would you do differently in this ecological assessment procedure and why? Are there other methods that you would use? If so, what are they, and why would you consider them?

4. What does this scenario suggest about Ms. Watson's use of a label (hyperactive) in assessment and problem solving in planning interventions? What are the implications regarding eligibility and placement of this student into special education settings?

Case Study 6–2

Julie is a fifteen-year-old Hispanic girl recovering from an automobile accident in which she sustained serious head trauma. She is now ready to return to her own junior high school after eighteen months of treatment at a rehabilitation hospital. Julie is confined to a wheelchair and has limited use of what was her dominant hand, making handwriting difficult. She has lost her ability to speak complex words and sentences. She has a communication board to help her communicate when her single-word utterances are not adequate to express herself. Prior to the accident, Julie was a normally functioning, academically capable, and popular student actively involved in school activities, including cheerleading and the drama department.

1. Using a junior high setting you are familiar with as a reference, conduct an ecological assessment to determine an appropriate instructional delivery and integration plan for Julie.

2. Determine possible procedures for assessing the home and family environments that could be utilized in planning home/school programming.

3. Consider cultural variables when planning home ecology assessment.

Case Study 6–3

Two kindergarten teachers at George Washington Elementary school provide pre-reading skills to students using a highly structured phonetic curriculum. The students are taught basic sounds such as hard/soft consonants and long/short vowels. These students then enter first grade, where teachers are using a whole-language approach that synthesizes reading and written language. The students are encouraged to use "inventive spelling" when attempting to write words they do not know how to spell correctly. The rationale for this approach is to promote the process of written expression and minimize the frustration of spelling to enhance positive attitudes toward writing. Second-grade teachers are using a curriculum that utilizes a phonetic approach to spelling and often lament that the students do not seem to know how to spell correctly. Consequently, a significant number of second-grade students are being referred for special education screening due to persistent difficulty in spelling.

1. What procedure would you use to assess the curriculum used in this school?

2. What curricular and instructional variables seem to be involved?

3. Do you think the second-grade students are displaying a mild form of learning disability associated with phonetic deficits? Why or why not?

4. Using the collaborative process worksheet presented in Chapter 2, how would you address this situation?

Key Vocabulary Terms

ecological assessment
analogue measures
self reports
direct observation
time sampling

event recording
error analysis
curriculum
parallel curriculum
community-based curriculum

specialized curriculum
criterion-referenced
   assessment
curriculum mapping
mediation assessment

verbal elicitor	activity catalogue	authentic assessment
curriculum-based assessment	momentary time sampling	hidden curriculum
checklists/rating scales	instruction	absent curriculum
interval recording	explicit curriculum	permanent products
duration recording	functional curriculum	skill probes

Chapter 7

Chapter Overview

Instructional and Behavioral Management Strategies

Chapter Objectives

After reading this chapter, the reader should be able to
1. List and describe four dimensions of instructional adaptation.
2. Define traditional and alternative instructional materials.
3. Explain traditional and alternative internalization, maintenance, and externalization instructional activities.
4. Discuss principles and components of academic learning time.
5. Discuss various approaches of peer-mediated instructional student grouping.
6. Describe comprehensive scheduling strategies for accommodating curricular and instructional adaptations.
7. List and describe various behavioral management strategies.

Introduction

As we saw in the previous chapter, ecological factors within a learning environment can have an impact on the way students learn. Once aware of these variables, educators must plan, develop, and implement effective classroom-based strategies that will facilitate meeting curricular goals. This process recognizes and accommodates individual differences of students. Consequently, it may be necessary to adapt the curriculum to meet the needs of students at risk. If this is the case, there are two important concepts for educators to consider.

One, equality must not be confused with equal opportunity. Equal opportunity does not mean treating every student the same way. However, neither does it mean that educators must prepare individualized lessons for each and every student. This would certainly appear as an daunting challenge for any teacher. Instead, educators must strive to provide students with equal opportunities to learn. This may mean simply providing a variety of instructional activities rather than a single method. While the content and methods may differ dramatically for some students with very special needs, overall, each student can be given an equal chance to learn with only minor variations of instructional activities offered. Some teachers might argue that using a "special" method is unfair to the rest of the class. First, we want to point out that fairness does not mean "sameness." To be "fair" does not mean treating everyone the same way, any more than "equal opportunity" does. Second, we propose that most, if not all, students could equally benefit from an alternative instructional method that is being implemented for specific student with a special need. Third, classroom teachers must be aware that the role of specialists such as special educators is to assist the classroom teacher in making such adaptions.

The second important concept educators must consider is what is meant by the *least restrictive environment* (LRE) and what it entails at the classroom level. The federal statute defines LRE this way:

> That to the maximum extent appropriate, students with disabilities, including children in public or private institutions or other care facilities, are educated with children who are not disabled and that special classes, separate schooling or other removal of students with disabilities from the regular educational environment occurs only when the nature of severity of the disability is such that education in regular classes with the use of supplementary aid and services cannot be achieved satisfactorily.

By first identifying the needs of the student at risk, the team can design curricula and then determine the most appropriate setting for delivering the curricula. Once it has been determine *what* the student needs to learn, the educational partnership must turn its attention to *how* it will be delivered.

Consequently, it is incumbent upon educators to have a repertoire of strategies for adapting instruction that can be readily implemented in regular classroom settings. This chapter will present an overview of various strategies for adapting instruction. A scheduling strategy to facilitate a variety of instructional activities will also be presented. This chapter concludes with an overview of proactive behavioral management techniques. The strategies presented in this chapter can generally be employed in a classroom by a teacher with little or no assistance from other individuals.

Instructional Management Strategies

Instructional management is determined and influenced by curricular goals. There must be a meaningful outcome for each learning experience. Furthermore, as we learned in the previous chapter, information obtained during ecological assessment can be used to identify specific needs and goals. These goals drive decisions educators make regarding what instructional activities will be implemented. As discussed in Chapter 3, ecological assessment during the problem-solving process provides valuable information on contextual variables that may be contributing to problematic behaviors or situations. Consequently, classroom teachers must utilize a variety of effective instructional techniques that will meet the needs of all students. A summary of effective instructional methods in mainstream and Chapter I classrooms (Crawford, 1989; Larrivee, 1989; Reynolds, & Larkin, 1987) are presented in Table 7–1. This profile is similar to an emerging body of evidence of effective teaching for all students (Brophy & Good, 1986). The strategies presented in this chapter reflect these effective instructional approaches. It is beyond the scope of this text to provide detailed descriptions of each strategy. To supplement this overview, a list of recommended readings is presented at the end of the chapter.

Educators must be aware that the learning process involves a series of steps. Instructional objectives will vary at each step, and therefore certain types of learning exercises are more appropriate than others. Complicating this process is the fact that a classroom with a diverse range of student abilities will require coordination of a variety of activities at different levels of intensity designed to meet students' individual needs. The management and coordination of instruction are based on matching objectives with appropriate learning activities that are implemented through empirically sound teaching behaviors.

Bickel and Bickel (1986) identified and examined a number of characteristics associated with effective instruction. Among these are (1) teacher behaviors during pre-instructional, instructional, and post-instructional activities (Berliner, 1984; Rosenshine, 1983; Rosenshine & Stevens, 1986; Stevens & Rosenshine, 1981), (2) organization of academic learning time (Wilson &

Table 7–1   Characteristics of Effective Instruction

1. Frequently providing constructive feedback to students.
2. Providing supportive and encouraging responses to students.
3. Asking questions that students have a high probability of answering correctly.
4. Implementing learning tasks that students can complete with high rates of success.
5. Effectively using classroom time for academic learning time.
6. Minimizing teacher intervention for discipline.
7. Rarely criticizing students.
8. Minimizing student and/or instructional transition time.
9. Maintaining student on-task behavior through effective management of academic learning time.
10. Carefully and systematically orienting students to the learning task and objective.
11. Utilizing a variety of student-grouping strategies such as peer tutoring and cooperative learning to maximize academic learning time.
12. Focusing on mastery of critical basic skills.
13. Providing systematic, direct instruction.
14. Communicating high expectations of students' performance.

Wesson, 1986), and (3) grouping of students (Dawson, 1987; Johnson & Johnson, 1986; Slavin & Stevens, 1991). Each of these characteristics can be utilized within four dimensions of adapting instruction to meet the needs of students at risk.

Four Dimensions of Instructional Adaptation

Given the needs of the diverse population of students who are at risk, teachers need a repertoire of strategies for adapting instruction in four dimensions: (1) teaching, (2) materials, (3) activities, and (4) student grouping. In Chapter 6 we defined instruction as specific behaviors and materials educators use to deliver curriculum. We also described the role of the classroom teacher as mediator, serving as a bridge between curriculum and student, using tools and methods to facilitate the learning process. There are a variety of instructional activities that can be integrated with effective teaching behaviors that will accommodate student needs as well as facilitate achieving instructional objectives at various stages of learning. These activities and strategies for adapting instruction must (1) be easy to implement, (2) be used for any student experiencing difficulty, (3) be based on the curriculum in the mainstream setting, (4) be used to teach students to transfer or generalize to other settings and tasks, (5) be applicable to group instruction, and (6) include systematic instruction of skills necessary for mastery (Idol, Paolucci-Whitcomb, & Nevin, 1986). The strategies presented in this chapter meet this criteria and are appropriate for *all* students, not only students at risk.

Teaching. Instructional objectives should dictate how teachers behave instructionally. Teachers, however, often put the proverbial cart before the horse by conceptualizing learning as a result or by-product of teaching. It is much more accurate to think of teaching behaviors as a process for facilitating what and how we want students to learn. Certain levels of learning and specific curricular goals will influence how instruction is managed and delivered.

A variety of instructional techniques can be incorporated as effective teaching behaviors. However, there currently exists a great deal of confusion regarding what term should be used to describe effective teaching behaviors (Gersten, Woodward, & Darch, 1986; Rosenshine & Stevens, 1986). Among the various terms, *direct instruction* is probably the most commonly used and recognized as well as the most misunderstood. The term has traditionally conjured the image of highly structured and scripted teacher-directed instruction (Larrivee, 1989) such as DISTAR (Becker & Carnine, 1980). We, however, present a conceptualization of direct instruction as a system of classroom organization and management, meaningful teacher-student interactions, and effective design of curriculum materials (Gersten, Woodward, & Darch, 1986). This instructional system may include other features, such as sequential instruction, flexible skill-level grouping, practice and feedback, and review of previously learned material (Larrivee, 1989).

The fundamental components of effective teaching behaviors in direct instruction consist of three stages: (1) model/demonstration, (2) guided practice, and (3) feedback (Rosenshine & Stevens, 1984, 1986). A teacher provides a clear demonstration of the steps in an instructional task by modeling the procedure to students. This generally incorporates a "think aloud" procedure by the teacher so students can "hear" what the teacher is thinking while completing the task.

The teacher then prompts or coaches students through two or three practice exercises during *guided practice*. Coaching may take the form of prompting students to perform a specific skill or asking questions. A teacher may also pose a problem or hypothesis that students are expected to answer by coming to their own conclusions following practice application of newly acquired skills. The teacher monitors student performance and provides constructive feedback. Guided practice can be organized as group or individual activities so students can complete experiments, simulations, games, and puzzles.

These fundamental components have evolved over time into more refined and discrete steps which include (1) daily review, (2) presentation, (3) guided practice, (4) corrective feedback, (5) independent practice, and (6) enrichment/review (Rosenshine & Stevens, 1986). These steps reflect the multidimensional aspect of teaching. Teaching is not solely a teacher-directed dissemination of information. It includes providing students with opportunities to be actively engaged in activities to practice and apply newly acquired skills, either collaboratively with other students or individually. Teaching also involves a time for reflection and enrichment to provide students with the opportunity to construct their own learning experiences.

A *constructivist* approach of learning is "more concerned with understandings achieved through relevant experience than with accumulated facts received from others" (Black & Ammon, 1992, p. 324). Teachers, however, often assume that students have the prequisite "tools" to construct their own learning experiences. Students who do not demonstrate proficiency in the use of fundamental skills are often referred to special education. Consequently, we do not conceive an "in-structivist" approach of education as pouring information into students. Instead, we envision effective instruction as a process in which teachers empower students to engage in meaningful learning experiences by creating strategic environments.

Strategic environments are created when teachers recognize instruction as an opportunity to model and teach strategic behaviors to meet the demands of the classroom (Lenz & Deshler, 1990) that facilitate the learning process. *Strategic behaviors* are systematic and efficient steps students take to complete a task or solve a problem (Welch & Link, 1990) and can be thought of as part of the absent curriculum. Strategic behaviors can be creatively used to construct meaningful learning experiences.

Direct instruction lends itself well to creating strategic environments. However, many students lack strategic behaviors in areas such as taking notes, using textbooks to locate and understand information, or express ideas in writing. Consequently, some of the academic difficulties encountered in classrooms are a result of inefficient or nonexistent strategic behaviors rather than lack of understanding of content.

Strategic interventions can be used to teach strategic behaviors to students to help them meet the demands of the classroom (Welch & Link, 1991). Strategic interventions are empirically based *metacognitive learning strategies,* characterized as steps producing systematic self-instruction that allows students to activate prior knowledge about cognitive resources to be applied to resolve a specific problem (Ellis & Lenz, 1987). Metacognitive learning strategies can be utilized in mainstream settings to meet the needs of all learners (Deshler & Schumaker, 1986).

A host of strategic interventions are readily available for teachers. A summary of metacognitive learning strategies is presented in Table 7–2. Strategy details are discussed later in this chapter.

Roehler and Duffy (1984) stated, "Direct instruction emphasizes instructional time and student opportunity to learn. As such, it is little more than efficient management of material, activities, and pupils" (p. 265). Teachers can adapt instruction during presentation and demonstrations as well as guided practice and independent practice to meet the needs of students at risk by implementing specific types of activities and tasks that employ various materials.

Materials.   Allen, Clark, Gallagher, and Scofield (1982) suggested that a low-cost method of adapting materials involves changing the format of the materials without changing the instructional task. Textbooks have been traditionally used as the primary means of disseminating information to students. As alluded to in our previous discussion on curriculum, textbooks

Table 7–2   Metacognitive Learning Strategies

PLEASE Strategy for Writing Paragraphs (Welch & Link, 1991)

A process-oriented writing intervention that incorporates a high-interest video presentation to model and demonstrate each step of the pre-writing planning, writing, and post-composition editing of paragraphs. An instructional support manual provides guided practice activities for each step.

GET-IT Strategy for Reading Comprehension (Welch & Link, 1992)

A high-interest video presentation is used to model and demonstrate each step of the strategy that includes pre-reading identification of important ideas, the parts of a textbook, location of information in the text, taking notes, and self-test procedures. An instructional support manual provides guided-practice activities for each step.

STRATEGIC INTERVENTION MODEL—The following learning strategies were developed at the University of Kansas.

Word Identification Strategy
This strategy teaches students a problem-solving procedure for quickly attacking and decoding unknown words in reading materials, allowing them to move on quickly for the purpose at comprehending the passage.

Paraphrasing Strategy
Students read a passage, ask themselves the main idea, and paraphrase the information.

First-Letter Mnemonic Strategy
Students learn how to design memorization aids for recalling lists and important information. HOMES is an example of a first-letter mnemonic strategy to recall the Great Lakes (Huron, Ontario, Michigan, Erie, and Superior).

Sentence-Writing Strategy
A strategy for composing four basic types of sentences (simple, compound, complex, and compound-complex) is taught to students.

Error-Monitoring Strategy
Students learn to proofread their written work and correct any errors in capitalization, overall appearance, punctuation and spelling.

Test-Taking Strategy
This strategy helps students allocate time for responding to test items. Students also learn how to carefully read instructions. Another step of the strategy helps students employ a process of elimination in answering questions.

are often the focus of curriculum. At the elementary level, a specific curriculum often utilizes a commercially published textbook to teach specific skills in spelling, arithmetic, and language arts. Entire courses at the secondary level revolve around a state- or district-approved textbook. Due to the numerous demands and challenges in the classroom, teachers often rely heavily on textbooks as the only instructional resource. While teachers are usually presented with a textbook that has been formally approved by state or district agencies, they are not told how to use the textbook. Instead, they are expected to use their professional judgement in determining appropriate use of the textbook.

Unfortunately, textbooks do not always adequately meet the needs of students at risk. It should be fairly obvious that culturally different students who do not speak English as a primary language and students with visual impairments will undoubtedly encounter difficulty reading textbooks. Consequently, teachers usually make adaptations for these students. Many teachers, however, continue to implement textbooks as the exclusive instructional tool for students experiencing less apparent problems. Some learners with learning disabilities have difficulty in the mechanics of word recognition that ultimately interferes with comprehension of the reading passage. Teachers also assume that students know the purpose for reading as well as how to efficiently use textbooks to accomplish a specific objective. Teachers often have unreasonable expectations for student use of textbooks. We propose that textbooks continue to be utilized as a valuable instructional resource but not necessarily as the only or primary resource. Furthermore, we suggest that teachers clearly demonstrate how to use textbooks efficiently while teaching the content. This includes showing students how to use an index and explaining the purpose of bold print or summary questions to facilitate acquisition of important concepts and information.

Audio/visual equipment and materials serve as alternative and supplementary instructional resources to textbooks. Films, video presentations, tape recordings, filmstrips, and slide presentations can visually illustrate or depict complex concepts or abstract ideas that may otherwise be difficult for students to understand. A potential risk, however, is that teachers will perceive and use audio/visual instruction as a passive activity. As with textbooks, it is unreasonable to expect information to leap out at students. Students must be actively engaged throughout the instructional process. Teachers must follow a series of steps to promote effective use of audio/visual materials. These steps include: (1) ask pre-viewing questions to activate prior knowledge, (2) define key terms or concepts prior to viewing, (3) pose specific questions in which students must obtain answers from the viewing activity, (4) highlight specific segments within the presentation to watch for, and (5) discuss questions and segments as post-viewing activities (Newman, 1981).

Activities.   Materials are usually incorporated within a number of activities designed to facilitate learning. Students learn when teachers spend time and energy organizing activities in which students are actively engaged in the instructional task (Berliner, 1984; Bickel & Bickel, 1986; Denham & Lieberman, 1980; Fisher et al., 1980). Carroll (1985) suggested that learning is a result of time spent on learning and the time needed to learn. This seemingly obvious tenet is the foundation of *academic learning time* (ALT) (Fisher et al., 1978). ALT originated in the 1950s in general education classroom settings and consists of three directly observable classroom components: (1) duration of instructional time, (2) student engagement in relevant instructional activities, and (3) student success rate (Wilson & Wesson, 1986). Significant academic gains of students in general education and special education classroom settings are related to these components (Rosenshine & Berliner, 1978; Stallings, 1980). Implementation strategies for each of the three components of ALT described by Wilson and Wesson (1986) have been summarized in Table 7–3.

Instructional activities designed to maximize student engagement throughout inquiry can be conceptualized as falling into three phases: internalization, maintenance, and externalization. An example from driver's education will be

Table 7–3 Implementation Strategies for Academic Learning Time

Increasing Actual Instructional Time

1. Schedule or allocate more instructional time.
2. Reduce or minimize transition time between activities.
3. Minimize free time or provide quasi-instructional activities (reading a magazine, listening to a recorded story) as leisure-time options.
4. Employ efficient error-correction procedures.
5. Organize nonacademic activities (passing out papers, taking attendance) to be efficient.

Maximizing Teacher-Directed Instructional Time

1. Use effective teaching behaviors of modeling and demonstrating
2. Balance teacher-directed instruction with individual seatwork.
3. Minimize irrelevant seatwork activities.

Increasing Students On-Task Rates During Teacher-Directed Instruction

1. Increase teacher questioning.
2. Implement activities that engage students and require active participation.
3. Use signals to gain student attention.
4. Reinforce or reward students who are actively engaged, and present them as a model for other students.

Maximizing Student Performance During Practice Activities

1. Provide clear, concise, and unambiguous instructions.
2. Employ self-correcting materials.
3. Use learning centers or study cubicles.
4. Incorporate novel and motivating activities.
5. Instruct students what they should do when they complete a practice activity.

used to illustrate each phase. *Internalization* is the dissemination and delivery of information or skills to the student. Internalization is generally divided into two parts: introduction and cognition. During *introduction,* students are presented with new information, such as a definition or description of a skill. For example, a drivers' education teacher may introduce the skill of parallel parking to students by describing when and how it is used with a diagram. It is during this phase that teachers present content to students through model and demonstration. *Cognition* involves activities that require students to actively seek information rather than merely receive information merely presented to them. Student inquiry as an instructional input activity (Jarolimek & Foster, 1981) represents an approach to learning whereby students literally construct their knowledge base through a variety of cognitive activities. The inquiry process begins by defining a problem, followed by asking a question, either by the teacher or the students themselves, as a hypothesis. Students are then responsible for collecting data and information. The data-collection process can be conducted by small teams of students or individually. For example, students in a drivers' education course may be assigned to watch a family member or friend with a current driver's license as he or she parallel parks a car. In this way, the teacher merely facilitates the acquisition of information. Once the data are collected, students evaluate the information before making a conclusion. Again, the evaluation and conclusion process can be accomplished by student groups or individual students. Although students may have a cognitive understanding of what parallel parking is and when it is used, they do not necessarily know how to do it.

Maintenance is the instructional process that allows students to develop and maintain skills and knowledge base acquired during the internalization phase. The maintenance phase of instruction involves mastery and fluency. During *mastery,* students are expected to comprehend a concept or use a skills with a marginal level of acceptability. For example, a novice driver may actually be able to parallel park a vehicle, but only after several labored attempts. In this case, the driver clearly understands the task of maneuvering the vehicle but is not necessarily proficient at it. Consequently, the second aspect of maintaining the newly acquired skill is developing *fluency.* Through repeated drill and practice, the student eventually becomes confident and skilled enough to complete a task at a higher level of efficiency.

Externalization is student demonstration of understanding of the information or skills through group and individual activities. Externalization is divided into the two parts of recall and application. *Recall* typically involves assignments or tests whereby students are expected to remember and indicate what they have learned. Depending on the objective, written assignments or tests may not be necessary. For example, a state or district CORE language arts curriculum may require a student to demonstrate an understanding of the eight parts of speech. The mandate does not, however, indicate exactly how the student must demonstrate understanding of this specific content area. Therefore, an oral or written test may be considered. The Department of Motor Vehicles usually requires drivers to demonstrate their understanding of written laws through the use of a written test. However, these state agencies accomodate non-readers by providing a reader and/or a scribe when necessary.

Application of skills requires students to use their newly acquired knowledge in a situation or task. Application may involve developing a product that can be used in *authentic assessment,* as described in a previous chapter. In the case of driver education, novice drivers are required to apply their skill while demonstrating their ability to parallel park a vehicle during a driving test. It is only after an individual is accomplished at all three levels of instruction that more complex or sophisticated techniques or applications can be incorporated.

There is no single best format for internalization, maintenance, and externalization, given the different levels of student ability and the various types of objectives at each stage of learning. The following section will briefly describe a variety strategies for modifying traditional internalization, maintenance, and externalization methods that can be used in teacher-directed, group, or individual learning formats that promote student inquiry.

Internalization: Lectures

Lecturing is a culturally entrenched and logistically efficient method of passing on information and values through talking. Teachers talk to a captive audience for most of the school day. Unfortunately, many students experience difficulty processing information that is presented aurally. This may be due to obvious conditions such as a hearing impairment or speaking a different language. Less obvious factors may be associated with attention deficits or learning disabilities. In any case, these students are less efficient at learning with their ears. Teachers can accommodate these students by implementing a variety of visually oriented assistive devices.

Graphic organizers can be used to graphically represent the relationship between topics (Lovitt, 1989; Moyer et al., 1984). As illustrated in Figure 7–1, a series of boxes and corresponding arrows can be used to illustrate the

Figure 7–1
Graphic
Organizer

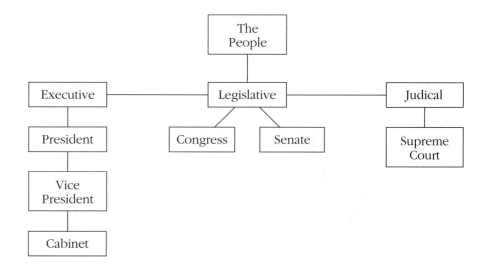

Figure 7–2
Acquisition
Outline

Name _____

SUBJECT: General Science

TOPIC: Fossils

OBJECTIVES: 1.   Define "fossil."

2.   Describe six ways a fossil can be formed.

3.   List four ways important information about the past
      can be obtained by studying fossils.

FOSSIL = Any naturally preserved part or trace of a plant or animal that
lived in the past.

Six Ways Fossils Are Formed

1.   Freezing

2.

3.

4.

5.

6.

Types of Information We Can Obtain from Fossils

1.   Fossil plants tell us about conditions in ancient times.

2.

3.

4.

sequence of steps in a given process, compare and contrast concepts, and present the cause and effect of a given event.

Acquisition outlines (Wood, 1991) help students readily identify the salient features of a lecture. This approach presents the subject, topic, and objective followed by a logical sequence of information. Using this map, students can take notes as they listen to the teacher presentation. This keeps both the student and teacher on track as both can monitor the progression of the presentation. Key points or terms are listed as "bullet statements" in one of three formats: complete, partial, or blank. A teacher can literally provide all of the information in a complete format that eliminates note-taking altogether. Students, therefore, have the option of jotting down personal notes rather than exerting effort and energy in writing down important information. As illustrated in Figure 7–2, teachers may elect, however, to provide partial acquisition outlines in which key terms or definitions are provided. This minimizes the possibility of students misspelling vocabulary words or omitting important parts of definitions. This procedure also requires students to attend to what the teacher is presenting. A blank format may simply list numbers or letters representing the number of topics to be covered in the presentation. Students then fill in the spaces with information presented by the teacher.

One variation on the acquisition outline is the K.I.M. sheet (Welch & Link, 1991) which is a modification of a note-taking format developed at Cornell University (cited in Alley & Deshler, 1979). The K.I.M. sheet is divided into three columns: one for the *K*EY WORDS, another for the *I*NFORMA-TION, and a third for *M*EMOS. As illustrated in Figure 7–3, a teacher may choose to list the key vocabulary terms in the KEY WORD column. As the teacher discusses each term, students record important information in the INFORMATION column while jotting down the page number the information may be located in the text or mnemonic devices in the MEMO column. Teachers might consider creating a large version of the K.I.M. sheet on the chalkboard using masking tape. In this way, the teacher can write the term or concept to be discussed in the KEY WORD followed by information in the INFORMATION column on the chalkboard. This form of prompting may eventually be phased out, once students demonstrate an understanding and mastery of the technique.

Students can employ a self-test procedure to review their notes by covering the INFORMATION and MEMO columns on their K.I.M. sheet with a blank piece of paper. Upon looking at the term or concept listed in the KEY WORD column, students attempt to recall and write as much information as they can on the blank sheet of paper. If they experience difficulty, they can slide the blank sheet of paper to the side, exposing the MEMO column to refer to mnemonic devices or a page reference. Once they have written what they recall, they can compare what they have written with what is on the K.I.M. sheet. If they continue to experience difficulty or confusion, they make a note in the MEMO column to get assistance.

Figure 7-3
K.I.M. sheet

Lincoln's Assassination	Ford's Theater – Washington, D.C.	Chap. 11 p. 312–313
	April 1865 – Civil War Over	President's "BOOTH"
	John Wilkes Booth actor southerner Revenge for South's loss	
Kennedy's Assassination	Dallas, Texas November 22, 1963 Shot in car	Chap. 11 p. 313
	Lee Harvey Oswald Conspiracy?	Compare + Contrast each for Friday Test.

Internalization: Textbooks

Simple and low-cost strategies for making textbooks user-friendly generally involve a series of teacher behaviors. These behaviors can be characterized as *advance organizers*. When assigning a reading passage, a teacher should state the objective of the reading task. Clearly articulate what students are expected to understand. An overview of key vocabulary terms is another important activity. Direct students' attention to words presented in italics or bold print as well as vocabulary lists at the end of a chapter. Outlining the major sections of a reading passage provides students with a sneak preview of the organization and chronology of the reading passage. Teachers can easily present a series of questions prior to reading to help students identify and target important information as they read. Prior to reading assignments, teachers should consider utilizing students' realm of experiences and prior knowledge that will enable them to approach the reading from a familiar context. For example, a teacher might discuss issues related to privacy prior to reading a chapter on the Bill of Rights for social studies. Students might discuss the importance of privacy associated with writing diaries, phone calls, and their bedrooms. In this way, teachers create a relationship between the students' lives and values with the reading passage to promote active engagement during reading. A generic worksheet can be developed consisting of each of the steps that can be checked off or filled in by students as they read. Providing spaces for taking notes on important concepts or terms is another option. To create continuity between note-taking during lectures, teachers may wish to allow students to use the K.I.M. sheet to take notes as they read.

Taped textbooks are an alternative to an exclusively visual presentation of text (Jones, 1975; Mayle & Riegel, 1979). Teachers are usually best suited as readers as they are familiar with the material and know what they want students to comprehend. Realistically speaking, though, most teachers lack the time, and therefore other adults or even students may serve as readers. A set of guidelines for recording textbooks adapted from Mayle & Riegel (1979) is presented in Table 7–4.

Other print materials such as *newspapers and magazines* can be inexpensive supplements or alternatives to textbooks. Textbooks can quickly become outdated, while newspapers and magazines provide almost instantaneously current information. Another advantage is the relatively low cost of newspaper and magazine subscriptions.

Internalization and Maintenance: Media and Computers

Teachers should not view audio/visual input as a passive activity in which information washes over students. The same type of advance-organizer activities used prior to reading assignments should be utilized before using any audio/visual media. The user-friendly nature and availability of video camcorders and videocassette recorders (VCRs) are especially appealing to teachers. Teachers can videotape their presentations or demonstrations that can be played as many times as necessary. A teacher can quite literally be in two places at one time. A small group of students can view the teacher on a video demonstration of the parts of a paragraph while the teacher works with another group of students on a different topic or task. Teachers can also use videotaped presentations to model note-taking skills. As the class watches a video lecture, the teacher can stop and start the video presentation using the pause button while showing on the chalkboard what student notes should look like. Instructional video programs can embellish teacher presentations and textbooks.

Audiocassette recordings can be used in many of the same ways a video recording can be used. Correct pronunciation and definition of vocabulary words or spelling tests and correction procedures can easily be recorded on a clearly labeled cassette. Instructions for activities can be tape recorded. Study questions from reading assignments can be recorded, followed by adequate

Table 7–4   Guidelines For Recording Textbooks

Recruiting and Training Readers

1. Post announcements in the school or school newsletter and senior citizen centers.
2. Ask teachers to nominate student candidates who are proficient readers and need opportunities for enrichment.
3. Ask for PTA volunteers.
4. Create an application form to keep track of applicants.
5. Hold an audition.
6. Model and demonstrate appropriate voice levels, pacing, and specific techniques.

Recording Techniques

1. Find a quiet place with rugs, upholstered furniture, and draperies to absorb ambient noise/echo.
2. Sit in a comfortable seat that does not face hard surfaces such as walls, windows, or doors to reduce echo or hollow-sounding tapes.
3. Place the microphone or tape recorder with microphone on a table slightly below the mouth approximately six to ten inches away.
4. Speak across the top of the microphone.

Reading Techniques

1. Announce the title, author of the book as well as the title of chapters/subsections.
2. Emphasize italics with your voice.
3. *Briefly* describe photographs, charts, tables, and graphs.
4. Read study questions at the end of the chapter *prior* to reading; this way they serve as an advance organizer for the listener.
5. Take a break every fifteen minutes to reduce voice fatigue.
6. Read in a normal voice and pace that is not too fast nor too slow.
7. Put a single chapter on a tape to create a volume of tapes and mark/label each tape.

space to allow students to record the oral response. As described before, entire textbooks can also be recorded.

Computers can be utilized for simulations, tutorials, demonstrations, and drill/practice. A handbook published by the Council for Exceptional Children entitled *Beyond Drill and Practice: Expanding the Computer Mainstream* (Russell, Corwin, Mokors, & Kapisovsky, 1989) provides teachers with various procedures that promote learner-centered, interactive activities on computers. The authors of the handbook characterize learner-centered software as: (1) allowing student choices in selecting goals and strategies; (2) providing constructive feedback; (3) promoting prediction and successive approximation; and (4) encouraging learning within a meaningful framework. Computers can be used for enrichment and remediation (Sheingold & Hadley, 1990). A number of computer software programs for instruction in arithmetic, reading, and language arts exist and can be utilized in general education classrooms. Many programs have been designed with specific student populations and disabling conditions in mind.

Internalization and Maintenance: Activities

Alternatives to traditionally passive instruction such as lectures and reading include physical activities and experiences. Science teachers know that reading about chemical reactions will be enhanced through lab experiments that allow students to experience what was presented in their text. Arithmetic has traditionally involved completing worksheets of operations that often seem unrelated to real life. Teachers may, for example, consider allowing students apply calculation of averages and percentages by recording daily temperatures that can be graphed and perhaps even reported to a local TV meteorologist. Role playing and simulations allow students the opportunity to experience some of the concepts or techniques presented in class or textbooks. Despite the cost and logistical considerations, field trips remain one of the most valuable learning activities. These, however, do not necessarily require exotic voyages to distant lands. A trip to the playground can serve as an appropriate biology laboratory.

Externalization: Written Products

Teachers have traditionally used written reports to assess student mastery and understanding. This practice, however, is based on the assumption that students are knowledgeable about that fundamental building block of written expression, the paragraph. Students are often unable to meet teacher expectations because they lack a strategic approach to the process of writing. Process-oriented writing (Bos, 1988; Englert & Rahpael, 1988; Graves, 1983) promotes steps in pre-writing, writing, and post-writing activities. The PLEASE strategy (Welch & Link, 1990) is a useful tool for teachers and students. The steps of the strategy are presented in Table 7–5. Teachers can use the PLEASE strategy as a management tool by placing the letter of each step on a posted calendar in the classroom to remind students when a specific step must be completed and turned in for review and feedback.

Written products do not need to be limited to formal reports or essays. One alternative approach is to allow students to create a newspaper front page complete with headlines to report on a specific topic. For example, a small team of students may "publish" a front page announcing the discovery of gold in California that includes salient information such as WHO, WHAT, WHERE, WHEN, and WHY for a U.S. history assignment.

Student journals can also be used to personalize learning activities. Teachers can assess student understanding of concepts presented in class by asking students to respond to them from a personal perspective. For example, a lesson on a topic as mundane as adjectives could include students' journal entries of a list of adjectives describing themselves. History lessons

Table 7–5   **The PLEASE Strategy for Writing Paragraphs**

P = PICK a topic.
L = LIST your ideas about the topic.
E = EVALUATE your list of ideas.
A = ACTIVATE your paragraph with a topic sentence.
S = SUPPLY supporting sentences.
E = END with a concluding sentence, and EVALUATE.

could require students to imagine what it would be like to be on the Mayflower and enter their thoughts in their personal diary. Teachers could specify that these diary entries must include some kind of factual information taken from class discussions or reading assignments. Dialogue journals written on microcomputers have been an effective instructional strategy for bilingual exceptional children (Goldman & Rueda, 1988). Personalization of writing tasks facilitate relationships between the teacher and students "estranged from the cultural context of the classroom" (p. 547), which in turn motivates students to continue writing.

The emergence of word processors has made a great impact on written expression. Macarthur (1988) described a number of features and impact of word processing on written expression. Students experiencing difficulty with handwriting, spelling, editing, and organization can use word processors to circumvent some of their frustration and failure. The visibility of the monitor and keyboard promotes the social context of a writing community in which students and teachers can interact during composition or editing.

Externalization: Oral Presentations

Oral presentation of information provides a viable alternative to students who, for one reason or another, cannot adequately express themselves in writing. Oral reports do not mean reading a paper aloud in front of the class. An oral presentation is the dissemination of information through speaking. Teachers should consider the various forms of oral presentations that bombard us every day as possible methods for instructional output activities. Producing radio programs using an audiocassette tape recorder in which a reporter presents information and conduct interviews is one possibility. Debates are another way of allowing students the opportunity of gathering and presenting information. An oral presentation of information can be as simple as asking a student to come up to the teacher or record into a tape recorder what they have learned.

Externalization: Products and Demonstrations

Fine arts, industrial arts, and home economics teachers routinely require students to demonstrate understanding and mastery of skills by producing some kind of product. While it may be unreasonable to expect students in a science class to create a nuclear reactor, it is feasible for them to create a model or poster depicting it. Students might also produce and perform plays depicting historical or literary events. The computer is a valuable tool for creating multimedia presentations (Sheingold & Hadley, 1990). Students are familiar and at ease with video technology. Allowing them to produce a video documentary or news broadcast is a viable and entertaining output method. Since the advent of instructional video, many filmstrips now gather dust in the school media center. Provide the filmstrip without the commercially published audio accompaniment and written transcript. Assign students to create their own written or recorded narrative to accompany each of the filmstrip frames. Artwork in the form of posters, charts, graphs, or murals is another viable means of demonstrating understanding.

Student Grouping.   Students are often grouped according to ability. This practice allows teachers to provide review and remediation for low achievers while increasing the pace and level of instruction for high achievers (Archambault, 1989). Dawson (1987) concluded from a comprehensive review of research literature that assigning students to groups or classrooms based on ability has little educational benefit. Furthermore, ability grouping often has a stigmatizing effect on students (Archambault, 1989). Despite these findings, and the fact that we live in a heterogenous society, ability grouping persists, largely due to a perceived lack of alternatives.

From a logistical standpoint, there are times when large-group instruction is more effective and appropriate than small learning groups. Large-group instruction is well suited for nonacademic activities such as providing an overview of the day's activities. It is also appropriate for introducing new concepts that do not require prior knowledge (Brookover, Beamer, Efthim, Hathaway, Lezotte, Miller, Passalacqua, & Tornatzky, 1982). Small-group instruction lends itself well to practice activities. It has logistical challenges for the teacher. The teacher cannot be in all places at one time and consequently must consider implementing a variety of peer-mediated instructional interventions to effectively manage small heterogenous student groups.

Peer-Mediated Intervention

The needs of students at risk can often be met through the use of *peer-mediated intervention,* a supervised technique in which students take an active instructional role with peers in a variety of learning environments. Peer-mediated instruction is a true embodiment of the spirit and premise of student-centered education. From a pragmatic perspective, educators are beginning to recognize that "students are a valuable, under-used educational resource" (Lynn, 1986, p. 62). Peer-mediated interventions are appropriate for group-practice learning activities.

Research suggests that peer-mediated procedures appear to be at least as effective as other instructional interventions. Furthermore, they are practical, as they can be implemented with relative ease by teachers in general classroom settings (Lloyd, Crowley, Kohler, & Strain, 1988). Such interventions have been effective with a variety of student populations including preschool children (Strain & Odom, 1986), low-achieving minority and disadvantaged children (Delquadri, Greenwood, Whorton, Carta, & Hall, 1986), students with mild disabilities (Maheady, Sacca, & Harper, 1988), and students with severe disabilities and autism (Haring, Breen, Pitts-Conway, Lee, & Gaylord-Ross, 1987; Rotholz, 1987). There are many approaches of peer-mediation; from these, three basic techniques emerge: peer tutoring, cooperative learning, and special friends/peer management.

Peer tutoring is conceptualized as an expert instructional delivery system in which a student provides direct instruction of academic or social skills to another student. It is expert in nature as it is hierarchial in its structure. One student with an expertise in a given area or skill teaches a peer. Peer tutoring can serve as supplementary resources in classrooms and community settings (McDonnell, Wilcox, & Hardman, 1991). This approach has been used extensively for many years, and there is considerable evidence to document its effectiveness with a wide variety of student populations and in various settings (Cohen, Kulik, & Kulik, 1982; Gartner & Lipsky, 1990; Topping, 1988).

Peer tutoring reflects the collaborative ethic in that all of the members of the school community appear to benefit from the interaction. Gartner and Lipsky (1990) cited numerous benefits of peer-tutoring for the students serving as tutors. Tutors appear to develop positive attitudes toward school as well as their own self-confidence and self-esteem (Sasso & Rude, 1988). An early comprehensive, meta-analysis of sixty five peer-tutoring programs conducted by Cohen, Kulik, and Kulik (1982) revealed that both the tutor and tutee made significant, positive gains in academic and social areas. Peer tutoring is equally beneficial to teachers. Levin (1984) reported that the use of peer tutors was more cost-effective than using computer-assisted instruction and reducing class size.

A number of guiding principles for creating and implementing peer-tutoring programs have been developed (Greenwood, Whorton, & Delquadri, 1984; Jenkins & Jenkins, 1987; Sprague & McDonnell, 1984; McDonnell, Wilcox, & Hardman, 1991) and are summarized in Table 7–6. Moncur (1991) suggested that the first year of such programs should serve as a "trust-building pilot test" in which the primary objective and responsibility of the peer tutor is to serve as a special friend. In this way, prospective peer tutors become familiar with the prospective tutee at a personal level as well as with the classroom environment and teacher expectations.

Critical factors associated with the potential effectiveness of peer tutoring must be continuously monitored and considered. Shapiro (1988) cautioned that educators must strive to ensure the competency of the tutor, encourage and facilitate effective data-collection procedures by tutors in monitoring student progress, and consider the effect of peer pressure on student performance. Educators must be aware of the possible effect of perceived status differences between tutor and tutee (Voeltz, 1982).

Table 7–6   Guidelines for Developing and Implementing Peer-Tutoring Programs

1. Recruit peer-tutor candidates through nominations from classroom teachers and school counselors.
   a. Briefly explain the role and responsibility of peer tutors.
   b. Ask teachers and counselors to identify high-achieving students who need enrichment opportunities or students with low-self-esteem who could benefit from leadership roles.
2. Interview peer-tutor candidates.
   a. Provide an application to collect important demographic information on the candidates such as name, address, phone number, age, class schedule.
   b. Ask candidates why they want to be a peer tutor.
   c. Ask candidates what they would do in a given situation such as when the tutee makes an error.
3. Provide training to peer tutors.
   a. Demonstrate what tasks they are to carry out.
   b. Demonstrate data-collection procedures.
   c. Demonstrate prompting, correction, and reinforcing procedures.
   d. Explain certain characteristics of the disabling condition without divulging confidential information.
4. Monitor peer-tutoring program on a regular basis.
   a. Observe peer-tutoring interactions.
   b. Provide a summary report form to the peer tutor to record anecdotal information
   c. Consult with teachers/cousnelors and ask for feedback.
   d. Conduct periodic discussions with the peer tutor and, when appropriate, the "tutee" to assess the peer-tutoring process.
5. Reward and acknowledge peer tutors.
   a. Provide academic course credit to peer tutors when possible.
   b. Provide certificates of appreciation.
   c. Host an appreciation "banquet" or party to honor peer-tutor efforts.

Cooperative learning involves heterogeneous groups of students working collaboratively to meet specific instructional and social objectives. It can be an effective means of developing student social skills as well as academic skills. Cooperative learning provides students with the opportunity to meaningfully interact with peers who have disabling conditions while providing supplementary academic support (Nattiv, 1988; Slavin, 1990; Slavin, Madden, & Leavey, 1984). Johnson and Johnson (1986) summarized the benefits of cooperative learning in terms of improving student achievement, motivation, attitude, and social interactions between nondisabled students and their peers with disabilities.

Spotlight: Classwide Peer Tutoring and Academic Learning Time

Greenwood (1991) provided a comprehensive analysis of time, engagement, and achievement of at risk students and non-risk students in which classwide peer tutoring was implemented. Early studies suggested that classwide peer tutoring increased students' (1) time spent working with specific instructional materials, (2) level of engagement, and (3) daily and weekly performance on curriculum-based assessment. A longitudinal study employing experimental and control groups in inner city schools revealed that students from low socioeconomic backgrounds made significantly higher gains on the Metropolitan Achievement Test than an equivalent control group. Curiously, students from higher socioeconomic groups consistently demonstrate higher rates of time spent and time engaged in academic activities.

There are numerous cooperative-learning methodologies (Kagan, 1989; Nattiv, 1988, 1990). Seminal work in the subject has been led by Slavin (1990) and Johnson and Johnson (1986). Nattiv (1988, 1990) has characterized its salient features as consisting of individual accountability, interdependence in reward structure, tasks, roles, and materials, and social skills development.

Johnson and Johnson (1986) described four basic components of cooperative learning: positive interdependence, individual accountability, collaborative skills, and group processing. *Positive interdependence* reflects the collaborative ethic in that individual success is inextricably linked to group success by sharing resources, materials, and expertise. Specific roles of each student are complementary in that individual tasks must be successfully completed in order to complete the over-arching group task. Each individual is *accountable* by having individual tasks that interface with the group task. Furthermore, individual accountability is assured by assessing the individual's performance. Individual scores can be averaged to derive a group score. Students must effectively use *collaboration skills* in interpersonal communication, conflict management, decision making, and problem solving. These are lifelong skills that are as important as academic skills and that must be modeled by educators and parents. Consequently, cooperative-learning objectives often include a social or collaboration component (for example, allowing everyone to participate or minimizing arguments) as well as an academic objective (for example, listing and describing five major inventions from the Industrial Revolution). *Group processing* allows the team to assess how successful they were in reaching academic and social objectives. Collective identification of group strengths and weaknesses provides the team with valuable information that can be used to make decisions and plans that will facilitate the efficient functioning of the partnership. Group processing might be

Cooperative learning allows small groups of diverse students the opportunity to learn academic and interpersonal skills.

facilitated by using a written survey at the end of each cooperative-learning activity. The survey, using a simple yes/no format, could include questions such as the following: Did the group reach its goal? Did the group have fun? Did each individual contribute to helping the group as a whole? With the teacher as facilitator, the group should discuss factors that influenced the group response to each processing-assessment question and design appropriate plans for addressing them.

Student teams-achievement divisions (STAD) is a cooperative-learning technique developed by Slavin (1986). Following a teacher-directed lesson, heterogeneous learning teams of four students work together to complete worksheets and other practice activities. Each student is individually assessed through homework assignments/quizzes. Individual improvement points are awarded on the basis of achievement gain from previous assignment/quizzes and are averaged to derive a team score. Similarly, *team-assisted individualization* (TAI) (Slavin, Leavey, & Madden, 1986) consists of heterogeneous groups of four to five students. This cooperative learning technique was designed to be used in developing arithmetic skills and is effective in promoting social interactions between diverse student groups and self-management. Using regular curriculum materials, students are primarily responsible for managing materials, scoring answers, and keeping records. Using a curriculum-based assessment procedure, students work on specific content and tasks at their own level and pace. Teachers introduce and demonstrate skills to a group while other groups are working together as a team. Students work on their own, receiving peer-tutorial assistance as needed. Team members also score each other's work. A team score is calculated according to the average number of lessons completed and the accuracy on unit tests. Salend and Washin (1988) reported that the TAI approach was successfully implemented with disabled adjudicated youth. Most of the same procedures have been implemented in a cooperative-learning program for reading and composition by Madden, Slavin, and Stevens (1986).

Guidelines for establishing and maintaining cooperative-learning groups are provided in Table 7–7. For detailed descriptions of procedures, readers are referred to Johnson and Johnson (1986).

Special friends/peer management strategies are generally used to promote social integration of students with disabilities through programs designed to develop relationships based on social and leisure interactions (Haring, Breen, Pitts-Conway, Lee, Gaylord-Ross, 1987). Special-friends procedures and peer management have been effective in improving the attitude of nondisabled students toward disabled peers and social behaviors of students with disabilities in academic and social settings (Haring, Breen, Pitts-Conway, Lee, & Gaylord-Ross, 1987; Strain & Odom, 1986). This form of peer-mediated intervention has also been effective in facilitating transition and integration of students with severe disabilities into mainstream classroom settings. Classmates support their peers with disabilities as they become familiar with routines, schedules, class rules, and interactions with other students and teachers (Stainback & Stainback, 1990).

Strain and Odom (1986) viewed peers as a resource that could be used to circumvent some of the difficulties associated with teacher-mediated social interventions. They recognized that social interactions were often interrupted when teachers intervened. Furthermore, they determined that it was difficult for teachers to monitor and facilitate social interactions of several children in a classroom setting. The role of special friends usually revolves around mutually appealing leisure and recreational activities in which a nondisabled peer will share a treat (eg. ice cream, pizza) or engage in an activity (playing video games, taking walks) with a student who has a disability (Haring et al., 1987).

Scheduling

Given the array of special needs within a diverse student population, teachers must organize a schedule and management plan that will incorporate instructional activities that are both teacher-directed and student-focused, yet accommodate individual student needs at a variety of ability levels. The schedules and management plans presented here have been designed to easily implement an ecological approach of using existing resources in the

Table 7–7   Guidelines for Establishing and Maintaining Cooperative-Learning Groups

Specifying Objectives

1. Clearly state instructional objectives that include criteria (i.e., identify and list five interventions from the Industrial Revolution).
2. Clearly state collaborative objectives that promote interpersonal skills (i.e., each member will contribute one piece of information and the group will not argue during the twenty-minute activity).

Forming Cooperative-Learning Groups

1. Groups of two to three should be used when inexperienced students are working within a limited amount of time and materials.
2. Carefully assign students to groups. Create a balance of ethnic background, ability level, and gender. Carefully consider in which group to place students with special needs so they are readily accepted rather than isolated.
3. Determine duration of working together. Duration can range from an entire year to completion of an academic unit.
4. Form groups according to the task. One group might be well suited for math activities but unsuitable for language arts. Be flexible in determining group membership and makeup.
5. Facilitate positive interdependence by "jigsawing" where roles and materials are distributed in such a way that team members must cooperate (i.e., one textbook, one pencil, one pair of scissors, a reader, a note-taker).

Promoting Individual and Group Accountability

1. Award individual points/grades for completion of tasks.
2. Award points to the group for completion of tasks.
3. Combine individaul and group points for final grade.
4. Award bonus points to each member of the group when individual objectives/assignments are completed correctly.

Monitoring and Intervening

1. Monitor individual student behaviors and intervene when necessary.
2. Provide task assistance to group.
3. Teach collaborative problem-solving skills when groups encounter disputes.
4. Provide opportunities for each group to reach closure by assessing their individual and group performance. The results of the closure process can serve as instructional and/or collaborative objectives for subsequent group sessions.

Using the 4×4 management plan, a teacher can monitor guided practice activities for a small group of students.

school and home, effective teaching behaviors and peer-mediated instruction in mainstream classroom settings or instructional support settings.

4×4 Management Plan.   The method known as the *4×4 management plan* is a matrix of four separate blocks of instructional activities that rotates approximately every fifteen to twenty minutes. This management plan can be used in all academic content areas including physical education and the fine arts. Approximately five minutes are spent as a large group to describe the various activities students will engage in during each instructional block of time. After an overview, the class is divided into fourths so students can be heterogenously grouped into one of four blocks. One block is the *teacher-directed* (TD) instructional activity. The teacher may model or demonstrate a specific skill to approximately one-fourth of the class during the TD block. The *group or guided practice* (GP) block allows the teacher to either conduct guided practice, as described earlier in the chapter, with the same group of students, or allow the students to work together as a group or in small groups. The group-practice approach lends itself well to cooperative-learning activities. Students can work individually and at their own pace during the *individual practice* (IP) block. The IP block is well suited for drill and practice worksheets. Students may also work on completing individual products or projects that might be included within a portfolio as part of the authentic assessment process. Classrooms with an array of well-organized *learning centers* can be used effectively either during the IP block or during the *review/enrichment* (RE) block. The RE block allows students the opportunity to either review their work or engage in activities that embellish the learning process. It can also be used to provide additional time to complete assignment or worksheets, review and evaluate completed work, and participate in enrichment activities on the skill or concept that has been the focus of attention throughout the 4×4 block. The RE block can be modified to allow a team-teacher or a paraprofessional (classroom aide) to reconvene students and provide feedback or check work. When used in this way, it provides an effective implementation of team teaching whereby both the students and teachers are given more opportunities to interact during the learning process. Figure 7–4 depicts an example of the 4×4 scheduling plan for an English lesson.

Teachers can, of course, modify the 4×4 schedule in a number of ways. The rule of thumb, however, is to maximize academic learning time by providing opportunities for teacher-directed instruction and practice with feedback. One modification would be the rescheduling of the review/enrichment block as a large-group activity for the whole class on the following day. This would essentially create a 3×3 management plan, with a single block of time allocated for review or enrichment. Finally, an "hourglass" approach begins with a large group with teacher-directed activities, followed by dividing the class into two groups. A teacher or an instructional aide can continue to provide guided practice to one group while the other group completes individual practice or drill activities. After fifteen to twenty minutes, the groups shift activities, allowing the teacher or instructional assistant to work with the other group. The instructional period concludes by reconvening the group to engage in review or enrichment activities.

The following example has been provided to demonstrate how a teacher might incorporate all of the techniques that have been presented thus far in this chapter. In this example, Mr. Enfield, a sixth-grade teacher, is preparing a cross-curriculum unit on presidential elections. Among the twenty-five students are a Vietnamese refugee named Tran who speaks little English, a girl named Pam who has severe learning disabilities that restrict her reading abilities, and Tony, who is wheelchair-bound with cerebral palsy.

For reading and social studies, Mr. Enfield is embellishing a chapter of the district-approved social studies textbook that examines presidential elections with articles from news magazines and video "clips" from national news broadcasts. He is providing advance organizers consisting of vocabulary terms and specific questions designed to locate WHO, WHAT, WHERE, WHEN, and WHY information for the reading and video activities during teacher-directed instruction. Mr. Enfield will determine the extent to which students understand important concepts from the reading and video presentations by staging debates. Teams of students will address specific issues from a particular election during a mock debate. Students are expected to compare and contrast the debates of 1860, 1960, and 1992 in a written paper. They have the option of writing a formal report or a

READING COMPREHENSION

	Group 1	Group 2	Group 3	Group 4
9:00 9:15	**RE** Use yesterdays vocabulary in your own story	**TD** Introduce: cause & effect	**GP** Use text to identify cause/effect on characters	**IP** Worksheet: Identify cause/effect
9:15 9:30	**TD** Introduce concept of cause/effect	**GP** Use text to I.D. cause/effect on crisis of characters	**IP** Worksheet: Identify cause/effect	**RE** Journal entry - Describe cause/effect in personal experience
9:30 9:45	**GP** Using text - I.D. cause/effect of crisis on characters	**IP** Worksheet: I.D. cause/effect	**RE** Journal entry: Describe cause/effect with personal experience	**TD** Continue discussion: Cause/effect using journal entries
9:45 10:00	**IP** Worksheet: I.D. cause/effect	**RE** Journal entry - Describe cause/effect in personal experience	**TD** Introduce tomorrow's topic: Compare/contrast	**GP** Edit each other's work

MODIFIED 4×4 format

9:00 9:15	TEACHER DIRECTED INSTRUCTION MODEL/DEMONSTRATE NEW SKILL TO WHOLE CLASS		
	˅	˅	˅
	Group 1	**Group 2**	**Group 3**
9:15 9:30	Group Practice	Group Practice	Group Practice
9:30 9:45	Individual Practice	Individual Practice	Individual Practice
9:45 10:00	Review/Test	Review/Test	Review/Test

Figure 7–4
4×4 Management Plan

newspaper article. For math, students will be required to devise their own rating scale to assess each other during a simulated debate. The rating scale will convert raw data in the form of points into averages and percentages. The students will also construct their own grading scale based on these averages and percentages. A lesson plan for Mr. Enfield's cross-curriculum activity is presented in Figure 7–5.

Learning Centers.   Individualized instruction and individual practice activities can be facilitated through the use of *learning centers*—characterized as specified locations in the classroom that generally accommodate one to two individuals to enter instructional activities at varying levels. Students can proceed here at their own pace. Learning centers can be organized around specific content or skill areas such as social studies, math, language arts, and life skills. Teachers should consider the following guidelines (Mercer & Mercer, 1985; Stephens, 1977) to create effective learning centers.

Work Space
Learning centers should be designed to accommodate one to two students. Students can either work individually or in dyads to facilitate peer tutoring. Countertops, small tables, or even two individual student desks can provide adequate room to work. Ideally, learning centers should be strategically located in the peripheral areas of the classroom to minimize disruption of large- or small-group instructional activities.

Organization
Learning centers must be organized in a manner that facilitates efficient use and transition while at the same time are pleasant in appearance. Color codes, icons, and symbols are often useful, especially when schedules are posted in the room indicating when students are scheduled to be working at a specific station. For example, a math learning center may consistently use a blue color for worksheets to match the blue color code on the posted schedule. Codes such as A1 or +1 on a manilla folder in a file located at the learning center contains the first addition worksheet. A list or matrix of worksheets can be laminated to the front of the folder and students can record their scores and mark off completed worksheets. The teacher can easily monitor student progress and provide feedback using such folders. A box or storage container such as a collapsible, accordion-style file can be used to keep individual student file folders.

Instructions
Clear and simple instructions are a necessity, as most students will be working independently. The instructions should provide an objective or goal statement for the activity, which may also include a mastery criteria (such as to correctly change at least eight out of ten improper fractions to mixed fractions). Instructions should also include a list of the necessary materials for the activity.

Figure 7–5
Lesson Plan for Cross-Curriculum Activity

SOCIAL STUDIES: Presidential Campaigns and Debates

	Reading	Writing	Arithmetic	Oral Language	Comments/Notes
Teacher-directed	Advance organizer for Chapter 6 Time mag + video clips	Compare/contrast 1860/1960/1992 issues and debates	Develop poll & evaluation sheet to determine debate winner Look at Gallup polls	Look at speaking styles (glittering generalities, bandwagon, etc). Define terms and illustrate with video	Tony: Dictate written essay
Group practice	Research & I.D. issues for your candidate (newspaper or mag.)	PICK topic LIST ideas on topic EVALUATE list of ideas	Devise debate rating scale Create a poll	Form debate teams & plan strategies Assign students to (A) Lincoln/Douglas (B) Bush/Clinton & Perot	
Individual practice	Vocabulary worksheet	Begin written assignment: ACTIVATE + SUPPLY + END/EVALUATE	Worksheets to convert raw data to averages and % scores of rating and poll results	Make individual notes for debate arguments	
Evaluation procedures		Existence, form, & function of topic sent, 3 supp. sent, & concluding sentence	Students calculate debate/poll winner and write brief report of data	Rate debate team using student-generated rating forms and polls	
Comments/notes	Pam: Taped text	Tran: Make poster with study buddy containing bullet statements Tony: Dictate paper			Tony: Serve as debate moderator Pam & Tran: Collect & collate rating/poll data

Pam = Non-reader with learning disabilities   Tran = Vietnamese student with limited spoken English
Tony = Student with cerebral palsy affecting fine motor control/handwriting

Materials

An array of readily available materials can be used in learning centers. Newspapers, magazines, and maps are useful in social studies learning centers. Almost any object from the home can be used for instructional activities or storage. Poker chips, beans, or golf tees in pegboards can be used as manipulatives for arithmetic activities. A deck of playing cards can be used in a multitude of basic-operation activities. Milk cartons, plastic containers, or cupcake baking pans can be used to store materials. Index cards can be used as flash cards and stored in a recipe-card box. A question, definition, or math problem can be printed on one side with the answer printed on the other. Peer-tutoring dyads can use the dual-sided flash cards during practice drill exercises designed to enhance student response fluency. Use of acetates or laminated materials and grease pencils/markers allow materials to be recycled and used several times. Students' responses on individual worksheets that have been laminated or placed within an acetate envelope can be wiped clean after they have been self-checked for accuracy using an answer key and the score recorded. In addition to these "low-tech" items, learning centers can employ high-tech materials such as computers, interactive laser discs, filmstrip projectors, and audiocassette and/or videocassette players.

Correction and Recording Procedures

Learning centers often employ self-correcting techniques that will provide immediate feedback to the student and allow for accurate, daily recording of student progress. Acetates or laminated materials are especially useful as self-correcting materials. Answer keys may also be provided on audiocassettes. For example, correct spelling of spelling words, answers for math worksheets, and terms for definitions can be recorded on an audiocassette to be played back and listened to on headphones. A chart or matrix of a specific set of tasks or worksheets can be developed and placed in the student file folder. Students can record their scores on the chart. The teacher can quickly and efficiently monitor student progress and provide direct feedback to students this way.

Check-in and Check-out Periods.   Allotting a period of time at the beginning and/or end of the school day allows teams of educators to monitor student readiness as well as conduct routine business (Adamson, Cox, & Schuller, 1989). A *check-in period* is time when a teacher, paraprofessional, itinerant, or peer tutors/special friends can prepare a student for the day's activities. Daily logistic activities such as taking attendance, collecting meal money, or daily announcements can occur during check-in time. Additionally, special monitoring or preparation of students at risk can be supervised easily. This typically involves establishing an academic or behavioral objective for the day. Check-in periods also serve as a last-minute homework-completion check.

A *check-out period* is an opportunity to ensure that students have their assignments and materials necessary to complete their work (e.g., textbooks, worksheets) as well as check for understanding of the assignment. The check-out period is also a time when teachers can monitor and chart daily behavior, recording slips that the student has accumulated over the course of the day. Students and designated professionals may meet during the check-out period to review the extent to which students successfully met their academic and/or behavioral objectives for the day. The time may also serve as   reflective moment for students to record thoughts and feelings in daily journals. Check-in and check-out periods can be implemented in secondary settings as well by requiring students to report to their homeroom or student advisor.

Behavioral Management Strategies

We began this chapter by considering how the classroom environment can have an impact on learning. Similarly, ecological factors can influence student behaviors. Consequently, it is important for educators to understand that behavior problems are not always the result of some internal or pathological condition within a student. Factors within the classroom may actually contribute to inappropriate student behavior. Effective teacher behaviors, appropriate use of materials, student grouping, and scheduling can maximize appropriate learning and behavior as well as minimize inappropriate behavior or inefficient learning.

Managing behavior has traditionally been a reactive process in which teachers respond to inappropriate behaviors. A proactive approach to behavior management is more efficient, given the diverse student population in a classroom setting (Gettinger, 1988). Such a proactive approach is typified by three characteristics: (1) preventing inappropriate behaviors by anticipating potentially negative situations, (2) implementing effective instruction that promotes achievement and on-task behavior, and (3) focusing on group dimensions of classroom management. As such, proactive management is the synthesis of instructional and behavioral strategies. The instructional strategies described earlier lend themselves to effective management of behavior. It is beyond the scope of this chapter to provide a comprehensive description of behavioral management strategies. Readers are referred to additional resources at the end of the chapter for detailed descriptions of practical behavior strategies. Additionally, there is a very small segment of the student population with significant behavior needs that require extensive behaviorial interventions. In cases such as this, specialists will work closely with classroom teachers and parents. There are, however, a number of strategies that teachers can easily implement on their own that will promote appropriate behavior.

Classroom Rules

Establishing classroom rules allows a teacher to explicitly state expectations regarding appropriate behaviors. The process of establishing rules should include a rationale so students understand why some behaviors are or are not appropriate. Rules should also be proactive in that they effectively anticipate likely problems (Rhode, Jenson, & Reavis, 1992). Classroom rules essentially outline the teacher's expectations and the consequences for the student who does not meet them. Following is a summary of guidelines for developing and implementing classroom rules (Morgan & Jenson, 1988; Rhode, Jenson, & Reavis, 1992; Rockwell, 1993).

- *Minimize the number of rules that are essential.* A large number of rules makes enforcement difficult and increases the number of opportunities for noncompliance.

- *Clearly state and post the rules.* Language must be clear and not subject to individual interpretation. Avoid ambigous words. Use descriptive words. The rules should be placed prominently for easy reference.

- *State rules positively.* Teachers should indicate what they want students to do rather than what not to do.

- *Involve students in the development of the rules.* Students will have a vested interest and sense of personal responsibility and accountability when they are included in the process of establishing rules.

- *Teach the rules to students.* Teachers must employ the effective teaching behaviors described in this chapter to help students understand the rules.

- *Tie the rules to consequences.* Students should understand the positive outcomes of complying with rules as well as the negative consequences for not following rules.

- *Carefully choose rewards and punishments.* Be sure to select positive and negative consequences you can deliver.

- *Be consistent.* Follow through on the positive and negative consequences you described to the students.

Antecedent Strategies

An *antecedent strategy* is another proactive approach to managing behavior. As its name suggests, this strategy is employed before a positive behavior in order to maintain and increase its frequency (Rhode et al., 1992). It is an approach common in business, where it is used to motivate and reward employees for increased performance. Antecedent strategies can be equally effective in classroom settings. For example, a teacher might award a coupon for ten minutes of free time on the computer for completing individual seatwork activities. There are three basic steps for effectively implementing antecedent strategies (Rhode et al., 1992). First, clearly articulate what you want students to do, and be sure they understand your expectations (such as turning in math homework on time for five consecutive days). Second, explain the outcomes if they meet your expecations (for example, students who turn in their math homework on time for five consecutive days will get to watch a video on Friday afternoon). Third, immediately provide the positive feedback and reward (you might announce, "Great! This group of students who turned in their fifth day of math homework on time may now go to the back of the room and watch a video").

Surface-Management Techniques

Surface-management techniques (Long & Newman, 1980) are proactive strategies that are easily implemented in a classroom. One example is *reducing distractions*. Students are often distracted by objects that become playthings (such as rubber bands, or pencils) or by events in or outside the classroom (a truck being unloaded outside the window or the class gerbil moving in its cage). Pulling the shade or relocating the student are simple approaches that minimize the potential for becoming distracted. Establishing *routines* can also minimize the risk of inappropriate behavior. Fixed schedules make tasks predictable, especially during transition between activities. *Proximity* to a student allows the teacher to be a physical reminder of appropriate behavior. Moving a student closer to the teacher's desk facilitates monitoring and as well as immediate response to inappropriate behavior when it does occur without major disruption of instruction. The use of *signals* such as eye contact, facial expressions, and writing a student's name on the board can be effective. A simulated traffic light can be used as a signal. A green light indicates the class as a whole is behaving appropriately. Replacing the green light with a yellow light cautions the class that behavior is marginal. A red light indicates behavior is unacceptable and consequences are forthcoming. *Positive appeal* is a technique that reinforces and models appropriate behavior. A teacher can acknowledge the appropriate behavior of one student, which behavior in turn is used as a model for a student who is not behaving appropriately. For example, a teacher might say, "I like the way Michelle is quietly working at her desk with her hands to herself. Michael, I want you to work quietly and keep your hands to yourself the way Michelle is doing."

Reductive Strategies

Despite best efforts to create proactive behavioral management systems, teachers will encounter student behaviors they will want to reduce or eliminate. *Reductive strategies* can be used to stop inappropriate excessive behaviors and encourage their replacement by appropriate actions (Rhode, Jensen, & Reavis, 1992). Most teachers and parents are familiar with this approach, as it often involves the word "don't" (for example, "Don't talk to your neighbor," or "Don't talk with your mouth full."). Paradoxically, reductive strategies have the potential of being extremely effective. Consequently, they are commonly but inefficiently used. Effectiveness of reductive strategies is based on a request for appropriate behavior followed by immediate reprimand if the student does not comply. The request should be descriptive so students have a clear understanding of your expectations. For example, "Keep your hands and your feet to yourself," is much more effective than, "Don't bother your neighbor." A teacher may need to make the request a second time. Guidelines for making effective requests (Rhode et al., 1992) are summarized in Table 7–8.

The "Sure I Will" program (Rhode et al., 1992) is a simple one that promotes compliance and reminds teachers to reinforce appropriate behavior. As the teacher asks a student to do something, the student responds by saying, "Sure I will," followed by complying with the request. This approach appears to be effective in initiating specific student action while minimizing arguing and noncompliance. If the student has not complied with the teacher request after five to ten seconds, the teacher issues a second request that is prefaced with, "I need you to . . ." and waits for another five to ten seconds for compliance. If the student complies after the second request, the teacher provides

Table 7–8 Guidelines for Effective Teacher Requests.

- **Make a single statement.** State your expectations (e.g., I want you to sit quietly in your seat) rather than asking a question (e.g., Don't you think you should work quietly at your desk?). Be sure to make a single request rather than series of requests that increase the possibility of noncompliance.

- **Use "do" more than "don't."** Requests that use the word "do" are proactive and establish expectations. An overabundance of "don't" requests may suggest that classroom rules are unclear or ineffective.

- **Stay close.** Walk around the room to monitor behavior. Keep in close physical proximity to the students when making a request. This minimizes shouting or pointing.

- **Use appropriate speaking tone and volume.** A quiet voice will indicate you are in control rather than out of control emotionally. Be nonemotional by simply stating your request rather then expressing your frustration.

- **Use appropriate wait time.** Allow five to ten seconds for students to comply. Do not interrupt the wait period.

- **Request twice.** Ask a student to comply only two times. Students will learn to manipulate teachers and parents if it is clear that the person making the request is not serious about compliance. Consequently, teachers and parents fall into the trap of, "I've had to ask you a hundred times to stop talking."

- **Reinforce and acknowledge compliance.** Be sure to reinforce compliance verbally and/or physically through facial expressions.

242   Part 2   *The School*

some kind of reinforcement. A preplanned reductive consequence is applied if the student does not comply after the second request.

Reductive Consequences.   The term *reductive consequences* means simply penalties for noncompliance. An effective application of reductive consequences is the "What If?" chart posted in front of the classroom (Rhode et al., 1992). This chart displays preplanned positive and negative consequences. The reductive consequences listed include a description of how much and how long each consequence will be applied. The list of penalties increase in severity. For example, a verbal warning from the teacher is less negative than the loss of free time, which is less negative than a phone call to parents. The "What If?" chart can and should include positive preplanned consequences as well. Positive consequences may include additional free time, a praising phone call home, eliminating one night of homework, or watching a video.

Token Economies

Tokens are symbolic representations, analogous to the use of money, that when earned can be exchanged for something of value to students (Alberto & Troutman, 1990). A token can be a tangible object (such as a poker chip or play money) or a symbol (such as a checkmark or happy face) that is easy to manage, meaning it can be awarded efficiently and immediately. Tokens must be something that cannot be counterfeited. Earned tokens can be exchanged for privileges such as playing computer games or for prizes such as pencils. Typically, students earn tokens over the course of a week and exchange them at a "store" at the end of the week. For example, points can be awarded to an individual or groups of students using the "Sure I Will" strategy that are later exchanged for a privilege.

Contracts

A written *contract* serves as an agreement between teacher and student that earning a reward is contingent upon display of specific behaviors. For example, a teacher and student may agree that the student is entitled to play a computer game if the student completes in-class work. Alberto and Troutman (1990) listed a number of benefits in using contracts. A written contract ensures that each party understands and agrees to specific goals and procedures. Contracts are useful in that they can be kept on file to document specific objectives and procedures during parent-teacher conferences. Contracts also reflect collaboration in that the process actively involves the student. Finally, a contract facilitates individualized intervention based on need.

Contracts may require an initial investment of time and effort that often results in significant dividends. They should not be used as a bribe or a crutch. Instead, they should be designed to initially augment motivation and gradually be faded, allowing the appropriate behavior or outcome to evolve as the motivating factor. Rhode et al., (1992) provided a list of six steps for developing and implementing contracts:

1. Define and describe the specific behavior (for example, John will speak with a calm voice and without hurtful or obscene words).

2. Mutually agree upon and select reinforcers.

3. Define and create contract criteria that is accumulative in nature.

4. Include a bonus and penalty cause.

5. Negotiate the terms.

6. Create and sign a written document of the agreed upon terms.

The Hero Procedure

Morgan and Jenson (1988) astutely point out that many classroom teachers are reluctant to single out one or two students by rewarding them for appropriate behaviors when the majority of the class consistently behaves according to classroom rules. The *hero approach* was developed to address this legitimate concern by letting a student earn a reward for the entire class by behaving correctly. For example, Michael has had difficulty working quietly at his desk. He talks to others and is disruptive by leaving his seat. The teacher will award Michael and each member in the class a token if he can remain in his seat without talking during the seatwork activity. This technique reflects basic principles of positive interdependence as it encourages individual accountability within a group setting. Furthermore, it is in the interest of the entire group to make sure that Michael meets the objective. Consequently, collaborative peer support is positive rather than negative.

Classroom-Level Management System

A hierarchy of behaviors and rewards that students move through is known as a *classroom-level management system.* As in token economies, specific privileges are earned at various levels of appropriate behavior. The lowest level is associated with fundamental behaviors such as staying in one's seat, keeping hands and feet to oneself, and refraining from aggressive behaviors. Students performing at this level receive regular schoolwide privileges such as going to recess and limited use of classroom activities/equipment such as computer games. Subsequent levels are accumulative in nature, requiring maintenance of previous level skills as well as additional and more complex behaviors. Privileges also increase at each level. For

Peers can assist each other in promoting appropriate behaviors through various behavior management strategies.

example, in addition to demonstrating the behaviors at the lowest level, a student may also exhibit good citizenship such as picking up waste paper and throwing it away without being asked, or engaging in quiet activities after assigned work has been completed. Students at this level earn additional privileges such as free time. The highest level of expectations may include collaborative problem solving and assisting peers in meeting individual or group objectives.

Self-Monitoring and Self-Evaluation Strategies

Self-monitoring strategies require students to observe and supervise their own behavior (Zirpoli & Melloy, 1993). They are taught to collect data regarding the occurance or nonoccurance of a specific behavior. The data-collection process appears to improve students' awareness of their own behavior, often resulting in improvement of student conduct and performance. Self-monitoring strategies can also be coupled with token economies or contracts. Typically, an audiotape that emits a tone cues the student to see if he or she was behaving appropriately or inappropriately. The student then marks a data-collection sheet.

Students compare their behavior with a predetermined standard during *self-evaluation strategies* (Cole, 1987, cited in Zirpoli & Melloy, 1993). After reviewing and learning classroom rules, students and teachers assess student behavior using a Likert-type rating scale every ten minutes. The student and teacher compare their assessment ratings. Points or tokens are earned for appropriate behavior.

Anger-control training is an effective strategy that can be used to help students monitor and control their own frustration and aggression (Zirpoli & Melloy, 1993). This approach involves self-instruction in which a student utilizes self-statements in four stages: (1) preparation for provocation, (2) impact and confrontation, (3) coping with arousal, and (4) reflecting on the provocation (Novaco, 1979). Another form of anger-control training utilizes some components of the self-evaluation techniques already described. The "hassle log" is a structured questionnaire that can be used during role playing (Goldstein, 1988). Students learn to identify the antecedents, behavior, and consequences associated with an episode. The data collected on the questionnaire is used to help students problem solve by devising alternative reactions for future incidents.

Chapter Summary

An array of strategies that can be implemented in general education classrooms is readily available for teachers to accommodate the needs of a diverse student population. The actual curricular content may vary from student to student, depending on individual needs. Curricular adaptation may, however, be realistically implemented within the larger framework of the explicit curriculum in a manner that can accommodate all learners. There are four dimensions of instructional adaptations: teaching, materials, activities, and student grouping. Effective teaching includes model and demonstration of skills followed by practice and enrichment activities. Strategic environments are created when teachers clearly illustrate how to use strategic behaviors to problem solve and meet the demands of the classroom. Materials are the medium in which content is presented. Materials may need to be adapted to meet the needs of students at risk. Activities fall into three broad categories: internalization, maintenance, and externalization. Internalization is the introduction and explanation of a concept or skill. Students practice using the new skill during maintenance activities. Finally, students demonstrate their mastery through externalization activities such as written tests or other products. Teachers must consider an array of strategies for modifying each of these three categories in order to meet the needs of students at risk.

Students may be grouped in various ways during instructional activities. Peer tutoring, cooperative learning, and special friends/peer management are three examples of peer-mediated instruction that may be used to group students. Scheduling systems must be incorporated to facilitate achieving curricular and instructional objectives. Instructional activities must dictate the schedule that will allow teachers to conduct teacher-directed, group-practice, and individual studies. Learning centers are effecient in providing individualized instructional activities.

A proactive approach of managing behavior involves combining effective instructional strategies with preventative measures that promote and faciliate appropriate student behaviors. Classroom rules efficiently establish teacher expectations of student behaviors and citizenship. Antecedent strategies can be used to reward positive and appropriate behaviors. Various surface-management techniques are low-cost approaches for managing behavior. Reductive strategies are used to reduce inappropriate behaviors by reducing distractions, establishing routines, using signals for warnings and transitions, and making a positive appeal for specific appropriate behaviors. These reductive strategies use reductive consequences, which are penalties for noncompliance. Token economies use tangible items or symbols that are earned and then used to purchase privileges. Contracts are written agreements that outline specific behaviorial objectives and consequences. The hero procedure is a strategy that employs the entire class to monitor the group and/or individual behavior. Classroom-level management systems utilize a hierarchy of structured guidelines for behavior with privileges that are earned for compliance. For individual cases, self-monitoring or self-evaluation strategies are used by students to collect data on their own behavior.

Case Study 7–1

Mrs. Pierce is a first-year teacher in a fourth-grade classroom of thirty-five students. The students in Mrs. Pierce's class demonstrate varying levels of math skills, ranging from students who have not mastered addition and subtraction to those who are beginning to work with division of one-digit divisors and fractions. Each day, Mrs. Pierce presents instruction to the entire group by putting examples on the board and calling on various students to come forward to work sample problems. Then, all students work on their seatwork assignment while Mrs. Pierce sits at her desk and assists students who come forward for assistance or to have their completed seatwork assignments checked. Seatwork assignments consist of completing faded ditto worksheets.

During seatwork time, students are lined up seven or eight deep, blocking the teachers' view of the remainder of the class. Over half of the students do not complete their assignments each day, taking homework with them, and of these, only half bring in their completed homework the next day. There is considerable inappropriate behavior, including shooting spitwads, passing notes, and doodling on desks. Almost daily, a scuffle erupts among the students waiting in line for Mrs. Pierce's help. Two students who are most disruptive and who seldom complete their seatwork and homework are students who receive reading assistance in a resource room. Mrs. Pierce believes that these students are the "troublemakers" of the class, and that they instigate classroom problems. Mrs. Pierce has requested that these boys receive additional time in the resource room for assistance in math.

1. Form small groups and use the collaborative process worksheet presented in Chapter 3 to conduct an ecological assessment and develop an appropriate action plan that can be used to help Mrs. Pierce adapt the instructional procedures and activities in her classroom.

2. How might students be grouped to facilitate academic learning time?

3. What are some scheduling alternatives that might be implemented by Mrs. Pierce?

4. What are some alternative evaluation and grading procedures presented in Chapter 6 that Mrs. Pierce might use?

5. What behavioral management strategies might be considered?

6. What are the implications of Mrs. Pierce's request for additional resource time for the students currently receiving special education support?

Case Study 7–2

The state and district curriculum competencies mandate that students must demonstrate an understanding of the three branches of government (executive, legislative, and judicial). However, the state and district do not indicate how students must demonstrate their understanding. You are preparing a social studies unit on the checks and balance of the U.S. government that describes the roles and functions of each branch of government. Carlos is one of your students. He recently arrived in this country with his family and speaks very little English but seems to understand what is slowly spoken to him. Tara has a learning disability that interferes with her reading comprehension and spelling. Stanley has difficulty staying on-task during individual, seatwork activity. He often becomes frustrated in class, which is displayed in aggressive behavior such as knocking over chairs or abusive language when he cannot complete an assignment.

1. How would your teaching be adapted to meet the needs of all the students in your classroom?

2. How would you adapt materials in your class to meet the needs of these students in your classroom?

3. What internalization, maintenance, and externalization activities would you consider implementing?

4. What forms of student grouping might you consider?

5. How would you use the 4×4 management plan to organize the instructional process?

6. What behavioral management techniques would you consider using for the entire class and for Stanley?

7. Using examples from Chapter 6, what evaluation and grading strategies might be considered to assess student achievement?

Key Vocabulary Terms

parallel curriculum
functional curriculum
community-based curriculum
specialized curriculum
direct instruction
constructivism
strategic environments
strategic behaviors
strategic interventions
academic learning time (ALT)
internalization
maintenance
externalization
graphic organizers
taped textbooks

peer-mediated intervention
peer tutoring
cooperative learning
special friends/peer
  management
learning centers
authentic assessment
4×4 management plan
teacher-directed (TD)
  instruction
group/guided practice (GP)
individual practice (IP)
review/enrichment (RE)
check-in/check-out periods
tokens

surface management
  techniques
classroom-level management
hero procedure
contracts
reductive strategies
reductive consequences
self-monitoring/self-
  evaluation strategies
metacognitive learning
  strategies
antecedent strategies
reducing distractions
anger-control training

Suggested Readings

Cooperative Learning

Johnson, D. W., & Johnson, R. (1991). *Learning together and alone: Cooperation and competition, and individualization.* 3d ed. Englewood Cliffs, NJ: Prentice-Hall.

Johnson, R., & Holubec, E. (1990). *Circles of learning: Cooperation in the classroom.* 3d ed. Edina, MN: Interaction.

Madden, N. A., Slavin, R. E., & Stevens, R. J. (1986). *Cooperative integrated reading and composition: Teacher's manual.* Baltimore, MD: John Hopkins University, Center for Research on Elementary and Middle Schools.

Slavin, R. E. (1983). *Cooperative learning.* New York: Longman.

Slavin, R. E. (1990). *Cooperative learning: Theory, research, and practice.* Englewood Cliffs, NJ: Prentice-Hall.

Learning and Teaching Strategies

Lovitt, T. C., (1984). *Tactics for Teaching.* Columbus, OH: Merrill.

Saski, J., Swicegood, P., & Carter, J. (1988). Notetaking formats for learning disabled adolescents. *Learning Disability Quarterly, 6,* 265–271.

Schumaker, J. B., Deshler, D. D., Alley, G. R., Warner, M. M., & Denton, P. H. (1982). Multipass: A learning strategy for improving reading comprehension. *Learning Disability Quarterly, 5,* 295–304.

Strategies for Adapting Instruction and Managing Classrooms

Cangelosi, J. S. (1993). *Classroom management strategies: Gaining and maintaining students' cooperation.* New York: Longman.

Lovitt, T. C. (1991). *TRIP: Translating research into practice: Adapting Materials.* Salt Lake City, UT: Utah Learning Resource Center.

Wood, J. (1991). *Adapting instruction for mainstreamed and at risk students.* 2d ed. Columbus, OH: Merrill.

Strategies for Behavior Management

Rhode, G., Jenson, W. R., & Reavis, H. K. (1992). *The tough kid book: Practical classroom management strategies.* Longmont, CO: Sopris West, Inc.

Rockwell, S. (1993). *Tough to reach/tough to teach: Students with behavior problems.* Reston, VA: Council for Exceptional Children.

Zirpoli, T. J., & Melloy, K. J. (1993). *Behavior management: Applications for teachers and parents.* Columbus, OH: Merrill.

Chapter 8

Chapter Overview

School-Based Partnerships

Chapter Objectives

After reading this chapter, the reader should be able to
1. Name three types of school-based consultation programming.
2. List guidelines for establishing and evaluating school-based consultation programs.
3. Name three types of team teaching.
4. List guidelines for establishing and evaluating team teaching.
5. Enumerate the characteristics and functions of case-management teams.
6. List guidelines for establishing and evaluating case-management teams.
7. Describe the composition and function of a multidisciplinary student service-delivery team.
8. Delineate the components of an individualized education program.
9. Explain methods for planning and implementing effective multidisciplinary team meetings for developing individual education plans.
10. Describe the functions and characteristics of effective staff development.
11. List guidelines for implementing and evaluating staff-development programs.

Introduction

The previous chapter described a variety of classroom-based strategies that could be implemented primarily by a single professional. This chapter will examine several aspects of educational partnerships in which two or more professionals collaborate to provide services in a variety of settings within the school. We begin by discussing partnerships that are implemented at a micro-level, generally involving a one-on-one collaborative interaction. This section is followed by a broader perspective at the macro-level in which partnerships consist of more than two professionals and are implemented schoolwide.

Micro-Level School-Based Partnerships

School Consultation Programs

A definitive overview of consultation was presented in Chapters 1 and 3. As a review, collaborative consultation is conceptualized here as an indirect service-delivery approach in which professionals with diverse expertise generate creative solutions to mutually defined problems. The school consultation programs highlighted here will reflect a variety of theoretical models. This chapter will include some examples and guidelines for establishing school-based collaborative consultation programs. The role of consultant can be assumed by a variety of professionals such as special education teachers, remedial teachers, school psychologists, social workers, guidance counselors, speech and hearing specialists, or school administrators (Idol, 1988).

Behavioral Consultation.   The *behavioral consultation* model has been successfully implemented in school settings. This model is an indirect service-delivery approach in which the consultant provides assistance to a consultee rather than delivering interventions directly to a client. Behavioral consultation incorporates a systematic method for solving educational problems (see Chapter 3) with the research-validated technology of behavioral analysis (Goodwin, 1975).

The primary goal of behavioral consultation is to produce change in the client's (typically the student) behavior within the context of social, emotional, and educational domains (Sheridan & Kratochwill, 1991). As discussed in Chapter 6, there may be ecological factors contributing to the client's behaviors. Consequently, the behavioral intervention may focus on the environment as well (Gettinger, 1988). A secondary goal of behavioral consultation is to promote changes on the part of the consultee (usually the teacher). This may involve enhancing the consultees' knowledge base or range of skills (Kratochwill & Bergan, 1990) to addresses an immediate and also perhaps future need. Within this framework, the client is likely to be the beneficiary of behavioral consultation by empowering the consultee with a new repertoire of skills (Sheridan & Kratochwill, 1991). Typically, the types of interventions recommended by the consultant include (1) behavioral management techniques for modifying students' inappropriate behaviors; (2) strategies for modifying instruction, curriculum, and evaluation/grading procedures; (3) ways of adapting the learning environment; and (4) facilitating home/school partnerships.

The goals of behavioral consultation may also be expanded to include producing organizational change (Sheridan & Kratochwill, 1991). This typically involves promoting effective communication and problem-solving skills of individuals within the learning environment through staff development. In this way, a consultant enhances the skills of educators in areas such as communication between administrators and teachers or teachers and parents. This approach may also focus on training educators how to use problem-solving steps to address issues or difficulties encountered in the school setting. The consultant may facilitate organizational change by utilizing an ecological or systems approach, identifying available resources within the school that could be used to address a need. Here a systemic analysis and examination of human resources, technology, information, physical, and financial resources might be utilized in developing a school-based intervention or program (Driscoll, 1984; Maher & Bennett, 1984). For example, the consultant may identify two school-based needs: (1) the need for peer-mediated intervention in a special education classroom and (2) the need for mental health programming to enhance students' self-esteem. The consultant may then coordinate a peer-tutoring program with the school counselor and special educator to provide positive, esteem-building experiences for students serving as peer tutors with students with severe disabilities. In this way, the systemic needs of the special education teacher and school counselor are met while meeting the needs of students.

Resource/Consulting Teacher. The *resource/consulting teacher (R/CT)* (Idol, 1989) can provide both direct and indirect services. Typically, direct services are provided by a special education teacher in support settings such as a resource room. The R/CT conducts a variety of assessment measures (see Chapter 6) to plan and deliver instructional and/or behavioral interventions in the support setting. Generalization of newly acquired skills is monitored by the R/CT as students are integrated into mainstream settings. The responsibilities of the R/CT require a portion of the day to be allocated for indirect services. The types of indirect services offered by the R/CT are many, and include (1) conducting ecological assessments, (2) developing and implementing alternative instruction and curricula (3) assisting and supporting classroom teachers through consultation, and (4) monitoring student progress. Indirect services may also include implementing peer-mediated interventions (see Chapter 7), developing and conducting staff development, and establishing home/school programs (see Chapter 10).

A resource/consultant teacher consults with two classroom teachers who are team teaching.

Whether using a behavioral consultant or resource/consulting teacher, there are a number of precepts that both the consultant and the consultee must keep in mind (Reynolds & Birch, 1988). Classroom teachers seeking consultative assistance are ultimately in charge of the student, situation, and collaborative problem-solving procedure. While both parties have diverse expertise and knowledge bases, the two parties are co-equals, and therefore status problems (e.g., tenure, years of experience, advanced degrees) should not arise. A menu of alternatives, rather than a single plan, must be generated and considered. The focus of the problem solving should be on the student and/or instructional situation. Written action plans outlining goals, methods, and responsibilities should serve as a contractual agreement. Finally, a consultee has the right and obligation to share evaluative observations and conclusions with the consultee.

Peer Collaborative Consultation.   We do not wish to imply that educational partnerships can be accomplished only through the direct participation of special support personnel such as special education teachers or school psychologists. On the contrary, the *peer collaborative consultation* approach exemplifies the fact that many teachers have the expertise and knowledge base to provide assistance to their peers. In this approach, classroom teachers meet with a peer to utilize a structured dialogue consisting of self-questioning, summarization, and prediction as a means of generating classroom interven-

Spotlight: Resource Programming and Direct/Indirect Consultation

Schulte, Osborne, and McKinney (1990) randomly selected and placed a total of sixty-seven students with learning disabilities from eleven elementary schools into one of four service delivery programs: resource once a day (RR1), resource twice a day (RR2), consultation with direct instruction by a special education teacher in a mainstream setting (C/D), and consultation with indirect services (C/I). The Woodcock-Johnson Tests of Achievement were used as a pre- and post-intervention norm-referenced measure. A criterion-referenced reading test developed by the school district was used as a post-intervention measure. Teacher satisfaction was assessed by using the Consultation Evaluation Questionnaire (Erchul, 1987). In both the C/D and C/I conditions, consultants worked with classroom teachers to identify instructional and behavioral objectives as well as develop curriculum and lessons. In the C/D setting, the consultant also provided direct instruction to individual or small groups of students in the classroom that included those with and without learning disabilities. The C/I intervention employed traditional, triadic consultation programming in which the teacher and consultant met to plan interventions and strategies implemented by the teacher. Results from a multivariate, repeated-measure, analysis of variance revealed that while students in all groups improved from pre-testing to post-testing, students in the C/D group made greater overall academic gains than the RR1 group. There were no significant differences between groups on the criterion-referenced measures. Responses on the CEQ revealed positive teacher attitudes toward both the C/I and C/D approaches. Results suggest that teachers in the C/D group perceived student outcomes to be significantly higher than teachers in the C/I group. The results of this study suggest that a resource/consultant teacher approach to service delivery contributed to the academic growth of students with learning disabilities and was viewed positively by classroom teachers.

tions for dealing with academic and behavior problems (Johnson & Pugach, 1991; Pugach & Johnson, 1988). Results from one investigation (Johnson & Pugach, 1991) suggested that this approach was effective in promoting greater tolerance for students of lesser cognitive abilities and generating classroom interventions. Participating teachers in the study reported that 86 percent of the strategies generated during the peer consultation were effective, resulting in a referral of only five of seventy students for consideration in special education programs. Using the peer collaboration approach as a model, a group of special education teachers created a structured dialogue protocol sheet known as the Cooperative Options Outcome Planner, or CO-OP (see Figure 8–1), that could be used by any combination of two individuals

---

COLLABORATIVE OPTIONS - OUTCOME PLANNER

Student's Name _____   Date _____

Parent's Name _____   Grade _____ Age _____

Parent's Phone # _____   Form Completed by _____

1. How would the situation/behavior be described? What are the antecedents?	2. What has been tried before to resolve the situation and what were the results?
3. Where and when does the situation or behavior take place and how long has it been occurring?	4. What is (or has been) an area of strength for the individual(s) involved?
5. What appears to motivate the person(s) involved and could this be used as a reinforcer?	6. What others are involved and how are they involved?

Figure 8 –1
Structured Dialogue Protocol Sheet

7. Describe/operationalize the desired outcome/behavior that includes criteria.	8. Brainstorm options:
9. How will progress be measured and recorded?	10. What roles and responsibilities will each participant have for implementation?
11. When and where will the follow up meeting take place?	12. Who should attend the next meeting?

Follow up meeting held on: _____

Report of outcomes:	Continued plan of action:

Figure 8–1
continued

(teacher-teacher, specialist-teacher, teacher-parent, specialist-specialist) to facilitate peer collaboration (Welch et al., 1990). The use of the CO-OP is not limited to student or academic matters. The form can be used to facilitate problem solving in an array of situations that include personal interactions with other individuals.

Activity 8–1

Conduct a simulated peer collaboration interaction with the Cooperative Options Outcome Planner (Figure 8–1), using either or both of the scenarios provided below. Assign one individual to play the role of the consultee and the other to play the role of the facilitator.

Scenario A [SPECIALIST-TO-TEACHER]

A classroom teacher is concerned about Johnny, an average, bright fifth grader who consistently forgets to bring any or all of his homework for any subject back to school. The teacher has called and written notes to the parents, who were supportive and appreciative of her concern and efforts. The problem, however, persists. The teacher has tried to use a point system to reinforce Johnny's desired behavior, but this doesn't seem to help. The teacher is consulting with the specialist for ideas.

Scenario B [SPECIALIST-TO-SPECIALIST]

A special education teacher consults with another special education teacher about a concern she has regarding the overbearing and somewhat abrasive conduct of a novice school psychologist during IEP meetings. In an attempt to "speed things up," the school psychologist often dominates the discussion instead of using effective interpersonal communication skills. Overwhelmed with a large caseload, he essentially "rattles off" test scores before running out the door, without participating in any further discussion. The concerned specialist has made subtle comments to the school psychologist during informal, casual conversation. When this didn't work, she asked the district supervisor to discuss the matter directly with him. The problem persists, but the special education teacher is worried that she will anger or alienate the school psychologist if she confronts him directly. The concerned specialist is at a loss as to what she should do and has sought the assistance of her friend and colleague.

1. To what extent did the consultee generate her own solutions?

2. Were appropriate interpersonal communication skills used during the process? If so, provide specific examples.

3. Did the protocol of the reflective dialogue keep the individuals focused on the task?

Guidelines for Establishing School-Based Consultation Programs

The following list of guidelines is a composite of recommendations to consider when establishing school-based consultation programs. These four areas, while not an exhaustive list of suggestions, are comprised of empirically based strategies (Idol, 1988; Zins et al., 1991) for practitioners and administrators.

System Entry. It is important to remember that implementation of an innovative service delivery within an existing system is a process. The process will require gaining initial support for the consulting program through changing perceptions and expectations on the part various constituencies within the school. An understanding of the existing cultural variables discussed in Chapter 5 is an important prerequisite. An awareness of the values, norms, and overall climate of the school, as well as knowing who the formal and informal leaders are, will facilitate efforts to solicit support from administration and the teacher constituency. Zins and Curtis (1984) suggested the following steps when seeking administrative support:

1. Involve all relevant administrators (e.g., building principal, district program coordinator).

2. Present a rationale for the consultation program.

3. Describe the types of data to be collected for program evaluation.

4. Establish formal and informal contractual agreements outlining the consultation services.

5. Plan for ongoing review and renegotiation.

6. Maintain open lines of communication.

7. Develop a formal job description of the consultant's role, responsibilities, and caseload.

The importance of this last step merits a closer examination. Clearly articulating the roles and responsibilities associated with consultation in a written job description is critical whether the program is to be delivered by a resource teacher, school psychologist, school counselor, or classroom teacher. A written job description that outlines duties and caseloads may minimize a number of potential barriers to implementing school-based consultation programs. Studies have shown that administrators' and classroom teachers' perceptions and expectations of resource teachers are largely incongruent with their actual practices (Dugoff, Ives, & Shotel, 1985; Friend & McNutt, 1987). Typically, administrators assume resource teachers will consult with teachers and parents *in addition* to their other direct service responsibilities. Despite an implicit expectation of resource teachers serving as consultants, many resource/consultant teachers are not given the opportunity to consult (Idol-Maestas & Ritter, 1985). This is largely due to teachers' misunderstanding of consultation and lack of time.

A job description should delineate the percentage of time a resource/consulting teacher is expected to engage in direct service and consultative service. Idol (1988) suggested that resource teachers who provide consultative services exclusively may be expected to serve up to thirty-five students. However, educators providing direct and indirect services might be expected to serve ten students during 50 percent time assignments for direct services and eighteen students during 50 percent time allotted for consultation, resulting in a total caseload of twenty-eight students (Idol, 1988). Individual states delineate caseloads, and job descriptions should comply with those guidelines. In addition to determining caseloads, direct services should be clearly defined. Typically, direct services include conducting formal/informal assessments, providing small-group instruction in special and/or mainstream settings, team teaching, and managing students' *individualized education programs* (IEPs). Indirect services should be outlined to include responsibilities such as classroom observation, one-on-one consultation with teachers and parents, and conducting staff-development programs. Securing the support of the faculty and other staff may best be initiated through an orientation presentation during a faculty meeting. The presentation should be informal and collegial, avoiding complex terminology. Specific topics should include a rationale for the consultation program (preferably presented by the building administrator), a definition and description of the consultation program, an overview of the collaborative problem-solving process, procedural steps for requesting assistance, and an opportunity to address any questions or concerns that might be raised (Zins et al., 1991). An additional goal of the presentation is to change teachers' existing perceptions and expectations of support-service personnel. An effective presentation will articulate the complementary role of the consultant working *with* teachers in meeting the needs of students at risk rather than perpetuating traditional roles and responsibilities associated with direct service delivery in segregated settings. In this way, teachers should come to see the consultant as a resource to them as well as to students with special needs.

Establishing Requests for Assistance.   An efficient procedure for requesting consultant assistance must be established. A central location, typically the administration office, should house a request form. This form should provide basic demographic data, including the name of the person requesting assistance, the date, and a general description of the situation including where and when it occurs (see Figure 8–2). A well-organized request form can be used throughout the entire consultation process by including additional space to record preliminary data collection (observation, interviews), ecological assessment data, and the actual action plan developed during the collaborative process. A final section is delineated for outcome and evaluation information. The entire two-sided form can be easily filed. The form also serves as documentation if formal referral is made for individual assessment of a student to determine eligibility for special education is deemed necessary.

Scheduling.   As discussed in Chapter 1, scheduling adequate time for educators to consult with each other is a major barrier to establishing and

Teacher's Name _____

Student's Name _____

Date _____ Grade _____ Subject Area _____ Room # _____

_____

Briefly list and describe the concerns you have for this student:

1.

2.

3.

4.

Of the concerns listed above, which <u>one</u> do you see as a priority?

At what specific time and location does the situation occur?

Regarding this situation/concern, what is (are) your goal(s)?

When is your preparation period or a convenient day/date and time to meet to discuss your concerns?

Day(s)/Date(s):   Period(s)/Time(s):

PLEASE TURN TO THE OTHER SIDE OF THIS PAGE

Figure 8–2
Request for Consultation Form

Action Plan

What has been tried previously to address this situation/concern, and what was the outcome(s)?

List possible alternatives/interventions:

Which of these interventions would you like to implement?

Observable objective:

Begin Date: _____   Follow up date: _____

Date of actual follow-up meeting: _____

Outcomes:

Revised action plan:

Figure 8–2
continued

implementing this type of educational partnership. A number of scheduling strategies (Idol, 1988; Pugach & Johnson, 1988; West & Idol, 1990) are presented in Table 8–1 for consideration. While some of these suggestions may not be feasible nor even necessary for a given school, they are included as possible options.

Program Evaluation.   Finally, a comprehensive evaluation plan must be developed to assess the impact of the consultation program. Collecting accountability data is useful here to (1) determine the impact of service through the assessment of outcome variables; (2) gather information about program strengths, needs, and areas in need of modification; (3) obtain information about consumer satisfaction; (4) assist with professional development; 5) chart progress toward program goals; and 6) determine patterns in the use of services (Zins & Curtis, 1984, p. 232).

Table 8–1   Scheduling Options for Implementing Consultation Programs

1. Employ a group of floating substitutes on a regular basis.
2. Rotate teaching responsibilities with consultation by scheduling certain days or portions of days (e.g., Monday mornings and Wednesday afternoons) for consultation and the remaining time for teaching.
3. At elementary schools, assign a consultant to a specific grade or cluster of grades (e.g., one special education teacher to work with grades K–3, another with grades 4–6).
4. At secondary settings, assign a consultant to one specific course and/or department at a time (e.g., one special education teacher to work directly with teachers in the science departments while another works exclusively with the English department).
5. Schedule special education teachers to "cover" general classrooms so classroom teachers can meet together. This also allows specialists an opportunity to observe students at risk in natural settings as well as to gain insights regarding the demands of the environment.
6. Schedule the building principal or support personnel (e.g., school counselor, social worker, school psychologist) to regularly conduct enrichment activities in a classroom setting.
7. Schedule specialized, departmental activities (e.g., art, P.E., music) or films/guest speakers for a large group of students to allow teachers in other departments time to meet.
8. Cluster larger groups of students working cooperatively or independently on similar assignments in a common setting (e.g., library, multipurpose room).
9. Utilize paraprofessionals and/or volunteers (e.g., parents/grandparents, community/ business leaders, retired teachers).
10. Alter the school-day schedule (e.g., one Friday afternoon each month, extend the school day for teachers by thirty minutes).
11. Designate one day per week or grading period for collaboration.

Idol (1988) conceptualized an evaluation process consisting of three components that would enable administrators and program coordinators to collect accountability data. The first component focuses on the *input variables* that contribute to the development of the program. The second examines *process variables* associated with the operation of the consultation program. The final component is concerned with assessing *program outcomes.*

Input Variables

Identifying input variables involves recognizing the antecedent conditions within the school that prompted the decision to develop a consultation program. Some examples of contributing factors include the number of requests for student referral to special education, instructional or classroom management styles of teachers, and the location and duration of specific problems (such as aggressive student behaviors on the playground or poor reading achievement in a specific grade). This phase is important, as these variables may ultimately serve as goals. For example, an existing condition of an inordinate number of requests for student referral to special education might be translated into a goal of reducing that number by 20 percent for one academic year.

Process Variables

Program evaluation must include assessing the process variables that affect the consultation program in operation. This is *formative evaluation* and involves examining factors such as the knowledge base of the consultant and consultee, the quality of interpersonal interactions, turnaround time following a request for assistance, the amount of time allotted and actually used for consultation, and the logistical coordination of program implementation. An example of assessing process variables (like expediency of response) is when the consultant records both the date and time a request for assistance is made and the date and time consultation occurs. Surveys and observations are utilized periodically to gauge the type and frequency of specific interpersonal communication skills exhibited during consultation.

Program Outcomes

There are a number of subdivisions that fall under program outcomes that can be used to evaluate consultation programs (Maher & Bennett, 1984). As mentioned, antecedent conditions listed as input variables can often be translated into goals used to assess program outcomes. Typically, this kind of *summative evaluation* focuses on goals related to improving student behavior and academic achievement (Fuchs et al., 1992). Program evaluation should also assess satisfaction of teachers (Zins et al., 1991). The types of procedures commonly used to measure these outcomes include teacher ratings, systematic observations, tests, interviews, and questionnaires (Fuchs et al., 1992). The *Consultation Evaluation Questionnaire* (Erchul, 1987) is a reliable and succinct instrument that measures three aspects of consultation programming: consultant characteristics, consultation process, and consultation outcomes. Another possible instrument is a twenty-item acceptability rating scale for consultation methods and procedures that was adapted from Von Brock and Elliott (1987).

Zins et al. (1991) included other operational goals that could be used as outcome-based measures of consultation programs. One is to minimize the number of students placed into special education programs by providing pre-referral services in classroom settings. The example in Figure 8–3 illustrates how outcome-based measures, coupled with accountability data, can be used to evaluate programs. Tracking the number of referrals and actual placements is a relatively easy measurement that can be used. Other methods include determining the number of requests for consultation and the number of completed psychoeducational evaluations. A related outcome-based goal is to enhance the skills of classroom teachers in meeting the individual needs of students at risk. Finally, the evaluation process must assess the cost effectiveness of the consultation program. Utilizing accumulated process-variable data, program developers can determine the cost effectiveness in terms of time and money expended on assistance in contrast to psychoeducational evaluation and actual placement into special education programs.

Figure 8–3
Program
Evaluation
Form

Task Force Committee Members:
    S. MARTIN   T. CHIN
    R. CAMPOS   D. SMITH

Identified Area(s) of Need/Concern:

1. # OF REFERRALS TO SPECIAL ED.

2. STUDENT PERFORMANCE ON MATH + READING CRITERION-REFERENCE TESTS

3.

Program Objectives:

1. REDUCE REFERRALS

2. INCREASE C.R.T. TEST SCORES

3.

Proposed Program Components:

1. SP ED TEACHER/CONSULTANT SUPERVISE 5 INSTRUCTIONAL ASSISTANTS WHO PROVIDE REVIEW

2. OUTCOME BASED EDUC + CROSS-GRADE GROUPING

3.

Figure 8–3
continued

Program Initiation Date: ___8/25/93___

Formative Operations Evaluation Date: ___11/22/93___

To what extent have program components been implemented to meet objectives?

Objective #1:   INST. ASST. HIRED & TRAINED

Objective #2:   O.B.E. INITIATED WITH CROSS-GROUPS

Objective #3:

_____

Summative Evaluation Date: ___5/25/94___

Outcome #1:   REFERRALS REDUCED BY 56%.

Outcome #2:   SIGNIF. GAINS IN MATH & READING IN GRADES
1, 5 & 6 – OTHER GRADES REMAIN SAME

Outcome #3:   TEACHER SATISFACTION SURVEYS GENERALLY
POSITIVE WITH LOGISTICAL SUGGESTIONS

Conclusions/recommendations:
EXAMINE GRADES 2, 3, & 4 INST. &
CURRIC. PROGRAMS

Team Teaching

A collaborative approach to managing learning environments with a diverse student population is *team teaching,* the joint responsibility of instruction by the simultaneous presence of more than one teacher (Bauwens, Hourcade, & Friend, 1989). Whereas team teaching does not meet the criteria of indirect service of collaborative consultation (West & Idol, 1990), it does reflect the basic tenets of the collaborative ethic and educational partnerships. In contrast to traditional "pull-out" programming where students receive services in segregated settings, team teaching may be thought of as "pull-in programs" where services are delivered jointly in mainstream settings (Gelzheiser & Meyers, 1990; Meyers, Gelzheiser, & Yelich, 1991). Team teaching is often a dynamic process in which ongoing modifications in instruction or curricula are made as roles and responsibilities of teachers evolve from class to class and from day to day (Nowacek, 1992). Typically, educators share teaching responsibility for instruction in a given academic subject such as reading or math for specific times each day. Teams consisting of general education teachers and special education teachers have been effective at the elementary level (Adamson, Cox, & Schuller, 1989; Adamson, Matthews, & Schuller, 1990; Self et al., 1991) and the secondary level (Harris, Harvey, Garcia, Innes, Lynn, Munoz, Sexton, & Stoica, 1988). As well as potential benefits to students, team teaching is advantageous to teachers in many ways. First, the presence of two professionals reduces the teacher-student ratio. Second, attempting to individualize instruction to meet the array of needs for a diverse group of students is logistically more feasible when two teachers are involved. Third, educators can enrich their own professional skills by observing each other. Finally, team teaching allows specialists to gain insight into the demands of general classroom settings while classroom teachers become sensitized to the needs of individual students and the challenges faced by specialists.

Team teaching, however, is not limited to general classroom teachers nor to classroom settings. A critical and often overlooked resource is the school librarian. Wesson and Keefe (1989) described how media specialists and special education teachers collaboratively developed and implemented a comprehensive model for teaching students library skills. The program involved assessing student needs, setting objectives, providing instruction with modification when necessary, and monitoring student progress.

There are three fundamental ways in which educators can provide instruction collaboratively in a learning environment: co-teaching, complementary instruction, and supportive learning activities (Bauwens et al., 1989). A traditional form of team teaching is *co-teaching*, which is defined as an instructional approach wherein two or more professionals share the responsibility of planning and delivering instruction and evaluation of student progress. While the members of the teaching team come to the classroom with their own skills and expertise, the team does not implement any special interventions or techniques that enhance the regular curriculum nor provide support for students experiencing difficulty.

Complementary instruction is a procedure in which the regular instruction delivered by the classroom teacher is "complemented" by supplementary resources and strategies provided by another professional. An example of this approach is when a specialist provides instruction on strategic interventions such as note-taking and essay composition skills that can empower *all* of the students in the classroom to meet the demands and expectations of the classroom teacher. A key characteristic to this type of team teaching is the maintenance of traditional roles. A specialist often provides the "complementary" instruction and usually has no other responsibilities in the classroom, while the classroom teacher maintains his or her primary role and responsibility of organizing the class, supervising instruction, establishing and maintaining classroom policies/procedures, and student evaluation. This approach can also serve as a form of micro-level staff development as teachers assimilate and implement new skills and strategies that are modeled in their classroom.

Supportive learning activities are provided by all members of the teaching team to students who are academically at risk or have disabilities requiring

Spotlight: Stratisticians and Team Teaching at the Secondary Level

The University of Utah developed a program designed to prepare "stratisticians" for educational partnerships in secondary settings (Welch & Williams, 1991). Teachers were trained how to create and implement learning strategies that could be co-taught in mainstream classrooms by classroom teachers and specialists using content from the course. As part of this program, a special education teacher used the Instructional Priority System (Welch & Link, 1991) to conduct an ecological assessment of a middle-school English class that included several students with learning disabilities. After written expression was chosen as a priority (identified in collaboration with the English teacher) the specialist provided complimentary instruction. Specifically, the PLEASE strategy for written expression (Welch & Link, 1990) was taught in the mainstream setting using class content. An analysis of pre- and post-intervention writing samples revealed a significant improvement in paragraph composition by students with and without learning disabilities. Following the complementary instruction, the English teacher adopted the strategy, which has allowed the special education teacher serving as stratistician to move to another classroom setting (Welch & Chisholm, in review).

additional support. Each member of the teaching team takes a turn at providing direct supplementary instruction to students at risk in the mainstream learning environment while the other team member works with and supervises the larger group. Special education and classroom teachers have successfully implemented supportive learning activities in reading and math instruction to students without disabilities, students academically at risk, and students with disabilities. Among the numerous benefits of this approach are (1) it prevents significant numbers of students from being inappropriately labeled as disabled, (2) it increases teacher skills, and (3) it provides teachers from both disciplines insight into the realities of their counterpart's responsibilities (Adamson et al., 1990; Adamson et al., 1989; Meyers et al., 1991). Self et al. (1991) described a cooperative teaching project in which the focus was prevention and support rather than remediation. Classroom teachers were primarily responsible for meeting the needs of students who were at risk while special education teachers, Chapter 1 teachers, and speech/language specialists provided direct supplementary support in the classroom. This approach of collaborative teaching resulted in significant gains for *all* students as the majority of students reached or surpassed district expectations without being classified or placed in segregated special education settings.

Guidelines for Developing Team Teaching.   The development of team-taught pull-in programs requires adequate time, ideally an entire year, for preparation and planning (Gelzheiser & Meyers, 1990). The following guidelines for establishing and maintaining team teaching have been collected from a variety of resources (Brann, Loghlin, & Kimball, 1991; Gelzheiser & Meyers, 1990; Nowacek, 1992) and are summarized here.

Scheduling

There are two important scheduling factors to consider when developing team-teaching programs. One, educators interested in team teaching must secure release time from other responsibilities. Typically, a special education teacher or school psychologist must find "windows of opportunities" within existing time frames. This includes allocating adequate preparation and conferencing time. Two, the team of teachers must confer with school administration and personnel directly involved in scheduling students class assignments. A logistically feasible number of students who would benefit most from being placed in a team taught classroom must be collaboratively identified and scheduled for that setting.

Defining Roles and Responsibilities

After educators have scheduled time to plan, they must clearly identify and articulate who is going to do what. This discussion is largely dependent on each participants' expertise and background. A number of questions must be addressed: Will one or both create lesson plans? Will both share instructional tasks with at risk students? Will the group of students be divided, or will both teachers serve all students by taking turns or "floating"? Who will determine classroom rules and implement discipline policies? What are the evaluation criteria and procedures, and will they be shared, divided, or remain the primary responsibility of one teacher? Will the classroom teacher focus on content while the specialist concentrates on strategies and remedial techniques? It is suggested that these types of questions and their answers be recorded on paper for future reference.

Identifying Potential Problems

To a large extent, identifying potential problems will transpire over the course of addressing the types of questions and issues just enumerated. However, many potential problems may be student-related and based on specific needs of the student. In this respect, the background and expertise of a specialist plays an important role in the planning process. Specifically, the classroom teacher must be apprised of the unique needs and characteristics of a student with disabilities that may affect the instructional process or environment by the specialist. Naturally, unexpected situations will arise, and both educators must clearly articulate a time, place, and procedure for collaborative problem solving.

Planning, Monitoring, and Modifying Instruction and Curriculum

Educators must review and determine what instructional format will be used at specific times and with particular curriculum. The team must consider how materials and instructional activities might be modified to meet the needs of students at risk. Instructional format will depend largely on the instructional task and objectives. Many of the types of strategies described in Chapter 7 might be considered for implementation.

Evaluating Team Teaching

Finally, the team must consider how the team teaching will be evaluated. A number of dimensions must be considered. First, the team must determine to what extent students successfully achieved academic and behavioral objectives. This can be accomplished through curriculum-based or criterion-referenced testing. Second, student and parent satisfaction of the team-teaching process must be considered. Surveys or interviews are relatively easy ways to implement such an assessment. It may be feasible to consider soliciting the assistance of other professionals such as counselors or administrators to facilitate this process. Third, the teachers must honestly assess their own performance and satisfaction of team teaching through discussion. It might be helpful for teachers to initially plan specific goals and objectives that can be used during the evaluation dialogue.

Potential Barriers to Team Teaching. Despite the potential benefits of team teaching, Bauwens et al. (1989) identified three potential barriers. First, time is most often cited as the greatest obstacle to team-teaching. Despite this concern, research has shown that pull-in programs conducted through team teaching actually increase teacher collaboration and interaction through brief meetings (Meyers et al., 1991). Implementation of creative scheduling strategies, as will be described in detail here, may minimize or circumvent time factors that impede team teaching. Second, a lack of cooperation is another potential obstacle. Developing a partnership can be intimidating, as it is a radical departure from the traditional, autonomous practice of teaching. Attitudes based on traditional roles of teaching are challenged by team teaching whereby teachers adopt new functions (Meyers et al., 1991). It is important to provide teachers with training directly related to educational partnerships that reflect the collaborative ethic prior to implementation of any team teaching. Third, teachers often express concern over increased workloads. This may be due to a perception based on traditional roles on the part of teachers that team teaching is an additional responsibility that will require additional work. This concern is usually resolved after teachers begin to adjust to their new roles and responsibilities.

A potential danger of team teaching is the misuse of having another professional in the room. Team teaching does not mean that teachers mutually agree to divide the curriculum lesson by lesson so that one is responsible for delivering the lesson and the other is free to leave the room to carry out other activities. Such an arrangement usurps the intent of sharing expertise and resources and is more like "tag-team teaching." Another plausible risk is the possibility of stigmatizing students who receive side-by-side programming within a mainstream setting. It has been reported, however, that this does not often occur when specialists are perceived as normal fixtures within the classroom, providing support services to all students (Gelzheiser & Meyers, 1990). Other issues that must be considered and addressed are related to delegating responsibilities. Using effective communication and conflict-management skills, issues such as grades, evaluation criteria, classroom rules, and discipline procedures must be discussed early in the planning and development phases of team teaching.

Scheduling and Managing Team Teaching

Perhaps one of the greatest challenges to team teaching has been the fact that administrators and teachers have clung to traditional methods of scheduling and classroom management. As much as educators may advocate for collaboration, they lament that the existing system will not allow it. In other words, teachers are not "freed" from their duties to work with colleagues. Teaming traditionally has been a logistical challenge because administrators and teachers continue to perceive delivery of services as something that occurs in specialized and segregated environments.

The *double class roll* approach places two teachers, often a general education and a special education teacher, in a single classroom. Each teacher has his or her own roll, or roster, of students. Each is primarily responsible for those students. A small number of students receiving special education support are on the special education teacher's roll but are receiving the direct services in a mainstream setting. The double roll allows a special education teacher to work collaboratively with a classroom teacher in a mainstream setting while still providing direct services to students with individualized education programs (IEPs). There are, essentially, two "classes" with two teachers within one learning environment. Again, a potential risk for the double-roll approach is to delegate roles and responsibilities in such a way that the classroom teacher works only with the typical students while the specialist interacts only with the students who have IEPs. Ideally, students are unaware of the separate class lists as teachers exchange teaching responsibilities so that each works with typical and atypical students. This in effect, creates a "double *role.*"

Effective instructional techniques combined with enhanced collaboration and communication allow teaching teams to provide direct services to students at risk in mainstream settings. Through observation and data collection, educators are empowered to make informed decisions in terms of the effectiveness of interventions. When performance data suggests that students are experiencing difficulty, the team of teachers may choose to seek the additional support and input of a case-management team (Self et al., 1991), described next.

Macro-Level School-Based Partnerships

A one-on-one relationship between two professionals, such as consultation or co-teaching, is a viable form of educational partnerships. There are, however, circumstances and situations in which a team approach may be more appropriate. Our discussion now moves from the micro-level of classroom environments in which teachers work in tandem with another professional to an examination of partnerships within the broader context of the school building. Here, at the macro-level, teams or groups of professionals collaborate to provide services to students at risk.

Case-Management Teams

A systematic process in which a support service network provides assistance to individuals seeking help is defined as *case management* (Weil, Karls, & Associates, 1985). A number of approaches have been developed in which teams of professionals design and implement service delivery (Morsink, Thomas, & Correa, 1991; Nevin & Thousand, 1986). While each type of case-management team shares some characteristics, each differs in terms of member composition and objectives. For example, the objective of some case-management teams is to develop interventions that will reduce the number of inappropriate referrals of students to special education. Another type of team may actually manage the case or educational program of students who are eligible for special education services. The common element threaded through all case-management teams is the collaborative process of a small group of individuals to develop and implement support services to teachers and students. Examples of these teams follow.

Teacher Assistance Teams.   A peer-support system for teachers utilizing systematic problem solving steps is a *teacher assistance team* (TAT) (Chalfant, VanDusenPysh, & Moultrie, 1979). A parent, teacher, or even student who is encountering academic or behavioral difficulty may request the assistance of the TAT. The TAT is generally comprised of three to four classroom teachers who are appointed, elected, or volunteer to serve on the committee. These members should have classroom experience, knowledge of curriculum and materials, and interest and skills in learning and behavior problems and individualizing instruction. They should demonstrate respect for peers and parents, and employ effective interpersonal communication skills (Chalfant et al., 1979). Typically, building administrators are not members of the TAT, although they may occasionally observe or be consulted by the team. Similarly, specialists such as special education teachers, counselors, and school psychologists do not usually participate as team members. These specialists may be invited by the TAT to periodically attend meetings when a unique situation that merits their expertise is addressed. The rationale for the makeup of classroom teachers is to create a sense of ownership and responsibility for the student and situation.

One member of the TAT serves as the team leader or case manager to schedule, coordinate, and facilitate the team's meetings and activities. After an individual completes an initial request for assistance form, the team leader reviews the information and informally meets with the person seeking assistance. A team meeting is scheduled, at which time the team leader reports the student's strengths and weaknesses, what type of interventions have been implemented thus far, and any other pertinent information such as test scores or observation data. The team follows the basic format of the collaborative process described in Chapter 3, or similar type of protocol such as the CO-OP form presented earlier in Figure 8–1. A secretary records possible interventions generated during brainstorming. Once the individual requesting assistance selects an intervention, the team collectively develops an action plan that includes evaluation criteria.

Activity 8–2

Using the collaborative process forms presented in Chapter 3 or the protocol of the CO-OP form presented in Figure 8–1, conduct a simulated TAT meeting. Assign individuals to play the role of the teacher seeking assistance, the role of TAT leader, and at least two other team members who are classroom teachers. Assume that the teacher requesting assistance has already met with the team leader for preliminary data collection and discussion of the following situation:

Ms. Heber is a young, first-year, single teacher at Kennedy Elementary School, which is located in a rural school district. Jack is a bright, well-behaved student who attempted to "set her up" with a young, single male friend of his family. At first, Ms. Heber thought Jack's good intentions were somewhat humorous and didn't take the situation seriously. Jack persisted in his efforts. Ms. Heber tried to explain she was appreciative of his efforts, but that she already had a boyfriend. She thought about calling his parents to discuss the situation, but was afraid that this would only make things worse. Jack became resentful and began to stop doing his work and became resistant and belligerent in class. He began to gain support and empathy from his classmates as they all wondered why "Ms. Heber hates Jack." Ms. Heber was very concerned about Jack and how the rest of the class was reacting, so she requested assistance from the school's TAT.

1. Did the TAT members effectively follow the general operating procedures for meetings?

2. Was effective interpersonal communication used throughout the meeting?

3. Was a plan of action consisting of specific objectives and and evaluation criteria generated?

Note: The authors wish to acknowledge John Mayhew for his assistance in providing this actual scenario.

Chalfant and Van Dusen Pysh (1989) reported the results of five program development studies that were conducted in seven states to identify effectiveness and challenges of ninety-six teacher-assistant teams that were in the their first year of operation. They reported that TATs can (1) improve student performance through a collaborative problem-solving approach with teachers; (2) create strategies for students without disabling conditions; (3) help teachers serving students with disabilities in mainstream settings who are also receiving additional pull-out services; and (4) serve as an effective screening device for referrals to special education. The teams were effective in reducing the number of referrals to special education as well as promoting faculty morale and communication. Teachers were, for the most part, satisfied with TATs, but problems and concerns were evident as well. Some teachers were perceived as being unwilling to admit that a problem existed and consequently reluctant to seek assistance or share their concerns with colleagues. Others were resistant to the additional responsibilities and accountability associated with serving on a TAT. Finally, many faculties did not appear to understand the role of the TAT or were not receptive to the idea.

Six recommendations for improving TAT effectiveness emerged from the data obtained from the ninety-six teams. These are summarized in Table 8–2.

Table 8–2   Recommendations for Improving TAT Effectiveness

Administrative Support

1. Building principals must provide overt support by providing adequate and regular time periods for team meetings.
2. Building principals must publically advocate utilization of the TAT as well as provide incentives and reinforcement for participants.
3. District and building administration must allow three to four years for a TAT to become an accepted and integral part of the educational community.

Faculty Support

1. TATs are more effective when the faculty are given an opportunity to accept or reject implementation of the program.
2. An effective adoption process involves providing training to the entire faculty, then allowing a vote for faculty members who choose to be placed on a ballot for election by their peers.
3. If training the entire faculty is not feasible, a one-hour orientation presentation may be useful in recruiting potentially interested individuals who may be willing to receive training.

Training

1. All TATs must receive training to ensure effective and efficient operation.
2. Training should provide hands-on experience in
   a. Analyzing problems.
   b. Establishing intervention goals.
   c. Effective communication.
   d. Efficient team-meeting management.

Team Procedures

1. Duration of TAT meetings should be no more than forty-five minutes.
2. Agendas should be used.
3. Verbal economy must be practiced.
4. Paperwork must be minimized.
5. Procedures must be clearly understood to facilitate a streamlined meeting.
6. Weekly, regularly scheduled meetings are perceived as part of the system more so than teams that meet on an ad hoc basis.

Table 8–2   continued

Networking

1. TATs are usually more effective when ongoing support (e.g., district-level monthly meetings) is provided to discuss and resolve issues.
2. District newsletters and/or in-service programs provide TAT members the opportunity to share ideas with each other.
3. The existence and availability of a support system is more important than a specific form of the support system.

Evaluation

1. The TAT must assess to what extent the team is effective in meeting teacher and student needs through data collection (surveys, interviews) and monitoring student performance.
2. Consumer satisfaction of TAT members and the teacher constituency must be included in the evaluation process.

A function of a TAT is not necessarily limited to reactive problem solving. A TAT can be proactive by identifying current needs and issues that may be potential problems or by evaluating schoolwide efforts and programs (Heron, Drevno, & Harris, 1992). For example, a TAT might be charged to assess the

Case management teams provide support through collaborative problem solving.

impact of an after-school work-completion program. Individual members might be assigned to collect data from various teachers by examining homework records or conducting interviews.

It is important to understand what the TAT is designed to do and not to do. The fundamental purpose of the TAT and any form of preferral invention (described later) is reduce the number of inappropriate referrals for special education services through collaborative problem solving. General and special education teachers often erreoneously characterize the TAT as a "hoop to jump through" before a student can be placed in special education. This perception clearly indicates a lack of understanding of the TAT and its role. The objective of the TAT is to generate interventions that will serve as an alternative to referral and placement in special programs. Additionally, a TAT cannot determine a student's eligibility for special education by labeling a child with a disabling condition nor by placing a child in a specific support setting such as resource room. If appropriate steps have been taken by the TAT to document unsuccessful prereferral interventions, the TAT may then recommend forwarding the case to another type of case-management team known as the multidisciplinary student service-delivery team (described later).

Prereferral Intervention Teams.   Like the TAT, an objective of preferral intervention teams is to minimize the number of inappropriate referrals of students for testing and placement in special education programs. This process redirects and reallocates time, money, and resources typically used for testing to direct intervention to settings where problem arise (Ysseldyke, 1991). The goal of a prereferral intervention team is to provide interventions through an indirect service-delivery approach to meet specific student needs in classroom settings (Graden, Casey, & Christenson, 1985).

There are two fundamental differences between the prereferral intervention team and a teacher assistance team (TAT). One distinction is the composition of the team. While a TAT is generally a peer group of classroom teachers, the prereferral intervention team is multidisciplinary, comprised of professionals from various fields such as educational psychology, social work, and special education. A second difference is that while a TAT may proactively identify schoolwide issues and needs as a task force, a prereferral intervention team is generally focused on the needs of an individual student who is a likely candidate for special support services.

Lloyd, Crowley, Kohler, and Strain (1988) reviewed the literature on the effectiveness of prereferral intervention teams. Acknowledging some methodological limitations of some studies, they concluded prereferral intervention appears to be effective in reducing the number of students referred for and placed in special education programs. Harrington and Gibson (1986) reported that prereferral teams were perceived by teachers as generally being effective and helpful.

The process is similar to other problem-solving approaches described already and begins with an initial consultation in which the educator requesting assistance and the team members identify and define the problem. The prereferral team incorporates an ecological perspective in viewing student needs while analyzing the problem. After environmental variables such as the classroom, teacher, instructional format, and curricula are considered, a menu of instructionally relevant interventions is collectively generated by the team. An action plan is developed and implemented. Data are collected through observation to evaluate the effectiveness of the intervention. If the intervention is not successful, the team discusses alternatives and makes additional recommendations for further action. The team reconvenes at a later date to review the progress of the revised action plan. Decisions are made to continue the intervention, modify the intervention, or refer the student to a multidisciplinary student-service delivery team for formal psychoeducational testing to determine eligibility for special education services.

Multidisciplinary Student Service-Delivery Teams. Results of psychoeducational testing are reviewed and interpreted by a *multidisciplinary student service-delivery team* composed of teachers, parents, and support personnel. Using formal and informal information, the team determines if a student's needs merit special education support. The team establishes annual goals and short-term objectives in developing an education program (Elliott & Sheridan, 1992; Strickland & Turnbull, 1990). While developing this program, members of the team must comply with federal, state, and district guidelines as they consider eligibility and develop the instructional program known as the individualized education program (IEP). The metaphor of a football team might be used to characterize the transdisciplinary student service-delivery team as it "huddles" to plan a strategy to reach the goal. In this case, the team identifies a number of goals designed to meet the specific needs of the student. The IEP is a long-term plan of action consisting of several parts. Like a football team deep in its own territory, the team will need to "pass deep" to get to the goal on the other end of the field. The first-letter mnemonic of PASS DEEP presented in Table 8–3 is a useful strategy for recalling the components of the IEP.

The IEP has the potential of serving as an effective tool in educational partnerships. In addition to being a communication link between the school and home, it is a mechanism for determining if meaningful progress is being made toward student goals and objectives (Huefner, 1991). It is critically important to understand that the objectives enumerated on the IEP drives service delivery. The type of services necessary to meet goals and objectives will dictate where the services will be provided and by whom. These types of decisions can be made only through meaningful collaboration. Consequently, the IEP is written prior to placement. Furthermore, an IEP for students in secondary schools must also include a transition plan. This component outlines specific objectives and activities that will prepare the student for passage from the secondary school setting to post-secondary environments such as the workplace or college.

Like a football team, the multidisciplinary student service-delivery team has several members with specific roles and responsibilities. The parent is the most important member of the team, serving as participant in instructional

Table 8–3   PASS DEEP: The components of an Individual Education Plan

P = Present Levels of Performance

Results of formal and informal assessment measures are reported. This includes scores from intelligence and achievement tests as well as curriculum-based assessment.

A = Annual Goals

Three to four broad objectives, usually in the areas of academics, behavior, and life skills, are listed as general statements of expectancies.

S = Short-Term Objectives

Measurable statements of incremental goals are listed as a means of achieving annual goals. Short-term objectives are comprised of three components: behavior, condition, and duration.

S = Specific Services

Any special support services (e.g. transportation, physical therapy, or counseling) necessary to achieve annual goals are listed.

D = Dates of Service Delivery

 Projected dates of initiation and completion of services are listed.

E = Extent of Regular Classroom Participation

To establish to what extent a child is placed in the least restrictive environment with nondisabled peers, short-term objectives must indicate which activities/services designed to meet annual and short-term objectives will be delivered in mainstream settings.

E = Evaluation Criteria

Ways of meeting specific short-term objectives are clearly described in terms that are measurable and observable, using formal and informal measurement techniques.

P = Persons Responsible for Service Delivery

Individuals responsible for specific services and activities are listed within the context of each short-term objective.

decision making and advocate for his or her child. As discussed in Chapter 5, federal and state laws outline procedural safeguards that protect the student and parent throughout the instructional decision-making process. The building principal is generally designated as the *local educational agency* (LEA) representative. The administrator officially represents the school and pledges resources toward meeting IEP objectives. The school psychologist plays an important role in administering, scoring, and interpreting a variety of intelligence and psychoeducational tests. The expertise of the school psychologist is equally important in identifying resources and appropriate interventions for meetings goals on the IEP. Many times, the special educator is seen as the logistical coordinator and manager of the IEP. The classroom teacher has an equally important role in providing ecologically relevant information that will enable the team to determine integration in the least restrictive environment as well as determine specific goals and interventions that will assist the student in meeting the demands of the criterion environment, the classroom.

There is a sequence of steps for conducting the IEP conference (Strickland & Turnbull, 1990). The IEP team meeting begins with introductions, followed by a review of the agenda and an explanation of the process. The case manager conducting the meeting must also ensure that the parents understand their due process rights. The team then reviews informal and formal evaluation data to determine a student's current level of performance. If assessment results indicate the student meets eligibility criteria for support services, the team mutually identifies specific areas requiring assistance. Once this has been established, specific annual goals and short-term objectives are developed. The most appropriate settings for service delivery are identified. Persons are then listed as being responsible for the delivery of services in a particular setting.

Elliott and Sheridan (1992) reviewed the literature regarding the effectiveness of multidisciplinary service-delivery teams. In their review, a number of problems were identified. Traditionally, input from various disciplines has been disproportionate, with school psychologists and special educators contributing the most and classroom teachers and parents contributing very little. Teams often employ an unsystematic approach of collecting and interpreting diagnostic information and a loosely constructed decision-making-planning process (Pfeiffer & Hefferman, 1984). The majority of time is generally spent on diagnostic decision making, with little time allotted to developing interventions (Ysseldyke, 1983). Fiedler and Knight (1986) reported that fewer than 25 percent of diagnostic recommendations tend to make their way into IEP goals. Furthermore, decisions regarding placement often precede development of goals and service-delivery plans (McKellar, 1991; Poland, Thurlow, Ysseldyke, & Mirkin, 1982).

McKellar (1991) suggested that parents and classroom teachers be provided with a pre-IEP meeting *advance organizer* (see Table 8–4). This

---

Table 8–4   **Advance Organizers for IEP Meetings**

1. What goals do you have for the student in specific academic subjects and/or social skills? What lifelong or independent-living goals do you have for the student?
2. What specific strengths or interests does this student have that might help in reaching these goals?
3. What types of assistance and/or strategies have been used in the past to achieve the goals listed above? What worked and why? What didn't work and why?
4. What kind of assistance/resources do you think the student will need to achieve these goals?
5. What kinds of skills, information, or resources do you have that might be used to help the student achieve these goals?

Source: Adapted from McKellar, N.A. (1991). Enhancing the IEP process through consultation. *Journal of Educational and Psychological Consultation, 2*(2), 175–187.

Activity 8–3

Conduct a simulated IEP meeting. Assign individuals to play the roles of the parent(s), local educational agency representative, school psychologist, classroom teacher, and special education teacher in developing an individual education plan for Janie. Use a variety of strategies and techniques described in this chapter to conduct an efficient and supportive meeting. The following information will be adequate in developing an IEP that addresses at least one annual goal for Janie:

Janie's chronological age is nine years and six months. Her current grade placement is the first grade. Her full-scale intelligence score is 68 while her verbal and performance IQ scores are 74 and 62, respectively. Janie suffered from smoke inhalation at the age of fifteen months and was comatose for three weeks. She experiences difficulty in letter formation, spelling, and reading recognition. Her mother is concerned about her spelling and handwriting as well as her self-esteem. Janie enjoys arithmetic and has mastered the four basic operations but has some minor difficulty with simple division involving two digits. She is shy, well-mannered, but very dependent on her mother and older sister. Janie is well-liked by her peers but has few friends her own age and has limited social interactions with children her own age. Her grade-equivalent scores are as follows: math = 2.1, spelling = 1.0, reading recognition = 1.0, and reading comprehension = 0.8. Error analysis suggests that Janie has not mastered hard/soft consonants nor long/short vowels. She has a tendency to reverse letters (b/d) and invert/rotate letters (u/n). She has mastered some basic sight words such as "exit." Her handwriting is immature in appearance.

1. To what extent were the parents involved in developing Janie's IEP? What might have been done differently?

2. What categorical label did the team use for Janie, and how relevant was it in developing her IEP? Using information presented in Chapter 2, would you consider Janie mildly disabled, moderately disabled, or severely disabled?

3. To what extent were responsibilities for meeting Janie's IEP goals shared, or was the bulk of the responsibilities delegated to a specific team member?

4. What were the various leadership roles during the meeting? What role did each member play in terms of facilitating the IEP development process?

5. How did the team determine to what extent Janie would receive educational services in mainstream settings?

outlines the purpose and agenda of the meeting as well as providing a menu of ideas that facilitate meaningful involvement on the part of parents and teachers. The advance organizer may also include some questions that parents and teachers can consider and address prior to the meeting that will enable them to participate in a meaningful and productive manner.

Van Reusen and Bos (1990) suggested that student involvement in the IEP process is, for the most part, either passive or nonexistent. An educational planning strategy employing the acronym IPLAN has been developed to allow students greater opportunity for meaningful participation in the IEP process (Van Reusen, Bos, & Schumaker, 1987). An entire curriculum teaches students to follow a five-step strategy:

I = INVENTORY your strengths, weaknesses + goals/interests.
P = PROVIDE your inventory information.
L = LISTEN and respond.
A = ASK questions.
N = NAME your goals.

This strategy has been effective with junior and senior high students with learning disabilities (Van Reusen, Bos, Schumaker, & Deshler, 1987).

Another useful tool that can be used prior to and during an IEP meeting is the *activities catalog* (Wilcox & Bellamy, 1987a, 1987b). This is particularly useful for parents of individuals with severe disabilities. A family reviews a menu of activities in three domains: leisure, personal management, and work. The family selects at least two to three activities within each category that promote social integration and suggest activities that increase access to or visibility in the community (McDonnell, Wilcox, & Hardman, 1991).

Zins and Curtis (1984) suggested that "many of the shortcomings of [multidiscplinary team] conferences might be overcome or minimized" if all of the participants utilized effective collaborative process skills (p. 236). The collaborative process described in detail in Chapter 3 is an efficient mechanism of instructional decision making for the multidisciplinary service-delivery team (Elliott & Sheridan, 1992). The process is a systematic plan for collecting and using assessment data that are student-centered.

Staff Development

Another example of school wide partnerships is staff development. The developers of Public Law 94-142 appear to have been aware of the impact the legislation would have on teachers by including Section 121a 380-387, which mandated comprehensive systems of personnel development (Cline, 1984). State and district agencies must design and implement continued professional development that will enhance educators' skills in providing services to students with special needs. Professionals and staff within the educational setting enhance their skills through additional, site-based training. Historically, staff development has been conducted by district and state office personnel or outside consultants. As the educational reform movement continues to emphasize site-based management, an evolving role of support personnel such as school psychologists and special educators will include providing ongoing technical assistance through staff development. Staff development truly exemplifies collaboration, as professionals share their expertise and resources with each other to address immediate and long-term needs. An integral part of effective schools (McDonnell, 1985), staff development is ongoing technical assistance that can be characterized in two fundamental forms: in-service and peer coaching.

In-Service.   A formally sanctioned group meeting of professionals in which new information or skills are presented is known as *in-service.* In-service is continuing education. Unlike preservice preparation programs at institutions of higher education, in-service is usually delivered in the school after educators have completed their degree or certification program. It often consists of a series of workshops conducted by teachers, special services personnel, building or district personnel, state personnel, faculty from colleges/ universities, or outside professional consultants. In-service is designed to disseminate information and skills that will be applied by educators. A school psychologist, for example, might demonstrate specific behavioral management strategies that teachers could readily implement in classroom settings. Sometimes the presentation is primarily in the form of consciousness raising. For example, a specialist might present a series of simulation activities emulating various characteristics of learning disabilities to create a sense of empathy on the part of teachers.

Paradoxically, teachers recognize the importance of in-service yet often view attending workshops as "only slightly more palatable and necessary than death and taxes" (Dillon, 1979, p. 43). This perception is largely based on the fact that in-service tends to be brief, a-theoretical, and irrelevant to life in the classroom—and therefore, the least effective method for professional growth (Gall, Haisley, Baker, & Perez, 1984; Smylie & Conyers, 1991). In-service typically consists of a single session in which a presenter (often from outside the school) offers information and then leaves without providing ongoing technical assistance (McDonnell, 1985; Schumker & Clark, 1990). Fullan (1990) suggested that staff development has not been successful because it is practiced so poorly. What, then, constitutes effective in-service?

Characteristics of Effective Staff Development.   Most research on staff development and in-service is largely based on descriptive surveys (Daresh, 1985). These surveys suggest a number of variables that contribute to effective in-service. A prerequisite step is conducting needs assessment. Results from ecological assessment and prereferral observations may serve as informal indicators of need. The use of multiple needs assessment measures such as interviews, surveys, and observation increase the probability of valid findings (Kuh, Hutson, Orbaugh, & Byers, 1980; Powers, 1983). The teacher constituency should be directly involved in the identification of specific content and skill areas that will be presented during the in-service (McDonnell, 1985).

The content of the staff development must relate to the conditions of teaching as well as to the needs of students (Epstein, Lockard, & Duaber, 1991).

Smylie and Conyers (1991) suggested that staff development should be reconceptualized as a work group, rather than a workshop to allow educators the opportunity to collaborate with colleagues as they develop new skills. Effective instructional techniques of demonstration, practice, and immediate feedback for teaching students new skills described in Chapter 7 are equally effective when helping teachers assimilate new strategies (Archer & Issacson, 1990; Gersten, Woodward, & Darch, 1986; Showers, Joyce, & Bennett, 1987). Effective in-service consists of four parts: (1) presentation of theory; (2) demonstration of the new technique; (3) practice in workshop settings; and (4) prompt, constructive feedback regarding participants' effort (Showers, 1987). The demonstration of new techniques should be directly related to and focus on teachers' needs (McDonnell, 1985). Consequently, effective design of the in-service training appears to matter more than where, when, or by whom in-service is provided (Showers et al., 1987). Participants are more likely to adopt techniques, materials, and strategies when the training incorporates a variety of "hands-on" activities (Powers, 1983). Furthermore, effective in-service incorporates one or two sessions solely dedicated to follow-through and feedback (Jones & Lowe, 1990; McDonnell, 1985). Accompanying materials should be self-instructional flowcharts or step-by-step instructions that an in-service participant can easily follow and implement in the classroom on his or her own upon completion of the in-service workshop. Sharp (1992) developed a number of guidelines for developing and implementing effective in-service that are presented in Table 8–5.

Peer Coaching.   Following an in-service presentation, professionals may begin to apply newly acquired skills through a supervised approach known as *peer coaching*. Ackland (1991) described two basic forms of peer coaching. One is coaching by experts, whereby a consultant with expertise in a given area observes educators and provides feedback on their performance. A second form is reciprocal coaching. Teams of teachers periodically observe

---

Table 8–5   Guidelines for Effective In-Service Workshops

1. Be sensitive to participants' personal needs by providing breaks and refreshments.
2. Create a realistic schedule so you don't have to rush through material, and adhere to that schedule.
3. Clearly state the objectives of the workshop, and provide a needs-based rationale.
4. Bring enough accompanying, self-instructional materials for all participants.
5. Provide legible handout materials and overhead transparencies.
6. Actively involve participants rather than read or talk at them.
7. Include fun activities.

Activity 8–4

Form teams of two individuals. Partners take turns modeling and demonstrating a specific skill to complete a task unfamiliar to the other (e.g., threading a needle, tying a hitch knot, arranging pieces on a backgammon board).

1. What behaviors did the peer coach exhibit that facilitated empathy, support, commoradary? How important is this to the individual learning a new skill?

2. How did the peer coach use effective interpersonal communication skills when providing feedback to the learner?

3. Was there a need for modifying the steps or learning process to facilitate the needs of the learner?

4. What are various educational skills that might be appropriate for teaching to colleagues through peer coaching?

each other implement new techniques while providing feedback, support, and assistance. Both forms of peer coaching serves five major functions: (1) facilitating companionship as teachers share successes and frustrations, (2) providing constructive feedback, (3) allowing the analysis of the application of the new skills to promote internalization and adoption, (4) determining methods of adapting new skills to meet the needs of particular students, and (5) promoting emotional and technical support (Showers, 1984).

Chapter Summary

Educational partnerships can be established within the school setting at two levels. The micro-level is characterized as one-on-one collaboration between two individuals, often within a classroom setting. This interaction may take place through consultation. Educators may choose from a variety of school-based consultation models and programs such as behavioral consultation, resource/consulting teacher, and peer collaborative consultation. There are four components for establishing school-based consultation programs. The first step is system entry, which requires careful cultural and systemic analysis of the school setting. Administrative and teacher support accompanied by an understanding of the roles and responsibilities of participants must be obtained before moving to the second step. Establishing procedures for requesting assistance is the second component and is the key to facilitating the logistical success of the program. Closely associated with this process is the third component, which requires scheduling of consultation services. A variety of scheduling strategies is available for consideration. Finally, the consultation program must include a comprehensive evaluation component that assesses specific outcomes and satisfaction of all participants.

Another micro-level approach of educational partnerships is team teaching. Team teaching is characterized as two teachers simultaneously providing direct instruction in a classroom. There are three fundamental formats: co-teaching, complementary instruction, and supportive learning activities. When planning any form of team teaching, partners must consider scheduling factors, defining roles and responsibilities of each teacher, identifying potential problems, planning instructional procedures and adaptations, and evaluating the entire operation using student outcomes and satisfaction surveys.

Another level of educational partnerships is at the macro-level, typically involving teams of professionals. These teams generally operate on a school-wide basis. A major function of case-management teams is to support and assist teachers in providing services to students at risk while minimizing inappropriate referral to special education services. The teacher assistance team and prereferral intervention team provide indirect services to professionals seeking assistance. The multidisciplinary student service-delivery team is usually composed of parents, teachers, special educators, school psychologists, and building administrators. The team is responsible for determining student eligibility for special education services and development of an individual education plan that outlines roles and responsibilities of each participant in service delivery.

Finally, staff development embodies the basic tenets of the collaborative ethic through formally held in-service workshops designed to share resources, information, materials, and strategies. Effective staff development addresses areas of need identified by educators and provides comprehensive training and feedback in promoting the application of new skills or procedures. Ongoing technical assistance is often provided through peer coaching to facilitate assimilation of newly acquired skills.

Case Study 8–1	Ms. Zimmerman, a resource-room teacher at Henry David Thoreau High School, approached a biology teacher, Mr. Judge, to discuss the possibility of team teaching. Her rationale was the fact that many of her students were in Mr. Judge's class. While he was generally supportive of accommodating her students, they were still experiencing difficulty in note-taking and test-taking, thus jeopardizing their chances for graduation. It was her hope that she could show the entire class how to take better notes and use some test-taking skills. Mr. Judge was also the track coach, and he welcomed the idea as a means of covering his afternoon classes when the track team had to travel. Ms. Zimmerman was pleased by his quick and enthusiastic response of providing her a copy of his lesson plans. She raised the possibility of taking fifteen minutes each class period to demonstrate note-taking skills. She knew her instructional assistant could manage her resource room for that period of time and had secured approval from the building principal to do so. The biology teacher responded by saying, "We don't have time to do remedial education . . . we have to get through the material. They should have had these skills by the time they got to their senior year. Besides . . . isn't that what you teach in your study skills

class?" In her desire to assist her students, Ms. Zimmerman did not attempt to persuade Mr. Judge. Instead, she took the materials he provided and returned to her classroom to review them. As she examined the lesson plans, she noticed that Mr. Judge divided the lessons and chapters between them. Coincidently, the days and lessons she was scheduled to team matched the track team's road-trip calendar. She also discovered she knew little or nothing about biology and realized she would need to spend considerable time to prepare.

1. What were examples of role conflict in this situation?

2. What steps that should have been followed by these two teachers? Refer to the guidelines for establishing and implementing team teaching presented in this chapter.

3. How might an evaluation plan look that could be implemented by these teachers to assess the impact of team teaching?

Case Study 8–2

The principal of Hidden Valley Middle School returned from a one-day in-service for district administrators on collaboration to announce during a faculty meeting that the school was going to establish a teacher-assistance team (TAT). During the faculty meeting, the principal indicated that the TAT would serve as a prerequisite step to facilitate referral to special education by easing the amount of testing and observation the school psychologist and special education teacher were conducting. The principal ended the meeting by announcing which four teachers would compose the team and handed them a three-page "manual" to study. These teachers were selected by the principal because they were young and energetic "go-getters" who, in the principal's estimation, could make the program work. The team met on an as-needed basis, whenever team members' schedules would accommodate. Meetings were held before and after school as well as during lunch. A total of ten meetings were held, during which only four teachers even requested assistance. A single student was considered by the team for nearly ninety minutes each meeting. Meetings could be characterized as an opportunity for the teachers seeking assistance to vent their frustration. The team often discussed the child's background and home environment as probable contributing factors. The cases typically involved behavior problems on which the team routinely recommended elaborate behavioral management programs that were often used in smaller, segregated special education settings. After nearly a month of frustration on the part of the teachers requesting assistance, the team reconvened to recommend that seven of the ten students reviewed be referred and placed into special education.

At the end of the school year, the team distributed a survey to assess the program's impact. Responses were overwhelmingly negative. Comments indicated that most teachers viewed the TAT as just another bureaucratic hoop to jump through to place problem students into special education. Some respondents indicated a resentment that "rookie" teachers were "trying to tell us how to handle our students." One survey anonymously revealed that seeking help from the team was like an admission of incompetence. Finally, one survey completed by one of the teachers who utilized the TAT lamented that the recommendations by the team were "pushed" on her and there was no follow-up or support to help her implement the intervention.

In reading the survey results, the team members became frustrated and voiced their resentment toward the faculty. Specifically, they didn't feel that the faculty appreciated their efforts, which were time-consuming and constituted an additional responsibility to their other teaching duties. After reviewing the evaluation results, one member indicated that he was not going to continue serving on the team. Consequently, the team as whole drafted a memo to the principal recommending that the program be discontinued.

1. Review the guidelines for establishing effective teacher-assistance teams presented in Table 8–2. What factors appear to have contributed to the inefficiency of the Hidden Valley Elementary TAT?

2. What misperceptions and behaviors on the part of the building principal may have contributed to the situation?

3. What cultural variables within the school building appear to have been ignored that may have contributed to the difficulties that were encountered?

4. After determining factors that contributed to the demise of the team, decide on specific recommendations that you might make to minimize the problems encountered.

Note: The authors wish to acknowledge John Mayhew's assistance in creating this case scenario.

Key Vocabulary Terms

behavioral consultation
resource/consulting teacher
  (R/CT)
formative evaluation
summative evaluation
peer collaborative
  consultation
prereferral intervention team
input variables

process variables
program outcomes
team teaching
co-teaching
complementary instruction
supportive learning activities
double class roll
multidisciplinary student
  service-delivery teams

individualized education
  program (IEP)
in-service
peer coaching
case management
teacher-assistance team (TAT)
local education agency (LEA)

Part 3

Home and Community

Chapter 9

Chapter Overview

The Home

Chapter Objectives

After reading this chapter, students should be able to
1. Describe the changing demographics of families today.
2. Identify changes in the relationship between the home and school over the century.
3. State conceptual and functional similarities of homes and schools.
4. Define parent involvement and home-school collaboration.
5. Report the empirical findings regarding parental involvement and home-school collaboration.
6. Identify practical issues in working with families.
7. Define various "hard to reach" families.
8. Outline issues surrounding involving diverse families.
9. Discuss Epstein's conceptual model as a framework for reconceptualizing the relationship between homes and schools.
10. Outline various principles of home-school collaboration.
11. Describe three models of home-school collaboration.

Introduction

"[T]o fail to know families . . . is to fail to know children"
(Conoley, 1989, p. 556).

Educational experiences are derived not only from schools, but also from the family and community. Therefore, it is generally understood that to meet the needs of students, a recognition of their contexts (where they come from, where they are) is imperative. Consistent with ecological theory, these three systems (school, home, community) are interrelated and simultaneously responsible for the education and socialization of our youth (see Chapter 3 for a review of ecological theory). Efforts to maximize the developmental experiences of students must therefore include significant persons from all three settings. Additionally, we must explore the potential partnerships within each each setting to maximize educational experiences. In Chapters 5 through 8, we discussed the school as well as school- and classroom-based interventions designed to assist students at risk. In the present and following chapters, we explore variables contributing to home-school and school-community partnerships and methods to promote effective relations among these critical systems.

The Changing Family

The "traditional family" is undergoing a significant change, such that families of today are markedly different from families of yesteryears. The transformation of the American family has occurred very rapidly over recent decades, and virtually every demographic characteristic imaginable has been altered. Several of the changes have produced more stressful living conditions for families and family members, including youth. Indeed, a number of the characteristics identified in Chapter 2 that may place students at risk for educational difficulties are related to changing demographics of families.

Natriello, McDill, and Pallas (1990) cited five key indicators associated with educationally disadvantaged children and youth, several of which are related to family variables. These indicators include (1) living in a poverty household; (2) being of a minority racial group; (3) living in a single-parent household; (4) having a poorly educated mother; and (5) having a non-English language background. They further estimate that at least 40 percent of children seventeen years old and younger experience any one (and often more) of these indicators, which may put them at risk for educational failure.

Family living arrangements are one demographic characteristic that continues to change dramatically. In 1955, 60 percent of all U.S. households consisted of a working father, a housewife mother, and two or more school-age children. In 1985, only 7 percent fit this pattern (Davis, 1991). Seventy percent of mothers of school-age children are now in the work force, as compared to 30 percent in 1960. Almost half of all marriages end in divorce. As of 1988, nearly 25 percent of all U.S. children were living in single-parent families (the mother in over 90 percent of these cases). Living in single-parent households is considered one of the major indicators for placing children at risk for educational failure (Educational Testing Service, 1992; Milne, Myers, Rosenthal, & Ginsburg, 1986). One-third of all marriages are now remarriages, and one out of four children has one or more stepparents (Braun & Swap, 1987).

Along with changing family characteristics, we are experiencing a general population shift in American society. For example, the number of all preschool children increased by more than 3 million between 1980 and 1990. This number is expected to decrease again by the year 2000; however, the number of elementary school children will continue to rise. Likewise, the number of secondary school youth will increase by the year 2000 (Davis, 1991). Beyond increases in total number of students entering elementary schools in the upcoming years, the percentage of minority children is projected to rise significantly. Some demographers project an almost 200 percent increase in the nation's population of African Americans by the year 2020 and an almost 300 percent increase in the Hispanic population. It is also estimated that by the year 2000, between 33 and 40 percent of our public school students will be representative of some ethnic/racial minority group, and many of these children will be poor (Children's Defense Fund, 1989; Davis & McCaul, 1991; National Center for Health Statistics, 1991).

The number of children living in poverty is also increasing. Almost one in four children now lives below the poverty line, and over half of the children living in single-parent households are poor (Braun & Swap, 1987). In fact, the rate of poverty among families with young children almost doubled between 1973 and 1986 (Children's Defense Fund, 1989). Being a member of a minority group significantly increases the chances of a child being poor. In 1987, 45 percent of all African American children and 39 percent of all Hispanic children were considered to be poor (Davis & McCaul, 1991).

The number of babies being born to unwed women is at the highest level in history, with the fastest growing group being fifteen- to seventeen-year-old mothers (Davis & McCaul, 1991). Teen pregnancy often perpetuates economic, social, and educational disadvantages for both the mother and child. Problems of teenage mothers and their children are exacerbated when they also experience other risk factors, such as being a minority, living below the poverty line, and failing to complete high school.

There also has been a steady increase in the number of reported child abuse cases in the United States over recent years. In 1989 approximately 2.4 million child abuse cases were filed with the National Committee for the Prevention of Child Abuse, with more than 400,000 of these reports involving sexual abuse. Also in 1989, state child protection agencies reported nearly 1,250 child abuse-related deaths, which represents a 38 percent increase over 1985. It is believed that these numbers may be underestimates of actual child abuse cases, as several may continue to go unreported.

Although the estimates vary, the numbers of homeless and "precariously housed" (Davis, 1991) children in the United States are rising dramatically. Young children in families represent the fastest growing single group of homeless in America. This problem places special demands on schools, as concerns regarding supervision, hygiene, nutrition, and health care may be related to a child's homeless situation.

The educational implications of these changing family characteristics are significant. It may seem simple for educators to blame families for children's failure to succeed in school. However, this belief is not only inaccurate, it is destructive (Swap, 1993). Rather than focusing on a *deficit model of families,* which focuses on problems or shortcomings of a family, we promote an *enhancement model,* whereby inherent assets and strengths of families are recognized. Likewise, in keeping with an ecological model, we recognize that schools and homes are interrelated and cannot be considered distinct and separate influences in a child's life. This has not always been the predominant belief, however. We turn now to a discussion of the changing relationship between homes and schools.

Historical Perspective of the Home within Education

The relationship between schools and families has changed dramatically over the course of history. In Colonial times, the home and school were kept separate, with distinct roles and responsibilities clearly delineated. Specifically, schools were responsible for educating children in the basics of reading, writing, and arithmetic. Families, on the other hand, were committed to shaping the moral character of their children. By the early nineteenth century, some organizations were formed to promote home-school collaboration (Kagan & Holdeman, 1989). Most of these initiatives took the form of integrating programs such as music, art, and kindergarten into the public school experience. The late 1800s saw a great increase in the kindergarten movement and in parent education (Berger, 1991), where schools provided instructional functions to parents on topics such as child care. (Information regarding contemporary views of parent education are presented in Chapter 10.)

Commitments to families expanded in the early 1900s with the community school movement. This movement had a significant influence on current family support programs. According to Kagan and Holdeman (1989), "though gaining only limited practical acceptance then, the movement legitimated the family, not solely the child, as the unit of service, predicting current trends toward serving the child and the family" (p. 2).

In the mid-1900s, tensions emerged between families and schools. The educational field became professionalized and bureaucratized, and school personnel began questioning parents' intrusion into what was considered "their domain." Educational budgets were slim, responsibilities were increasing, and schools began attending less to parents and social concerns and more to educating students in the basics. During the post-Depression and postwar era of the 1950s, schools were consolidated and many children began to travel long distances to and from school. This served to physically separate families and schools. School administrators took on strong leadership roles, and parents' power was reduced as they were no longer personally involved with their children's schools (Berger, 1991). School boards were generally accepted as representatives of parents and afforded power to make educational decisions. When parents were involved in the 1950s and early 1960s, they basically fulfilled modest, nonthreatening roles (e.g., bake sales, attendance on field trips), while the school maintained control.

The post-Sputnik era of the 1960s saw a heavy emphasis on science, math, and foreign language, with limited attention to serving families in need. However, parents began voicing interest in becoming involved in school decision making during the mid-1960s. At this time, schools began to see parent participation in key decisions such as budget, personnel, and curriculum. Also in the mid-1960s, the Head Start program was established by the Office of Economic Opportunity, which promoted various levels of parent participation.

Since the 1970s, attention to home-school collaboration efforts has flourished. A number of factors that gained prominence in the 1970s contributed to the renewed attention to families (Kagan & Holdeman, 1989). First, a number of legislative mandates demanded more involvement of parents. For example, Public Law 94-142 of 1975 included parents of students with disabilities in the development of Individualized Education Programs (IEPs), and Title I of the Elementary and Secondary Education Act (now called Chapter I) required parent participation on boards. Public Law 99-457 (1986) served as a downward extension of PL 94-142, and required that (1) the rights and protections of PL 94-142 be extended to children with disabilities age three through five; and (2) an *Individualized Family Service Plan* (IFSP) be developed to specify the intervention services necessary to meet the unique needs of the child *and family.*

A second factor that promoted increased parent participation in the 1970s was the "national ethos toward an ecological approach to serving children" (Kagan & Holdeman, 1989, p. 2). Educators, psychologists and bureaucrats began to realize that children and their environments influenced each other in a reciprocal manner, and that students could not be considered in isolation from their multiple ecologies. At this time, the Coleman report (Coleman et al., 1966) and related documents (Mostellar & Moynihan, 1972), citing research support for the significance of the home environment on school achievement, gained recognition. Also at this time, Gordon (1977) suggested three influential models of parent involvement: (1) the *family-impact model,* in which the school reaches out to the family through home visits or various techniques to increase communication; (2) the *school-impact model,* in which parents are involved (for example, in volunteer work and in serving on advisory boards) in efforts to change the schools to become more responsive to the needs of the home; and (3) the *community-impact model,* in which resources of the larger community (medical, psychological, and so forth) are used to facilitate a community-home-school partnership. These influences encouraged educators to widen the doors of the schoolhouse to serve students through partnerships with families and communities.

Third, a recognition of the benefits of prevention was experienced at that time. Based on empirical evidence in favor of early intervention, educators began to realize the importance of proactive models of service delivery. Head Start programs, which provided preschool programs and parent education, were funded around the United States. A final force in the improvement of home-school relations was the dramatic change in family life. As outlined at the beginning of this chapter, the demographics of American families have changed over the last decades, and this change did not occur overnight. Schools became sources of family support as the American family began to change.

Importance of Home-School Partnerships

The importance of establishing productive partnerships with families is clear. Schools are responsible to reach out to *all* families, whether they be wealthy or poor, Caucasian or of color, American or culturally different, headed dually or by a single parent. Peterson and Cooper (1989) stated it clearly:

> [P]arents take their child home after professionals complete their services and parents continue providing the care for the larger portion of the child's waking hours . . . No matter how skilled professionals are, or how loving parents are, each cannot achieve alone what the two parties, working hand-in-hand, can accomplish together" (pp. 229, 208).

Models emphasizing home-school relationships can be characterized as parental involvement or home-school collaboration. According to Christenson, Rounds and Gorney (1992), "*parent involvement* . . . is defined broadly to include various activities that allow parents to participate in the educational process at school and at home" (p. 190). Examples include parents volunteering to help in the school's computer lab and parents attending annual "Back to School" nights. On the other hand, "*home-school collaboration* refers to addressing parents' and teachers' concerns about children, engaging in problem solving . . . to resolve educational problems, and establishing a partnership" (Christenson & Cleary, 1990; p. 226). An example is parents meeting with teachers and a school-based specialist to identify specific problems a child is having and to mutually develop and share in the responsibility for a program to address the concern.

Although the disctinction between parent involvement and home-school collaboration is important, most of the existing literature discusses them interchangeably. We will follow this approach, keeping in mind that conceptual and practical differences exist.

Conceptual Rationale

Conceptually, both schools and families can be considered open systems (Conoley, 1987). Each is comprised of a number of subsystems (the student subsystem in schools; the sibling subsystem in families) that are related to and dependent on each other. Likewise, schools and families are interrelated and interdependent. In other words, the beliefs, attitudes, values, norms, practices, events and virtually every other variable in one setting (the home) affect and are affected by those present in the other setting (the school). Clearly, there is a significant and reciprocal relationship between the home and school settings that must be appreciated to maximize students' development and learning.

A hypothetical example may help illustrate the relationships within and between home and school systems. Parkside is a middle school in an upwardly mobile university community, Collegetown. Parents in Collegetown are generally well-educated and work at professional jobs (university professors, doctors, lawyers). The students at Parkside consistently score above national norms on standardized testing. Schools push for academic breadth and excellence by requiring courses in foreign language, advanced math and science, and humanities. A high priority is placed on college preparation. Parents at Parkside support and demand these high standards and practices. Contrast Parkside to Lincoln, an inner city, low socioeconomic school. Parents at Lincoln are primarily uneducated and of mixed racial and cultural background. Many parents are unemployed, or they work at the local tool and dye factory making minimum wage. Several families in the Lincoln catchment area have relocated from Puerto Rico, and English is not spoken in most homes. Gangs and drug use are high at Lincoln, with several students known to bring knives and guns to school. The school's efforts focus on survival functions, such as safety on the school grounds. These same priorities (survival and safety) are apparent in the homes and neighborhoods of students at Lincoln.

Functional Similarities

At the functional level, several similarities between homes and schools can be noted. In Chapter 5, we outlined several objectives of schools, many of which correlate positively with objectives families have for their children. At a basic level, both families and schools are concerned with socializing children and

Activity 9–1	Within homes and communities, there are a number of influences that affect schools' goals and activities. Likewise, within schools there are a number of variables that influence students' homes. Label one side of a sheet of paper "Home to School." Label the other side "School to Home." In a small group, identify "out-of-school" variables (those that occur in the home or community) that contribute to the climate and events within schools. List these on the first side of the paper. Then, brainstorm a list of "out-of-home" variables (those that occur in the school) that contribute to the home climate and activities. Write these on the other side of the paper. Are there any events or factors that are completely separate?

preparing them to be successful in society. Conoley (1987) identified other functional similarities and noted that "both schools and families teach, reward, punish, provide nurturance and sustenance, evaluate, and prepare for the departure of children" (p. 193). Schools also provide medical attention, nutrition, and mental health services to children. It seems clear that the greater the coordination among home and school, the greater the chance for optimal student outcomes.

Several examples highlight the manner in which functions taken on by schools overlap with those traditionally left to families. Many schools now offer free lunch programs for students from families on fixed or minimum budgets. Some even have breakfast offerings to ensure that students are nourished and "ready to learn." Several schools provide immunizations to students to promote children's health, and fitness programs are often required in physical education courses. After-school programs are also becoming more prominent in public schools to provide supervision to students whose parents work outside of the home after the school day ends.

Empirical Support for Educational Partnerships with Families

The empirical support for the development of home-school partnerships is voluminous. When parents are involved in their children's education, their children do better in school, and they go to better schools (Henderson, 1987). Parental involvement has been a central component of programs designed to improve educational outcomes for children at risk for school failure (Comer, 1984; Nye, 1989), to enhance the social development of students (Comer & Haynes, 1991), and to improve the academic performance of disabled learners in the regular classroom (Wang, Gennari, & Waxman, 1985). Studies have been conducted investigating effects on students, parents and teachers.

Students.   Reviews of the *parental involvement* literature suggest that parental participation in school affairs is related to several important benefits for students: increased achievement, better school attendance, better study habits, fewer discipline problems, more positive attitudes toward school, and more regular homework habits (Becher, 1986; Epstein, 1984). Other benefits of active parent involvement include positive effects on students' homework, perception of family and school ties (Epstein, 1982), and higher student grades (Fehrmann, Keith, & Reimers, 1987).

Much of the research has investigated in-home learning activities as means of involving parents in their child's education. Many of these programs involve reading activities in the form of parents reading to children, children reading to parents, or interactive practices. Studies indicate that home reading activities increase reading achievement (Becher, 1984; Goldenberg, 1987), with positive effects for children of all abilities and from all social classes (Searles, Lewis, & Morrow, 1982; Tizard, Schofied, & Hewison, 1982). Achievement gains have also been associated with home learning activities in subjects other than reading (Epstein, 1986; Mullen, 1989).

Parents.   Research on home and school connections has also indicated several effects on parents. First, it is clear that most parents want to know how to help their own child at home and how to stay involved in their child's education. This is true for parents of children from elementary through high school. Some research has suggested that over 90 percent of parents of elementary and middle-school students believed that the school should provide guidance on how to help at home (Dauber & Epstein, 1989; Epstein, 1986). Similarly, over 80 percent of parents of high school students reported the same beliefs (Dornbusch & Ritter, 1988).

Second, parents are strongly influenced by the teachers' practices, especially when the teacher is a "leader" in effectively involving parents (Epstein, 1985, 1986). Parents of these teachers are more likely to report that they (1) receive many ideas about how to help their child at home; (2) feel they should help their child at home; and (3) understand more about what their child was learning. They also rate the teacher higher in overall teaching ability and interpersonal skills. When engaged in collaborative home-school efforts, parents report that they communicate better with the school and are more willing to help with educational tasks (Christenson & Cleary, 1990; Epstein, 1987, 1991; Stevenson & Baker, 1987).

A third finding is that most parents cannot and do not participate at the school building (Bauch, 1988; Dauber & Epstein, 1989; Dornbusch & Ritter, 1988). Epstein (1986) found that only 4 percent of the elementary school parents were active at the school building twenty-five days or more each year. Few parents participate directly in school decision making as leaders or representatives of other parents through involvement on the PTA, advisory committees, or other activities. Over 70 percent never volunteer in official ways, and over 60 percent work full- or part-time during the school day. These findings have implications for the way in which parents can be involved. Although they likely have responsibilities that preclude their physical involvement in the school building, they could use information from audiocassette recordings, newsletters, videotapes, and other forms at home. In fact, all or most parents in all types of schools and at all grade levels express the need for clear communications about (1) their children's attendance, behavior, and academic progress; (2) the content of what their children are learning; and (3) how to help their children at home (Epstein, 1990a).

A fourth finding regarding parents concerns status variables (race, parent education, family size, marital status, grade level), which are often assumed to affect the home-school relationship. In fact, *school policies and teacher practices are more important than parental status variables in determining whether parents are an active part of their child's education* (Becker & Epstein, 1982; Dauber & Epstein, 1989). It is important to recognize that different parents respond in different ways to requests for involvement. For example, single mothers and mothers who work outside of the home are less likely to come to the school building than other parents, but are more likely to spend time with their children at home to help them in school activities (Epstein, 1990b).

Teachers.   Effects on teachers can also be summarized from the home-school partnership literature. When there is parental involvement at school, teachers report feeling positively about teaching and their school. Teachers who frequently involve parents in their children's education rate all parents (including less educated and single parents) as higher in helpfulness and follow-through than do other teachers. They tend to refrain from making stereotypical judgments about poor, less educated, or single parents (Epstein, 1990b).

Teachers in inner city schools often report that they want all parents to perform school-related activities at home in the elementary and middle grades. However, very few teachers initiate practices to help parents understand how to conduct such activities at different grade levels. There may be several reasons for this, including the increased number of teachers students face each day in the upper grades, students' greater interest in peers than in families, and the greater numbers of students for whom teachers are responsible (see later section of this chapter for a lengthier discussion of parental involvement in the upper grades). At the middle-school grades, teachers tend to blame parents for their generally low level of involvement (Epstein & Dauber, 1988; Leitch & Tangri, 1988).

Most research supports the contention that teacher variables, more than parent or student variables, contribute to the degree to which parents are involved in education (Leitch & Tangri, 1988). Teachers with a high sense of self-efficacy (that is, those who believe that they are competent and are performing a useful service) view parents as less threatening and are more open to working with them to solve learning and behavioral problems (Hoover-Dempsey, Bassler, & Brissie, 1987; Power, 1985). Alternatively, some teachers continue to view parents as a "nuisance" and fail to welcome them actively into the classroom or into their child's learning experiences. Thus, although benefits to teachers can be accrued when parents are active in education, teachers often dictate (at least in part) the actual level of parental participation. From a partnership perspective, teachers cannot be held solely responsible for engaging parents constructively in educational endeavors. Certain practices at the broader school level are necessary as well.

Despite research support for parental involvement practices, there are a number of issues facing parents and educators alike that limit home-school collaboration efforts. We will now explore these various issues.

Working with Families: Current Issues

Swap (1992) identified four barriers to effective programs involving families, including (1) a tradition of separation between home and school; (2) a tradition of blaming parents for children's difficulties; (3) changing demographic conditions; and (4) persistent school structures. Others have been described by Davis (1991), including lack of agreement over specific roles and responsibilities and false assumptions regarding parental interest. For ease of discussion, we will describe practical issues and issues involving diverse families as they relate to efforts at establishing and maintaining effective home-school partnerships.

Practical Issues

Practical or logistical barriers to greater parental involvement include lack of clarity regarding roles and responsibilities and unsupportive organizational structures.

Lack of Clarity.   Many teachers question the success of practical efforts to involve parents in learning activities at home, citing lack of parental time and expertise (Becker & Epstein, 1982). However, most parents, including single parents and working parents, want to know how to help their children at home and how to stay involved in their children's education (Epstein, 1990a, 1990b; Epstein & Scott-Jones, in press). In fact, most parents help their children with school-related tasks at home, but many do not know whether they are doing the right thing or doing things right (Dauber & Epstein, 1989).

Teachers and other school personnel are also uncertain of their own roles. They have reported that they do not know how to involve parents and still maintain their roles as "professional experts." Few school personnel receive guidance or structure to assist them in utilizing family resources, and few professional preparation programs include instruction or supervision related to parental involvement.

Unsupportive Organizational Structures.   Another important practical issue impeding the success of working with families is that the organizational structures currently in operation in many schools lack adequate flexibility to allow family involvement. Time constraints have been cited as an important reason for lack of parental involvement (Fine, 1984). The current structure of the school day poses another problem. In most American schools, students attend school from 8:30 to 3:00 (for example), with teachers scheduled to be active in the classroom all day long. Brief "breaks" may be available to teachers while their students eat lunch or receive specialized instruction in physical education or music, and these periods are typically spent grading papers, planning instruction, or returning phone calls. In a structure such as this, meetings after school or programs to include parents in learning activities at home are perceived as "extra" and not part of their "normal" job. Other school professionals as well (such as school counselors and school psychologists) cite limited time and high caseloads as reasons for working minimally with families (Carlson & Sincavage, 1987).

Another organizational barrier to working with parents is the lack of resources available to do so. Remember from our discussion in Chapter 3 that there are several levels at which school resources can be identified. Financial, informational, physical, human and technological resources can all be important in the development and implementation of effective parental involvement programs. However, they are often tied up in other school programs and thus fail to be utilized for home-school collaboration efforts.

Issues Involving Diverse Families

The importance of meaningful parental involvement is viewed as especially critical for families at risk. However, it is for these families and students that attempts at forming effective home-school partnerships have been least successful. Practical barriers often impede these families' abilities to become involved in the school building, including lack of transportation, family living arrangements, child care costs and inconvenient meeting times (Davis, 1991).

There are many diverse variations in families that can affect schools' efforts to establish meaningful partnerships. Some families are generally more

Activity 9–2

Several barriers may exist in the establishment of home-school collaborative programs. One of these is the attitudes some people may have about the separate responsibilities and tasks that "should" belong to homes and schools. In a small group, develop a list of these traditional responsibilities and tasks. In other words, generate a list of those things for which parents have traditionally been held responsible (e.g., ensuring that the student had breakfast; signing report cards). Then, generate a second list of those things for which educators have traditionally been held responsible (e.g., teaching addition; scheduling field trips). For each responsibility or task, describe the benefits and limitations of maintaining the traditional attitude.

difficult to involve than others. According to Epstein and Scott-Jones (in press), "hard to reach" families are "those whose physical, social, or psychological distance from the school raises extra barriers to productive overlap." Several conditions may exist to characterize families as "hard to reach." Families with diverse parental backgrounds, families with diverse structures and roles, and families of upper-grade students may all fall in this category (Epstein & Scott-Jones, in press).

Families with Diverse Parental Background.   Parents with relatively low levels of formal education and those for whom English is a second language are often uninvolved in their children's education. This may be because they feel uncomfortable in the school, they have had negative experiences in school settings, or they are unable to communicate with school personnel. There are a number of things that schools can do to increase involvement of these sometimes "difficult to reach" *families with a diverse parental background.*

Schools can help poorly educated parents locate and use social, health, and educational services in the community that they need in order to establish and maintain home environments that support learning. Some help parents enhance their own academic skills through adult basic education programs conducted at the school building or other convenient locations (Davidson & Koppenhaver, 1988). Likewise, intergenerational literacy programs have been employed to help parents and students learn to read together (Nickse, Speicher, & Buchek, in press). Uneducated parents, as all parents, are a heterogenous group. There are likely more differences than commonalities among them. An important key to developing programs to involve less educated parents is that activities be organized to meet their own unique and specific needs and abilities.

Oftentimes parents for whom English is a second language (or not spoken at all) and minority families are hard to reach because they have difficulty understanding and being understood by school personnel. Schools must acknowledge that communication is important with *all* families, including language minority families. Special bilingual staff, paid aides, or parent or other volunteers can be used as translators, liaisons, and resources to facilitate communication between parents and school personnel. In the upper grades, bilingual students can perform some of these roles (Epstein & Scott-Jones, in press).

Activity 9–3

In Chapter 3, we discussed various levels at which resources are available in school communities. On a sheet of paper, develop a matrix with five columns. Label the columns as follows: human, financial, informational, physical, and technological. In each column, list resources that can be used in the development and implementation of parent programs. Are these resources readily available to school personnel? Why or why not?

An important consideration in increasing and retaining the involvement of minority and non-English speaking parents is that they make participation easy (Inger, 1992). Programs can increase ease of involvement by providing babysitting, preparing materials and presentations in a common language, arranging meetings at convenient times and locations, and refraining from charging fees. To initiate involvement, personal, face-to-face communcation with the parents appear more successful than impersonal efforts such as letters, flyers, and announcements (Inger, 1992). To retain the involvement of minority parents, every meeting and event should respond to some needs or concerns of the parents. Likewise, nonjudgmental communication and respect for parents' feelings are important.

Families with Diverse Structures.   As articulated at the beginning of this chapter, the "traditional family" is changing. Families now look very different than they did in previous decades. Despite the increasing numbers of households with single parents, working parents, and different structures (stepparents, blended families, and noncustodial and foster situations), these families may still be relatively "hard to reach." As families continue to change, schools must have a wide range of responsive practices to keep all families informed and involved.

Families headed by single parents represent one group of *families with diverse structures* that may be difficult to reach. The problems of single-parent families are compounded if they fall into other "hard to reach" categories, such as poorly educated parents, limited English proficiency families, or working parents. However, it is a mistake to assume that if a child comes from a single parent household that the family is unwilling to be involved in educational activities. Research has demonstrated that compared to married parents, single parents are just as concerned about their children and spend more time helping their children at home, but spend less time in the school (Dauber & Epstein, 1989; Epstein, in press). In fact, teacher practices, not marital status, is more predictive of whether single parents are involved in their child's education. Teachers who frequently involve all parents in learning activities at home report that single parents are as able as married parents to help children successfully (Epstein, in press).

Obviously, all single parents are not identical. Some are well-educated and working; some are uneducated and poor. Some are male; some are female. Likewise, single parents are single for a variety of reasons (divorced, widowed, separated, never married), which produce different social, emotional, and economic conditions for the families. Also, parents likely undergo changes over time as a single parent (Epstein & Scott-Jones, in press). Newly single parents likely face different stressors than those who have experienced the situation for a longer period of time. Whatever the case, because they bear the responsibility of home-school connections alone, single parents may benefit from structured parental involvement practices (Espinoza, 1988) such as structured homework programs or consultation (see Chapter 10 for more discussion on specific and structured practices).

Working parents may be uninvolved in school-based activities and events because schools typically schedule them during the workday. Student assemblies, opportunities to volunteer, and meetings are often unavailable to working parents because of the traditional schedules used by schools. Some working parents are more flexible than others; however, it is necessary for schools to recognize the varying situations of parents if they want them to be involved actively. Efforts are being made in several states and cities to advance employers' understanding of the need to allow employees "flex time" to attend school events (Epstein & Casner-Lotto, 1988). Schools must also devise creative and flexible methods of accommodating working parents and creating alternative ways for them to become involved. For example, some volunteer activities may be completed at home during parents' free hours. Conferences can be scheduled for early morning or evening times, and events can be held on Saturdays or after dinner hours.

Working parents have a unique concern if their schedule does not permit them to be at home when the school day ends. Children of these parents are often called *latchkey children* (children who lack adult supervision for a few hours each day). Contrary to popular belief, there is no research to suggest that all such children are at risk for behavioral or emotional problems (Rodman, Pratto, & Nelson, 1985; Steinberg, 1986). After-school programs can support parents who work and can provide a mechanism for the parents to have daily contact with the school. Although still not common in public schools, after-school programs may become standard in many districts in the upcoming years (National School Boards Association, 1986).

Contemporary students may function within a range of additional alternative family structures, requiring educators to remain sensitive to a host of children's life situations. For example, many students may live with stepparents, siblings, extended family members (e.g., aunts or uncles), grandparents, or in blended or gay/lesbian families. Schools must also make efforts to reach out to noncustodial parents, fathers, and foster parents. These parents may need carefully worded invitations to get them to come to school for the first time, to feel welcome at the school, and to understand their role in helping the child succeed in school (Epstein & Scott-Jones, in press).

Families of Students in Upper Grades.   Although older children become more independent and peer-oriented than younger children, parents continue to exert a significant effect on their lives. Nevertheless, parental involvement in their children's education drops dramatically as they advance into the upper grades. Parents of older students are sometimes considered "hard to reach" primarily because most schools have not carried through with parental involvement activities across the grades (Epstein & Scott-Jones, in press).

Research demonstrates that teachers, parents, and students need better practices in the upper grades to create and continue productive school-family partnerships. Parents of students in the upper grades admit their lack of involvement at school but report being involved at home. Many parents, however, report that they do not know what to do to help their children as they approach middle school and beyond (Baker & Stevenson, 1986). Likewise, many students believe that their teachers do not want them to discuss schoolwork with their parents or that there is no reason to do so. This belief may stem in part from the fact that schools reduce their contacts with parents of students in the upper grades (Epstein & Scott-Jones, in press).

Various conditions may exist that discourage parents of older students from remaining involved in school activities. For example, some parents may have increased job responsibilities facing them once their children are settled in school. Others may have recently returned to work, with new time pressures and expectations. Others still have young children at home and perceive a more urgent need to remain involved with these children. It is also likely that parents of middle and high school students fail to receive ideas and guidance from school personnel on ways to remain involved or help their child with school.

It is clear that parents need information about helping their older children at school and methods for remaining involved in their education. The greatest changes in school and family connections come at transition times (from elementary to middle school and from middle to high school) (Epstein & Scott-Jones, in press). Efforts to keep parents involved at these critical junctures are particularly important. Activities, assemblies, and other events should be scheduled at times conducive to parents at least some of the time. Likewise, they should aim to help parents (1) understand adolescence and middle school organization, goals, and policies; (2) recognize early warning signs of poor school achievement; (3) prepare for teacher conferences with multiple teachers; (4) interpret test scores and report card grades; (5) volunteer in ways that are appropriate in the middle grades; (6) assist with homework; and (7) become involved with their child in course choices and career guidance (Epstein & Scott-Jones, in press).

Although issues and barriers will confront educators and families in their efforts to develop collaborative partnerships, it is clear that the benefits to students, parents, and school personnel far outweigh the difficulties. Thus, the relationship between families and schools is changing in contemporary education. Although various distinct practices can be suggested, it may be helpful to completely reconceptualize the role of parents and families as *partners* in educational activities.

Reconceptualizing the Role of the Home and Family in Education

Perhaps the most underutilized resource in the educational environment is the family. Significant individuals in the home setting can provide important and effective support in the education of students. To be meaningful, however, there is a "need for schools and families to modify their historical relationship and become partners in the education of all students" (Batsche, 1992, p. xv).

Overlapping Spheres of Influence Model

One meaningful way to reconceptualize home-school relationships is articulated by Epstein's (1987) *overlapping spheres of influence* model. Here (see Figure 9–1), the key environments that educate and socialize children are depicted as spheres that can overlap in their goals, resources, and practices. While the external structure of the model is one of overlapping spheres, the internal structure is comprised of interactions among the various members of school and family organizations that influence student learning and development. The model recognizes the interlocking histories of institutions that educate and socialize children (that is, school and home), and the changing and accumulating skills of the many individuals across these important settings.

Figure 9–1
Epstein's
Overlapping
Spheres of
Influence
Model

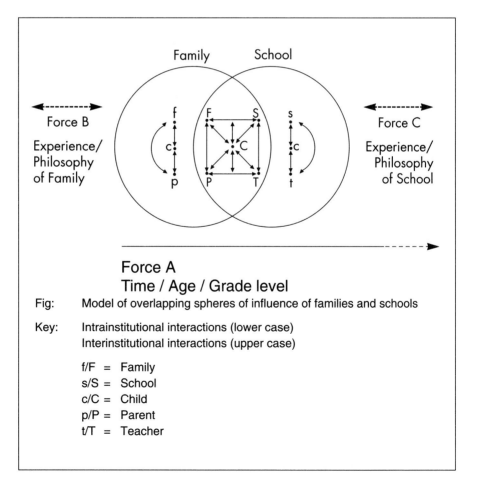

Fig:	Model of overlapping spheres of influence of families and schools
Key:	Intrainstitutional interactions (lower case)
	Interinstitutional interactions (upper case)

f/F = Family
s/S = School
c/C = Child
p/P = Parent
t/T = Teacher

Much of Epstein's model is based on Bronfenbrenner's (1979) ecological model presented in Chapter 3. That approach emphasizes the connections that occur between settings, such as the home and school. The ecological model emphasizes that personal development will be enhanced when exchanges between settings are bidirectional, with mutual trust and a balance of power. These are some of the characteristics that we have deemed important and necessary for partnerships.

Principles of Home-School Partnerships

Epstein (1992) described a number of basic perspectives that are important in the reconceptualized home-school relationship. First, *school and family connections are about children.* Consistent with the emphasis of this text, *students* must remain at the center of home-school programs. The main purpose of home-school partnerships is to help more students succeed in school. If relationships between schools and families remain positive, children will feel better about learning, work harder, and have more motivation to do well in school. Moreover, when strong partnerships are in place, problems with schoolwork or behavior can be managed in the early stages.

Second, *school and family connections are important at all grade levels.* Programs to promote partnerships between home and school must occur across all grade levels. Developmental and instructional changes occur from preschool to elementary school, from elementary to middle school, from middle to high school, and beyond. These transitional times present significant challenges to parents and students. Families need information about their children's school experiences across all grade levels, and schools need commitment from families to support educational goals as children move through the grades. If schools and families continue to forge partnerships at all grade levels and during transitions, children have better chances for educational success.

A third principle is that *school and family partnerships include all families.* Concerted efforts must be made to involve *all* families, not simply those that are easy to reach. Families of students who are at risk may be the most difficult to access, and may require the most clear, responsive, and specific communication regarding methods to help their children in school. Most families report that they would like to be involved in their child's education and that they need and want information on how to help their child be successful at school, but that they are not sure of the best way to help their child (Bauch, 1988; Dornbusch & Ritter, 1988; Epstein, 1986). This need for assistance and guidance likely increases as children progress through the school years. If home-school partnerships can be established and maintained early, continuous communication and interaction practices can serve to benefit students for the duration of their educational career and beyond.

Activity 9–4

Conceptually, most now agree that home-school collaboration is a desirable process in educational settings. A difficulty that exists in several schools is the lack of a clear vision regarding how the process might be implemented procedurally. In a small group, discuss what parental involvement and home-school collaboration efforts might look like in an "ideal" school. Who would participate? How would parents and families become involved? What would be some of the goals and objectives of a home-school program? How would participation be maintained? What would be the roles of teachers, administrators, school psychologists, school counselors, and special educators?

Fourth, *home-school partnerships are a process, not an event.* As with any attempt to establish effective educational partnerships, the development of home school programs takes time. Families and schools must strive to understand their mutual interests, develop trust, organize shared responsibilities, and take risks in the management of potential conflict. There must be time to assess needs, set goals, plan strategies, implement programs, evaluate program effects, and modify strategies to increase their effectiveness. Strong programs develop over time in a step-by-step process (remember the adage, "Think big, start small, go slow"). It has been estimated that schools must invest a minimum of three to five years for building strong home-school partnership programs. More time is necessary to ensure maintenance (Epstein, 1992).

A fifth principle states that *school-family linkages do not take the place of other school reform or school improvement initiatives.* It would be naive to suggest that home-school partnership programs can solve all of children's learning problems or increase school achievement. The learning process is much more complex than that. Rather, we suggest that the establishment of school-family linkages can support and enhance other school improvement efforts. Families are one resource of many that should be tapped to improve the educational experiences of students. They are necessary, but not sufficient in the overall efforts of educational restructuring initiatives.

Models of Home-School Programs

There are several models linking parents and educators that fall under the general umbrella of "home-school programs." In an excellent review, Swap (1992) described three types of models: school-to-home transmission, interactive, and partnership.

School-to-Home Transmission Model

The *school-to-home transmission model* encourages parents to adopt and support the values of schools, particularly those values and practices that lead to student success. The goals of this model are developed by school persons, and two-way communication is not a primary objective. This model has been summarized in the following way:

> Educators hope that parents will adopt an orientation that explicitly supports schooling and school personnel, and that they will either teach their children the social skills required for success in school and in life, and/or be responsive to the school's attempts to educate parents and children about these values and skills. (Swap, 1992; p. 59)

Most parental involvement programs in existence are based on the school-to-home transmission model. Examples are many, and include (1) parent training programs where parents are taught means of managing their child's behavior; (2) programs that ask parents to reinforce at home the values and attitudes deemed important at school; (3) lectures for parents on child development, talking to children, and helping with homework; and (4) "homework hotlines" for parents who have questions about homework (Swap, 1993).

Interactive Model

The *interactive model* recognizes that there are important and valuable differences between families and schools. Programs that espouse this model encourage open communication and stress reciprocal influences between homes and schools in the education of children. They are built on the premise of mutual respect between parents and educators, and they stress bidirectional learning and shared objectives.

Parental involvement models characterized as interactive in nature hold at least two primary objectives: to enhance students' successful achievement in the mainstream, and to value the goals and beliefs of the non-mainstream culture. Whereas in the school-to-home transmission model the school's primary cultural values and attitudes are emphasized to enhance students' success in mainstream society, the interactive model actively recognizes, respects, and supports the cultural diversity of students and families. Examples of the application of this model include "International Fairs" in schools with a diversity of cultures represented in its students, and inviting minority parents into the school to talk to students or to help teachers provide instruction. It is important to recognize that the inclusion of parents in this way not only provides support to school activities, but also transforms the culture of the school (Lightfoot, 1978). (See Chapter 5 for a broader discussion of school culture.)

Partnership Model

The *partnership model*, emphasized throughout this text, is based on mutual respect and an explicit, shared commitment to supporting the educational experiences of all students. This model views family-school relationships as essential to students' success. Parents are viewed as assets and resources in the development and implementation of strategies to promote success for all children.

To establish true partnerships between schools and families, the manner in which home-school relations are conceptualized must undergo a *paradigm shift* (Seeley, 1989). This refers to a fundamental reorganization of the way in which educators think about problems and solutions. It incorporates the idea that parents must be *empowered* to serve as active and meaningful participants in their child's education. *Empowerment* can be defined as "enabling experiences that (1) create opportunities for persons to work together in pursuit of a goal or interest and that (2) build upon and promote each partner's capabilities and capacities" (Dunst, Johanson, Rounds, Trivette, & Hamby, 1992; p. 159). Educational partnerships, then, are mutually empowering to both parents and educators.

Examples of the partnership model are Comer's (1980, 1988; Comer & Haynes, 1991) School Development Program and Levin's (1987) Accelerated Schools program. The School Development Program is presented in this chapter's "Spotlight." The Accelerated Schools program is described in Chapter 10's "Spotlight."

A parent educational program where parents learn specific skills that can be used in the home is an example of the school-to-home model.

Chapter Summary

Families are changing. To meet the needs of students most effectively, schools must become sensitive to these changes in demographic characteristics (for example, socioeconomic status, racial and cultural backgrounds, household composition) and restructure their programs to address these needs. In this chapter, we emphasized the importance of establishing home-school partnerships in an effort to maximize the outcomes for all students, including those at risk for educational failure.

The importance of home-school collaboration was predicated on several accounts. Conceptually, both homes and schools are considered systems that affect and are affected by each other. They both serve the same functional purpose: educating and socializing children. Empirically, the support for parental involvement and home-school collaboration is unequivocal. When parents are involved in educational endeavors, students, parents and teachers all benefit.

Although we now recognize the desirability of home-school partnerships, this was not always the case. Historically, the United States has seen varying degrees of permeability between homes and schools. In other words, depending on various social and political forces over the decades, the responsibilities between homes and schools has changed from *separate* (homes are responsible for nurturance, schools are responsible for teaching) to *sequential* (homes provide early enrichment, schools provide formal education), to *shared* (homes and schools both provide social and educational experiences simultaneously). Current issues in the establishment of home-school partnerships still focus on several practical and organizational barriers.

Educators face several special issues when attempting to establish working relationships with diverse families: Those with diverse parental background (such as minority and uneducated parents, and parents for whom English is a second language), those with diverse structures (such as single-parent households and those with parents working outside of the home), and those with students in the upper grades. Although these families may be considered "hard to reach" by many educators, it is safe to say that they are as interested in helping their children as "traditional" families. However, school personnel must be creative and flexible in establishing mechanisms to ensure their involvement.

The need for redefining the relationship between families and schools was described in detail. Epstein's (1987) overlapping spheres of influence model provides a heuristic aid for conceptualizing the reciprocal and dynamic nature of the interactions between families and school personnel. Several important principles and models were also described, which will serve as a foundation for the development and implementation of effective programs such as those discussed in Chapter 10.

Spotlight: School Development Program

The School Development Program is a comprehensive model project spearheaded by James Comer and the Yale Child Study Team in the mid-1960's. The schools originally targeted in the project were located in low-income neighborhoods and were 100 percent black, with 80 percent of the students benefiting from free- or reduced-lunch programs. The "Comer process" (Swap, 1993) is now being implemented in 150 schools in all parts of the United States.

The School Development Program consists of three mechanisms. The key element, the School Planning and Management Team, is a governance mechanism and is representative of all adult parties in the school (parents, teachers, administrators, professional support staff, and nonprofessional staff). The team carries out important management operations of development and implementation of a school plan, staff development, and assessment and modification. The second mechanism is a Mental Health Team that addresses developmental and behavioral needs of students by means of collaborative problem solving. The third mechanism is the Parent Program, which focuses primarily on supporting the social program of the school plan, enabling parents and staff together to facilitate the social development of students and to encourage them to do well socially as well as academically.

The Parent Program is implemented at three levels. Level 3 involves general participation of parents in activities such as holiday programs and other school events. Level 2 involves parents in day-to-day classroom and school activities. They participate meaningfully in important academic, social and behavioral functions, such as helping to carry out the academic and social programs in classrooms, assisting on field trips, and supporting behavioral and educational goals of students. Because of their day-to-day involvement, parents involved at this level become particularly knowledgeable about school needs and resources. At Level 1, parents are elected to participate on the School Planning and Management Team. In this capacity, they serve as a natural link to the communities in which schools are located. They serve with other adults from the school (i.e., teachers, professional and nonprofessional staff, and the principal), representing other parents in the development and implementation of a comprehensive school plan.

The School Development Model provides convincing evidence that the barriers of distrust between low-income, minority families and schools can be overcome. Several participating schools have received national recognition for achievement, and parents are involved effectively in several important roles (including curriculum development and school decision making). This exemplifies nicely the benefits of meaningful home-school partnerships.

Case Study 9–1

Lowell Elementary School is located in a suburban district with a mixture of middle class and upper-middle class patrons. The school staff is considered very stable, with an average of twelve years' experience across teachers. The principal (Mr. Daly) is supportive of the teachers, but rarely takes initiative in promoting new projects. Things at Lowell seem to run smoothly as is, and they have for a number of years.

The O'Connors moved into Lowell's catchment area at the beginning of the school year. Mrs. O'Connor was president of the PTA at her daughter's previous school. She also assisted teachers in the computer lab every Thursday afternoon and had a home-note system established with her daughter's teacher to maintain daily communication about her performance. She felt very positively about her relationship with the staff at their previous school.

The first day of school, Mrs. O'Connor made an appointment to visit with the principal of Lowell. Upon her arrival, Mr. Daly stated that "things are really busy the first day of school; I don't have much time and may get called out a lot!" They proceeded to talk with several interruptions. Midway through the meeting, Mrs. O'Connor asked Mr. Daly if she could observe the fourth-grade classroom in which her daughter would be enrolled. Mr. Daly responded immediately and firmly: "We don't do those sorts of things here." Mrs. O'Connor left feeling a bit confused and intimidated.

The next day when Stacy O'Connor returned from school, she reported that the work assigned in math was confusing. Apparently her teacher used a different approach to teaching than her previous teacher and Stacy had difficulty grasping the concepts being presented. Mrs. O'Connor called Ms. Shank (the fourth-grade teacher) to set up a meeting and work out a system whereby Stacy could be helped at home. Ms. Shank's response on the phone was surprising to Mrs. O'Connor: "I don't meet with parents until the first parent-teacher conference. This gives me the time to see where their children are at and prepare reports to inform parents of their child's standing in the class." Mrs. O'Connor hung up the phone, feeling angry and impatient.

1. What are some of the attitudes regarding home-school collaboration being conveyed by Mr. Daly, Ms. Shank, and Mrs. O'Connor? What practices (things they say and do) suggest that these attitudes exist?

2. Brainstorm ideas that Mrs. O'Connor could use to achieve her goals of becoming more actively involved in Stacy's education at her new school.

3. Brainstorm ideas that Mr. Daly, Ms. Shank, and others at the school could use to begin opening up to parents in a facilitative and constructive way.

Key Vocabulary Terms

deficit model of families
enhancement model of
  families
family-impact model
school-impact model
community-impact model
parental involvement

home-school collaboration
diverse parental backgrounds
diverse family structures
latchkey children
overlapping spheres of
  influence

school-to-home transmission
  model
interactive model
partnership model
paradigm shift
empowerment

Chapter 10

Chapter Overview

Strategies for Home-School Partnerships

Chapter Objectives

After reading this chapter, students will be able to
1. Discuss the importance of an open atmosphere in schools.
2. Describe activities that can be conducted at the district level to support families in education.
3. Outline the role of the school and school personnel in promoting parental involvement.
4. Identify the importance of effective communication and relationship building skills when working with parents.
5. Describe methods of improving communication with parents.
6. Outline the basic procedures for establishing parental involvement programs.
7. Identify various characteristics of effective home-school programs.
8. Explain five types of family involvement, with examples of each.
9. Present practical suggestions for implementing the five types of home-school programs.

In Chapter 9, we presented a foundation for home-school partnerships by reviewing conceptual, functional, and empirical rationales. In this chapter, we will describe practical guidelines and procedures by which to establish, maintain, and maximize various types of collaborative relationships between families and schools. As is the case in other forms of partnerships, home-school collaboration is not an end, but a means to increase the academic and social success of all students.

Establishing and Maintaining Home-School Partnerships

Establishing and maintaining effective, reciprocal relationships between schools and families is challenging. Such partnerships require effort on the part of parents to invest fully in the school, and they require effort on the part of educators to share authority with parents (Swap, 1993). Trust and open communication are the keys to initiating such partnerships and maximizing their potential once the components are in place.

Creating an Atmosphere of Openness

Parents have many diverse experiences with schools. Several parents remember their own elementary, middle, and high school years as times when their own parents and those of their friends were not actively involved in the school. Some parents may have negative memories of their schooling if they had difficulties with learning or behavior. Others are skeptical of communications that they receive from the school because they are used to hearing only bad news ("Samantha is failing in math;" "Please come and get Jason from school—he was in a fight on the playground.") Obviously, when parents are angry, skeptical, or apathetic, it is unlikely that they will "break down the schoolhouse doors" to become involved in a constructive and positive way. Thus, when trying to solicit the active involvement of all families, it is important that the school atmosphere be open, positive, and facilitative.

There are many ways to convey an atmosphere of openness in schools. Several concrete suggestions are provided in Table 10–1. In addition to these recommendations, educators should ask a series of questions to assess the message that is sent to parents. Honest and candid responses to the following questions may enable school staff to improve the atmosphere for increased parental interest.

What Is the District's Message to Parents?   Most school districts are replete with policies about virtually every activity and event that goes on in school buildings. An important piece of information is the policy that the district adopts regarding parental involvement. For example, the San Diego City School District formulated a comprehensive policy that has been approved by

Table 10–1 **Creating an Open Atmosphere in Schools**

1. Display signs that welcome visitors. Include welcome signs in various languages if the school has several families in which English is not the primary language.
2. Post a map that depicts where the office is located.
3. Arrange flowers, brightly colored murals, children's pictures, or photographs of teachers, students, and parents in the entrance hallway.
4. Designate a space for a parent center with accommodations for coffee, tea, or soft drinks.
5. Assign a parent to greet other parents at the entrance of the school at drop-off and pick-up times during the first week of school.
6. Develop a friendly and inviting greeting for secretaries to use when answering the phone.
7. Arrange for translators for parents who do not speak English.
8. Designate "visiting hours" when parents can come into the school to meet with the principal or spend time in their child's classroom. Allow parents to schedule visits if designated times are inconvenient.
9. Publish a school newsletter early in the school year to offer a welcome to all families.
10. Develop a parent-outreach program where trained parents visit other parents' homes to share information and "helpful hints."

the school board. Given its extensiveness and appropriateness as a model for all school districts, it is paraphrased here:

> The Board of Education recognizes the necessity and value of parent involvement to support student success and academic achievement. In order to assure collaborative partnerships between parents and schools, the board, working through the administration, is committed to
>
> a. involving parents as partners in school governance . . .
> b. establishing effective two-way communication with all parents . . .
> c. developing strategies and programmatic structures at schools to enable parents to participate . . .
> d. providing support and coordination for school staff and parents . . .
> e. utilizing schools to connect students and families with community resources. . . . (adapted from Swap, 1993, pp. 62–63)

Although district-level policy statements are not sufficient to ensure effective home-school connections, they can help individual schools activate family involvement programs. There are other important things that can happen at the district level also. Importantly, district administrators must provide more than "lip service" support for home-school collaborative efforts. For example, a commitment to fund parental involvement policies for at least three to five years (which is the minimum time required to effectively implement programs) can come from a district's central office. Likewise, district administrators can create and allow decision-making structures that bring parents and educators together through initiatives such as site-based management. Active and visible district support mechanisms such as these can provide the organizational means by which to initiate parental involvement programs.

What Is the School's Message to Parents?   As Zeldin (1990) aptly summarized, "State and district mandates can facilitate or diminish the change process, but ultimately, it is the school staff . . . who make the initiative work" (p. 29). A school's culture (as described in Chapter 5), generally sets the stage for effective and productive home-school relations. According to Swap (1993), "the school culture that would be most favorable to reaching out to parents is one in which the staff felt strong and secure, empowered to make important decisions about their work life, and eager for more information and resources that would help them to fully educate children" (p. 65).

It is the role of *all* individuals in the school building (including administrators, teachers, specialized staff, secretaries, bus drivers, coaches, lunchroom aides, and custodians) to promote an atmosphere of openness to parents. Thus, messages sent by all school staff, both formally and informally, should be considered important communications to families.

There are a number of ways that schools' messages are conveyed to parents. In their book, *Beyond the Bake Sale,* Henderson, Marburger, and Ooms (1986) describe signs posted on the doors of various schools. In a school in Great Britain, they identified a sign saying, "Parents are not allowed into the playground before school, during school hours, at dinner time, or after. If you wish to see the head teacher . . . you must ask the school keeper to make an appointment for you" (cited in Henderson et al., 1986, p. 64). Contrast that to a sign saying, "Welcome. We are glad you have come to visit. Please report to the office." (p. 63). The difference is obvious in these examples. In the first, the school seems to be adopting a defensive and closed stance toward parents. In the second, parents and others from the community are openly invited into the school, while still maintaining a "check-in" policy to monitor individuals' presence in the building.

In Chapter 5, we explored the various roles of principals, and suggested that they often set a particular tone or climate in the school. *Building administrators* can promote a climate of family involvement in several ways. For example, they can (1) create a school policy that invites parental participation; (2) hire teachers who enjoy and prioritize working with parents; (3) model proactive efforts to reach out to parents; (4) utilize "creative scheduling" in the school to ensure that appropriate times and places are available for parental activities; (5) support in-service and other training opportunities to enable staff to remain abreast of effective practices; and (6) encourage staff involvement in parent programs by providing incentives (Swap, 1993).

Research in the area of parental involvement supports the important role of building administrators. For example, Hauser-Cram (1983) found that there was significantly more parental involvement in second-grade classrooms when principals established an explicit policy encouraging it. Administrative policies in different schools promote various types of parental involvement. Leadership appears to be related to levels of parental involvement in schools (Epstein, 1987a).

The point of entry into educational endeavors for many parents lies at their child's classroom door. In other words, interest is generally first initiated via issues surrounding their own child's learning experiences. *Classroom teachers* obviously have a tremendous opportunity to invoke parental involvement in education.

There are a number of factors that contribute to a teacher's attempts to involve parents. In general, when teachers perceive that they are supported for parent involvement by their colleagues and by parents, they consider involvement programs more favorably. Size of classroom may also be a factor, as parent contacts by teachers of self-contained classes with limited numbers of students were found to be more frequent and diverse than contacts by other teachers (Epstein & Dauber, 1991).

Unfortunately, at the current time little attention is afforded to parental involvement and home-school collaboration in teacher preparation programs. Thus, teachers are often requested to work actively with parents, but are uncertain about the most effective way to approach this task. They may perceive parent outreach as an additional burden on their already full schedule.

There are several ways that teachers can be supported in their attempts to work with parents. For example, educators who are known to have expertise in effective home-school programs can collaborate with an individual or group of teachers and assist them to establish a management plan for parental involvement. The ecological problem-solving model presented in Chapter 3 provides a structured format by which this can be accomplished. Teachers can have opportunities to observe and model programs already in place, and should be given adequate time and resources to develop a meaningful program for use with their students and parents. They should also be excused to attend educative sessions such as courses, workshops, and conferences that provide practical knowledge and skills for parental involvement. If a school has adopted a particular family involvement program, teachers should be provided adequate knowledge and support to implement it with their students, and flexibility to mold various components to meet their needs.

Along with administrators and teachers, *specialized support staff* (school psychologists, school counselors, special educators, occupational and physical therapists, speech and language therapists, nurses) are important to the home-school link. School psychologists and counselors may have acquired special expertise in working with parents through their professional preparation programs. They may be especially instrumental in dealing with "difficult" or "hard to reach" parents. In some cases, their knowledge base with particular types of student problems will necessitate their involvement with certain parents. For example, if a parent becomes involved with school staff due to a concern with her daughter's social withdrawal and apparent depression, the school psychologist would likely be an invaluable participant. Special educators may have special knowledge about litigation and parents rights, and should be involved in cases where these types of issues may become apparent. Speech/language therapists and occupational/physical therapists also must work with parents to develop goals for students and ensure that the skills students learn at school transfer to the home.

What Messages Are Sent to Individual Parents?   The question pertaining to the type of message sent to parents must be asked of all educators and individuals in the school setting. Important aspects of messages include both the nature of statements (the actual words used) and the manner in which they are delivered (the tone, openness, and sincerity conveyed). Obviously, these often overlap to portray an especially positive or negative message to families.

Educators should monitor their exact communications to parents to gauge the nature of their statements. Oftentimes, teachers, administrators or support staff say things to parents that are insensitive, defensive, or unintended. For example, consider the impact a statement such as the following may have on a parent: "Michael is really different than the other kids. He's just really lazy when it comes to schoolwork!" Statements such as this may have the effect of degrading parents or widening the gap between them and the school. It is important to remember that most parents are emotionally invested in their child, and demeaning comments regarding their child are often taken personally.

One way of monitoring communications to parents is to keep the overall objective of *engaging parents* at the fore. In other words, it is important to approach all interactions as a potentially "win-win" situation, rather than a "win-lose" confrontation. This means that *each time* the home and school interact (verbally, in writing, through homework), a positive and inviting tone is conveyed. Take, for example, a parent who approaches a teacher and claims, "You're giving Suzie too much homework!" A defensive, critical, or otherwise negative response might be, "Well, Suzie *is* the lowest in the class and she needs the extra work! I can't keep the other kids at her level, and I simply don't have the time to spend with her one-on-one!" Contrast this to an open and inviting response such as, "I can see you're concerned about Suzie's homework. Let's take a look at where she's at and decide how we can meet her needs."

There are certain "killer phrases" that are often used with parents that can serve to cut off communication and therefore close the door for further collaboration (Henderson et al., 1987). These are often scapegoats ("My boss at the district office won't allow that," or, "It's against federal regulations") or cop-outs ("That won't work in our school," or, "There's no money for a program like that"). Other killer phrases are listed in Table 10–2. How many sound familiar? How many have you used in the past?

As emphasized in Chapter 4, there is more to communication than mere words. The manner in which the words are spoken and the message conveyed nonverbally are also powerful aspects of interpersonal

Table 10–2   **Killer Phrases**

1. That's a good idea, but . . .
2. It's against policy.
3. It's impractical.
4. It costs too much.
5. Let's sit on it for awhile.
6. That's not our problem.
7. The district superintendent won't allow it.
8. It's too hard.
9. That's not the way we do it.
10. Let's form a committee to discuss it.

Source: Adapted with modifications from Henderson, Marburger, & Ooms (1987, p. 67).

communication. The active listening and relationship building skills described in Chapter 4 are extremely important when interacting with parents.

When interacting with parents, it is important that communication be bidirectional. Thus, educators must be good listeners. You will recall that active listening skills can be remembered with the acronym CAPS. These skills include clarifying, attending, paraphrasing, and summarization.

Clarification is important to ensure that parents understand exactly what is meant. Specific and concrete examples help clarify messages for parents. For example, if you would like a parent to understand that his child has difficulty sitting still, you might describe observations during a twenty-minute independent work time (for example, child got out of his seat three times to sharpen his pencil, throw paper away, and look at the class gerbil; he talked to a peer for four minutes; he approached teacher two times to ask permission to go to his hallway locker). These types of concrete statements with specific behavioral referents are more clear than a statement such as, "Your child is simply hyperactive!"

Attending is the second active listening skill, and includes the SHARE behaviors: Sit squarely/have an open posture; Acknowledge parents' statements;

**Activity
10–1**

Fold a sheet of paper in half vertically. Label the left column "Killers" and the right column "Motivators." With a small group of other students, write the killer phrases listed in Table 10–2 in the left column. Generate a list of others that you have used or heard used and add them to the list. For each killer phrase, identify why the message impedes communication and collaboration. In other words, what makes it a "killer phrase"? In the right column, rewrite the phrase so that it conveys a positive and inviting tone. In other words, change the killer phrase to one that motivates action.

Relax; use Eye communication. It is recommended that readers review these skills in Chapter 4. The main advantage of attending is that it conveys to parents the message that you care about what they are saying and that you want to understand their viewpoint.

Paraphrasing is the third component of good listening, and involves restating in your own words the main points of a parent's statement. For example, a parent might describe numerous issues associated with homework completion (for example, her daughter refuses to begin homework, does not know the assignments, fails to have the necessary books or tools, works sporadically). An appropriate paraphrase in this example might be, "It sounds like homework is a difficult time at your house, as your daughter tries very hard to avoid it altogether."

Summarization is the final active listening skill. It is extremely important to use with parents, as it "pulls together" several key points of a discussion and ensures that all participants understand and agree upon what was said. Summarization also strengthens communications by emphasizing those issues in need of attention.

Advanced relationship building skills are also important when interacting with parents. These include the GRACE behaviors of genuineness, reflection, acceptance, concreteness, and empathy. These skills are critical to promote an atmosphere of respect and openness to parents. They convey the message that parents are worthwhile and valued in the school. Readers are referred to Chapter 4 to review these skills and relate them to working with parents.

How Are Opportunities for Communication Established?   A final question that educators must ask concerns the opportunities parents have to communicate with the school. This includes formal and informal outlets available to parents to invite two-way communication.

One of the most effective ways to initiate communication with parents is through informal mechanisms such as social events and gatherings. Following an extensive two-year study of urban schools, Swap (1990) concluded that "when there has not been a history of parent involvement . . . activities that promote pleasant social encounters and exchange of information among adults are indispensable. These activities, usually supplemented by food and informal conversation, provide a mechanism for parents and teachers to develop an acquaintance as 'just people' . . . these types of activities signal a mutual interest in establishing adult relationships on behalf of the child and in breaking down the barriers between home and school" (p. 110). Informal

| Activity 10–2 | Review the advanced relationship-building skills of Genuineness, Reflection, Acceptance, Concreteness, and Empathy described in Chapter 4. On a sheet of paper, provide a definition for each one. Then generate at least three concrete examples of each as it might be used with parents. |

social events can promote an atmosphere of openness, caring, and trust that is necessary to carry out mutual programs in the future. They can be considered the "essential lubrication for more serious interventions" (Davies, 1990, p. 42).

Informal activities that engage parents with educators can be presented in a variety of ways. Some examples include a multicultural potluck dinner with entertainment, adult and child activities in a nearby park on a Saturday afternoon, family member breakfasts, welcoming "coffee hours" for new families, and holiday celebrations (Swap, 1993). Suggestions for increasing the success of informal events are presented in Table 10–3.

There are a number of formal mechanisms by which to communicate with parents. Some (such as conferences and consultations) will be discussed in a later section of this chapter. At this time we describe additional basic forums for communication between home and school, including "Open House" nights, newsletters, report cards, and school-home notes.

Most parents and educators are familiar with Open House night at schools. Inviting parents in to the school to see classrooms and discuss expectations with their child's teacher provides an excellent opportunity to allow parents to experience schools firsthand. When conducted at the beginning of the school year, they can send a message of interest in involving parents in collaborative exercises throughout the year. They can also be used to (1) learn from parents what goals they have for their child; (2) identify possible resources that may be provided from home; and (3) develop strategies for continued communication between parents and school staff.

A key to effective communication between parents and the school is regularity. In other words, one-time events such as an open house or informal potluck-in-the-park are important, but not sufficient to ensure open communication. Rather, the dialogue must continue throughout the school year. One method of promoting ongoing communication is through newsletters. Monthly newsletters

Table 10–3 Suggestions for Increasing the Success of Informal Events

1. Provide a two- to four-week notice of upcoming events.
2. Prepare personal invitations in parents' native language.
3. Schedule some events on weekends, evenings, or other times conducive for working parents.
4. Send reminders home.
5. Provide transportation and child care to families in need of these services.
6. Have refreshments available; an informal meal is especially inviting.
7. Plan events carefully (e.g., seating arrangements, open discussions) to promote informal communication between parents and school personnel.
8. Evaluate events by asking parents and school staff their perceptions. Use feedback for planning future events.

can, for example, announce school activities, identify academic goals, report schoolwide achievement test scores, and celebrate successes of students, teachers, staff, or parents. Letters or articles can also be solicited from parents or representatives of the Parent-Teacher Association to ensure that their voices be heard.

Report cards are an additional type of formal communication that can be very effective in keeping parents abreast of their child's performance. When used properly, they can be instrumental in monitoring the progress of an individual child over the course of a school year. We believe, however, that report cards are too infrequent and contain little functional information that can help parents understand precisely what their child is doing in school. Thus, more regular and informative communications through mechanisms such as a home-note should supplement report cards.

School-home notes (discussed again later in this chapter) are daily, written communications between teachers and parents that provide information regarding a student's academic performance or behavior. An important feature of home notes is their bidirectional communication potential. In other words, parents can be informed not only of their child's performance in the note. They can also be encouraged to provide comments to the teacher or other school staff to ensure that an active dialogue continues. Likewise, home notes should not only report negative behaviors or difficulties the child is having, but should be structured so that positive comments can be highlighted. School-home notes will be described in greater detail in a later section of this chapter.

Basic Procedures for Establishing Programs

As is evident from the previous and ensuing discussions, home-school collaboration, like all forms of collaboration, is a process that evolves. It is neither an event nor an end; rather, it is a means of enhancing the educational experiences of all children. The method of involving parents in individual schools must be determined by the needs of the constituencies and the resources available. Whatever form they take, the same eight basic steps, presented in Table 10–4, can be followed to enhance their success (Henderson et al., 1987).

Table 10–4   **Procedures for Establishing Home-School Programs**

1. Provide at least half-time coordination for activities.
2. Assess together the needs and resources.
3. Develop a common understanding about the roles parents and staff will play.
4. Recruit parents actively; select and assign them carefully.
5. Provide training for parents and staff.
6. Establish several communication channels and keep them open.
7. Provide continuing support services for parent activities.
8. Allow frequent opportunities for evaluation and feedback.

Source: Excerpted from Henderson, Marburger, & Ooms (1987, pp. 46–49).

Characteristics of Effective Programs

Some characteristics of home-school programs that can increase their effectiveness are presented in Table 10–5. In general, effective parental involvement programs consider the *cost-return ratio*. The cost of a program (in terms of monetary, personal, and time expenses) should be in line with returns and available resources. In other words, when setting up a volunteer program, educators might ask, "Is it worth the time, effort, and money? Do the benefits outweigh the costs?"

A second important characteristic of effective programs is that they be *minimally intrusive*. Programs that ask teachers to completely reschedule their day or planned activities, or that ask parents to take on roles that are uncomfortable or unrealistic are doomed for failure. A program should not consume all of a teachers' or parents' time or overtake effective programs already in operation. Rather, it should serve as an asset to existing educational programs.

Third, home-school programs should *empower* parents and teachers. Parents should feel that the program is in their best interest and in the best interest of their child. For example, they must see the merit of developing parenting skills, learning about their child's school experiences, or meeting with school personnel to set up a contract for their child. They should feel that their cooperation and assistance are valued and vital to program success.

Table 10–5   Components of Effective Home-School Programs

Successful programs
1. Are designed with the expectation that parents will be involved.
2. Tailor activities to meet the needs of the particular parents involved.
3. Include a variety of types of parental involvement.
4. Utilize creative and flexible program activities.
5. Communicate expectations, roles, and responsibilities.
6. Consider staff skills and available resources.
7. Recognize variations in parents' skills.
8. Are characterized by a balance of power so that parents are involved in decision making and administrative decisions are explained.
9. Provide increased opportunities for interaction.
10. Expect problems but emphasize solutions.
11. Empower parents and school personnel.
12. Are minimally intrusive.
13. Are clear and specific.
14. Are designed with obtainable goals and objectives.
15. Have an acceptable cost-return ratio.
16. Assess parents' and school personnels' perceptions of programs.

Likewise, teachers should believe that having parents involved also benefits them in their educational efforts, and that they are equipped to elicit parental support and assistance in the future.

Ease of implementation is a fourth important component of effective programs. To be effective, the program should have clear and specific parameters regarding what will be done, how the procedures will be implemented, when and where the program will be run, and who will be involved. Clear, specific program guidelines will enhance ease of implementation and facilitate successful application.

Fifth, successful programs *match goals, purposes, and activities.* When deciding to implement a parental participation program, schools must initially outline the specific objectives it wishes to attain. The activities to involve parents that follow should be related directly to achieving the stated goals and objectives of the program. For example, if a school wishes to increase communication with families and the community, activities such as hotlines, newsletters, memos to businesses, conferences, home notes, and invitations to visit the school are likely to meet with success. Activities that would not be appropriate in this case are those that ask parents to help make bulletin boards or monitor the playground. While these activities are worthwhile and meaningful in some situations, they do not support the overall program goals of increasing communication with a range of school patrons.

In a discussion of a comprehensive family-school collaboration project, Weiss and Edwards (1992) identified three additional major barriers to collaborative relations. First, they suggested that schools and families typically fail to establish ongoing routines for sharing information, developing educational plans, and addressing problems. Second, various differences between families and schools (including racial, cultural and socioeconomic differences) create real or assumed barriers. Third, Weiss and Edwards discuss the limited conceptions that are held about the roles that parents could play in the school as a major deterrant to collaborative home-school partnerships. It appears that establishing ongoing and open communication, respecting and capitalizing on differences (rather than allowing them to serve as barriers), and expanding the various ways that parents can be involved are central to maximize family involvement.

Types of Family Involvement

In a comprehensive and oft-cited approach to school and family connections, Epstein (1987a, 1987b) identified five main types of parental involvement. Each type of home-school program is valuable; no one is inherently superior to any other. Rather, as with any partnership discussed in this text, immediate situations and presenting issues should dictate the type of program that is most appropriate at any given time. We present the five types of programs with concrete examples and suggested practices.

Basic Obligations of Parents

The first type of home-school program addresses the basic needs of parents in providing the nutrition, health care, parenting skills, and child care appropriate for their children. Parents perform the early child-rearing obligations that prepare children for school and continue their responsibilities through childhood and adolescence. Once children are school age, parents must ensure that they have the basic supplies, time, and space to complete schoolwork. In a survey conducted by Epstein (1986), over 97 percent of parents reported that their children had the school supplies they needed, and over 90 percent said the children had a regular place where they could do homework.

Because parents vary in their experiences and abilities, schools can take active roles in helping parents understand and develop positive home

Spotlight: Accelerated Schools Program

The Accelerated Schools Program, designed by Levin (1987), is an experimental program that offers a comprehensive approach to school reform and parental involvement. The program was initially implemented in 1986 in two low-income schools in California, but now involves more than 150 schools in 17 states. The mission of this program is to move each student into the educational mainstream by the end of the sixth grade. The three cornerstones of the model include (1) an interdisciplinary accelerated curriculum; (2) instructional practices that promote active learning; and (3) an organizational model characterized by the participation of administrators, teachers, and parents.

In the Accelerated Schools Program, every student receives individualized objectives, with periodic assessment of progress toward the specific objectives. Parental involvement is perceived as critical to the overall goals of the model. Educators and parents are committed to creating a school culture in which all students can be successful. Parents are engaged in school-based steering committees; in setting expectations for students; in establishing an agreement specifying the obligations of parents, students, and school staff; and in providing academic assistance to their children. They serve as volunteers, paid aides, and teachers of their own children. Of particular importance is the emphasis placed on academic achievement; parental involvement is perceived as a means of contributing to the primary mission of schools (i.e., educating students), rather than an indirect activity.

Research continues to be conducted on the Accelerated Schools Program. In several schools implementing the model, students' achievement test scores are rising significantly. Although the scores are not all reaching the national average, the model seems to be promoting meaningful types of parental involvement, thus increasing academic performance and establishing important changes in the educational structure of schools.

conditions for their children's learning. Thus, one important form of service within this framework is parent education programs. *Parent education* is defined as "a systematic and conceptually based program, intended to impart information, awareness, or skills to the participants on aspects of parenting" (Fine, 1980, pp. 5–6). This type falls under the rubric of the school-to-home transmission model (Swap, 1992) described in Chapter 9. In general, parent education models depend on lectures and discussions to disseminate information, heighten awareness, and change attitudes (Kramer, 1990). The goals of parent education typically include helping parents achieve greater self-awareness, improve parent-child communication, make family life more enjoyable, and attain useful information on child development (Fine, 1980). Schools may furthermore provide programs that are designed to meet parents' needs beyond those directly related to child care (such as courses to allow parents to obtain their GED or classes in English as a second language).

Parent education is typically considered an umbrella that subsumes more specific approaches to working with parents (including parent training and parent-teacher consultation). Some basic characteristics of parent education include limited involvement with parents' personal problems, a limited scope of interpersonal communication, and predetermined number and length of sessions (Sheridan, 1993). As one element of a parental involvement program, parent education can provide a mechanism to get parents into the school building and help them feel connected to the school.

Suggested Practices.   A number of strategies can be implemented to improve the effectiveness of parent-education programs. Perhaps the most critical is to ensure that the programs offered are responsive to the needs of parents they are meant to reach. Some form of *needs assessment* can be instrumental in determining the specific topics or skills that interest parents. A needs assessment can be conducted through interviews with parents, surveys, or group meetings, and should request parents to respond with concrete ideas regarding the types of programs that would be of greatest help. This process may be time-consuming; however, it is critical in maximizing the overall meaningfulness and effectiveness of parent education efforts. All parents should have an opportunity to respond to a needs assessment. Once the data is gathered, programs should reflect the parents' priorities. For example, an advisory committee (including both educators and parents) might be established to analyze the findings from the needs assessment, review the priorities mentioned by a number of parents, and develop and evaluate programs. Swap (1992) suggests identifying a chair or co-chair of parent education committees who can take or share responsibility for calling and leading meetings, and coordinating tasks such as identifying and securing necessary resources, identifying potential speakers, and publicizing activities. This co-chair responsibility might be best served if shared by parent and school representatives.

Once needs and interests are identified, a program should be developed that covers chosen topics adequately. There are a number of ways that the program can be delivered. For example, parents may meet hourly once a week for eight weeks to learn about behavioral parenting techniques. Other formats include half-day workshops, videotape presentations, and evening discussions. Models, hands-on practice, feedback, written materials, homework, and group interaction are all important to enhance parents' understanding of information (Kramer, 1990).

A common pitfall of parent education programs occurs when educators plan several single-session activities on various divergent topics. Although several topical areas can be covered in this way, the session format does not allow adequate depth into any one area. Different groups will often attend the sessions, so parental involvement is sporadic and does not continue over time. Also, this approach is very time-consuming because each activity requires different leaders, separate outreach efforts, and individualized organization (Swap, 1992). Although the information provided may be interesting and stimulating, noninteractive approaches rarely lead to changes in parents' attitudes or behaviors.

As one means of improving family involvement in schools, parent education programs may be enhanced by including activities that are of interest to both parents and educators. For example, teachers and parents both might be interested in developing creative ways to integrate learning activities into everyday activities. A Saturday morning workshop on this topic, with hands-on demonstrations and opportunities for parents and teachers to try out new techniques together, can serve the dual purpose of disseminating information to interested parties and engaging parents and teachers in meaningful dialogue. This type of program is preferable to one that invites parents into the school to see only other parents, an outside "expert" discussing discovery learning, and a school-based organizer.

An important, logistical consideration to increase the effectiveness of parent education programs involves addressing parents' concerns with child care, transportation, and scheduling. When possible, babysitting services should be available in the school at the time of events. Seeking student volunteers from upper grades or parent or teacher representatives to tend children whose parents are participating in the program may be possible in some settings. Scheduling preferences can be polled in the needs assessment, as can transportation needs. Whenever possible, carpooling and ride-sharing opportunities should be coordinated in the planning stage.

It is common practice for educators to become excited about a number of potential programs and try to cover them all in a short period of time, such as one school year. However, as with any partnership program, it is important to "start small and go slow." As expressed by Swap (1992), "it is better to offer a few high-quality, well-planned activities than to provide a lot of mediocre events . . . excellent programs are the best way to recruit parents for future activities" (p. 68). If conducted appropriately and effectively, programs will become not only desirable, but essential in promoting the overall goals of educational settings. Resources may then continue to be available to offer quality programs over several years.

Basic Obligations of Schools

The second type of home-school collaboration model articulates the *basic obligations of schools*. In a basic sense, schools have an obligation to inform parents about school programs and their children's progress, so school-to-home communications are important at this level. Common examples of this type of home-school connection include report cards, memos, notices of special events, school-home notes, and conferences.

Surprisingly, large numbers of parents are excluded from some of the most basic, traditional communications from schools. According to Epstein (1986), over one-third of parents surveyed had no conference with their child's teacher the previous year, and two-thirds never talked to a teacher by phone. Although most teachers (over 95%) report that they communicate with their students' parents, most parents do not believe that they are involved in meaningful or frequent communications with teachers about their child's progress (Epstein, 1986).

Good, open communication between the home and school is the key to parental involvement, and is considered by some to be necessary for student success. According to Swap (1992), "the key to good communication is an attitude that welcomes parents as adult peers in a context of mutual respect . . . each respects the other's contributions and expertise; boundaries are clear . . . conflicts are dealt with openly and respectfully; and contacts are rewarding" (p. 69).

School-home notes (also referred to as "daily report cards") provide an effective means of communicating with parents. As mentioned earlier, these notes are daily written communication between teachers and parents that provide information regarding a student's academic performance or behavior. They can take many forms, including a brief, half-page document on which teachers can tally occurrences of target behaviors (such as work completed or on-task behaviors) or lengthier, open-ended forms on which teachers and parents can write comments to each other. Due to their flexible format, school-home notes are appropriate for students at any grade level. A sample school-home note for preschool and primary aged children is shown in Figure 10–1.

The benefits of school-home notes are many (Kelley, 1990; Kelley & Carper, 1988). First, they serve to establish communication between parents and teachers, promoting a collaborative problem-solving approach. They provide parents with frequent feedback and typically focus on positive rather than negative behavior. Furthermore, school-home notes are time and cost efficient. Because consequences are generally delivered at home, they require little teacher time and do not require significant alterations in teaching style. Parents often have access to a wider variety of reinforcers than do teachers, so programs using notes are likely to be effective. Some researchers have also

Figure 10–1
Sample home-
school note for
primary
students

DAILY HOME NOTE					
NAME		**DATE**			
PARENT'S INITIALS					
BEHAVIORS	**MON**	**TUE**	**WED**	**THUR**	**FRI**
UNSATISFACTORY= AVERAGE= GREAT=					
COMMENTS:					
TEACHER'S PHONE PARENT'S PHONE					

suggested that delayed reinforcement via a home-based treatment program may enhance generalization of treatment effects.

School-home notes typically incorporate a positive reinforcement system, whereby consequences for attainment of goals are delivered at home. Take the example of Stephen, a fourteen-year-old ninth-grade student with organizational difficulties. In a conference between Stephen's teachers and parents, "getting to classes on time at least five out of six periods per day" was targeted as a behavioral goal. It was agreed that each teacher would sign the school-home note if Stephen arrived to class on time. At the end of the school day, Stephen was to show his completed note to his mother. A tally chart was kept at home. Each day Stephen met his goal, he earned one token for the video arcade. Whenever Stephen accrued five tokens, he was allowed to go to the local mall and cash in his tokens on video games.

In many schools, the *parent-teacher conference* is the primary forum for communication. There are two main types of parent-teacher conference: group and individual (Epstein, 1988). *Group conferences* include "back-to-school nights," workshops or discussions on special topics, or grade/class-room-level meetings. These are used to discuss with groups of parents the programs, policies, and issues of importance to large numbers of parents and students. In *individual conferences,* the focus of attention is on one individual student. These conferences may be convened to discuss the student's work or progress, to increase a parent's understanding about the child's performance, to increase the teacher's knowledge about the child, or to identify academic or other problems that need improvement. Individual conferences may be *informal,* where parents come to school unannounced before or after school, or *formal,* where meetings are scheduled on a "free" day, in the evenings, or at any time at the request of the teacher or parent. Both group and individual conferences (formal and informal) are important at all grade levels.

Traditionally speaking, most parent-teacher conferences are "information giving"—that is, they are structured to provide to parents information regarding their child's classroom, schoolwork, and curriculum. We believe that conferences can be a vehicle to forge home-school partnerships if the format is one of "information sharing." In other words, the flow of information disseminated in conferences should be bidirectional. The knowledge that parents have about their child can be critically important to a teacher's attempts to educate the child. Likewise, observations and experiences that a teacher has with a student can assist parents who attempt to help their child with learning activities at home.

Suggested Practices.   There are a number of practices that can be employed to increase the effectiveness of school-to-home communications. The most basic requirement of a good communication device is that it be understood by its consumers (that is, parents). In some schools, this will mean sending notices, memos, and other written communications in more than one language to inform non-English-speaking families of school issues. Likewise, it may mean supplementing written communications with phone calls to ensure that nonliterate parents are privy to necessary information.

A comprehensive text providing practial recommendations for establishing school-home notes is available in Kelley (1990). In general, there are eleven steps in designing and using a school-home note program. First, it is important to conduct a parent-teacher conference to discuss the student's problems and identify goals. The problem-solving worksheet provided in Chapter 3 can serve as an invaluable tool in these problem-solving meetings. Second, using the information discussed in the conference, parents and teachers should work together to define the target behavior to increase. Common behaviors include following directions, turning in homework, remaining on-task, and interacting appropriately with peers. Third, small goals should be set to allow the child to experience success quickly and frequently.

Once these preliminary steps are completed, the teacher and parent together should design the school-home note. On the note, a place for the child's name, date, and signatures (of teacher[s], student, and parent) are important. Each note will have a different format, but should list or define the target behaviors clearly. Readers are referred to a text by Kelley (1990) for examples of various formats.

Fifth, responsibilities of teachers, students, and parents should be well-articulated. Sixth, the reward system should be established. Both daily (short-term) and weekly (long-term) rewards are helpful to maintain a student's interest in the program. Chapter 7 describes various other considerations for establishing effective reward systems. The next step of setting up a school-home note requires that the program be explained to the child in a positive and constructive way.

The eighth step for utilizing school-home notes suggested by Kelley (1990) is to collect baseline data. This is done by completing the notes for approximately one week without rewarding behavior. Parents and teachers thus know how the child is performing and can help determine short-term goals. Ninth, teachers and parents should provide frequent verbal feedback and praise to the student as they review the note daily. Tenth, it is extremely important that parents follow through with promised consequences each time the child attains an agreed upon goal. The final step for using school-home notes is to fade the system when the behavior improves and the program goals are met.

School personnel can work with parents to support and improve policies to inform parents, students, and the community at large about school activities and events. Schools can schedule conferences at times convenient for all parents, including those who work outside the home or have other personal or family-related responsibilities. Administrators and parent groups can encourage businesses to provide parents with release time, flex-time, or other special time allocations to attend meetings at school during the morning or afternoon.

Conferences can serve important, meaningful roles, or they can be "perfunctory rituals" (Epstein, 1988). A number of important procedural details are suggested in Table 10–6 to improve their effectiveness. Likewise, administrators can (1) initiate a review of conference policies with central administration, teachers, parents and union representatives to provide adequate teacher release time and flexibility for conferences; (2) model a welcoming attitude

Table 10–6   Suggestions for Improving Conferences

Before the Conference

1. Make efforts to establish a relationship with parents prior to the conference. Informal social events, such as those discussed under the heading of "How Are Opportunities for Communication Established" (p. 325) can be of assistance.
2. Send early notification about the conference (two to three weeks prior to its scheduled time, if possible). Try to add a personal note to a formal notice and offer some flexibility in appointment schedules.
3. Schedule an adequate amount of time to cover the concerns or topics in need of discussion.
4. Plan an agenda, which might include a list of questions, concerns, specific information about test scores, report card grades, attendance records, homework completion, or classroom behavior. Be sure to allow at least half of the time for parental input and questions. Prioritize concerns and ideas to discuss, expecting that you will have time to deal with only one or two.
5. Assist parents to plan for the meeting by providing a form on which they can list questions or concerns.
6. Arrange for transportation, babysitting at the school, translators for non-English-speaking parents, evening hours, and conferences for noncustodial parents.
7. Assemble the necessary materials (e.g., paper, writing utensils, student papers, test scores, etc.) for easy accessibility during the conference.
8. Practice in anticipation of difficult moments, particularly if negative information or conflicts are likely. Good listening and communication skills are essential in conferences with parents, especially those that feel angry or threatened or try to make school staff feel that way. In-service training that identifies key skills and provides opportunities to practice difficult situations can be helpful. It might also help to try out ideas and language on a colleague who can provide constructive feedback.
9. Set the stage for the conference by providing a physical comfortable environment for parents. Two or three adult-size chairs and privacy are minimum requirements. If possible, refreshments are a "nice touch."

During the Conference

1. Clarify the agenda by identifying issues or questions that are important to school staff and to parents. Time the conference carefully to give each parent equal time.
2. Seek the parents' expertise about their child. Appreciate the uniqueness of each child in a sincere way.
3. Avoid jargon.
4. If shortage of time seems to be pressuring you and the parent during the conference, schedule another meeting. The conference can be continued on a different day, evening, or over the telephone.
5. If the conference results in plans for action, decide on how follow-up will occur.
6. Conclude the conference on a friendly note.

Table 10–6   continued

After the Conference

1. The parent and school staff should talk with the student about the conference, emphasizing the positive information that was exchanged and areas in need of improvement.
2. When specific plans for improvement are established during the conference, continued home-school communication is critical. This may include communication about the student's instructional program, additional work to be completed at home with assistance or supervision, and periodic evaluations of the student's progress.
3. Evaluate the conference by soliciting information from parents and school personnel regarding satisfaction with time use, quality of information obtained and given, knowledge gained about the family or school, specific plans to help the student, arrangements for follow-through, willingness to attend future meetings, and other suggestions for improving conferences.
4. Monitor the rate of parent attendance, adequacy of scheduled time and space, needs of parents revealed in conferences, and utility of forms used to plan for and evaluate conferences.
5. Administrators can synthesize the evaluation from parents and school staff and discuss suggested changes with staff. School personnel can collaboratively locate, adopt, and redesign procedures to establish meaningful, productive, and effective conference formats.

toward parents; (3) make available a small budget for refreshments and duplication costs for conferences; and (4) create partnerships with media to publicize scheduled conference days and with businesses to support parent participation (Swap, 1992).

Parental Involvement at School

The third type of home-school program is concerned with *parental involvement in the school* itself. This is defined as the participation of parents in children's school events. At least two divergent types of procedures can be described that exemplify parental involvement at school. These include volunteering and consulting with school staff.

Volunteering.   Parental involvement in the form of *volunteering* is likely one of the most obvious and direct ways to help children to realize that their school and home lives are connected (Swap, 1992). Examples of volunteering activities include parents attending rallies, sporting events, or other at-school functions; chaperoning field trips or class activities; assisting in the school library; or serving as tutors in their native language for bilingual students. Parental involvement at the school in this way can have a major impact on the school, on parents, and on students. Schools benefit because well-conducted volunteer programs can extend what the school can accomplish. For example, a school may request parents to assist in the coordination of a computer lab or school library. This can extend the hours that these educational settings are open, and increase the number of students who can utilize them. Consequently, teachers who would otherwise be responsible for monitoring the learning environment are free to assist students directly.

Parents themselves have been shown to benefit from their active involvement within the school setting. In some inner city schools, involvement in the school sparked an interest in volunteers or aides to return to school and enabled them to gain meaningful employment (Comer & Haynes, 1991). However, in most schools, these kinds of activities are conducted by relatively few parents who can come to the school during the school day. The realities of parents' lives outside of school must be recognized when requesting assistance in the school. Over 40 percent of mothers surveyed by Epstein (1986) worked full-time, and 18 percent worked part-time. Over 70 percent of parents were never involved in activities assisting the teacher or other school staff. Only about 4 percent (about one or two parents per classroom) were highly active at school for twenty-five days or more per year.

Consultation with School Staff.   Another important way that parents can participate meaningfully in their children's education is by *consulting with school staff*. This often involves a parent attending school to meet with a specialist and teacher to discuss difficulties of their child. *Conjoint behavioral consultation* (CBC) is an extension of traditional teacher or parent behavioral consultation as discussed in Chapter 3. It is defined as "a systematic, indirect form of service delivery, in which parents and teachers are joined to work together to address the academic, social, or behavioral needs of an individual for whom both parties bear some responsibility" (Sheridan & Kratochwill, 1992, p. 122). CBC is designed to engage parents and teachers in collaborative problem solving with the assistance of a school-based consultant (such as a school psychologist or special educator). At times, the problems targeted in CBC will occur in both the home and school (such as noncompliance); in others, the problem may be specific to only one setting (such as lack of work completion).

A conceptual model of CBC is presented in Figure 10–2. As depicted, the interconnections between home and school systems are critically important in CBC. A simultaneous, conjoint model is preferable because services are provided by a specialist to parents and teachers *together*. CBC can facilitate parent-teacher communication and invoke a philosophy of shared responsibility in educational decision making. Various process and outcome goals of conjoint (parent-teacher) behavioral consultation are presented in Table 10–7.

The stages of CBC problem solving are similar to those utilized in the ecological model presented in Chapter 3. However, in CBC, the entire

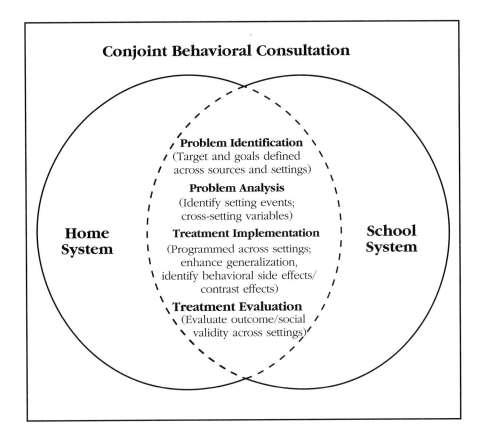

Figure 10–2
Conceptual model of conjoint behavioral consultation

Table 10–7 **Process and Outcome Goals of Conjoint Behavioral Consultation**

Process Goals

1. Increase communication and knowledge about family (e.g., family history, medical information, prior treatments, etc).
2. Improve relationship among the child, family (mother and father), and school personnel.
3. Establish home-school partnership.
4. Promote shared ownership for problem definition and solution.
5. Increase parent (mother and father) and teacher commitments to educational goals.
6. Recognize the need to address problems as occurring across, rather than within settings.
7. Promote greater conceptualization of a problem.
8. Increase the diversity of expertise and resources available.

Table 10–7   continued

Outcome Goals

1. Obtain comprehensive and functional data over extended temporal and contextual bases.
2. Establish consistent treatment programs across settings.
3. Improve the skills, knowledge, or behaviors of all parties (i.e., family members, school personnel, and the child-client).
4. Monitor behavioral contrast and side effects systematically via cross-setting treatment agents.
5. Enhance generalization and maintenance of treatment effects via consistent programming across sources and settings.
6. Develop skills and competencies to promote further independent conjoint problem solving between the family and school personnel.

Source: Sheridan, S. M., & Kratochwill, T. R. (1992).

process is implemented with parents and teachers together. In CBC, behaviors are assessed and treated across both home and school environments to maximize desired effects. Specifically, parents and teachers work together to (1) identify the problem(s) to be targeted in consultation, (2) identify factors across settings that might influence the attainment of the problem solution, (3) design and implement a treatment plan to be implemented at home and school, and (4) evaluate its success across settings making modifications as needed (Sheridan & Kratochwill, 1992). Specific stages and objectives of CBC are listed in Table 10–8.

Empirical support for CBC is growing. It has been found to be effective in increasing the social initiation behaviors of withdrawn children (Sheridan, Kratochwill, & Elliott, 1990; Sheridan, 1992), enhance work completion and accuracy in underachievers (Galloway & Sheridan, 1992; Galloway & Sheridan, in press), and resolve irrational fears in a kindergarten student (Sheridan & Colton, in press). Likewise, in a survey of nationally certified school psychologists, CBC was rated as significantly more desirable than working with parents or teachers alone, or delivering direct services to children for a number of problem types (Sheridan & Steck, 1993).

Suggested Practices.   There are a number of things that educators can do to increase the effectiveness of parent volunteer programs. First, it is important to extend the number of parents active at school by encouraging all parents to assist in some way, and not just the small cadre who are already motivated. This can be done via active outreach activities and surveys early in the school year soliciting interest and involvement. Educators can invite parents to become involved on vacation days, early in the morning, and after

Table 10–8	**Stages and Objectives of Conjoint Behavioral Consultation**

I. Problem Identification
   A. Define the problem(s) in behavioral terms
   B. Identify important contextual, environmental, and cross-setting conditions that affect the behavior
   C. Provide a tentative strength of the behavior across settings
   D. Discuss and reach agreement on a goal for behavior change across settings
   E. Establish a procedure for collection of baseline data across settings

II. Problem Analysis
   A. Evaluate and obtain agreement on the baseline data across settings
   B. Conduct a functional and conditional analysis of the behavior across settings
   C. Identify setting events (events that are functionally related, but temporally or contextually distal to the target behavior), ecological conditions, and other cross-setting variables that may affect the target behavior
   D. Design an intervention plan, including specification of conditions to be changed and the practical guidelines regarding treatment implementation
   E. Reaffirm record-keeping procedures

III. Treatment Implementation
   A. Monitor implementation of the intervention
   B. Provide training to parents and teacher if necessary
   C. Assess behavioral side effects, and contrast effects
   D. Determine need for immediate revisions in plan
   E. Continue data collection procedures

IV. Treatment Evaluation
   A. Evaluate treatment data to determine if the goals of consultation have been obtained across settings
   B. Evaluate the effectiveness of the treatment plan across settings
   C. Discuss strategies and tactics regarding the continuation, modification, or termination of the treatment plan
   D. Discuss strategies for maintenance and generalization of treatment gains

school and work hours. Likewise, methods should be created that allow parents to fulfill some volunteering responsibilities during nonschool hours, such as reviewing curriculum or collecting materials for science projects on a Saturday afternoon.

Effective volunteer programs contain some common components (Swap, 1992). First, to be effective, a volunteer program should have a coordinator to identify needs, arrange training, and monitor the program implementation. Second, they contain a method to ascertain the interests and skill levels of parents, as well as the needs of teachers, administrators and specialists. One-page questionnaires can be developed to assess parents' abilities, or volunteer "job

Activity 10–3

Get into a group of three or four members representing different educational disciplines. Consider yourselves part of a high school team whose objective is to increase parental involvement as aides in school activities. Develop a "job description" that can be used to solicit active parental participation in school events.

After completing the job description, consider the following questions: What difficulties might you encounter when attempting to get parents of high school students involved in school activities? What incentives can be offered? Once parents express interest, what actions should be taken to increase the success of the parent volunteer program? Who is responsible for what?

descriptions" can be developed and sent to parents to solicit interest (Office for Community Education, 1989—in Swap, 1992). Third, effective programs devise a method to match volunteers or aides and their supervisors. Fourth, they orient and train volunteers. Training may include a general orientation to the school and the volunteer position, but it must also include specific and detailed descriptions of the job objectives, procedures, and expectations. Some schools have published volunteer manuals to summarize useful information and help orient new volunteers. A fifth characteristic of effective volunteer approaches is that they monitor the program. For example, the coordinator is a likely person to stay in touch with school personnel and volunteers to assess effectiveness, identify problem areas, troubleshoot solutions, and assess further needs. Finally, good volunteer programs celebrate contributions and communicate them to others. Some schools have special recognition dinners where certificates or awards are presented to volunteers and educators who demonstrate commitment to making programs work.

A number of suggested practices can be made when consulting with parents as well. Many of the recommendations regarding conferences can be generalized to consultation sessions (see Table 10–6). The primary differences between parent-teacher conferences and home-school consultation lie in the purpose, structure, and outcomes of these practices. Specifically, whereas conferences can be scheduled and conducted for a myriad of reasons, consultation meetings should be focused specifically on identifying means of helping a student attain desired academic, social, or behavioral outcomes. Therefore, consultation sessions should follow a standard format to guide and structure the problem-solving efforts. Procedural guidelines and interview forms are available to facilitate the implementation of consultation with parents and school staff (Sheridan, Kratochwill, & Bergan, in press).

Parents Assisting Their Children in Learning Activities at Home

There are several activities that can be considered under the rubric of *parental involvement with learning activities at home*. In a general sense, this is defined as parents participating with children to build academic skills at home.

Examples include parents assisting their children complete homework, establishing a reading program at home, providing enrichment experiences for their child in the community, and reinforcing attitudes regarding learning that are being taught at school. All of these activities are designed to support the child's success in school. Three specific approaches that parents can take in assisting their child with learning activities at home are homework assistance, home tutoring, and enrichment activities (Jenson, Sheridan, Olympia, & Andrews, 1994).

Homework Assistance.   Time spent on homework has important and positive effects on achievement, whether measured by grades or by test scores (Anderson, 1986; Cooper, 1989; Fredrick & Walberg, 1980; Keith, 1982; Rutter, Maughan, Mortimore, Ouston, & Smith, 1979). Achievement gains have been associated with homework that (1) is graded or commented upon, (2) contains positive comments, (3) is followed by consequences versus no consequences, and (4) is reviewed or checked by parents (Keith, 1987). Long-term and cumulative academic gains have been associated with an efficient homework program for handicapped, gifted, at-risk, and low achieving students (Chadwick & Day, 1971; Fredrick & Walberg, 1980; Harris & Sherman, 1974; Paschal, Weinstein, & Walberg, 1984; Rousseau, Poulson, & Salzberg, 1984). Homework may also have compensatory effects; that is, less able students can compensate for lower ability through increased home study (Polachek, Kniesner, & Harwood, 1978).

Parents can assist students in completing homework in a number of ways. Most basically, they can provide resource materials in the home environment, such as reference books, dictionaries and other academic tools. Whereas specific parental behaviors (e.g., encouraging homework completion, discussing homework topics) have been suggested, no empirical support exists attesting to their relationship to academic achievement. Parental factors that have been found to be related to homework performance of high school students include parents' knowing the student's whereabouts outside of school, and parents' monitoring of school performance (DiPrete, 1981). This suggests that broad levels of awareness and supervision by parents are important for high school students' homework behaviors.

Several commercial materials are available for parent training related to homework problems. These include *Winning the Homework War* (Anesko & Levine, 1987), *Homework Without Tears* (Canter & Hausner, 1987), *Homework Helpers* (Kuepper, 1987), *Mindmovers: Creative Homework Assignments Grades 3-12* (Hart & Rechif, 1986) and *Do it Yourself Homework Manual: A Sanity Saver for Parents* (Olympia, Jenson, & Neville, 1990). While the empirical support for most of these programs is limited, they offer practical suggestions and important guidelines for parents to assist their children with homework.

The *Teachers Involve Parents in Schoolwork* (TIPS) interactive homework process was developed to allow teachers to help all families stay informed and involved in their children's learning activities at home, and to help students complete homework in order to promote school success (Epstein, Jackson, & Salinas, 1992; Epstein & Salinas, 1991, 1992). With the TIPS process, homework

Homework assistance programs provide parents with tools and strategies that can be used at home.

is conceptualized as a three-way partnership involving students, families, and teachers. Prototype materials are available for math (grades K–5), science (grade 3), and language arts, science and health (middle grades). The materials feature homework assignments that require students to talk to someone at home about things they are learning at school, and provide a structured means for parents to provide written feedback to teachers. Thus, TIPS homework is primarily the students' responsibility, requires interaction between students and their parents, and enables students to share with parents things they are learning at school.

Home Tutoring.   There is both empirical and intuitive support for the utilization of parents as tutors of their own children (Leler, 1983). In a review of the literature, Leler (1983) identified eighteen well-designed studies of home tutoring. All studies involved parents of elementary aged children. Of these, thirteen produced positive results on one or more achievement variables, and five showed no difference between involved and uninvolved families. Especially noteworthy is the fact that a number of the projects involved low-income minority or poorly educated parents, suggesting that the benefits of home tutoring are not restricted to mainstream parents and students.

Home Educational Enrichment.   Home enrichment activities have a positive effect on both parents and students. Epstein (1983) identified five types of parental practices that stimulate home learning. These include reading to children and having children read to parents; encouraging home discussions; providing informal learning activities through the use of games and common household items; establishing contracts for parents to supervise assignments; and teaching parents how to tutor or make learning materials for student use at home. Research on home educational enrichment supports the practice. Teachers who promote such parental practices report perceptions of improved basic skills in students, better parent-teacher cooperation, and more useful parent-student interaction (Epstein & Becker, 1982). Students gained more in reading achievement and reported more positive attitudes about school, more regular homework habits, and more similarity between the home and school (Epstein, 1984). Finally, when involved in home educational enrichment practices, parents reported feeling as though they should help their child at home, understanding more of their child's academic expectations, and communicating more positively with school. They also rated teachers' overall abilities more favorably and felt more positive about the school and home learning activities when involved in home educational enrichment practices (Epstein, 1983; Searls, Lewis, & Morrow, 1982).

In a meta-analysis of twenty-nine controlled studies of programs designed to increase the educationally stimulating qualities of the home environment, Graue, Weinstein, and Walberg (1983) found that school-based home instruction programs produce large positive effects on students' learning. These authors concluded that the significant results were obtained due to (1) extended quality and quantity of academic instruction; (2) increased efficiency and motivation for classroom learning with parental support; (3) lessened television viewing; and (4) encouraged family relations in a constructive and supportive environment.

It is important to note that parental enrichment practices at home are more important than their educational or occupational status in influencing children's performance (Tangri & Moles, 1987). Children from multi-ethnic areas, where parents are primarily non-English speaking, and who exhibit learning difficulties have also been shown to make striking gains when engaged in the enrichment practice of reading to their parents (Huang, 1992; Tizard, Schofied, & Hewison, 1982).

Suggested Practices.   Consistency and coordination among parents and teachers is important to increase the effectiveness of parental practices at home. In programs designed to enhance the effectiveness of homework, teachers and parents can share the tasks of (1) identifying the nature of homework problems; (2) developing an effective homework program to be used across home and school settings; (3) monitoring systematically the effects of the intervention on academic and nonacademic skills; (4) determining the need for modification in the homework program; and (5) evaluating overall outcome in relation to its stated objectives. It is the teacher's basic responsibility to ensure that homework is assigned in a clcar and meaningful way. Students are responsible to see that homework assignments are understood and that the necessary materials are brought home to complete the work in that setting. Finally, parents must have available an appropriate place for homework to be completed, preferably one that is free from distractions and equipped with the necessary supplies (Olympia, Sheridan, & Jenson, 1994).

When invoking a home tutoring or enrichment program, some form of parent training is essential. Specifically, parents should be trained in procedures to prepare their child for learning; ask questions and encourage their child to ask questions; praise their child for learning; and correct their child without criticism. Parents can be taught the importance of interactive book reading, and procedures by which they can maximize their children's understanding of written materials (Taverne & Sheridan, in press). Maintaining regular contact with parents who engage in home tutoring and home enrichment is important to enhance continued student learning.

Parental Involvement in Governance and Advocacy

Epstein's (1987a, 1987b) fifth type of home-school collaboration model refers to parent participation in educational governance and advocacy. This includes involvement in the PTA/PTO, advisory councils, advocacy groups, Chapter I programs, committees or teams at school, and site-based teams. Schools can help parents perform these tasks by offering information and training in decision making and communication skills.

Swap (1992) outlined three types of parental involvement in decision making. The first is *federally mandated advisory councils* at the school or district level. This includes parent advisory councils and program-specific committees such as Title I and Chapter I. In general, these committees continue to be dominated by principals who set the agenda and have final authority in decision making (Malen & Ogawa, 1988; Williams, 1989). A second format for parent involvement in decision making is the federally mandated *participation of parents of children with special needs*. Public Law 94-142 and its extensions mandate that parents be actively involved in the development of individualized education plans (IEPs; see Chapter 5 for more information on PL 94-142 and IEPs). However, although the law specifies that parents be active, equal participants in decisions about their child's educational program, this is not usually the case (Brinckerhoff & Vincent, 1986).

A third format for involving parents in decision making is through locally initiated *school-community planning or management councils*. For example, Malen and Ogawa (1988) described site-based governance councils in Salt Lake City that incorporated four important factors: (1) councils were located within the school; (2) councils were given broad jurisdiction and formal policy-making authority; (3) parents, teachers, and the principal had equal voting power; and (4) council members received training in group dynamics and school-site councils. However, these researchers found that despite these important structures, the traditional pattern of principal-professional control and decision making was not altered.

The P.T.A. meeting is a traditional approach of parental involvement in school governance.

There is limited research on the relationship between parental involvement in governance and advocacy and student achievement. What is available, however, fails to demonstrate a significant link. In other words, parental involvement in school- or district-based decision making does not appear to be related to student performance. This may be because, as highlighted in our earlier discussion, parental involvement at this level continues to be more rhetoric than reality (Swap, 1992).

Suggested Practices.   A minimal requirement to parents' success in decision making is that school personnel share an ethic that values parental participation as advocates and decision makers. A significant part of that ethic is the belief that school personnel *need* parents to be involved at this level; they "need the advice, strengths, perspective, and resources that parents can provide to pursue their common vision" (Swap, 1992, p. 76). It is also important for parents to accept the fact that when they are involved in helping school personnel make important educational decisions, they are accountable for school successes and limitations.

Training must be available to parents to maximize their involvement on school boards and councils. This may include information regarding the school's operation, staffing patterns, and organizational structure. Likewise, communication skills training and hands-on assistance in acquiring problem-solving skills are important. Specialists within the school such as the school psychologist or counselor may be especially instrumental in designing and implementing programs to support parents in this way.

Chapter Summary

The importance of involving families in their children's education is gaining increased recognition. In many places, however, the parental involvement movement continues to be one of rhetoric rather than reality. In this chapter, we described methods of establishing and maintaining home-school partnerships and provided concrete examples of various typologies of parental involvement practices.

Before initiating concrete partnership programs with families, schools should establish various activities that make parents feel accepted and welcome in the educational environment. An "atmosphere of openness" is necessary to make the school a comfortable and inviting place. This type of atmosphere is influenced by messages parents receive from several levels, including the district, school, and individuals with whom personal contact is made (teachers, administrators, bus drivers). The manner in which communications reach parents (what is said and how it is conveyed) has a significant effect on their subjective feelings of the school and their role in their child's education. The interpersonal skills examined in Chapter 4 are essential for use with parents.

There are a number of key considerations worthy of attention when developing programs for parents. Factors such as the cost-return ratio, intrusiveness of the program, implementation requirements, and program objectives interact to enhance or limit its effectiveness. A number of additional important characteristics of effective home-school programs are outlined in Table 10–5.

Finally, Epstein's (1987a, 1987b) five types of family involvement were described, with specific examples and suggested practices. The types of involvement—basic obligations of parents, basic obligations of schools, parental involvement at school, parents assisting their children in learning activities at home, and parental involvement in governance and advocacy—each have their own objectives and representative strategies. It should be recognized that no one type of program is superior to the others. All serve discrete purposes that are important to specific school and family situations. The needs and

Activity 10–4

Divide a sheet of paper into five sections. Label each section with the different types of parent involvement based on the Epstein model. Now think about your prospective or current role in the schools. In each section, write down three or four activities falling under that heading that you could do to encourage parental participation. When you are finished, get together with others and share ideas. Which are feasible and which are not? Why? What can be done to increase their utility and effectiveness in school settings?

resources of the school, families and community must be considered when determining the type of program most appropriate at any given time.

| **Case Study 10–1** | Mountain Crest Middle School is situated in a central-city, low-SES community comprised of many minority families. Many students live in single-parent households, and most parents work at blue-collar jobs with various schedules (some work "graveyard" shifts; others work at all times of the day). In the two-parent households, both parents are typically employed. Child care is often shared with extended family (such as grandparents); however, several children are responsible to care for themselves when the parents are absent. Parents or other guardians rarely attend school functions, including conferences, meetings or informal events. Likewise, little effort is expended to inform parents of school events or curricular objectives. When parents do come to school, it is usually in response to behavioral or academic problems, such as their child being in jeopardy of expulsion or failing. |

Teachers in the school are generally hard-working and competent; however, the school continues to perform well below average on standardized tests. Services and funds are very limited. As the new school year approaches, school staff decide that increased parental involvement in the school may be one way to improve the school climate. Thus, the administrator establishes an ad hoc team to work on identifying a goal and procedures to increase home-school collaboration.

1. Use the collaborative process worksheet (see Chapter 3) to develop a specific program or approach for improving the home-school relationship.

2. What are some barriers to home-school programs in this school (see Chapter 9)?

3. Which components of effective programs should be integrated into a home-school model in this case?

4. Which issues surrounding involvement of minority parents and parents of upper-grade students are present in this case?

Key Vocabulary Terms

cost-return ratio
empower
parent education
needs assessment
basic obligations of schools
school-home notes
parent-teacher conference
group conferences

individual conferences
informal conferences
formal conferences
parental involvement in the
  school
volunteerism
conjoint behavioral
  consultation (CBC)

federally mandated advisory
  councils
school-community planning
  or management councils
consulting with school staff
teachers involve parents in
  schoolwork (TIPS)

Chapter 11

Chapter Overview

The Community

Chapter Objectives

After reading this chapter, the reader should be able to
1. Define school-community partnerships.
2. Describe the three models of school-community partnerships.
3. Discuss the three objectives of school-community partnerships.
4. Describe various vocational programs used in school-community partnerships.
5. Enumerate the characteristics of effective school-community partnerships.

Introduction

We have examined the school and home as settings for establishing educational partnerships to promote lifelong learning. The community is included as another important learning environment. The word *community* is derived from the Latin word *communis,* which means "common." The context and circumstances of local life, including the provision and consumption of goods and services, cultural traits, and the interactions of individuals, families, and organizations are held in *common* (Warren, 1978). Therefore, beyond its geographic identity, the community "is a place of reference and belonging (Chaskin & Richman, 1993, p. 207). In this sense, community represents shared culture and resources that have a profound influence on the learning experiences of children and youth.

The relationship between the school and community is paradoxical in many respects. On one hand, schools are perceived as the primary agent for educating children and therefore is isolated from the community as a whole. The assumption is that "learning" is a static experience that takes place within the confines of schools under the expertise of professional educators. Using a broader, ecological approach, we believe that a school is merely one environment for learning. There are, in fact, more suitable and authentic settings than a school building for meaningful educational experiences. On the other hand, schools and the community are symbiotic in nature as students under the charge of educators will ultimately become tomorrow's community. Furthermore, most of the values of the community at large influence the educational experience of students through continued socialization. Therefore, it is in the best interest of the community as a whole to become active partners with educators to invest in the future of children and thus enhance the economic climate and enrich the social resources of our society (Sheridan, in press).

However, as we have seen in previous chapters, educators are facing growing challenges associated with an evolving society and family. More and more responsibility is being placed on the school for addressing the diverse needs of students. Jehl and Kirst (1993) documented the function of schools today as a response to various political, social, and economic reform initiatives throughout history. For example, school lunch programs were developed due to the economic depression of the 1930s. New school programs were developed in the 1960s to provide equal opportunities for children of all races. Similarly, special education was mandated to provide a free and appropriate education to students with disabilities in the 1970s. In the 1980s and 1990s, schools and educators have been expected to take greater roles in drug and sex education, with a particular emphasis on the AIDS epidemic. It is, however, unrealistic to expect schools alone to deal with the growing array of problems placing children at risk (Jehl & Kirst, 1993; NASBE, 1992). Likewise, the community cannot be expected to meet these challenges alone. We propose forging school-community partnerships that may take on a variety of forms and functions mutually beneficial to both arenas.

School-Community Partnerships

The term *school-community partnerships* conjures many different images. Social workers may envision welfare agencies working with school officials and educators to provide mental and physical health services to students. The owner and operator of a business might think of a partnership in terms of providing in-kind services or resources to a school, such as computers. Similarly, a business setting for work experiences may be what vocational educators perceive as a school-community partnership. A special education teacher might use a supermarket or mass transit system as a classroom to teach independent-living skills to students with disabilities. While these examples have different objectives, they all have common elements that characterize school-community partnerships.

We define a *school-community partnership* as an interactive exchange of ideas, resources, services, and expertise between educational and noneducational agencies in a variety of settings that mutually address the needs of students and the community as a whole by enabling students to become meaningful participants in their community. There are three basic approaches or models this partnership can take. Services and resources are available in a variety of settings, including the home, as part of the *interagency model* of school-community partnerships. This means that students may receive support services provided by several agencies not directly related to the educational system in a number of environments or in a single setting.

The *school-based model* is an approach in which services and programs are generally administered and disseminated from the school building. In this model, community agencies or business organizations collaboratively provide resources and services, but the focal point is at the school. The *community-based model* facilitates services and programs outside the school environment, wherein students receive services in settings such as businesses or specific agencies.

The models and approaches differ in terms of their service-delivery objectives, that is, whether those objectives are educational, social and health, or vocational. *Educational objectives* focus on facilitating academic and developmental growth of students. This may take the form of a school-business alliance in which a business "adopts" a school to provide financial support that will finance certain programs and/or materials. Other kinds of educational objectives may include increased literacy for adult learners, dropout prevention, citizenship and community service, or enhanced functional life skills for students with disabilities. The emphasis of *social and health objectives* is to provide services and programs that address the physical and mental health needs of students. This type of school-community partnership may provide drug education, anti-gang instruction, nutritional assistance, teen pregnancy support services or after-school programs such as latchkey groups. *Vocational objectives* target job and career needs of students by

Table 11–1	**Service-Delivery Objectives of School-Community Partnership Models**

	School-Based	**Community-Based**	**Interagency**
Educational Objectives	Literacy programs Drop-out prevention Adopt-a-school	Citizenship programs Special education	Community-based education

Social and Health Objectives	Teen pregnancy
	   prevention programs
	Drug education
	Anti-gang programs
	Nutrition programs
		After-school programs
		Latchkey programs
			Social, welfare, and
			   family-service
			   programs
			Youth-in-custody

Vocational Objectives	Career education	On-the-job training	Career education

providing career education in or out of the school building and hands-on experiences in actual work settings.

Government agencies such as social services, private businesses, and community volunteer service organizations can team up with schools to meet any or all of these types of objectives. Naturally, there will be some degree of overlap between model and service delivery objectives. Table 11–1 illustrates the array of school-community partnerships and the context in which different disciplines and agencies may collaborate to meet the needs of students.

We do not espouse a specific model, as each has its own objectives as well as its merits and shortcomings. Instead, we propose that each school and its community consider the most appropriate mechanism to serve their own unique needs. Therefore, it is incumbent upon educators and members of the community to carefully consider specific models as they relate to various educational contexts.

Interagency Collaboration

Interagency collaboration received considerable attention during the 1970s and 1980s (Peterson, 1991). It is actually a component of both school-based and community-based partnerships by virtue of the fact that two or more agencies are interacting to provide services to students. What differentiates this type of school-community partnership from other models is the setting. In this model, no specific setting is the target of coordinated efforts. Instead, a host of agencies may autonomously provide services in any number of settings. Many

Activity 11-1	Form small groups to establish an interagency school-community partnership. Using the collaborative process worksheet from Chapter 3, identify a common school-community issue, and then use the ecological problem-solving approach to develop a hypothetical school-community program. Establish specific social/health objectives. Delegate certain members of the group to represent a community agency. If at all possible, solicit the participation of actual business and/or community members for this activity.

times, the service actually delivered is based on the label children and youth receive as they enter the support system (Soler & Shauffer, 1993). For example, a student may be categorized as seriously emotionally disturbed. While that student may receive academic services from the educational system, a specific source of funds allocated for students within this category may allow a mental health agency to provide additional services. In this sense, the two organizations, the school and mental health agency, "cooperate" by providing their own specialized service. This approach often results in fragmented service-delivery programs that do not necessarily reflect the collaborative ethic described in Chapter 1.

One example of how agencies have attempted to reduce this type of fragmentation is described by Soler and Shauffer (1993). The National Institute of Mental Health developed the Child and Adolescent Service System Program (CASSP) to focus on service delivery rather than developing new technologies for treating mental illness. CASSP provides mini-grants and technical assistance to states or mental health agencies to improve service delivery. These grants and assistance programs focus on integrating services from education, mental health, health, welfare, and juvenile justice agencies.

School-Based Approaches

School-based approaches of school-community partnerships are defined as a model in which the school is the primary site for the administration and dissemination of academic, social, and health services to children and youth (Chaskin & Richman, 1993). In this model, the school is linked to at least two or more agencies to collaboratively deliver services to students (Kirst, 1993). The *school volunteer* is a common form of community involvement (Gonder, 1981) whereby individuals outside the school such as employees, parents, members of community service groups, or college/university students provide direct or indirect service to students. For example, a volunteer may work directly with a student to improve reading skills or indirectly support learning experiences by collating the written stories of students to be compiled in a bound publication.

An individual business or organization can *adopt-a-school* to address a particular need in a specific school (Sheridan, in press; Tangri & Moles,

1987). For example, a local bank may pay for a newspaper subscription that can be used to embellish social studies courses. Businesses may also adopt-a-school by sponsoring field trips or providing guest speakers. School-based programs, however, can go beyond meeting only academic needs of students. Because schools are often easily accessible to children, many health and social service agencies have begun to implement school-linked services where schools are the primary site of service delivery (Jehl & Kirst, 1992; Kirst, 1992).

There are many advantages *and* disadvantages of school-based approaches to community partnerships (Chaskin & Richman, 1993). A benefit of the school as the hub of service delivery is its established role in the community combined with the fact that it has existing space and facilities. Schools also offer an existing administrative structure to provide and coordinate social

Schools and local businesses may forge partnerships to raise funds to support school projects.

Activity 11–2	Form small groups to establish school-based community partnership. Using the collaborative process worksheet from Chapter 3, identify a common school-community issue, and then use the ecological problem-solving approach to develop a hypothetical school-community program. Establish specific academic objectives. Delegate certain members of the group to represent a business or community agency. If at all possible, solicit the participation of actual business and/or community members for this activity.

and health services. There are, however, potential problems associated with school-based programming that must be considered. Institutional rigidity on the part of one agency may result in controlling other participating agencies. In other words, the mission or agenda of one agency may overshadow other constituencies. Another potential drawback is the possibility that disenfranchised students and parents may not take advantage of services provided in an institution they associate with failure and frustration. Furthermore, schools are struggling to maintain their own mission with dwindling resources and may be unable to fulfill additional responsibilities of school-linked programs. Finally, the "community" of the school may not necessarily reflect the familial, religious, and cultural spheres of the community at large.

Community-Based Approaches

A community-based approach of education partnerships involves a coordinated system of services and organizations outside the school environment linked together to provide an array of settings, resources, expertise, and services to meet the needs of students (Chaskin & Richman, 1993). This approach expands the boundaries of schools to include businesses, agencies, and other organizations. The complexity of coordination can range from a simple interaction between a single teacher and employer to a governance board consisting of representatives from public and private agencies. As described previously, community-based approaches of school-community partnerships can address academic, social/health, and vocational needs of students.

Academic Objectives. Academically focused programs provide learning experiences for students that embellish developmental growth. A traditional example of community-based learning experiences to meet academic goals is the *field trip.* During visits to authentic settings, students can see concepts discussed in class actually applied in natural settings. For example, students learning about forms and functions of government during social studies courses can witness the legislative process by visiting and observing legislative sessions. The sciences also lend themselves to field trips by allowing students to conduct experiments in natural settings or observing scientists in action. Some schools are beginning to implement community service projects as a component to the overall curriculum. In programs such as these, students' perspectives of civic duty and citizenship are broadened by contributing part of their time and energies to a specific activity outside school.

As discussed in previous chapters, curricula may include functional life skills that prepare children and youth to independently carry out everyday social, personal, and vocational tasks (Gajar, Goodman, & McAfee, 1993; Wimmer, 1981). These skills are especially critical for students with disabilities. While some programs may be designed to prepare students with disabilities for jobs, other aspects of community-based programs teach students how to become independent and meaningful members of the community. In this case, the community can, quite literally, become a classroom. Community-based programs for students with disabilities use authentic settings such as mass transit systems and supermarkets to develop a variety of abilities, including survival reading and consumer math skills (McDonnell, Wilcox, & Hardman, 1991). For example, students learn to read the labels of products and calculate how much the items on a grocery list will cost. In programs such as these, the special education teacher becomes an important "public relations" liaison with employers and other individuals in the community. Similarly, the role of the paraprofessional, as discussed in Chapter 5, often involves supervision and coaching of students in community settings.

Another critically important type of school-community partnerships with academic objectives are programs designed to keep students in school. Schools and organizations have worked together to establish drop-out prevention programs in which part of the curriculum includes a *work-study program*. Students earn money on the job, but can keep the job only if they remain in school. This type of partnership could be perceived as having an overlap of academic and social objectives.

Social and Health Objectives.   Community-based models can be used to provide social and health services to students at risk. As discussed in Chapter 2, children and youth face a growing barrage of social and health challenges that may have an adverse effect on their learning experience. Similarly, Chapter 5 described the general role of schools as providing academic services to students. This, however, is difficult to accomplish when students come to school with a host of social and health needs. Consequently, educators have traditionally turned to other agencies to provide services targeting physical and mental health needs of students. The National School Board Association has taken the official position that neither the schools nor the community can address these issues alone (NSBA, 1991).

Vocational and Career Objectives.   Vocational and career programs prepare students for post-educational employment and career opportunities. Most of these programs are implemented at the secondary school level and range in complexity from occasional field trips to steady, paid jobs for

Spotlight: Project Achievement Program

Project Achievement was a joint venture by the Detroit Public Schools and the International Institute of Metropolitan Detroit, a multicultural social service agency funded by the United Way of Southeastern Michigan (Charney, 1993). The project was designed to provide early intervention at the elementary school level to address academic and behavior problems in bilingual schools. Since the program began in 1985, seven to nine schools have participated each year, involving a total of thirty support groups that served 248 children in second through sixth grades. A support group consisted of four students from various ethnic groups serving as role models and six underachievers of the same ethnic group. Role models were required to have a grade point average of 3.0 and leadership abilities. Underachievers had less than a 2.0 grade point average and were referred by school counselors and school teachers. Participating students signed a contract for a targeted grade point average. No more than two aggressive children were placed in groups, and the other referred students were either passive learners or experienced attention problems. During group sessions, group workers conducted discussions, role plays, and rehearsals on topics such as getting along with peers and teachers, and handling anger or fear. Over a six-year period, 30 percent of the underachievers ($n=39$) improved their grade point averages from D to C while only 18 percent ($n=7$) of a control group reached a C average. The majority of citizenship grades either improved or remained at a satisfactory level. On a behavior rating scale, 87 percent of the students demonstrated improved relationships with peers and adults and reduction of aggression and frustration.

students (Sheridan, in press). Programs typically involve a two-year commitment in which students work at their own pace to master specific objectives (Gonder, 1981). There are several models of vocational education programs. Our brief overview of these models is an adaptation of a description provided by Gajar et al. (1993).

Career education has been practiced since the 1970s. The premise of career education is to provide a related set of experiences in authentic settings. It includes academic and instructional components such as reading, problem solving, functional math, and following directions. In essence, career education is a synthesis of traditional academically oriented skills with work skills that enable young adults to be competent workers. *Work-study programs* consist of two parts: attending classes and performing paid work outside the classroom. The objective of employment opportunities is to provide income so the student can continue educational programs. In some instances, work-study is primarily a financial assistance program, while in

Spotlight: A Hospital-School Partnership for Child-Protection Services

In 1989 representatives from the Department of Pediatrics, Community Relations, and Social Work Services from the General Pediatrics Clinics of Mount Sinai Hospital located in East Harlem, New York, hosted a meeting with school principals and guidance staff to identify and discuss health care needs of children that affected the school system. In the context of a discussion on parents' substance abuse, school officials voiced concern regarding child abuse and neglect as a consequence of "crack" use. As a result of this discussion, hospital staff proposed establishing an ongoing forum for educators coupled with a pilot program of a hospital-school district child-protection committee. The project was funded by the hospital by its educational and community outreach programs. Four permanent members of the committee consisted of the school district's director of pupil personnel and three hospital staff members. The hospital's chairperson of the Child Protection Committee, the child-protection coordinator, and the social worker from the Community Relations Department voluntarily met with administrators and educators at monthly meetings at the central district office. The meetings were designed to provide ongoing indirect consultation, identify early need for family intervention, and develop intervention strategies. Summative evaluation consisting of anecdotal data suggested that improved communication and collaboration between the school district and hospital had evolved. Comments suggested that school personnel felt "less isolated" when dealing with these overwhelming problems. A greater understanding of what kind of evaluation and intervention the hospital could and could not provide also emerged. It was also discovered that teachers were unable to leave their classrooms to participate in the committee meetings and that on-site child protection committees were needed. Finally, it was further determined that many school personnel were unaware of this available resource. Although the model had its limitations, both agencies recognized the need for this type of collaboration and implemented the network economically. Through the efforts of this pilot program, both educational and health care agencies had a better understanding of how to collaborate in providing services to children and youth at risk (Mulack, Cohen, & Teets-Grimm, 1992).

other programs the experience of learning a skill is the focus. *Employment-site instruction* often reflects traditional on-the-job training or apprenticeship programs. *Experience-based career education* (EBCE) is intended to serve as a transition between the school experience and work in the community (Bucknam & Brand, 1983). Students earn academic credit in off-campus sites

Spotlight: A Postsecondary Vocational Project for Young Adults with Mild Disabilities

A federally funded project in Maryland provided postsecondary vocational experiences for sixty-six individuals with learning disabilities and mild mental retardation ranging in age from eighteen to thirty years (Neubert, Tilson, & Ianacone, 1989). Of this group, 59 percent were female and 44 percent had a learning disability. The program consisted of seven activities: (1) intake and processing personal information; (2) an eight-week course that included vocational assessment, community-based career exploration, and job-seeking skills; (3) job tryouts at community sites; (4) job-search support; (5) placement and follow-up; (6) a job club: and (7) job change and advancement support. Participants received a minimum of one follow-up visit per week during the first month of employment. After the first month, project facilitators conducted biweekly visits or phone contacts and implemented quarterly surveys for data collection. After six months, 76 percent of the participants were still employed and 64 percent after one year. Despite the general positive outcomes of the project, 92 percent of the participants experienced some type of task-related problem, such as less than acceptable productivity during part of their employment and 71 percent experienced some kind of interpersonal conflict on the job. Regardless of these setbacks, most participants successfully continued their employment and learning experience.

where curricula is delivered through experiences as the foundation for learning academic subjects.

School-Business Partnerships.   A common form of community-based partnerships is the alliance of schools and business. The National Center for Education Statistics reported that 40 percent of the public schools had some type of formal partnership with an outside institution, and in urban areas, 54 percent of those partnerships were with businesses (National Center for Educational Statistics, 1989). In a recent survey of Fortune 500 companies,

| Activity 11–3 | Form small groups to establish a community-based partnership. Using the collaborative process worksheet from Chapter 3, identify a common school-community issue, and then use the ecological problem-solving approach to develop a hypothetical school-community program. As a group, decide what type of objectives your program will have (academic, social/health, or vocational). Delegate certain members of the group to represent a business or community agency. If at all possible, solicit the participation of actual business and/or community members for this activity. |

A parent and business leader work together as a team to teach students skills on donated computer equipment.

all but 7 of 305 respondents reported an involvement with education (Kuhn, 1990). The support ranged from contributing money, offering students part-time jobs, contributing materials or equipment, to loaning executives to schools. A common form of school-business partnerships is the "adopt-a-school" approach discussed earlier, in which a business forms a relationship with a specific school to provide materials, equipment, or financial support.

Spotlight: Comprehensive School-Community Partnerships

The Santa Ana Unified School District of Santa Ana, California, has effectively implemented a variety of school-community partnerships to address an array of academic, social/health, and vocational needs (Santa Ana Unified School District, 1993). The district is in an urban area near Los Angeles and has forty-three schools with a total enrollment of 48,406 students. Hispanic students comprise 86 percent of the student population. The percentage of students with limited English proficiency is 67 percent. The district recognizes it cannot meet the diverse needs of its students alone through traditional funding formulas. Science and com-

continued on the following page

continued

puter programs are supported by large business organizations such as McDonnell Douglas and W.R. Grace Corporation. Instructional television programs from the CNN newsroom and the A & E Classroom are used to enrich reading, language arts, science, social science, and health curricula. After-school recreation programs and clubs have been established with organizations such as Boy Scouts, Girl Scouts, Boys and Girls Club, and the Department of Parks and Recreation. A culturally appropriate parent conference and workshop was sponsored by ITT Canon. "Healthy Tomorrows" is a school-based health and social service program that provides direct health care and intervention education through collaborative efforts of nine public and private agencies. A mobile van unit is part of the program, and over 900 students have received services to date. The "Santa Ana Parent Project" was developed in collaboration with the Santa Ana Police Department and School Police Services. The project is designed to help parents limit their children's involvement in drug and gang-related activities. Business, city, and community members are invited to participate in the "Principal for a Day" program as classroom tutors, science fair judges, and fundraisers. Approximately 136 businesses are involved in individual school-business partnerships. Over 350 community and business volunteers are active participants in the districts' "Stay in School" program. A total of 147 students with disabilities were placed in paid employment opportunities in over ninety-seven sites.

Establishing School-Community Partnerships

Most educators philosophically embrace the value of school-community partnerships but are legitimately concerned about how to go about making it a reality. As discussed earlier in Chapter 5, the existing structure of the school, with its prescribed roles and responsibilities of educators, does not easily facilitate this type of partnership. Consequently, coordination of school-community partnerships is often fragmented with a standard operating procedure of "it's not my job" leaving the job undone. There are, however, effective coordinated service programs that can serve as models for schools attempting to establish partnerships with the community.

Characteristics of Effective School-Community Partnerships

The literature reveals a number of characteristics of successful collaboration between schools and community (Ascher, 1990; Kirst, 1991; Soler & Shauffer, 1993). A summary of specific characteristics is presented in Table 11–2. However, there appears to be an overarching umbrella of five fundamental components common to successful school-community partnerships (Clark, 1992).

Table 11–2   Characteristics of Effective School-Community Partnership Programs

Successful school-community partnerships
1. Have a mission statement that guides the partnership.
2. Utilize a coordinating committee to oversee the operations of the partnerships.
3. Involve parents and children throughout all phases of service delivery.
4. Make clear that the school is a partner, but not in charge.
5. Use both top-down and bottom-up administration.
6. Develop service plans to meet the needs of students and/or their families.
7. Have service plans that are managed by an individual or group of individuals.
8. Provide accessible intake locations.
9. Link services to additional school restructuring efforts.
10. Move beyond crisis management and early intervention to prevention and development programs.
11. Cross professional and bureacratic boundaries to offer coherent services, often at nontraditional hours or in nontraditional settings.
12. Provide staff with time, training, and skills necessary to build relationships of trust and respect.
13. Utilize systems of accountability.
14. Include dispute-resolution procedures.
15. Include evaluation procedures.

First, successful school and community partnerships have a shared vision that is formally articulated in a written mission statement that includes specific goals. Second, while the partnership must have top-down and bottom-up decision making through coordination committees, successful programs have visible administrative commitment and support. Third, there must be a willingness to cross traditional institutional boundaries. Fourth, due to flexibility in operational contexts, there must be a willingness to subordinate traditional roles and adopt new ones. Finally, successful partnerships have continually open lines of two-way communication.

Clark (1992) pointed out that nearly 80 percent of school-community partnerships are initiated by the school. Therefore, as discussed in Chapter 5, it is likely that traditional roles of educators will evolve to include greater collaboration with constituencies within the community. For example, the building administrator's role will include writing grants while enlisting the services and support of community groups or businesses. Classroom teachers will no longer be isolated to the confines of their classroom with interactions limited to social conversation in the faculty lounge with colleagues. Teachers may actually have a team of adjunct faculty that will make significant contributions to the learning experiences of students in and out of the classroom.

Table 11–3   School-Community Partnership Resource List

Organizations

Association of School/Business Partnership Directors
PO Box 923
Norwalk, Connecticut 06852
  This organization provides school district administrators with workshops and materials such as articles, training modules, evaluation tools, and data on exemplary programs.

Center for Workforce Preparation and Quality Education
1615 H Street N.W.
Washington, D.C. 20062-2000
  This center was established by the U.S. Chamber of Commerce and serves as a clearinghouse for local chambers of commerce interested in partnerships to improve education.

Committee for Economic Development (CED)
477 Madison Avenue
New York, New York 10022
  The CED is an independent research and education organization composed of more than 200 business and education leaders. The mission of this group is promote reform and stable growth with rising living standards for all.

National Alliance of Business (NAB)
1201 New York Avenue N.W.
Suite 700
Washington, DC 20005
  The NAB works with businesses, government agencies, and community groups to promote educational reform through its Center for Excellence in Education.

National Association of Partners in Education (NAPE)
209 Madison Street
Suite 401
Alexandria, Virginia 22314
  NAPE is an organization comprised of representatives from business, education, community groups, and individuals who work to enhance the education of children. The organization provides materials and training for school-business-community partnerships.

National Center for Research in Vocational Education
1995 University Avenue
Suite 375
Berkeley, California 94704-1058
  This research center is interested in all aspects of vocational education programs. It provides information to the public and private sectors.

Table 11–3 continued

National Community Education Association (NCEA)
801 North Fairfax Street
Suite 209
Alexandria, Virginia 22314
    The NCEA was founded in 1966 and supports community involvement in education, interagency partnerships, and lifelong learning opportunities for everyone in the community. The organization publishes a journal, newsletter, training materials, and offers technical assistance to communities.

National Dropout Prevention Center
Clemson University
Clemson, South Carolina 29634
    This center collects and disseminates information about community-school partnerships designed to reduce the school dropout rate. It provides technical assistance to develop prevention programs and maintains an on-line database of dropout-prevention information entitled FOCUS.

Publications

At-Risk Youth in Crisis: A Handbook for Collaboration between Schools and Social Services

Linn Benton Education Service District and ERIC Clearinghouse on Educational Management (1991).

ERIC Clearinghouse on Educational Management
University of Oregon
1787 Agate Street
Eugene, Oregon 97403-5207
    This is a five-volume series that promotes interagency agreement and procedures for schools to follow in managing crisis situations with students at risk.

LINK-UP: A Resource Directory—Interagency Collaborations to Help Children Achieve

National School Boards Association
1680 Duke Street
Alexandria, Virginia 22314
    This directory describes partnerships linking local school boards with other agencies. Part I provides an overview of the necessity and issues surrounding interagency collaboration. This section also outlines implementation procedures and critical questions to ask before implementing any partnership. Part II is comprised of descriptions of 171 programs grouped under categories such as adjudication, child care/ latchkey children, health care, homelessness, employment, interagency communication, health care, parenting, staff development, and stay-in-school programs. The directory includes samples of interagency agreements, policy statements on confidentiality, and parental permission forms.

Table 11–3 continued

Business and the Schools: A Guide to Effective Programs
Diana Wyllie Rigden (1992)
Council for Aid to Education
51 Madison Avenue, Suite 2200
New York, New York 10010

Business/School Partnerships: A Path to Effective School Restructuring
Diana Wyllie Rigden (1991)
Council for Aid to Education
51 Madison Avenue, Suite 2200
New York, New York 10010

Both of these books provide useful information, guidelines, and materials for companies and schools interested in establishing partnerships. Materials include goal setting, costs, management, and evaluation procedures.

Source: Adapted from The ERIC Review (1992), Volume 2, Issue 2.

Specialized support personnel may also need to establish partnerships with individuals or organizations outside the school in the same tradition of social workers and vocational education teachers.

Individual schools and communities do not need to feel that they are reinventing the wheel nor carrying the bulk of work alone. A wealth of resources and information on funding and program development from government and private agencies exist. The U.S. Department of Education, in conjunction with the Educational Resources Information Center (ERIC) and Office of Educational Research and Improvement provide invaluable resources that can be used by schools and communities. A sample of organizational and informational resources is provided in Table 11–3.

Strategies for Establishing School-Community Partnerships

Collaboration was characterized earlier in this text as having mutual benefit for all parties involved. Consequently, it is incumbent upon educators to clearly articulate why establishing school-community partnerships with an agency or business will be beneficial for them. This is a pragmatic reality that must be addressed in early stages of establishing partnerships with community agencies or organizations. It may be an appropriate public relations event that can be considered as a tax-deductible contribution. Partnerships often create additional work force for employers at reduced or no cost. There are two levels at which school-community partnerships can be established: micro-level and macro-level.

Micro-level partnerships usually involve the efforts of a single teacher and classroom in a somewhat informal arrangement. For example, a special education teacher of students with moderate to severe disabilities may approach the owners or managers of businesses to create settings for learning opportunities. The manager of a supermarket might be asked if six to eight students can come to the store with peer tutors and paraprofessionals to practice their money-identification and shopping skills by locating and budgeting grocery items from a written list. The operator of a shoestore at a nearby shopping mall might be asked if a student can help with minor cleaning or stocking of shelves. Teachers who are interested in forming informal, micro-level partnerships can follow some simple guidelines to help establish and maintain the relationship.

First, seek and obtain permission from the building administrator by carefully describing the nature of the partnership. Second, draft a succinct letter of introduction on school stationery, carefully outlining the proposed partnership. This letter should include a description of benefits to the employer and to the students. The letter should also explain liability issues and how the students will be supervised. For example, the letter might state that the school insurance will protect the employer from any liability in case of an accident. The letter should also indicate that a peer tutor or paraprofessional will accompany the student throughout the learning experience. Third, work out schedules with the employer and students. Fourth, create a written agreement to be signed, documenting the components of the partnership that include roles and responsibilities of each participant. Fifth, maintain regular, ongoing communication with the employer to assess the situation and make any necessary modifications. This can be done through written forms or phone calls. Finally, acknowledge the cooperation of the community partner through thank-you letters to them and their immediate supervisor. Teachers may also consider sponsoring an appreciation banquet or social event to publicly acknowledge the partner.

Macro-level partnerships between the school and community are larger in scale. They may involve either large segments of the student population or the entire school. This level of partnerships usually requires substantial financial and human personnel investment on the part of the business. Consequently, strategies for establishing and maintaining macro-level partnerships are more complex. Hart (1988) recommended four strategies that reflect the ecological approach to collaboration presented throughout this textbook.

Identify Common Issues.   The first strategy is the identification an issue shared by the school and a community constituency. This step embodies problem identification and goal formulation. It is a process that can occur at many levels: classroom, school, district, or the community at large. For example, a high school counselor may recognize that a number of seniors are failing to graduate simply because they are not completing homework assignments. Or local employers may voice concern to school boards and the local press about the diminishing pool of high school graduates that comprise the work force.

Recruit Community Agencies. The second strategy is to recruit those community sectors with an interest and resources that might be utilized. This process involves an ecological analysis of existing factors that may be contributing to the problem as well as identification of resources that can be used to address these variables. Upon closer examination, the counselor and school psychologist may discover that many of the students at risk of not graduating lack fundamental learning strategies to help them with writing or reading assignments. Consequently, these students fail to complete their work, which in turn jeopardizes their chances for graduation and, ultimately, employment.

Identify Objectives and Make a Plan. The third strategy involves establishing a formal governing board consisting of representatives from the community agency, parents, and the school to identify a specific objective as well as establish procedures for decision making and allocation of resources. It is during this step that a plan is developed and implemented. While assessing existing resources, it is discovered that many employees at a nearby computer software plant are former teachers. Furthermore, the software company is currently developing computer-assisted instruction for written language. Through the coordination of the special education teacher, the company might be solicited to contribute computers and software as well as a few employees to serve as volunteers to train teachers how to use the software in an after-school work-completion program. Employees and teachers may volunteer one day a week to provide tutorials in the use of learning strategies to complete homework assignments.

Form Governing Committees. Fourth, form committees to oversee and evaluate the activities. The school counselor may work with the faculty as a whole to identify students who are at risk due to incomplete homework. The school psychologist and special education teacher might develop a rotating schedule of teachers and employees to work each day. The public relations and staff-development personnel at the computer software company could work with the school principal, counselor, special educator and PTA president to brainstorm the logistical operation of the program. Volunteer teachers earn career-ladder credit for these efforts. Using grade point averages, attendance records of program participants, and the number of graduating seniors, the coordinating committee will be able to ascertain the impact of the program. A satisfaction survey can also be developed and distributed to volunteer employees and parents.

Acknowledgment

After a school-community partnership has been successfully implemented, it is important that the community organization be publicly acknowledged for its contributions. There are a number of ways appreciation can be expressed. For example, an individual special education teacher who has established a partnership with one or two businesses for a community-based programs can write letters of thanks to the local managers and to their respective regional supervisors. Schools can provide photo opportunities that public relations departments can use in corporate newsletters, reports, or advertisements. A district may also wish to acknowledge participating businesses and agencies through a thank-you banquet or press releases to the local media.

Chapter Summary

The community is one of three learning environments examined in this text. Community is broadly conceptualized as the context and circumstances of local life, such as the provision and consumption of goods and services, cultural traits such as values and norms, and the interactions of individuals, families, and organizations held in common by a group of people. Therefore, beyond its geographic identity, the community is a reference point for a sense of identity.

School-community partnerships are an interactive exchange of ideas, resources, services, and expertise between educational and noneducational agencies in a variety of settings that mutually address the needs of students and the community as a whole by enabling students to become meaningful participants in their community. There are three basic approaches or models this partnership can take. The interagency model provides services from various agencies in one or more settings. This model requires extensive coordination to minimize fragmentation of assistance. A second model of school-community partnerships is school-based, wherein programs and services are primarily delivered at the school. The third model is community-based, wherein students often receive services in settings outside the school. Micro-level partnerships are less structured, more informal relationships that involve a single teacher and a small number of community partners. Macro-level partnerships are more complex, involving a significant investment of time, money, and personnel. Consequently, formal written plans and governing boards are necessary for efficient management of macro-level partnerships.

Each model can have one or more specific objectives. Educational objectives focus on academic or developmental achievement of students. Social and health objectives address the overall welfare of students. Social programs may focus on anti-gang programs or dropout prevention. Programs may include providing mental health services such as counseling, or health services such as anti-drug education programs. The third type of service-delivery objective is vocational. In this context, partnerships are formed to prepare children and youth for meaningful employment through career education or community-based learning experiences such as on-the-job training programs.

Key Vocabulary Terms

community
school-community
   partnerships
interagency collaboration
school-based partnerships
community-based
   partnerships

educational objectives
social and health objectives
vocational objectives
career education
school volunteers
adopt-a-school programs
field trip

work-study programs
employment-site instruction
experience-based career
   education (EBCE)
micro-level partnerships
macro-level partnerships

Part 4

Educational Partnerships:
The Future

Chapter 12

Chapter Overview

Future Issues

Chapter Objectives

Upon completing this chapter, students will be able to

1. Discuss various research areas in collaboration in need of investigation.
2. Describe the pre-service and in-service needs regarding preparation in collaborative partnerships.
3. Outline policy issues as they relate to collaboration.
4. Explore the ethical issues of privacy, informed consent, and confidentiality as they relate to students, parents, and educators.
5. State the important issues of educational collaboration in the upcoming years.

Introduction

The importance of educational partnerships has been stressed throughout this textbook, and their applications are numerous. However, it would be misleading to imply that the formation and implementation of collaborative relationships will occur without issues. In Chapter 1, we began this text by outlining not only the benefits of partnerships, but also the barriers. Although the practical barriers discussed in that chapter can be significant, we believe that they can be overcome with concerted effort and persistence. In this chapter, we will discuss broader issues that may affect educators' abilities to develop working partnerships within the school, and between the school, homes, and communities in which they participate.

There are several empirical, professional, and sociopolitical issues facing educators today that affect partnerships directly. They include limited research, lack of emphasis in professional preparation programs, conflicting educational policies, and ethical dilemmas. These issues may seem overwhelming and too "big" for individual educators to tackle. However, let us preface the discussion by stating that these issues can be resolved, one at a time, if the collaborative ethic is truly valued in progressive educational environments.

The issues can be addressed at several levels. Some broad ones, such as those dealing with professional preparation, are currently being addressed in several institutions of higher education. On the other hand, local efforts at staff development can also be beneficial to prepare inservice educators in collaborative problem solving. Likewise, issues surrounding archaic policies that may conflict with collaboration are being addressed by local educational agencies, as well as by individuals and teams of educators. In partnership with families and community agencies, educators can work together to identify the issues most important to their attempts at establishing a collaborative program. Using the ecological problem-solving model, they can develop programs to address those factors that hinder collaboration in their setting. This proactive approach will clear the way for future collaboration by tackling the barriers and allowing productive work to begin.

Research Issues

There are a number of important research issues that need to be resolved as the practice of collaboration within educational partnerships becomes more common. Although educators have been discussing collaborative processes and practices for some time now, it is important to recognize that the empirical basis for such practices is wanting. We have been careful to recommend research-validated practices throughout this text. For example, in our discussion of ecological assessment, classroom-based strategies, school-based partnerships, and home-school-community models, emphasis was placed on those practices that have been subject to empirical scrutiny. However, there remain several questions regarding the manner in which these practices can contribute to the educational experiences for students at risk.

Fuchs et al. (1992) conducted an extensive review of 119 research publications on the effectiveness of consultation programs. The majority of studies used systematic observation or questionnaires. The surveys typically measured teacher attitudes. While it is important to determine teacher satisfaction with consultation models, it is equally important to assess student outcomes. But very few investigations used student outcomes, such as achievement scores, to assess the impact of consultation. Furthermore, most of the studies were conducted in kindergarten through eighth-grade settings.

As presented in Chapter 3, our ecological problem-solving model is based on the behavioral consultation model of Bergan, Kratochwill, and their colleagues (Bergan & Kratochwill, 1990; Kratochwill & Bergan, 1990; Kratochwill, Elliott, & Rotto, 1990). While some important and sound research has been conducted in the area of behavioral consultation (see review in Chapter 3), one must be cautious in generalizing these research findings to practices involving teams. Some research adapting the behavioral consultation framework to prereferral teams was conducted by Graden, Casey, and Bonstrom (1985), attesting to the appropriateness of the model in educational teamwork. These researchers measured outcome by investigating number of referrals, evaluations, and placements in special education prior to, during, and after the implementation of the problem-solving team model in six schools. General support for the model was documented in four of the six schools during the implemetatation year. Specifically, referrals to the child study team and special educational assessment and placement decreased when consultation services were available. Follow-up (that is, post-implementation) data are available for only three schools, and only one of the three maintained low rates of special eduation referrals, evaluations, and placements. While this is important research, the investigators did not assess educational outcomes for individual or groups of students, nor did they evaluate processes within the team model that may have contributed to or detracted from its effectiveness.

Research is guided by theory, and should have implications for practice. The theoretical underpinnings of our approach to collaboration cuts across behavioral and ecological-systems principles. To begin an empirical investigation, theoretically derived *research questions* should be developed. Research questions are important to focus a research study or series of research projects. They can be organized in terms of whether they are primarily concerned with outcomes or processes. *Outcome-based research* is concerned with the effects of a variable (such as an intervention or a type of collaboration) on the persons for whom it is intended (such as a student or group of students). *Process-based research* is concerned with what happens within a situation (such as collaborative teams or team-teaching interactions) that may increase or decrease a technique's effectiveness. There are a number of both outcome- and process-based research questions that need to be addressed in the area of collaborative educational partnerships with students at risk. The following questions are general and are not meant to represent the entire range of research to be conducted in the field of collaboration. Indeed, you will likely think of more as you read these questions and the remainder of this chapter.

Outcome questions:

1. What are the effects of different types of collaboration on individual students or groups of students at risk?

2. Are certain types of collaborative partnerships more effective than others?

3. Are some forms of collaborative partnerships differentially effective for students at risk due to different demographic characteristics (e.g., minority, disabled, low-SES, single-parent family)?

4. Are certain components of collaboration more important than others for addressing the educational needs of students at risk?

5. Can educational partnerships effectively address the range of difficulties experienced by students at risk?

Process questions:

1. What are the important interactive practices that contribute to effective collaborative partnerships?

2. What is the most effective way to delineate roles and functions within collaborative teams?

3. Which roles and functions are required and which are secondary in an effective partnership?

4. How can educators effectively overcome barriers and challenges to establishing partnerhips?

5. What are some methods to maintain collaborative partnerships over time?

Activity 12–1

On a sheet of paper, develop two columns and title them "Outcome Questions" and "Process Questions." In a small group, generate a list of research questions under each heading. The questions should be developed from the theories, research findings, and collaborative practices you have read about throughout this text. After completing the chapter, get together with the group members and generate more questions. Share the lists with other classmates to realize the range of research needs and opportunities in collaboration.

Outcome-Based Research

As suggested in Chapter 1, programs established through collaborative models undoubtedly have several goals, including the pooling of resources, increased communication, efficiency in decision making, and staff development. The entire ecological model, however, is based on the premise that the *student* is central. That is, the needs of and services to students are the primary objectives. Therefore, research directed at investigating the outcomes of collaboration on individuals or groups of students at risk must be conducted. There are several methods of conducting outcome-based research, and many variables that can be measured. For example, investigators can make comparisons between schools using a collaborative model and those that do not, keeping records on such student-related outcomes as standardized test scores, truancies, tardies, work completion, graduation rates, or dropout rates. Indeed, multiple outcome measures in these studies are beneficial.

An alternative outcome-based research model employs a small group of subjects (such as four to six) and studies them intensively. *Single subject research designs* are concerned with individual students or small groups of students and their responsiveness to specific, well-controlled programs. Although they do not allow for broad conclusions to be made about a larger population of students, they help in determining with some degree of confidence the types of programs that are most effective with subjects presenting similar characteristics. The advantages to using single-subject designs are outlined in Table 12–1.

Table 12–1	**Advantages to Single-Subject Designs in Collaboration Research**

1. They allow the researcher to control certain factors that might otherwise contaminate experimental procedures.
2. Repeated measurement of important variables in collaboration allows the researcher to modify the design and/or procedures as data are gathered.
3. The scientific study of individual differences allows researchers to specify relevant subject characteristics and their relationship to programs.
4. They can be used where more experimentally rigid control procedures cannot be exercised (such as schools), so they permit evaluation of programs within the ecological setting in which behaviors are naturally occurring.
5. They can be internally valid, which allows researchers to conclude that educational programs, rather than other occurrences, produced certain effects.
6. They provide a useful way to combine quantitative and qualitative data.
7. The data generated in single subject designs can be reported through graphs and figures, which facilitates communication between the researchers and educators whom the research is meant to assist.

In single subject designs, the effectiveness of collaboration and educational programs is generally determined by several interrelated components. These include *degree* or amount of change in the student or students following the implementation of the intervention. *Immediacy* is investigated by looking at how quickly change occured with the onset of a program. Additional concerns when measuring effectiveness are *maintenance and generalization* of student change once intervention strategies are no longer in place. In other words, effective programs should produce changes that are meaningful and that continue even after the program is discontinued.

There are several considerations that must be kept in mind when conducting outcome-based research. First, the procedures used in the study must be clear and specific. Therefore, the components of collaboration (namely, consultation teams, team teaching, home-school-community program, and so forth) must be clearly defined and operationalized. That is, the specific practices of collaboration must be articulated. This will allow future researchers to replicate the procedures, and educators reading the research to identify exactly what must be done in their school to adopt a similar model. It is not enough to state in research that "collaboration" occurred, or even that "consultation" or "parental involvement" was the intervention used. *Operational definitions,* complete with descriptions of what those interventions looked like, are necessary (see Chapter 3 for a review of operational definitions).

A second consideration when developing outcome-based research is the sample of students for whom the intervention is designed. This sample will determine in part the target of the study (for example, whether increased academic productivity or school attendance is the focus) and the type of collaboration used to address the target. Thus, if improved social skills among minority, bilingual second graders is the focus of the study, the program developed will likely include individuals who can communicate effectively with the students. When very similar students are the focus of an intervention study, it is inappropriate to generalize the findings to other groups who are dissimilar to the research group.

Most collaborative approaches discussed throughout this text entail several components. For example, the ecological problem-solving model explored in Chapter 3 is complex, and includes several stages (problem definition, ecological analysis, plan development and implementation, and plan evaluation). Although we emphasized the importance of each stage in addressing problems and making decisions, it is possible that some issues may be dealt with more simply and effectively with less complex models. It is important to begin researching the types of issues that are most effectively addressed with a collaborative model, and those that are most effectively addressed with other methods. It may also be possible to "streamline" the model in some cases by identifying the exact and unique contribution that each stage makes in the total problem-solving process.

Process-Based Research

As suggested earlier, process-based research is concerned with understanding what happens within interactions or situations. There is clearly a wealth of directions that process research within collaborative educational partnerships can take. One such direction is investigating processes that contribute to or detract from effectively functioning teams. Unfortunately, much of the research investigating factors that increase acceptability or preferences in consultation is based on hypothetical situations or self-reports and surveys. For example, a resercher may show a group of teachers a videotape of a consultant and consultee in a problem-solving interview and ask them to rate their perceptions of the interaction or behaviors of the actors. In other research, the investigator may circulate hundreds of surveys and ask respondents to report on their preferences for various ways of handling classroom problems, including referral to special education, teaming, or consultation. Still other researchers have asked experts to rate the characteristics of "effective consultants." It is important to realize that none of these research approaches actually investigate live educators dealing with real problems. They fail to observe actual behaviors of educators as they deal with problems in classrooms or tackle issues within teams. Therefore, the results must be interpreted cautiously. It is necessary for researchers to begin studying real educators, dealing with real issues, to understand empirically those practices that contribute to effective and ineffective problem solving.

In Chapters 1, 3, and 9, barriers to various forms of collaboration were discussed. Clearly, educators will face several challenges when forming and implementing educational partnerships. These may include interpersonal difficulties such as resistance or interpersonal conflict; logistical constraints such as scheduling and time considerations; or professional issues such as competing agendas, lack of skill, or different philosophical beliefs. An important process issue concerns the effect that these barriers may have on the overall capability of a system to utilize a collaborative approach. Likewise, it is essential to empirically investigate means of overcoming these barriers if collaborative educational partnerships are to become a viable model of service delivery for students at risk.

Although a basic tenet of collaboration is that the partners are coequal and share in the ownership of problems and solutions, it is not correct to assume that all will be responsible for carrying out various aspects of the model. Rather, it is assumed that in an efficiently run team, roles and responsibilities are delegated to individuals most suited to carry them out. Yet the most appropriate way for work teams to specify responsibilities is not clearly understood. There are also roles that members may take within the group to enhance communication, such as keeping discussions on topic and clarifying statements. These "maintenance roles" (Johnson & Johnson, 1991) are believed to be important to aid the functioning of collaborative teams, but they have not been studied empirically. It is necessary to investigate the various roles that educational partners assume both within and outside of meetings, and to study their relationship to outcomes of collaborative problem solving.

Action Research

Action research is a special form of process research. It is defined as "a form of self-reflective inquiry undertaken by participants in social (including educational) situations in order to improve the rationality and justice of (a) their own social or educational practices, (b) their understanding of these practices, and (c) the situations in which these practices are carried out" (Carr & Kemmis, 1983, p. 58). Action research can take many forms and may be "intentionally idiosyncratic, personalized, and contextual . . . [as] questions for study emerge from needs which are unique to individuals in particular settings" (Kyle & Hovda, 1987, p. 171). Action research allows educators and preprofessionals to meaningfully apply theory (Kosmidou & Usher, 1991). In this way, practitioners are not merely the consumers of research, but are researchers themselves to improve their knowledge regarding curriculum, teaching, and learning (Dowhower, Melvin, & Sizemore, 1990). Miller and Pine (1990) suggested that in addition to allowing educators to discuss, reflect, and analyze their own teaching, action research provides the opportunity to make significant contributions to educational improvement and the research literature through classroom research. Researchers are often outsiders who conduct experimental research that may be artificial in nature, given the realities of classrooms, resulting in limited generalization into actual practice (Kosmidou & Usher, 1991). Therefore, action research has the potential to resolve "the dilemma between formal ivory tower research and the issues of day-to-day practice" (Dowhower et al., 1990, p. 33) while serving as a powerful learning tool in professional preparation programs.

Action research has a long history and has been effectively used in teacher education programs and staff development (Liston & Zeichner, 1990; Oja & Pine, 1987; Ross, 1987). Recently, it has been used to help educators develop their own skills in working with students at risk (Gove & Kennedy-Calloway, 1992). Traditionally, it has been primarily a reflective process for teachers and teacher candidates. This introspection has focused on identifying evidence of personal and professional growth. While this process is illuminating, it often does not provide empirical evidence of impact, especially at the student level. Therefore, action research should be supplemented with experimental investigations to assess the effects of collaborative interventions on student outcomes.

Professional Preparation Issues

The National Association of State Boards of Education (NASBE) commissioned a two-year study of the status of special education within the context of the educational reform movement. As part of that study, a set of thirteen operating assumptions have evolved to guide the efforts of the NASBE task force. Among these assumptions are the following:

> To the extent that teachers are trained and socialized to expect that there are two types of students (and teachers)—normal and special—general education teachers will perceive that they are incapable of teaching special students.
>
> Many student needs can be met by regular teachers, with support, who have broad training in instructional strategies that meet diverse student needs. (Roach, 1991, p. 4)

These assumptions appear to have profound implications for teacher educators and in-service program providers. The first assumption may well be an accurate depiction of current teacher-education programs and in-service practices. If this is so, educators must consider if current practices are counterproductive to educational reform. The latter assumption is based on the premise that support is, in fact, readily available to classroom teachers from other professionals such as special education teachers and school psychologists. Existing educational structures would suggest otherwise, as teachers are often isolated in facing the overwhelming challenge of teaching students with special needs. This is a disservice to both the student and teacher. The integration of students with disabilities will be a difficult task given large class size and the national emphasis to achieve academic excellence (Sapon-Shevin, 1987). While classroom teachers may recognize the potential values of integrating students with disabilities on philosophical, legal, and moral grounds, most face their new roles and responsibilities for this student population with little or no support and inadequate preparation (Welch, 1989).

A basic tenet of the collaborative ethic is that teachers, special educators, school psychologists, counselors, and administrators are expected to communicate and "co-labor" to meet the educational and social needs of all students. As articulated throughout this text, effective collaboration requires several skills and attitudes including the ability to take the perspective of others, speak a common language, manage conflict, conceptualize school problems in a broad fashion, and share resources, knowledge, and skills. A major barrier to the establishment of collaboration in the schools, however, is that key individuals involved in partnerships are often not prepared to carry out this role. There are two important issues at hand; the preservice preparation of educators, and the continuing professional development of educators in schools.

Preservice Preparation

Few educators graduating from professional preparation programs have exposure or experience in teaming, collaboration, consultation, partnerships, or serving students at risk. They enter the work force ill-equipped to function in conjunction with other educators, parents, and support staff. They may find, for example, that they do not understand the terminology used or practices of other professionals in schools. They may have questions or problems but be unaware of the most appropriate person to approach, or the procedures by which to access assistance or services. To collaborate effectively, specific practices and techniques must be explored, modeled, and rehearsed at the preparatory level (Pugach & Allen-Meares, 1985). Yet, most educational training programs continue to espouse an isolated model of preservice preparation (Allen-Meares & Pugach, 1982; Prasse & Fafard, 1982).

Institutions of higher education must be aware of similarities and relationships among disciplines, and provide coursework and applied experiences for prospective professionals that will facilitate collaboration (Golightly 1987; Humes & Hohenshil, 1987). Interdisciplinary training can be useful for promoting a common language, knowledge base, and an understanding of the diverse and complex functions of schools. Familiarity with roles, responsibilities, and techniques among related professions can enhance delivery of services to students at risk (Blaine & Sobsy, 1983; Golightly, 1987; Welch, Sheridan, Fuhriman, Hart, Connell, & Stoddart, 1992).

The most effective way of providing opportunities for preservice professionals to interface, communicate, and collaborate is only beginning to be explored. Didactic coursework can provide a knowledge base on the roles and functions of various individuals within schools, and allow students to begin considering ecological considerations in educational services. However, it is likely to be more beneficial to provide relevant and applied ("hands-on") opportunities for students to work through cases in a structured manner. Although practical experiences will likely enhance students' learning, they will also add elements of complexity. For example, conisderable amounts of time will be necessary for student teams to work through the ecological problem-sovling model to a level of competence. A great deal of direct observation and immediate feedback is necessary, which adds to the number of faculty members required to fulfill these roles. Scheduling becomes difficult if some programs offer night classes routinely, and some offer courses only in the daytime. Course credits and student enrollment become an issue if students need certain classes to graduate, and a "collaboration" course taught in a different educational department (or different college altogether) is not among them. Indeed, the range of difficulties that may be encountered in integrating collaborative training into university programs are only beginning to be recognized. The challenges may be particularly salient at present, given the infancy of some of the notions regarding collaboration as an educational philosophy.

Welch et al. (1992) described the efforts of one university to address these critical issues and preservice needs. A unique interdisciplinary course was developed at the University of Utah and is team-taught by faculty members from the departments of Educational Administration, Educational Psychology, Educational Studies, and Special Education. Individual faculty members across departments with teaching and research interests in educational collaboration and problem-sovling conduct the course. The purpose is

Activity 12–2

In small groups comprised of individuals representing different educational fields (e.g., teachers, special educators, administrators, school psychologists), address the following questions:

1. What are the benefits of a preservice collaboration course offered to individuals from various educational disciplines? What are the drawbacks?

2. What topics should be included to enhance the desirability of such a course?

3. Who should be responsible for teaching the course?

4. Who should be required to take it?

5. What are some of the challenges in developing and participating in a course such as this (you may be able to use personal experience here!). What can be done to meet these challenges?

to provide prospective teachers, special educators, school psychologists, counselors, and administrators insights into conceptual and practical components of collaborative problem-sovling and conflict management. A primary intent is to provide students with a unique interdisciplinary training experience, wherein the elements of collaboration, problem-sovling, shared decision making, and conflict management are operationalized and practiced in simulated role-play activities. The overall objective is to prepare preservice professionals to function as effective collaborators in educational settings upon completion of their respective graduate programs.

An important element of many collaborative models is the use of paraprofessionals. Jones and Bender (1993) conducted a comprehensive review of literature regarding the utilization of paraprofessionals in special education. They reported that the majority of research "addresses peripheral issues" such as descriptions of how paraprofessionals are used while providing inadequate empirical evidence of efficacy. Very few studies examine the efficacy of paraprofessionals in terms of student outcomes. Of those studies that do, most are dated and employ questionable methodology. In their concluding remarks, Jones and Bender suggested that research on the utilization of paraprofessionals within the context of the regular education initiative and inclusion movement is needed.

As more and more schools begin to utilize paraprofessionals, a number of important questions must be addressed. These questions include the following: Who should train and certify paraprofessionals? How will the use of paraprofessionals impact case loads for special education teachers? Who will supervise paraprofessionals? How will formative and summative evaluation be used to assess the effectiveness of paraprofessionals? What is the role of teacher unions?

Staff Development

Although models for preservice preparation in collaboration are being developed, there are a number of educators in the field for whom this continues to be a novel approach. Even if groups of students leave their preparation programs with the knowledge and ability to serve in collaborative partnerships, their skills will quickly dissipate if they are not developed and used in the field. Unless the system is responsive and reinforces individuals for this unique and important skill area, the resources will go unnoticed. For these reasons, staff development (such as in-services and workshops) for existing educators are essential. Unfortunately, once in the field, few opportunities for staff development in this important area are available.

There is some literature suggesting practices to increase the effectiveness of staff training. Smylie and Conyers (1991) suggested that staff development should be reconceptualized as a *work group*, rather than a workshop, to allow educators the opportunity to collaborate with colleagues as they develop new skills. Staff development should be organized in such a way that models are used to present new information, strategies, and materials, followed by hands-on practice activities (Howey, 1985). Clear and explicit objectives based on sound theoretical principles should guide the staff-development program through carefully planned activities that provide practice, feedback, and support for transfer of learning new skills (Jones & Lowe, 1990). Merenbloom (1984) maintained that active involvement of the participants during sustained and sequential effort is a key component to successful staff development. The content of in-service must relate to the conditions of teaching as well as to the needs of students (Epstein, Lockard, & Dauber, 1991). Necessary support materials and ongoing technical assistance must be readily available to educators at the building level as they begin to implement the new skills that they have assimilated (Howey, 1985).

In general, information provided in staff-development activities should be presented in a clear and succinct manner. Background theory may help set the stage for models to be presented, and research findings are helpful to support the recommended procedures. However, the majority of time should be spent discussing *how* to engage in relevant practices. Written materials are useful to ensure that educators receive important information, but they are not sufficient to develop skills. Live and videotaped examples and demonstrations are helpful to depict topics under discussion and to stimulate dialogue. Enactment of the procedures by participants through role plays or simulated case experiences are desirable to provide personal exposure and practice. Observation by leaders and immediate feedback can be used to further refine educators' skills. Whenever possible, groups of diverse educators and patrons of the school community (such as administrators, teachers, social workers, counselors, and parents) should be invovled in staff-development experiences together. An efficient way to train an entire school staff is to work with one core group of educators, which then becomes responsible for providing identical training experiences to the remainder of the school body.

Spotlight: Site-Based Transdisciplinary Educational Partnerships

To address the preservice needs of educators across disciplines, a three-year, federally funded project entitled Site-Based Transdisciplinary Educational Partnerships (STEP) was initiated at the University of Utah (Welch & Sheridan, 1993). Students from special education, educational studies, educational administration, and educational psychology were allowed to fulfill part of their respective field practica and/or internship requirements by working collaboratively in a cooperating public school setting. In the STEP experience, students worked as teams with their counterparts in the school to form educational partnerships in meeting the needs of students at risk.

The primary objectives of the STEP project were to (1) instill the collaborative ethic at the preservice level to facilitate transdisciplinary collaboration in the schools; (2) provide prospective educators supervised site-based learning experiences in team-based ecological problem-solving; and (3) prepare prospective educators with a knowledge base and skills to understand the process of change within the context of site-based school reform and restructuring. Working with cooperating educators in three urban and suburban school districts, the transdisciplinary cohorts developed and implemented projects at the building level designed to meet the needs of students at risk. Students were placed at exemplary school sites for two academic quarters to complete the collaborative project. Using an ecological problem-solving framework, students conducted a systems analysis to identify an area of need with regard to delivering services to students at risk. An ecological problem-solving worksheet was used by teams to structure the process of problem identification/definition, ecological analysis, development of action plan, and evaluation.

Transdisciplinary teams met during a quarter-long seminar to explore the collaborative ethic and ecological problem-solving approach. Action plans were developed as teams integrated their conceptual and operational knowledge base with skills practiced in the school sites. Action plans were implemented under the supervision of the building administrator the following quarter. Each action plan included an evaluation component to assess the effectiveness of the program. The range of project possibilities included creating home-school partnership programs, implementing team-teaching, developing teacher assistance teams, and establishing peer-tutoring programs.

It is not enough to provide skill-building experiences in time-limited in-services or workshops and expect the behaviors to carry over into the everyday operation of the school. At least two additional things must occur. First, specific responsibilities and tasks must be delegated to persons who will follow through on setting up meetings and establishing programs. Second, changes must occur in the traditional structure of school systems. Specifically, existing policies must be changed or new ones put into place to allow collaborative educational partnerships to develop to fruition in the school.

Policy Issues

Throughout this text we have tried to describe various research-validated models to promote collaborative educational partnerships. Frustrations with current practices have encouraged educators to find different ways to accomplish the changing tasks facing them, and the collegial practices emphasized herein have withstood numerous field tests pointing to their practical utility. However, policies at the local, state, and federal levels are not always supportive of "best practices." In the case of collaboration, for example, there likely remain many policies that contradict the basic principles of shared responsibility and interdependence. In collaborative partnerships, educators are most productive when they work together to pool resources, brainstorm ideas, develop plans and evaluate programs. However, several schools and districts continue to evaluate their staff on independent practices such as isolated classroom teaching or services delivered. In fact, it is possible that in some places, educators could be penalized (directly or indirectly) by engaging in collaborative activities.

Much of the service delivery provided in schools is based on labeling children. It has been argued that Chapter I of the Education Consolidation and Improvement Act of 1981 labels children unnecessarily (Natriello, McDill, & Pallas, 1990). It has a complicated funding formula in which monies are allocated to districts that, in turn, distribute funds to schools, which must select students to receive services. The selection process, in essence, imposes a label of poverty for children who otherwise would not receive support services. Chapter I services, like resource programming in special education, often employs a "pull-out" service-delivery model. These programs also contribute to the delineation of responsibilities between classroom teachers and specialists (Natriello et al., 1990).

Likewise, special education is primarily conceptualized and practiced as a remedial treatment. Rather than employing a proactive or preventative approach, most special education services are provided only after a student is eligible. By this time, the student has experienced considerable failure and frustration as well as risking possible stigmatization of being labeled as disabled. Moreover, students who are found ineligible often fail to receive individualized interventions, and their needs continue to go unmet. Special education is often perceived as a separate subsystem within the larger framework of the educational system, creating artificial and somewhat arbitrary boundaries due to separate rules, regulations, funding streams, facilities, and teacher training (Roach, 1991).

Activity 12–3

In a small group, try to identify as many formal school policies as you can. For example, policies regarding number of hours teachers should spend in a classroom, extracurricular responsiblitiies, and staff evaluation might be considered. If you do not have experience working in a school, consider policies of your most recent work setting. Highlight those that may conflict with the establishment and maintenance of collaborative partnerships as defined in this text. Now rewrite the policies so that collaboration can occur within the parameters of the policy.

Policies concerning the roles of "itinerant staff" also exist. These are staff members who provide contractual or part-time service to a school, and they often rotate to several schools as part of their responsibilities. School psychologists, speech and language technicians, and school nurses are examples. Although funding resources usually require such patterns of service delivery, the inclusion or exclusion of these individuals in school-based partnerships may significantly affect the overall efficiency and effectiveness of teams. Policies require that the resources provided by these important team players be shared among several sites, but this paradoxically limits their availability. The end result is that often these itinerant staff are perceived as "outsiders" to the school and not integral to its overall function. There may even be situations where these staff are purposefully excluded from school-based teams. We believe that these are unhealthy and ineffective attitudes and practices. For example, a school psychologist may be an essential ingredient on a team grappling with issues of underachievement or childhood depression. A nurse will be important on cases that present health, nutrition, or medication issues. Policies that limit the utilization of support staff on school-based teams should be reexamined and modified to invite their involvement.

In Chapter 1, practical and logistical issues were presented as barriers to collaborative problem-solving. It was suggested that organizational structures be put into place to allow for the development and implementation of productive educational partnerships. These include changes such as providing release time for teachers to attend meetings, using "floaters" or support personnel to assist in the implementation of programs, rescheduling the academic year, or rewriting educators' contracts to allow more preparation and staff-development opportunities. However, these practical changes at the local school level will be short-lived and of little benefit to others until they are turned directly into educational policies.

Ethical Issues

Dealing with an array of school, classroom, and student difficulties can be both challenging and intriguing. Although it may seem apparent, it is important to state that individuals involved in educational partnerships are responsible for behaving professionally and ethically within and outside formal meetings. Most professional associations have codes of ethics that set a standard for how professionals within that profession should behave. These include acting in ways that ensure the rights of students, parents, educators, and schools. As an example, the general principles of the American Psychological Association's code of ethics are presented in Table 12–2. Perusing these principles, one can see that they can easily pertain to all individuals invovled in educational collaborative relationships. In this context, however, the principles related to privacy, confidentiality, and informed consent deserve special attention. We will now address each of these in greater detail.

Table 12–2 General Principles of the American Psychological Association's Code of Ethics

Principle	Interpretation
A: Competence	"[R]ecognize the boundaries of particular competencies and the limitations of expertise . . . provide only those services and use only those techniques for which they are qualified."
B: Integrity	"[S]eek to promote integrity in the science, teaching, and practice . . . honest, fair, and respectful of others."
C: Professional and Scientific Responsibility	"[U]phold professional standards of conduct, clarify professional roles and obligations, accept appropriate responsibility for behavior, and adapt methods to the needs of different populations . . . consult with, refer to, or cooperate with other professionals and institutions to the extent needed to serve the best interests of . . . recipients of services."
D: Respect for People's Rights and Dignity	"[A]ccord appropriate respect to the fundamental rights, dignity, and worth of all people . . . respect the rights of individuals to privacy, confidentiality, self-determination, and autonomy"
E: Concern for Others' Welfare	"[S]eek to contribute to the welfare of those with whom they interact professionally."
F: Social Responsibility	"[Be] aware of professional and scientific responsibilities to the community and the society in which they work and live . . . apply and make public knowledge . . . in order to contribute to human welfare."

Students' Rights

Central to educational partnerships is the student or group of students for whom teams are responsible. In school settings, students are the primary clients of services. Therefore, decisions made on behalf of students must be concerned first and foremost with their educational, physical, social, and emotional well-being. Partnerships comprised of several relevant individuals allow this by adding increased objectivity, expertise, and "checks and balances" to the decision-making process.

The student's *right to privacy* must be acknowledged throughout the collaborative problem-solving process. This means that only topics related to the concern at hand should be explored. Take for example Stephen, a fourth-grade student who demonstrates chronic problems with reading. He attends school regularly, has no difficulties in other academic areas, and puts forth a great deal of effort to learn to read. While it will be helpful to know if there is a family history of reading problems and the strategies tried in the past, there is virtually no reason to delve into Stephen's home life to try to uncover "deep-rooted" problems or issues unrelated to reading.

Issues of *confidentiality* are intricately related to privacy. Educators in problem-solving partnerships must commit to keeping all discussions regarding a student or students strictly confidential. In other words, the problems, actions, and interventions regarding students that are uncovered or explored during collaborative interactions should not be shared with others. At no time should a student's name be shared to illustrate problems or treatment plans. In fact, it is a breach of confidentiality to indicate to others outside the collaborative team that a certain student has even been identified by the team as in need of attention.

Informed consent of clients is a necessary activity in ethical practice. This requires that individuals who are the recipients of services be informed of the planned activities (assessment, intervention, evaluation) at an appropriate level (using language or communication which they can understand) prior to their implementation, *and* provide their consent (acknowledge formally that the activities are acceptable to them). In work with minors or adult students with disabilities, informed consent is most generally considered a right of parents. However, it is becoming more widely accepted that

Activity 12–4	In a small group, review the APA Ethical Principles in Table 12–2. Insert the words "educators should" at the beginning of each interpretive statement (column at the right side of the table). With your peers, identify ways that these principles apply to educators in collaborative partnerships. In which situations might these principles cause difficulties in schools? How can these situations be handled to ensure adherence to the ethical code?

students also have an inherent right to be informed of programs that will affect their lives. There is some debate over whether minor students and students with disabilities are able to make intelligent decisions about treatment programs designed to improve their well-being, so parental consent generally supersedes child consent. It is recommended, however, that students be informed of programs that will affect them, and their consent be obtained whenever possible. This becomes more important as the student's age, developmental level, and intellectual capacity increases. For example, beyond informing the older student of a program and gaining his or her consent, it may also be important to involve him or her in the entire problem-solving process as much as possible.

Parents' Rights

In Chapters 9 and 10 and elsewhere throughout this text, we emphasized the importance of involving parents actively in educational programs. Ideally, this will begin before any "problems" arise, and parents' rights regarding privacy, confidentiality, and informed consent in relation to collaborative programming will be understood throughout. We have stressed the pragmatic reasons for parental involvement in this text, including the benefits of increased ownership for educational goals, effective communication between schools and families, and continuity of programs. Parents also have legal rights in regard to their children's education that dictate in part the way they are treated by school personnel.

The Buckley Amendment (Family Education Rights and Privacy Act of 1974) granted parents the right of access to educational records and placed restrictions as to who else could obtain access to their child's records. Public Law 94-142 gave parents of disabled students and students suspected of having a disability rights to examine records related to the identification, evaluation, and educational placement of their child. It also gave parents the right of prior notice of any change in the identification, evaluation, or educational program of their child and required informed consent. Collectively, these laws gave all parents the right to review educational records concerning their child, and the right to be active in decisions regarding their child's school program.

The interpretation of these laws as they pertain to educational collaboration differs across districts. Some districts, for example, interpret the Buckley Amendment to require parental permission for a teacher to discuss difficulties of a student with a consultant or problem-solving team. In some districts, a request for consultation must be initiated formally as the required first step in referral for a special education evaluation (Hughes, 1986). This practice is not recommended, as it implies that the evaluation will ensue and limits the preventive nature of collaboration.

The issue of informed consent as it relates to parents is central to the activities of problem-solving teams. We addressed this earlier in relation to student rights. Whereas obtaining informed consent from students is considered "best practices," it is the educator's ethical (and in some cases, legal) responsibility to obtain informed consent from parents of students for whom individualized programs are being developed and implemented. This is not to say that some early discussions of student difficulties cannot occur between educators in efforts to prevent more serious problems from arising. However, when extensive behavioral assessments (such as ongoing observations; parent, teacher, student ratings; multiple interviews) are planned or intrusive interventions are developed, parents must be informed of the activities and provide written consent acknowledging their acceptance. Regarding student interventions, Piersel (1985) suggested that "as the identified plan to resolve student problems intrudes into the educational environment, involves aversive procedures, or permits the student to be identified as different, informed consent is necessary" (p. 274). Thus, common procedures that are used with several students or that are generally accepted and approved educational practices will not require parental consent (Hughes, 1986).

Involving parents early in their child's education minimizes the legal or ethical entanglements that may arise as their child's difficulties require intervention. However, when parents are included in various aspects of educational problem-solving and decision making, their right to privacy must be maintained. It is not appropriate to conduct extensive, in-depth parent and family histories unless the case clearly warrants it. In general, only those issues related to the identified problem should be investigated. Further, only individuals trained in clinical interviewing (such as school psychologists) should attempt such sensitive practices. In all cases, only the information that relates directly to the student's demonstrated difficulty should be shared with others, and only with the consent of the parent. This will ensure confidentiality of private information.

Educators' Rights

The rights of privacy, confidentiality, and informed consent discussed in relation to students and parents extend also to educators. To engage in productive, effective collaborative activities, these rights must be recognized and respected. While all educators have rights to be treated fairly and professionally in their work setting, the present discussion pertains primarily to those educators who have the most direct responsibility for the student or students in question. In most cases, this will be the classroom teacher.

In many cases, problems are brought to the attention of a consultant or team of collaborative educators by a classroom teacher. For example, a teacher may have an unruly group of students or a highly inattentive and unproductive individual student in his classroom. At least initially, this teacher will be the primary provider of information regarding the problems demonstrated in his classroom. It is essential that the teacher feel comfortable disclosing information about the problem to the consultant or the team, and trust that his or her own privacy will not be invaded. For example, questions about the teacher's personal life events such as a death or recent divorce and the effect on his or her energy level in the classroom are an inappropriate invasion of privacy.

While questions about an educator's personal life are inappropriate during collaborative meetings, it will obviously be important to obtain some information about teaching style, classroom management, or student-teacher interactions. The extent and quality of information shared by teachers may be affected by the degree to which they feel it will be kept confidential. For example, they may feel reticent to admit that they do not understand how to manage a group of oppositional students if they believe this information will be spread throughout the school building and to parents. Other information shared by educators within the consultation or team meeting should also be kept confidential, and it is good practice to begin each meeting by reminding all individuals that discussions should remain within the group.

When educators become involved in collaborative relationships, they should be informed of the central aspects of the partnership. This includes the fact that it is voluntary, that they may be asked to carry out parts of an assessment or intervention plan, and that they have the right to reject what is recommended by the consultant or educational team (Gutkin & Curtis, 1990). The need to be involved in group or individual meetings which may in some cases involve skill training should be explored. It is also important to allow other educators to assist in the identification of the problem and development and implementation of a plan. Other characteristics of collaboration are outlined in Chapter 1, and these may be reviewed to ensure that all partners are fully informed of the procedures before agreeing to participate. Informed consent ensures that all participants understand the process and agree to become involved without coercion.

Schools' Rights

The importance of student, parent, and educator rights are straightforward. However, the rights of the school are often left unconsidered. In a thoughtful article on ethical issues in consultation, Hughes (1986) argued that there are many necessary services and limited funds in most educational settings. According to Hughes, "The employing school system is entrusted by the community with the responsibility for making decisions regarding the allocation of limited resources" (p. 494). If collaborative problem-sovling is to be touted as the primary educational service-delivery model in schools, educators have an ethical responsibility to evaluate the outcomes of their services and remain accountable for the expenditure of time, material, human, financial, and other resources used in collaborative programs.

Future Directions

The future of collaboration, educational partnerships, and services for students at risk is immense. With changing trends in technology and preservice preparation, more opportunities face educators than ever before. We envision changes in these areas as critical to the advancement of services for students at risk.

Technology as a field is expanding rapidly. Within educational applications, computerized instruction, interactive video, and electronic communication are just a few examples of resources that are available to educators. Whereas workbooks and ditto sheets were once considered state-of-the-art instruction, it is now possible to allow students to learn interactively with indiviudalized instruction designed to meet their unique learning needs and receive immediate feedback while sitting at a computer terminal. Educators can access educational databases, library card catalogs, and even colleagues around the country through electronic mailboxes and computer modems. Video technology has also allowed educators to demonstrate model programs and disseminate information graphically. With modern innovation, technological capabilities and applications are changing almost daily. This has implications for schools and school programs, including those designed by and for collaborative teams. For example, as schools become better equipped with technological resources, a technology specialist may become an important staff person. Likewise, educators within the school may be required to become better prepared to use equipment such as computers and video camcorders, and even seek grants to purchase new equipment for educational purposes. Certainly, they will be responsible for integrating technology into their curricula to better prepare students for the 21st century.

Preservice preparation programs are also changing to meet the changing educational environment. Some issues were addressed earlier in this chapter. We believe that in the future there will be more educational preparation programs requiring collaboration across departments such as Special Education, Regular Education, Educational Administration, Educational Psychology, Rehabilitative Services, and Social Work. It is also likely that classroom-based instruction will be just one aspect of training in collaboration. For example, practicum experiences at training sites such as "Professional Development Schools" (Holmes Group, 1986, 1990) may be required of all students exiting educational certification programs. Technology will also become increasingly important in preservice programs, as prospective educators will be required to teach using the latest technological innovations. And with satellite programs and "long-distance learning" opportunities, advancements in the preparation of educators in rural sites are likely.

The importance of home-school-community partnerships was emphasized in Chapters 9 through 11. While these are certainly current issues, they

Activity 12–5

Earlier in this chapter, research issues were discussed and several questions were posed. Now that you have completed reading this text and this chapter, make a list of additional research directions in the areas of collaboration, educational partnerships, and serving students at risk. Try to develop questions that address both outcomes and processes. Compare your list to those of other students. What can you conclude about what is known and not known in these areas?

also can be considered 'future directions' in that the role of the school in relation to families and community agencies will continue to change in the upcoming decades. This is particularly true as the demographic characteristics of students and families entering the school system continue to change (see Chapters 2 and 9 for a review). For example, comprehensive health, social, and educational services may soon be housed in public schools in some districts. This development could serve an important preventive purpose, and be a cost-efficient method of minimizing duplication of costly services across several community agencies. However, it will require important changes in the way educators approach their responsibilities to families and students.

Chapter Summary

Throughout this book, we have documented the relevance of educational partnerships to meet the needs of students at risk. Indeed, collaborative partnerships can take many forms, and should be determined by the needs of specific students at specific times. It must be recognized, however, that the collaborative approaches presented in the text are not a panacea; that is, they are not intended to solve all problems facing educators today. There are circumstances when alternative forms of decision making will be necessary. For example, if a gang member brings an automatic pistol to school or a group of students stage a riot, immediate administrative decision making would seem appropriate. That is not to say that these issues are too difficult or complicated for educational partnerships, but immediate independent action is sometimes necessary. Once the crisis is addressed, however, a collaborative team may well convene to establish preventive measures for future conflicts.

There are a number of additional issues surrounding the formation and implementation of educational partnerships. Continued research is necessary to investigate both the outcomes and processes embedded within collaboration. A number of important research questions are yet to be answered, and different research methodologies will be appropriate to investigate these areas thoroughly. Professional preparation, both at the preservice and in-service levels, should address the readiness of both the individuals responsible for collaboration, as well as the system in which these individuals function.

Various policy issues were discussed in relation to collaborative partnerships. First, there are likely to be mandates in several educational settings that may interfere with the implementation of collaboration. As educators work to change these existing policies, there will be a need to develop and institutionalize new policies that provide opportunities for collaboration to occur. While this may seem rather straightforward, it is likely "easier said than done." Finally, a number of ethical issues were explored (including the rights of the student, parent, educator and school) in efforts to raise readers' awareness of their responsibility to act professionally and ethically at all times.

The future of education and educational collaboration is not certain. We do not purport to have a crystal ball providing us with a vision of what to expect in the twenty-first century. Yet, we have our own vision. Our vision is based on a growing commitment shared by many teachers, special educators, administrators, school psychologists, school counselors, social workers, and parents. This commitment is one of providing the best and most appropriate educational experience for *all* students, regardless of race, gender, color, age, or disabling condition. We believe that a meaningful and effective way of enhancing these experiences for students is through educational partnerships. We hope that you share our vision.

Case Study 12–1

A team of educators at Prince High School convened in a collaborative team meeting at the request of Mrs. Paul, the vice-principal. Mrs. Paul expressed concern to the team about the number of phone calls she had been receiving from parents whose children were failing Mr. Stark's advanced history class. Students in the classes expressed to their parents that Mr. Stark assigned large numbers of assignments without clearly stating the objectives or criteria for passing. They said that he was often out of the classroom and provided little or no assistance or feedback on their work. Exams were given weekly; however, students were not provided with information on what to study or feedback on how they performed.

In the team meeting, representative teachers, a school counselor, a special educator, and Mrs. Paul discussed the information they had regarding the students failing the class and the concerns raised by parents about Mr. Stark. Most students in the class were honors students and were passing their other classes. A review of school records indicated that there were no pervasive problems with truancies or absences. Mr. Stark is also the head football coach in the fall and the head track coach in the spring. His athletes are generally well trained and his teams are often undefeated.

One member of the team, Ms. Stacy, is also a neighbor of Mr. Stark. She reported that he recently separated from his wife and often appeared intoxicated in the evenings. Other school members complained that his appearance at school was unprofessional, as he often arrived late and appeared disheveled. They further noted that he is frequently seen in the teacher's lounge talking on the telephone to his wife or lawyer, or working on football plays. This was his first year teaching an honors history class; prior to this, he was head of the physical education department and taught P.E. classes at a large high school in a neighboring district. The team decided that before they went on, a meeting with Mr. Stark was in order.

1. What are some of the ethical issues facing the team at Prince High School?

2. What are some potential violations to Mr. Stark's right to privacy?

3. In a meeting with Mr. Stark, what procedures for informed consent should be followed?

4. What additional ethical guidelines should be followed in this case?

Key Vocabulary Terms

research questions
outcome-based research
process-based research

single subject research
  designs
operational definitions
right to privacy

confidentiality
informed consent
action research

References Chapter 1

Algozzine, B., & Ysseldyke, J. E. (1981). Special education services for normal children: Better safe than sorry. *Exceptional Children, 48,* 238–243.

Bauwens, J., Hourcade, J. J., & Friend, M. (1989). Cooperative teaching: A model for general and special education integration. *Remedial and Special Education, 10,* 17–22.

Berman, P., & McLaughlin, M. (1977). *Federal programs supporting educational change: Vol. II. Factors affecting implementation and continuation* (R-1589/7-HEW). Santa Monica, CA: Rand.

Boyer, E. L. (Ed.) (1983). *High school: A report on American secondary education.* New York: Harper & Row.

Christenson, S. L., Ysseldyke, J. E., & Algozzine, B. (1982). Institutional constraints and external pressures influencing referral decisions. *Psychology in the Schools, 19,* 341–345.

Committee For Economic Development. (1987). *Children in need: Investment strategies for the educationally disadvantaged.* New York: Committee for Economic Development.

Curtis, M. J., & Curtis, V. A. (1990). The intervention assistance model. *Trainer's Forum, 10* (1), 3–4.

Curtis, M. J., & Meyers, J. (1988). Consultation: A foundation for alternative services in the schools. In J. L. Graden, J. E. Zins, & M. J. Curtis (Eds.), *Alternative educational delivery systems: Enhancing options for all students* (pp. 35–48). Washington DC: National Association of School Psychologists.

Duke, D., Showers, B., & Imber, M. (1980). Teachers and shared decision-making: The costs and benefits of involvement. *Educational Administration Quarterly, 16,* 93–106.

Elmore, R. F. (1987). Reform and the culture of authority in schools. *Educational Administration Quarterly, 23,* 60–78.

Epps, S., Ysseldyke, J. E., & Algozzine, B. (1983). Impact of different definitions of learning disabilities on the number of students identified. *Journal of Psychoeducational Assessment, 1,* 341–352.

Friend, M., & Cook, L. (1990). Collaboration as a predictor for success in school reform. *Journal of Educational and Psychological Consultation, 1,* 69–86.

Fullan, M. (1985). Change processes and strategies at the local level. *Elementary School Journal, 85,* 391–421.

Fullan, M., & Pomfret, A. (1977). Research on curriculum and instruction implementation. *Review of Educational Research, 47,* 335–397.

Gallessich, J. (1985). Toward a meta-theory of consultation. *The Consulting Psychologist, 13,* 336–354.

Gartner, A., & Lipsky, D. K. (1987). Beyond special education: Toward a quality system for all students. *Harvard Educational Review, 57,* 367–395.

Goodlad, J. (1983). *A place called school: Prospects for the future.* New York: McGraw-Hill.

Graden, J. L., Casey, A., & Christenson, S. L. (1985). Implementing a prereferral intervention system. Part I: The model. *Exceptional Children, 51,* 377–384.

Gutkin, T. B., & Curtis, M. J. (1990). School-based consultation: Theory, techniques, and research. In T. B. Gutkin & C. R. Reynolds (Eds.), *The handbook of school psychology.* 2d ed. (pp. 577–611). New York: Wiley.

Idol, L., Paolucci-Whitcomb, P., & Nevin, A. (1986). *Collaborative consultation*. Rockville, MD: Aspen.

Idol-Maestas, L., & Ritter, S. (1985). A follow-up study of resource/consulting teachers: Factors that facilitate and inhibit teacher consultation. *Teacher Education and Special Education, 8,* 121–131.

Kratochwill, T. R., Sheridan, S. M., Carrington Rotto, P., & Salmon, D. (1992). Preparation of school psychologists in consultation service delivery: Practical, theoretical, and research considerations. In T. R. Kratochwill, S. N. Elliott, & M. Gettinger (Eds.), *Advances in school psychology.* Vol. VIII (pp. 115–152). Hillsdale, NJ: Erlbaum.

Kurpius, D. J., & Lewis, J. E. (1988). Assumptions and operating principles for preparing professionals to function as consultants. In F. West (Ed.), *School consultation: Interdisciplinary perspectives on theory, research, training, and practice* (pp. 143–154). Austin, TX: Association of Educational and Psychological Consultants.

National Commission on Excellence in Education. (1983). *A nation at risk.* Washington, DC: U.S. Government Printing Office.

National Governors' Association. (1986). *Time for results: The Governors' 1991 report on education.* Washington, DC: National Governors' Association.

Office of Educational Research and Improvement. (1988). *Youth indicators, 1988: Trends in the well-being of American youth.* Washington, DC: U.S. Department of Education.

Olsen, L. (1986, January). Effective schools. *Education Week*, pp. 11–21.

Phillips, V., & McCullough, L. (1990). Consultation-based programming: Instituting the collaborative ethic. *Exceptional Children, 56,* 291–304.

Pugach, M. C. & Allen-Meares, P. (1985). Collaboration at the preservice level: Instructional and evaluation activities. *Teacher Education and Special Education, 8,* 3–11.

Schaeffer, E. C., & Bryant, W. C. (1983). *Structures and processes for effective collaboration among local schools, colleges, and universities: A collaborative project of Kannapolis city schools.* Charlotte, NC: University of North Carolina-Charlotte.

Self, H., Benning, A., Marston, D., & Magnusson, D. (1991). Cooperative teaching project: A model for students at risk. *Exceptional Children, 58,* 26–33.

Sheridan, S. M., & Kratochwill, T. R. (1991). Behavioral consultation in educational settings. In J. W. Lloyd, N. N. Singh, & A. C. Repp (Eds.), *The Regular Education Initiative: Alternative perspectives on concepts, issues, and models* (pp. 193–210). Sycamore, IL: Sycamore.

Sheridan, S. M., & Welch, M. (1991). An interdisciplinary course in educational problem-solving and conflict management. *The Consulting Edge, 2* (2), 3–7.

Skrtic, T. M. (1987). An organizational analysis of special education reform. *Counterpoint, 8,* 15–19.

Smith, R. C., & Lincoln, C. A. (1988). *America's shame, America's hope: Twelve million youth at risk.* Chapel Hill, NC: MDC, ERIC Document Reproduction Service No. 301 620.

Stainback, W., & Stainback, S. (1990). *Support networks for inclusive schooling: Interdependent integrated education.* Baltimore, MD: Brookes.

Villa, R. A., & Thousand, J. S. (1988). Enhancing success in heterogeneous classrooms and schools: The powers of partnership. *Teacher Education and Special Education, 11,* 144–154.

Villa, R. A., Thousand, J. S., Paolucci-Whitcomb, P., & Nevin, A. (1990). In search of new paradigms for collaborative consultation. *Journal of Educational and Psychological Consultation, 1,* 279–292.

Walker, L. J. (1987). Procedural rights in the wrong system: Special education is not enough. In A. Gartner and T. Joe (Eds.), *Images of the disabled/disabling images* (pp. 98–102). New York: Praeger.

Waugh, R. F., & Punch, I. F. (1987). Teacher receptivity to system-wide change in the implementation state. *Review of Educational Research, 57,* 237–254.

Webster, M. (1981). *Webster's new collegiate dictionary.* Springfield, MA: G. & C. Merriam Company.

Welch, M., & Hardman, M. L. (1991). Initiating change: One university's response to teacher education reform and the education of students with disabilities. *Teacher Education and Special Education, 14,* 228–234.

Welch, M., Sheridan, S. M., Hart, A. W., Fuhriman, A., Connell, M., & Stoddart, T. (1992). An interdisciplinary approach in preparing professionals for educational partnerships. *Journal of Educational and Psychological Consultation, 3,* 1–23.

West, J. F. (1990a). Educational collaboration in the restructuring of schools. *Journal of Educational and Psychological Consultation, 1,* 23–40.

West, J. F. (1990b). The nature of consultation vs. collaboration: An interview with Walter B. Pryzwansky. *The Consulting Edge, 2* (1), 1–2.

West, J. F., Idol, L., & Cannon, G. (1989). *Collaboration in the schools: An inservice and preservice curriculum for teachers, support staff, and administrators.* Austin, TX: Pro-Ed.

Will, M. (1986). *Educating children with learning problems: A shared responsibility.* A report to the secretary. Washington, DC: US Department of Education.

William T. Grant Foundation, Commission on Work, Family, and Citizenship (1988). *The forgotten half: Non-college youth in America.* Washington, DC: William T. Grant Foundation.

Wolfensberger, W. (1972). *Normalization: The principles of normalization in human services.* Toronto: National Institute of Mental Retardation.

Ysseldyke, J. E., Algozzine, B., & Epps, S. (1983). A logical and empirical analysis of current practices in classifying students as handicapped. *Exceptional Children, 50,* 160–166.

Ysseldyke, J. E., Algozzine, B., Richey, L., & Graden, J. L. (1982). Declaring students eligible for learning disability services: Why bother with the data? *Learning Disability Quarterly, 5,* 37–44.

Ysseldyke, J. E., Algozzine, B., & Thurlow, M. L. (1992). *Critical issues in special education.* 2d ed. Boston: Houghton Mifflin.

Zins, J. E., Curtis, M. J., Graden, J. L., & Ponti, C. R. (1988). *Helping students succeed in the regular classroom.* San Francisco: Jossey-Bass.

Chapter 2

Aksamit, D. (1990). Mildly handicapped and at risk students: The graying of the line. *Academic Therapy, 25* (3), 277–287.

Algozzine, B., Schmid, R.E., & Conners, R. (1978). Toward an acceptable definition of emotional disturbance. *Behavior Disorders, 4,* 48–52.

Algozzine, B., & Ysseldyke, J.E. (1983). An analysis of the incidence of special class placement: The masses are burgeoning. *Journal of Special Education, 17,* 141–147.

Baca, L. M., & Almanza, E. (1991). *Language-minority students with disabilities.* Reston, VA: Council for Exceptional Children.

Benavides, A. (1983). *Prereferral assessment of high-risk predictors for limited-English-proficient students.* Unpublished research study. Southern Illinois University at Carbondale.

Benavides, A. (1988). High-risk predictors and prereferral screening for language-minority students. In A. A. Ortiz, & B. A. Ramirez (Eds.), *Schools and the culturally diverse exceptional student: Promising practices and future directions* (pp. 19–31). Reston, VA: Council for Exceptional Children.

Bender, W. N. (1992). *Learning disabilities: Characteristics, identification, and teaching strategies.* Boston: Allyn & Bacon.

Bryan, T., Bay, M., Lopez-Reyna, N., & Donahue, M. (1991). Characteristics of students with learning disabilities. In J. W. Lloyd, N. N. Singh, & Repp, A. C. (Eds.), *The regular education initiative: Alternative perspective on concepts, issues, and models* (pp. 113–132). Sycamore, IL: Sycamore.

Bryan, T., Bay, M., Shelden, C., & Simon, J. (1990). Teachers' and at risk students' stimulated recall of instruction. *Exceptionality, 1,* 167–179.

Bucci, J. A., & Reitzammer, A. F. (1992). Collaboration with health and social service professionals: Preparing teachers for new roles. *Journal of Teacher Education, 43,* 290–295.

Burstein, N., & Cabello, B. (1989). Preparing teachers to work with culturally diverse students: A teacher education model. *Journal of Teacher Education, 40*(5), 79–81.

Coleman, M. C. (1992). *Behavior disorders: Theory and practice.* Boston: Allyn & Bacon.

Cooper, D. H., & Speece, D. L. (1990). Maintaining at risk children in regular education settings: Initial effects of individual differences and classroom environments. *Exceptional Children, 57,* 117–126.

Correa, V. I. (1989). Involving culturally diverse families in the educational process. In S. H. Fradd & M. J. Weismantel (Eds.), *Meeting the needs of culturally and linguistically different students: A handbook for educators* (pp. 130–144). Boston: College-Hill.

Cuban, L. (1989). The at risk label and the problem of urban school reform. *Phi Delta Kappan, 10*(70), 780–784, 799–801.

Donahue, M. (1987). Interactions between linguistic and pragmatic development in learning disabled children: Three views of the state of the union. In S. Rosenberg (Ed.), *Advances in applied psycholinguistics.* Vol. 1 (pp. 126–179). Cambridge: Cambridge University Press.

Drew, C. J., Logan, D. R., & Hardman, M. L. (1988). *Mental retardation: A life cycle approach.* Columbus, OH: Merrill.

Duran, R. P. (1989). Assessment and instruction of at risk Hispanic students. *Exceptional Children, 56,* 154–159.

Fleischner, J., & Van Acker, R. (1990). Changes in the urban school population: Challenges in meeting the need for special education leadership and teacher preparation personnel. In L. M. Bullock & R. L. Simpson (Eds.), *Critical issues in special education: Implications for personnel preparation* (pp. 73–91). Denton: University of North Texas.

Fradd, S. H. & Weismantel, M. J. (1989). *Meeting the needs of culturally and linguistically different students: A handbook for educators.* Boston: College-Hill.

Frymier, J. (1989). *A study of students at risk: Collaborating to do research.* Bloomington, IN: Phi Delta Kappa Educational Foundation.

Frymier, J., & Gansneder, B. (1989). The Phi Delta Kappa study of students at risk. *Kappan, 71,* 142–146.

Gay, G. (1981). Interactions in culturally pluralistic classrooms. In J. A. Banks (Ed.), *Education in the 80s: Multiethnic education* (pp. 42–52). Washington, DC: National Education Association.

Glenn, C. (1988). The next step in urban education. In D. P. Doyle & B. S. Cooper (Eds.), *Federal aid to the disadvantaged: What future for Chapter 1?* (pp. 205–215). New York: Falmer.

Gollnick, D. M., & Chinn, P. C. (1990). *Multicultural education in a pluralistic society.* 3d ed. Columbus, OH: Merrill.

Greer, J. V. (1990). The drug babies. *Exceptional Children, 56,* 382–384.

Gross, C. R., Wolf, C., Kunitz, S. C., & Jane, J. A. (1985). Pilot traumatic coma data bank: A profile of head injuries in children. In R. G. Dacey, R. Winn, & R. Rimel (Eds.), *Trauma of the central nervous system* (pp. 19–26). New York: Raven.

Hardman, M. L., Drew, C. J., Egan, M. W., & Wolf, B. (1993). *Human Exceptionality: Society, School, and Family.* Boston: Allyn & Bacon.

Hardman, M. L., McDonnell, J., & Welch, M. (1993). A closer look at the Individuals with Disabilities Education Act: An IDEA whose time has come? (In review)

Henley, M., Ramsey, R. S., & Algozzine, R. (1993). *Characteristics of and strategies for teaching students with mild disabilities.* Boston: Allyn & Bacon.

Hernandez, H. (1989). *Multicultural education: A teacher's guide to content and process.* Columbus, OH: Merrill.

Huefner, D. S. (1993). Federal and state legislation. In S.B. Thomas (Ed.), *Yearbook of education law* (pp. 247– 281). Topeka, KS: National Organization on Legal Problems of Education.

Kaskinen-Chapman, A. (1992). Saline Area Schools and inclusive community concepts. In R. A. Villa, J. S. Thousand, W. Stainback, & S. Stainback (Eds.), *Restructuring for caring and effective education: An administrative guide to creating heterogeneous schools* (pp. 169–186). Baltimore: Paul H. Brooks.

Kavale, K., & Forness, S. (1985). *The science of learning disabilities.* San Diego: College-Hill.

Kennedy, M. M., Jung, R. K., & Orland, M. E. (1986). *Poverty, achievement and the distribution of compensatory education services.* Washington, DC: U.S. Government Printing Office.

Kluckhohn, C. (1968). Queer customs. In J. H. Chilcott, N. C. Greenberg, & H. B. Wilson (Eds.), *Reading in the sociocultural foundations of education* (pp. 29–38). Belmont, IL: Wadsworth.

Kotlowitz, A. (1991). *There are no children here.* New York: Doubleday.

Lipsky, D.K., & Gartner, A. (1989). Building the future. In D. K. Lipsky & A. Gartner (Eds.), *Beyond separate education: Quality education for all* (pp. 255–290). Baltimore: Paul H. Brookes.

McCann, R. A., & Austin, S. (1988, April). *At risk youth: Definitions, dimensions, and relationships.* Paper presented at the annual meeting of the American Educational Research Association, New Orleans, LA.

Medden, B. & Rosen, A. (1986). Child abuse and neglect: Prevention and reporting. *Young Children, 41*(4), 26–30.

Meier, F. E. (1992). *Competency-based instruction for teachers of students with special learning needs.* Boston: Allyn & Bacon.

Mercer, C. D. (1991). *Student with learning disabilities.* 4th ed. Columbus, OH: Merrill.

Mercer, J. (1973). The pluralistic assessment project. *School Psychology Digest, 2,* 10–18.

Morrow, R. D. (1987). Cultural differences: Be aware! *Academic Therapy, 23*(2), 143–149.

Morsink, C. V., & Lenk, L. L. (1992). The delivery of special education programs and services. *Remedial and Special Education, 13,* 33–43.

National Center for Education Statistics. (1992a). *Digest of education statistics.* U.S. Department of Education, Office of Educational Research and Improvement. Washington, DC: U.S. Government Printing Office.

National Center for Education Statistics (1992b). *The condition of education.* U.S. Department of Education, Office of Educational Research and Improvement. Washington, DC: U.S. Government Printing Office.

National Commission on Excellence in Education. (1983). *A nation at risk: The imperative for educational reform.* Washington, DC: U.S. Government Printing Office.

National Institute on Drug Abuse. (1990). Washington, DC: U.S. Government Printing Office.

Natriello, G., McDill, E. L., & Pallas, A. M. (1990). *Schooling disadvantaged children: Racing against catastrophe.* New York: Teachers College Press.

New partnerships: Education's stake in the Family Support Act of 1988. (1989). Statement of the American Public Welfare Association, Center for Law and Social Policy, Center for the Study of Social Policy, Children's Educational Leadership, National Alliance of Business, National Association of State Boards of Education, National Governors' Association.

Ornstein, A., & Levine, D. (1989). Social class, race, and school achievement: Problems and prospects. *Journal of Teacher Education, 40*(5), 17–23.

Ortiz, A. A. (1987). The influence of locus of control and culture on learning styles of language-minority students. In M. J. Johnson & B. A. Ramirez (Eds.), *American Indian exceptional children and youth* (pp. 9–16). Reston, VA: Council for Exceptional Children.

Ortiz, A. A., & Garcia, S. B. (1988). A prereferral process for preventing inappropriate referrals of Hispanic students to special education. In A. A. Ortiz, & B. A. Ramirez (Eds.), *Schools and the culturally diverse exceptional student: Promising practices and future directions* (pp. 6–18). Reston, VA: Council for Exceptional Children.

Ortiz, A. A., & Polyzoi, E. (1988). Language assessment of Hispanic learning disabled and speech and language handicapped students: Research in progress. In A. A. Ortiz, & B. A. Ramirez (Eds.), *Schools and the culturally diverse exceptional student: Promising practices and future directions* (pp. 32–44). Reston, VA: Council for Exceptional Children.

Ortiz, A. A., & Yates, J. R. (1988). Characteristics of learning disabled, mentally retarded, and speech-language handicapped Hispanic students at initial evaluation and re-evaluation. In A. A. Ortiz, & B. A. Ramirez (Eds.), *Schools and the culturally divers exceptional students: Promising practices and future directions* (pp. 51–62). Reston, VA: Council for Exceptional Children.

Pai, Y. (1990). *Cultural foundations of education.* Columbus, OH: Merrill.

Pallas, A. M., Natriello, G., & McGill, E. L. (1989). The changing nature of the disadvantaged population: Current dimensions and future trends. *Educational Researcher, 59,* 16–22.

Passow, A. H. (1970). Deprivation and disadvantage: Nature and manifestations. In A. H. Passow (Ed.), *Deprivation and disadvantage: Nature and manifestations* (pp. 15–51). Hamburg, West Germany: UNESCO Institute for Education.

Pellicano, R. R. (1987). At risk: A view of social advantage. *Educational Leadership, 44*(6), 47–49.

Plata, M. (1990). *Assessment, placement, and programming of exceptional pupils: A practical approach.* Reston VA: Council for Exceptional Children.

Polloway, E. A., & Smith, J. D. (1983). Changes in mild mental retardation: Population, programs and perspectives. *Exceptional Children, 50,* 142–157.

Reschly, D. J. (1988). Minority overrepresentation and special education reform. *Exceptional Children, 54,* 316–323.

Reynolds, M. C. (1991). Classification and labeling. In J. W. Lloyd, N. N. Singh, & A. C. Repp (Eds.), *The regular education initiative: Alternative perspectives on concepts, issues, and models* (pp. 29–41). Sycamore, IL: Sycamore.

Reynolds, M. (1989). Students with special needs. In M. C. Reynolds, (Ed.), *Knowledge base for the beginning teacher* (pp.129–142). New York: Pergamon.

Sadker, M. P. & Sadker, D. M. (1991). *Teachers, schools, and society.* New York: McGraw-Hill.

Sailor, W. (1989). The educational, social, and vocational integration of students with the most severe disabilities. In D. K. Lipsky & A. Gartner (Eds.), *Beyond separate education: Quality education for all* (pp. 53–74). Baltimore: Paul H. Brookes.

Slavin, R. E. (1989). Students at risk for school failures: The problem and its dimensions. In R. E. Slavin, N. L. Karwelt, & N. A. Madden (Eds.), *Effective programs for students at risk* (pp. 3–17). Boston: Allyn & Bacon.

Smith, C. R. (1983). *Learning disabilities: The interaction of learner, task, and setting.* Boston: Little, Brown and Co.

Spindler, G. D. (1963). Education in a transforming America. In G. D. Spindler (Ed.), *Education and culture* (pp. 132–147). New York: Holt Rinehart & Winston.

Stodolsky, S., & Lesser, J. (1967). Learning patterns in the disadvantaged. *Harvard Educational Review, 37*(4), 546–593.

Strather, D. (1986). Practical applications of research: Suicide among the young. *Phi Delta Kappan, 67*(10), 756–759.

U.S. Department of Education (1991). *Thirteenth annual report to Congress on the implementation of the Education of the Handicapped Act.* Washington, DC: U.S. Government Printing Office.

Twenty-Three Code of Federal Resulations (C.F.R.) 300.5 (7) (1984).

U.S. Department of Education (1990). *Twelfth annual report to Congress on the implementation of the Education of the Handicapped Act.* Washington, DC: U.S. Government Printing Office.

U.S. Department of Health, Education, and Welfare (1977, August 23). Education of Handicapped Children (Implementation of Part B of the Education of Handicapped Act). *Federal Register, 42*(173), 42478.

Viadero, D. (1990, September 5). Study of drug-exposed infants finds problems in learning as late as age 3. *Education Week,* p. 15.

Walker, J. L. (1987). Language and curriculum development for American Indian handicapped children. In M. J. Johnson & B. A. Ramirez (Eds.), *American Indian exceptional children and youth* (pp. 17–23). Reston, VA: Council for Exceptional Children.

Wehlage, G. G., & Rutter, R. A. (1987). Dropping out: How much do schools contribute to the problem? In G. Natriello (Ed.), *School Dropouts: Patterns and policies* (pp. 70–88). New York: Teachers College Press.

Wehlage, G. G., Rutter, R. A., & Turnbaugh, A. (1987). A program model for at risk high school students. *Educational Leadership, 44*(6), 70–73.

Wetzel, J. R. (1987). *American youth: A statistical snapshot.* Washington, DC: William T. Grant Foundation Commission on Work, Family, and Citizenship.

Wicks-Nelson, R., & Israel, A. C.(1984). *Behavior disorders of childhood.* Englewood Cliffs, NJ: Prentice Hall.

Wood, J. W. (1992). *Adapting instruction for mainstreamed and at risk students.* New York: Merrill.

Yacobacci-Tam, P. (1987). Interacting with the culturally different family. *Volta, 89*(5), 46–58.

Ysseldyke, J. E., Algozzine, B., & Thurlow, M. (1992). *Critical issues in special education.* Boston: Houghton Mifflin.

Zins, J. E., Curtis, M. J., Graden, J. L., & Ponti, C. R. (1988). *Helping students succeed in the regular classroom.* San Francisco: Jossey-Bass.

Chapter 3

Algozzine, B., & Ysseldyke, J. E. (1981). Special education services for normal children: Better safe than sorry. *Exceptional Children, 48,* 238–243.

Babcock, N. L., & Pryzwansky, W. B. (1983). Models of consultation: Preferences of educational professinals at five stages of service. *Journal of School Psychology, 21,* 359–366.

Barrios, B. A., & Hartmann, D. P. (1988). Recent developments in single-subject methodology: Methods for analyzing generalization, maintenance, and multicomponent treatments. In M. Hersen, R. M. Eisler, & P. M. Miller (Eds.), *Progress in behavior modification.* Vol. 22 (pp. 11–47). Newbury Park: Sage.

Bergan, J. R. (1977). *Behavioral consultation.* Columbus, OH: Charles E. Merrill.

Bergan, J. R., & Kratochwill, T. R. (1990). *Behavioral consultation and therapy.* New York: Plenum.

Bergan, J. R., & Tombari, M. L. (1975). The analysis of verbal interactions occurring during consultation. *Journal of School Psychology, 13,* 209–226.

Bergan, J. R., & Tombari, M. L. (1976). Consultant skill and efficiency and the implementation of outcomes of consultation. *Journal of School Psychology, 14,* 3–14.

Brown, D., & Schulte, A. C. (1987). A social learning model of consultation. *Professional Psychology: Research and Practice, 18,* 283–287.

Caplan, G. (1970). *The theory and practice of mental health consultation.* New York: Basic Books.

Christenson, S., Ysseldyke, J. E., & Algozzine, B. (1982). Institutional constraints and external pressures influencing referral decisions. *Psychology in the Schools, 19,* 341–345.

Curtis, M. J., & Meyers, J. (1988). Consultation: A foundation for alternative services in the schools. In J. L. Graden, J. E. Zins, & M. J. Curtis (Eds.), *Alternative educational delivery systems: Enhancing options for all students* (pp. 35–48). Washington DC: National Association of School Psychologists.

Erchul, W. P. (1987). A relational communication analysis of control in school consultation. *Professional School Psychology, 2*, 113–124.

Erchul, W. P. (1992). On dominance, cooperation, teamwork, and collaboration in school-based consultation. *Journal of Educational and Psychological Consultation, 3*, 363–366.

Erchul, W. P., & Chewning, T. G. (1990). Behavioral consultation from a request-centered relational communication perspective. *School Psychology Quarterly, 5*, 1–20.

Erchul, W. P., Hughes, J. N., Meyers, J., Hickman, J. A., & Braden, J. P. (1992). Dyadic agreement concerning the consultation process and its relationship to outcome. *Journal of Educational and Psychological Consultation, 3*, 119–132.

Fuchs, D. & Fuchs, L. S. (1989). Exploring effective and efficient prereferral interventions: A component analysis of behavioral consultation. *School Psychology Review, 18*, 260–283.

Gallesich, J. (1985). Toward a meta-theory of consultation. *The Counseling Psychologist, 13*, 336–354.

Graden, J. L., Casey, A., & Christenson, S. L. (1985). Implementing a prereferral intervention system. Part I: The model. *Exceptional Children, 51*, 377–384.

Graden, J. L., Zins, J. E., & Curtis, M. J. (1988). *Alternative educational delivery services: Enhancing instructional options for all students.* Washington, DC: National Association of School Psychologists.

Gutkin, T. B. (1986). Consultees' perceptions of variables relating to the outcomes of school-based consultation interactions. *School Psychology Review, 15*, 375–382.

Gutkin, T. B., & Curtis, M. J. (1990). School-based consultation: Theory, techniques, and research. In T. B. Gutkin & C. R. Reynolds (Eds.), *The handbook of school psychology.* 2d ed. (pp. 577–611). New York: Wiley.

Gutkin, T. B., & Hickman, J. A. (1988). Teachers' perceptions of control over presenting problems and resulting preferences for consultatin versus referral services. *Journal of School Psychology, 26*, 395–398.

Henning-Stout, M. (1993). Theoretical and empirical bases of consultation. In J. E. Zins, T. R. Kratochwill, & S. N. Elliott (Eds.), *Handbook of consultation services for children* (pp. 15–45). San Francisco: Jossey Bass.

Idol, L., Paolucci-Whitcomb, P., & Nevin, A. (1987). *Collaborative consultation.* Austin, TX: Pro-Ed.

Kazdin, A. E. (1981). Acceptability of child treatment techniques: The influence of treatment efficacy and adverse side effects. *Behavior Therapy, 12*, 493–506.

Kratochwill, T. R., & Bergan, J. R. (1990). *Behavioral consultation in applied settings: An individual guide.* New York: Plenum.

Kratochwill, T. R., Sheridan, S. M., & Van Someren, K. R. (1988). Research in behavioral consultation: Current status and future directions. In F. West (Ed.), *School consultation: Interdisciplinary perspectives on theory, research, training, and practice* (pp. 77–102). Austin, TX: University of Texas Press.

Kratochwill, T. R., & Van Someren, K. R. (1985). Barriers to treatment success in behavioral consultation: Current limitations and future directions. *Journal of School Psychology, 23*, 225–239.

Mannino, F. V., & Shore, M. F. (1975). The effects of consultation: A review of empirical studies. *American Journal of Community Psychology, 17*, 275–282.

Mannino, F. V., & Shore, M. F. (1986). History and development of mental health consultation. In F. V Mannino, E. J. Trickett, M. F. Shore, M. G. Kidder, & G. Levin (Eds.), *Handbook of mental health consultation* (DHHS Publications No. ADM86-1446, pp. 3–28). Washington, DC: U.S. Government Printing Office.

Martens, B. K., & Witt, J. C. (1988). Expanding the scope of behavioral consultation: A systems approach to classroom behavior change. *Professional School Psychology, 3,* 271–281.

Medway, F. J. (1979). How effective is school consultation: A review of recent research. *Journal of School Psychology, 17,* 275–282.

Medway, F. J., & Updyke, J. F. (1985). Meta-analysis of consultation outcome studies. *American Journal of Community Psychology, 13,* 489–505.

Public Law 94–142. Education of All Handicapped Children Act of 1975 (20 U.S.C. and 34 C.F.R.).

Ponti, C. R., & Curtis, M. J. (August, 1984). Effects of consultation on teachers' attributions for children's school problems. Paper presented at the annual meeting of the American Psychological Association, Toronto, Canada.

Pray, B., Kramer, J. J., & Lindskog, R. (1986). Assessment and treatment of tic behavior: A review and case study. *School Psychology Review, 15,* 418–429.

Pryzwansky, W. B., & White, G. W. (1983). The influence of consultee characteristics on preferences for consultation approaches. *Professional Psychology: Research and practice, 14,* 457–461.

Reinking, R. J., Livesay, G., & Kohl, M. (1978). The effects of consultation style on consultee productivity. *American Journal of Community Psychology, 6,* 283–290.

Schmuck, R. A. (1990). Organization development in the schools: Contemporary concepts and practices,. In T. B. Gutkin & C. R. Reynolds (Eds.) *The handbook of school psychology.* 2d ed. (pp. 899–919). New York: Wiley.

Schmuck, R. A., & Runkel, P. J. (1988). *The handbook of organization development in schools.* 3d ed. Prospect Heights, IL: Waveland.

Sheridan, S. M. (1992). Consultant and client outcomes of competency-based behavioral consultation training. *School Psychology Quarterly, 7,* 245–270.

Sheridan, S. M., & Kratochwill, T. R. (1991). Behavioral consultation in educational settings. In J. W. Lloyd, N. N. Singh, & A. C. Repp (Eds.), *The regular education initiative: Alternative perspectives on concepts, issues, and methods* (pp. 193–210). Pacific Grove, CA: Brooks/Cole.

Sheridan, S. M., Kratochwill, T. R., & Elliott, S. N. (1990). Behavioral consultation with parents and teachers: Delivering treatment for socially withdrawn children at home and school. *School Psychology Review, 19,* 33–52.

Stokes, T. F., & Baer, D. M. (1977). An implicit technology of generalization. *Journal of Applied Behavior Analysis, 10,* 349–367.

Tindal, G., Parker, R., & Hasbrouck, J. E. (1992). The construct validity of stages and activities in the consultation process. *Journal of Educational and Psychological Consultation, 3,* 99–118.

Wenger, R. D. (1979). Teacher response to collaborative consultation. *Psychology in the Schools, 16,* 127–131.

West, J. F. (1990). Educational collaboration in the restructuring of schools. *Journal of Educational and Psychological Consultation, 1,* 23–40.

West, J. F., & Cannon, G. S. (1988). Essential collaborative consultaiton competencies for regular and special educators. *Journal of Learning Disabilities,* 56–63.

West, J. F., & Idol, L. (1987). School consultation (Part I): An interdisciplinary perspective on theory, models, and research. *Journal of Learning Disabilities, 20,* 388–408.

West, J. F., Idol, L., & Cannon, G. (1989). *Collaboration in the schools: An inservice and preservice curriculum for teachers, support staff, and administrators.* Austin, TX: Pro-Ed.

Witt, J. E., Martens, B. K., & Elliott, S. N. (1984). Assessing the acceptability of behavioral interventions used in classrooms. *Psychology in the Schools, 20,* 510–517.

Ysseldyke, J. E., Algozzine, B., & Epps, S. (1983). A logical and empirical analysis of current practices in classifying students as handicapped. *Exceptional Children, 50,* 160–166.

Ysseldyke, J. E., Algozzine, B., Richey, L., & Graden, J. L. (1982). Declaring students eligible for learning disability services: Why bother with the data? *Learning Disability Quarterly, 5,* 37–44.

Zins, J. E., Curtis, M. J., Graden, J. L., & Ponti, C. R. (1988). *Helping students succeed in the regular classroom.* San Francisco: Jossey-Bass.

Zins, J. E., & Ponti, C. R. (1990). Best practices in school-based consultation. In A. Thomas & J. Grimes (Eds.), *Best practices in school psychology-II* (pp. 673–693). Washington, DC: National Association of School Psychologists.

Chapter 4

Berger, C. R. & Calabrese, R. J. (1975). Some explorations in initial interaction and beyond: Toward a developmental theory of interpersonal communication. *Human Communication Research, 1,* 99–112.

Brammer, L., & Shostrom, E. (1982). *Therapeutic psychology: Fundamentals of counseling and psychotherapy.* 4th ed. Englewood Cliffs, NJ: Prentice-Hall.

Conoley, J. C. (1981). Emergent training issues in consultation. In J. C. Conoley (Ed.), *Consultation in schools: Theory, research, procedures.* New York: Academic.

Cormier, W. H., & Cormier, L. S. (1985). *Interviewing strategies for helpers: Fundamental skills and cognitive behavioral interventions.* Monterey, CA: Brooks/Cole Publishing Company.

Dustin, D., & Ehly, S. (1984). Skills for effective consultation. *School Counselor,* 23–29.

Egan, G. (1986). *The skilled helper: A systematic approach to effective helping.* 3d ed. Monterey, CA: Brooks/Cole.

Fine, M. J. (1990). Facilitating home-school relationships: A family-oriented approach to collaborative consultation. *Journal of Educational and Psychological Consultation, 1,* 169–187.

Fine, M. J., Grantham, V. L., & Wright, J. G. (1979). Personal variables that facilitate or impede consultation. *Psychology in the Schools, 16,* 533–539.

Friend, M. & Cook, C. (1992). *Interactions: Collaboration skills for school professionals.* New York: Longman.

Hawryluk, M. K., & Smallwood, D. L. (1986). Assessing and addressing consultee variables in school-based behavioral consultation. *School Psychology Review, 15,* 519–528.

Ivey, A. E. (1988). *Intentional interviewing and counseling: Facilitating client development.* 2d ed. Monterey, CA: Brooks/Cole.

Johnson, D. W., & Johnson, F. P. (1991). *Joining together: Group therapy and group skills.* 4th ed. Englewood Cliffs, NJ: Prentice-Hall.

Kirby, J. (1985). *Consultation: Practice and practitioner.* Muncie, IN: Accelerated Development, Inc.

Kohr, M. A., Parrish, J. M., Neef, N. A., Driessen, J. R., & Hallinan, P. C. (1988). Communication skills training for parents: Experimental and social validation. *Journal of Applied Behavior Analysis, 21,* 21–30.

Miller, G. R. (1978). The current status of theory and research in interpersonal communication. *Human Communication Research, 4,* 164–178.

Myers, G. E., & Myers, M. T. (1985). *The dynamics of human communication.* New York: McGraw-Hill.

Sheridan, S. M., Salmon, D., Kratochwill, T. R., & Carrington Rotto, P. J. (1992). A conceptual model for the expansion of behavioral consultation training. *Journal of Educational and Psychological Consultation, 3,* 193–218.

Small, J. (1974). *Becoming naturally therapeutic.* Austin, TX: Eupsuchian.

Webster, M. (1981). *Webster's new collegiate dictionary.* Springfield, MA: G. & C. Merriam.

West, J. F., & Cannon, G. S. (1988). Essential collaborative consultation competencies for regular and special educators. *Journal of Learning Disabilities, 21,* 56–63.

Chapter 5

Allington, R. & McGill-Franzen, A. (1989). Different programs, indifferent instruction. In D. K. Lipsky & A. Gartner (Eds.), *Beyond separate education: Quality education for all* (pp. 75–97). Baltimore: Paul H. Brookes.

Banks, J. A. (1993). Multicultural education: Historical development, dimensions, and practice. *Review of Research in Education, 19,* 3–50.

Baptiste, H. P. (1992). Conceptual and theoretical issues. In H. C. Waxman, J. W. deFelix, J. E. Anderson, & H. P. Baptiste, Jr. (Eds.), *Students at risk in at-risk schools* (pp. 11–32). Newbury Park, CA: Corwin.

Barth, R. S. (1988). School: A community of leaders. In A. Lieberman (Ed.), *Building a professional culture in schools* (pp. 129–147). New York: Teachers College Press.

Barth, R. S. (1990). *Improving schools from within: Teachers, parents, and principals can make the difference.* San Francisco: Jossey-Bass.

Brown v. Board of Education, 347 U.S. 483 (1954).

Bucci, J. A., & Reitzammer, A. F. (1992). Collaboration with health and social service professionals: Preparing teachers for new roles. *Journal of Teacher Education, 43*(4), 290–295.

Castallo, R. T., Fletcher, M. R., Rossetti, A. D., & Sekowski, R. W. (1992). *School personnel administration: A practitioner's guide.* Boston: Allyn & Bacon.

Castandea v. Packard, 648 F.2d 989, 1007 (1981).

Clark, D. L., & Meloy, J. M. (1989). Renouncing bureaucracy: A democratic structure for leadership in schools. In T. J. Serviovanni & J. A. Moore (Eds.), *Schooling for tomorrow: Directing reform to issues that count.* Boston: Allyn & Bacon.

Code, L. (1991). *What can she know? Feminist theory and the construction of knowledge.* Ithaca, NY: Cornell University Press.

Conoley, J. C., & Gutkin, T. B. (1986). Educating school psychologists for the real world. *School Psychology Review, 15,* 457–465.

Crowson, R. L., & Porter-Gehrie, C. (1980). The discretionary behavior of principals in large city schools. *Educational Administration Quarterly, 16*(1), 45–69.

Cusick, P. A. (1992). *The educational system: Its nature and logic.* New York: McGraw-Hill.

Devaney, K. & Sykes, G. (1988). Making the case for professionalism. In A. Lieberman (Ed.), *Building a professional culture in schools* (pp. 3–22). New York: Teachers College Press.

Dianda, M. R. (1993, April). Success For All in schools serving limited-English-proficient students. Paper presented at the annual meeting of the American Educational Research Association, Atlanta.

Dickinson, D. J., & Bradshaw, S. P. (1992). Multiplying effectiveness: Combining consultation with counseling. *The School Counselor, 40,* 118–124.

Ehly, S., & Dustin, R. (1989). *Individual and group counseling in schools.* New York: Guilford.

Elias, M. J., & Clabby, J. F. (1984). Integrating social and affective education into public school curriculum and instruction. In C. A. Maher, R. J. Illback, & J. E. Zins (Eds.), *Organizational psychology in the schools: A handbook for professionals* (pp. 143–171). Springfield, IL: Charles C. Thomas.

Elmore, R. F. (1987). Reform and the culture of authority in schools. *Educational Administration Quarterly, 23*(4), 60–78.

Elmore, R. F. (1989, March). *Models of restructured schools.* Paper presented at the annual meeting of the American Educational Research Association, San Francisco.

Erickson, F. (1987). Conceptions of school culture: An overview. *Educational Administration Quarterly, 23* (4), 11–24.

Feiman-Nemser, S. & Floden, R. E. (1986). The culture of teaching. In M. C. Wittrock (Ed.), *Handbook of research on teaching* (pp. 505–526). New York: Macmillan.

Fradd, S. H., Weismantel, M. J., Correa, V. I., & Algozzine, B. (1990). Insuring equity in education: Preparing school personnel for culturally and linguistically divergent at-risk handicapped students. In A. Barona & E. E. Garcia (Eds.), *Children at risk: Poverty, minority status, and other issues in educational equity,* (pp. 237–256). Washington, DC: National Association of School Psychologists.

Fullan, M. (1993). *Change forces: Probing the depths of educational reform.* New York: Falmer.

Fullan, M. (1985). Change processes and strategies at the local level. *Elementary School Journal, 85*(3), 391–421.

Garcia, E. E. (1990). Language-minority education litigation policy: "The law of the land." In A. Barona & E. E. Garcia (Eds.), *Children at risk: Poverty, minority status, and other issues in educational equity* (pp. 53–64). Washington, DC: National Association of School Psychologists.

Garcia, E. E. (1993). Language, culture, and education. *Review of Research in Education, 19,* 51–98.

Gerler, E. R., Ciechalski, J. C., & Parker, L. D. (1990). *Elementary school counseling in a changing world.* Ann Arbor, MI: ERIC Counseling and Personnel Services Clearinghouse.

Gollnick, D. M., & Chinn, P. C. (1990). *Multicultural education in a pluralistic society.* 3d ed. Columbus, OH: Merrill.

Goodlad, J. I. (1984). *A place called school.* New York: McGraw-Hill.

Gutkin, T. B., & Conoley, J. C. (1990). Reconceptualizing school psychology from a service delivery perspective: Implications for practice, training and research. *Journal of School Psychology, 28,* 203–223.

Haberman, M. (1991). The pedagogy of poverty versus good teaching. *Phi Delta Kappan, 73* (4), 290–294.

Hanson, E. M. (1990). *Educational administration and organizational behavior.* 3d ed. Boston: Allyn & Bacon.

Hardman, M. L., McDonnell, J., & Welch, M. (1993). A closer look at the Individuals with Disabilities Education Act: An IDEA whose time has come? (in review).

Hart, A. W. (1990). Personal communication.

Hart, A. W. (1993). *Principal succession: Establishing leadership in schools.* Albany, NY: State University of New York Press.

Hendrick Hudson District Board of Education v. Rowley, 458 U.S. 176 (1982).

Hocutt, A. M., Martin, E. W., & McKinney, J. D. (1991). Historical and legal context of mainstreaming. In J. W. Lloyd, N. N. Singh, & A. C. Repp (Eds.), *The regular education initiative: Alternative perspectives on concepts, issues, and models* (pp. 17–28). Sycamore, IL: Sycamore.

Huefner, D. (1991). Judicial review of the special education program requirements under the Education for All Handicapped Children Act: Where have we been and where should we be going? *Harvard Journal of Law and Public Policy, 14,* 483–516.

Jones, K. H., & Bender, W. N. (1993). Utilization of paraprofessionals in special education: A review of the literature. *Remedial and Special Education, 14*(1), 7–14.

Jones, R., Sheridan, S. M., & Binns, W. (1993). School-wide social skills training: Providing preventive services to students at risk. *School Psychology Quarterly, 8,* 57–80.

Lau v. Nichols, 414 U.S. 563 (1974).

Lezotte, L. W. (1989). School improvement based on effective schools research. In D. K. Lipsky & A. Gartner (Eds.), *Beyond separate education: Quality education for all* (pp. 25–38). Baltimore: Paul H. Brookes.

Lieberman, A., Saxl, E. R., & Miles, M. B. (1988). Teacher leadership: Ideology and practice. In A. Lieberman (Ed.), *Building a professional culture in schools* (pp. 148–166). New York: Teachers College Press.

Lipsky, D. K., & Gartner, A. (1989). The current situation. In D. K. Lipsky & A. Gartner (Eds.), *Beyond separate education: Quality education for all* (pp. 3–24). Baltimore: Paul H. Brookes.

Lipsky, D. K., & Gartner, A. (1992). Achieving full inclusion: Placing the student at the center of educational reform. In W. Stainback & S. Stainback (Eds.), *Controversial issues confronting special education: Divergent perspectives* (pp. 3–12). Boston: Allyn & Bacon.

Lee, V. E., Bryk, A. S., & Smith, J. B. (1993). The organization of effective secondary schools. In L. Darling-Hammond (Ed.), *Review of research in education* (pp. 171–267). Washington, DC: American Education Research Association.

Maeroff, G. I. (1993). *Team building for school change: Equipping teachers for new roles.* New York: Teachers College Press.

Madden, N. A., Slavin, R. E., Karweit, N. L., Dolan, L. J., & Wasik, B. A. (1993). Success For All: Longitudinal effects of a restructuring program for inner-city elementary schools. *American Educational Research Journal, 30*(1), 123–148.

McLaughlin, M. W., & Yee, S. M. (1988). School as a place to have a career. In A. Lieberman (Ed.), *Building a professional culture in schools* (pp. 23–44). New York: Teachers College Press.

McNeil, L. M. (1986). *Contradictions of control: school structure and school knowledge.* New York: Routledge & Kegan Paul.

Miller, L. (1988). Unlikely beginning: The district office as a starting point for developing a professional culture for teaching. In A. Lieberman (Ed.), *Building a professional culture in schools* (pp. 167–184). New York: Teachers College Press.

Mills v. District of Columbia Board of Education, 348 F. Supp. 866 (D.D.C. 1972).

Moll, L. (1988). Education Latino students. *Language Arts, 64,* 315–324.

Murphy, J. (1991). *Restructuring schools: Capturing and assessing the phenomena.* New York: Teachers College Press.

National Center for Education Statistics. (1992). *Digest of education statistics.* Washington, DC: U.S. Department of Education, Office of Educational Research and Improvement.

Natriello, G., McDill, E. L., & Pallas, A. M. (1990). *Schooling disadvantaged children: Racing against catastrophe.* New York: Teachers College Press.

Owens, R.G. (1987). *Organizational behavior in education.* Englewood Cliffs, NJ: Prentice-Hall.

Pai, Y. (1990). *Cultural foundations of education.* Columbus, OH: Merrill.

Partin, R. L. (1993). School counselors' time: Where does it go? *The School Counselor, 40,* 274–281.

Pease-Alvarez, L., Espinoza, P., & Garcia, E. (1991). Effective schooling preschool settings: A case study of LEP students in early childhood. *Early Childhood Research Quarterly, 4,* 153–164.

Pennsylvania Association for Retarded Citizens v. Pennsylvania, 343 F. Supp. 279 (E.D. Pa. 1972).

Pickett, A. L. (1991). *Restructuring the schools: The role of paraprofessionals.* Washington, DC: Center for Policy Research, National Governors' Association.

Ralph, J. (1990). Identifying the problem of educationally disadvantaged students. In J. H. Johnston & K. M. Borman (Eds.), *Effective schooling for economically disadvantaged students: School-based strategies for diverse student populations* (pp. 3–30). Norwood, NJ: Ablex.

Ramirez, J. D., & Merino, B. J. (1990). Classroom talk in English immersion, early-exit and late-exit transitional bilingual education programs. In R. Jacobson & C. Faltis (Eds.), *Language distribution issues in bilingual schooling* (pp. 61–103). Clevedon, England: Multilingual Matters.

Resnick, L. B., & Klopfer, L. E. (1989). *Toward the thinking curriculum: Current cognitive research.* Alexandria, VA: Association for Supervision and Curriculum Development.

Rice, G. E., & Smith, W. (1993). Linking effective counseling and teaching skills. *The School Counselor, 40,* 201–206.

Roach, V. (1991, October). Special education: new questions in an era of reform. *Issues in Brief: National Association of State Boards of Education, 11*(6), 1–7.

Rossman, G. B., Corbett, H. D., & Firestone, W. A. (1988). *Change and effectiveness in schools: A cultural perspective.* Albany, NY: State University of New York Press.

Rothstein, L. F. (1990). *Special education law.* New York: Longman.

Schein, E. (1985). *Organizational culture and leadership.* San Francisco: Jossey-Bass.

Schon, D. A. (1988). Coaching reflective practice. In P. Grimmett & G. Erickson (Eds.), *Reflection in teacher education.* New York: Columbia Teachers College Press.

Silver, C. B. (1973). *Black teachers in urban schools.* New York: Praeger.

Skrtic, T. M. (1991). *Behind special education: A critical analysis of professional culture and school organization.* Denver: Love.

Stainback, S., & Stainback, W. (1992). Schools as inclusive communities. In W. Stainback & S. Stainback (Eds.), *Controversial issues confronting special education: Divergent perspectives* (pp. 29–43). Boston: Allyn & Bacon.

Stringfield, S., & Yoder, N. (1992). Toward a model of elementary grades' Chapter 1 effectiveness. In H. C. Waxman, J. W. deFelix, J. E. Anderson, & H. P. Baptiste, Jr. (Eds.), *Students at risk in at-risk schools* (pp. 203–221). Newbury Park, CA: Corwin.

Thompson, R. (1992). *School counseling renewal: Strategies for the 21st century.* Muncie, IN: Accelerated Development, Inc.

Tugend, A. (1984). College counseling is inadequate. *Education Week, August 10, 29,* 7.

Vacc, N. (1981). Program evaluation activities of secondary school counselors in New York. *Measurement and Evaluation in Guidance, 14,* 21–25.

Villa, R., Thousand, J. S., Paolucci-Whitcomb, P., & Nevin, A. (1990). In search of new paradigms for collaborative consultation. *Journal of Educational and Psychological Consultation, 1*(4), 279–292.

Wade, S., Welch, M., & Jensen, J. B. (1994). Teacher receptivity to collaboration: Levels of interest, types of concern, and school characteristics as variables contributing to successful implemention. *Journal of Educational and Psychological Consultation* (in press).

Walker, L. J. (1987). Procedural rights in the wrong system: Special education is not enough. In A. Gartner & T. Joe (Eds.), *Images of the disabled/disabling images* (pp. 97–116). New York: Praeger.

Waugh, R. F., & Punch, K. F. (1987). Teacher receptivity to systemwide change in the implementation stage. *Review of Educational Research, 57*(3), 237–254.

Welch, M. (1989). A cultural perspective of the third wave of educational reform. *Journal of Learning Disabilities, 22,* 537–540.

Welch, M. (1993, February). Educational partnerships in teacher education: Reconceptualizing how teacher candidates are prepared for teaching disabled students. Paper presented at Annual American Association of Colleges for Teacher Education conference, San Diego.

Welch, M., & Egan, M. W. (1993). *These are our kids!* (Videocassette). Salt Lake City, University of Utah, Department of Special Education, Educational Tele-Communications.

Welch, M., & Hardman, M. L. (1991). Initiating change: One university's response to teacher education reform and the education of students with disabilities. *Teacher Education and Special Education, 14*(4), 228–234.

Williams, A., & Welch, M. (1993, November). *The site-based transdisciplinary educational partnerships project.* Paper presented at the Teacher Education Division of the Council for Exceptional Children, 15th Annual Conference, Cincinnati.

Ysseldyke, J. E., & Algozzine, B. (1982). *Critical issues in special and remedial education.* Boston: Houghton Mifflin.

Ysseldyke, J. E., Algozzine, B., & Thurlow, M. L. (1992). *Critical issues in special education.* Boston: Houghton Mifflin.

Chapter 6

Abdin, L. (1983). *Parenting stress index.* Charlottesville, VA: Pediatric Psychology.

Achenbach, T. M. (1978). The child behavior profile I. Boys aged 6–11. *Journal of Consulting and Clinical Psychology, 46,* 478–488.

Achenbach, T. M., & Edelbrock, C. S. (1979). The child behavior profile II. Boys aged 12–16 and girls aged 6, 11, and 12. *Journal of Consulting and Clinical Psychology, 47,* 223–233.

Alessi, G. (1988). Direct observation methods for emotional/behavioral problems. In E. S. Shapiro & T. R. Kratochwill (Eds.), *Behavioral assessment in schools: Conceptual foundations and practical applications* (pp. 14–75). New York: Guilford.

Allington, R. L., & McGill-Franzen, A. (1989). Different programs, indifferent instruction. In D. K. Lipsky, & A. Gartner (Eds.), *Beyond separate education: Quality education for all* (pp. 75–98). Baltimore: Paul H. Brookes.

Bagnato, S. J., Neisworth, J. T., & Capone, A. (1986). Curriculum-based assessment for the young exceptional child: Rationale and review. *Topics in Early Childhood Special Education, 6* (2), 97–110.

Bertalanffy, L. (1968). *General systems theory: Foundations, development, applications.* New York: Braziller.

Blankenship, C., & Lilly, M. S. (1981). *Mainstreaming students with learning and behavior problems: Techniques for the classroom teacher.* New York: Holt, Rinehart & Winston.

Caldwell, B. M., & Bradley, R. H. (1978). *Home observation for measurement of the environment (HOME) manual.* Little Rock, AR: University of Arkansas.

Delquadri, J., Greenwood, C. R., Whorton, D., Carta, J. J., & Hall, R. V. (1986). Classwide peer tutoring. *Exceptional Children, 52,* 535–542.

Deshler, D., & Schumaker, J. (1986). Learning strategies: An instructional alternative for low-achieving adolescents. *Exceptional Children, 52,* 583–590.

Deno, S., Mirkin, P., & Shinn, M. (1978). Behavioral perspectives on the assessment of learning disabled children. In J. Ysseldyke (Ed.), *Synthesis of the knowledge base: Identification and assessment of learning disabled children* (Monograph No. 2). Minneapolis, MN: University of Minnesota, Institute for Research on Learning Disabilities.

Edelbrock, C., & Achenbach, T. M. (1984a). The teacher version of the child behavior profile I. Boys aged 6–11 (unpublished).

Edelbrock, C., & Achenbach, T. M. (1984b). The teacher version of the child behavior profile II. Boys aged 12–16 and girls aged 6–11 and 12–16 (unpublished).

Ellis, A. K., Mackey, J. A., & Glenn, A. D. (1988). *The school curriculum.* Boston: Allyn & Bacon.

Epps, S., & Tindal, G. (1987). The effectiveness of differential programming in serving students with mild handicaps: Placement options and instructional programming. In M. C. Wang, M. C. Reynolds, & H. J. Walberg (Eds.), *Handbook of special education: Research and practice—Learner characteristics and adaptive education.* Vol. 1 (pp. 213–248). New York: Pergamon.

Fuchs, L., Deno, S., & Mirkin, P. K. (1984). The effects of frequent curriculum-based measurement and evaluation on pedagogy, student achievement, and student awareness of learning. *American Educational Research Journal, 21,* 449–460.

Goodlad, J. (1983). What some schools and classrooms teach. *Educational Leadership, 40* (7), 8–19.

Graden, J. L., Casey, A., & Christensen, S. L. (1986). Implementing a prereferral intervention system: Part I. The model. *Exceptional Children, 51,* 377–384.

Gresham, I. M., & Davis, C. J. (1988). Behavioral interviews with teachers and parents. In E. S. Shapiro, & T. R. Kratochwill (Eds.), *Behavioral assessment in schools* (pp. 455–493). New York: Guilford.

Hendrix, D. (1987). Grading the LD student: With so many solutions, why are there still problems? *LD FORUM, 12* (2), 1–3.

Hoover, J. J. (1987). Preparing special educators for mainstreaming: An emphasis upon curriculum. *Teacher Education and Special Education, 10,* 58–64.

Komoski, K. (1990). Needed: a whole-curriculum approach. *Educational Leadership, 47,* 72–78.

Kratochwill, T. R., & Bergan, J. R. (1990). *Behavioral consultation in applied settings: An individual guide.* New York: Plenum.

Kratochwill, T. R., & Sheridan, S. M. (1990). Advances in behavioral assessment. In T. B. Gutkin, & C. R. Reynolds (Eds.), *The handbook of school psychology.* 2d ed. (pp. 328–364), New York: Wiley.

Lentz, F. E. (1988). Direct observation and measurement of academic skills: A conceptual review. In E. S. Shapiro & T. R. Kratochwill (Eds.), *Behavioral assessment in schools: Conceptual foundations and practical applications* (pp. 76–120). New York: Guilford.

MacMillan, D., Keogh, B., & Jones, R. (1986). Special education research on mildly handicapped learners. In M.C. Wittorck (Ed.), *Handbook of research on teaching.* 3d ed. (pp. 686–724). New York: Macmillan.

Maher, C. A., & Bennett, R. E. (1984). *Planning and evaluating special education services.* Englewood Cliffs, NJ: Prentice-Hall.

Maruyamn, G., Deno, S., Cohen, C., & Espin, C. (1989). *The School Characteristics Survey: An "effective school" based means of assessing learning environments.* Paper presented at the annual meeting of the American Educational Research Association, San Francisco.

McLoughlin, J. A., & Lewis, R. B. (1981). *Assessing special students.* Columbus, OH: Merrill.

McDonnell, J., Wilcox, B., & Hardman, M. L. (1991). *Secondary programs for students with developmental disabilities.* Boston: Allyn & Bacon.

McNergney, R. F., Medley, D. M., & Caldwell, M. S. (1988). Making and implementing policy on teacher licensure. *Journal of Teacher Education, 39,* 38–44.

Messick, S. (1984). Assessment in context: Appraising student performance in relation to instructional quality. *Educational Researcher, 13* (3), 3–8.

Miller, J. H., & Milan, C. P. (1987). Multiplication and division errors committed by learning disabled students. *Learning Disabilities Research, 2* (2), 119–122.

Reynolds, M. C. (1984). Classification of students with handicaps. In E. W. Gordon (Ed.), *Review of research in education.* Vol. 11 (pp. 63–92). Washington, DC: American Educational Research Association.

Saudargas, R. A. (1983). *State event classroom observation code*. Knoxville, University of Tennessee. Department of Psychology (available from the author).

Schalock, R. (1986). *Transitions from school to work*. Washington, DC: National Association of Rehabilitation Facilities.

Stainback, W., & Stainback, S. (1983). A severely handicapped integration checklist. *Teaching Exceptional Children, 15* (3), 168–171.

Stanley, S. O., & Greenwood, C. R. (1981). *CISSAR: Code for instructional structure and student acdemic response: Observer's manual*. Kansas City: University of Kansas, Juniper Gardens Children's Project, Bureau of Child Research.

Thurlow, M. L., & Ysseldyke, J. E. (1980). *Instructional planning: Information collected by school psychologists vs. information considered useful by teachers* (Research Rep. No 29). Minneaplis, MN: University of Minnesota, Institute for Research on Learning Disabilities.

Tucker, J. A. (1985). Curriculum-based assessment: An introduction. *Exceptional Children, 52,* 199–204.

Vasa, S. F. (1981). Alternative procedures for grading handicapped students in the secondary schools. *Educational Unlimited, 3* (1), 16–23.

Vasa, S. F ., Steckelberg, A. L., & Asselin, S. B. (1981). *Accommodating the mildly handicapped student in the regular secondary classroom: A resource Guide*. Lincoln: University of Nebraska.

Voeltz, L. M., Kishi, G. M., & Brennan, J. (1981). *SIOS: Social interaction observation system*. Unpublished document, Honolulu: Hawaii Integration Project, Department of Special Education, University of Hawaii.

Welch, M., & Link, D. P. (1992). Informal assessment of paragraph compostion. *Intervention in School and Clinic, 27* (3), 145–149.

Wiggins, G. (1989). Teaching to the authentic test. *Educational Leadership, 46* (7) 41– 47.

Ysseldyke, J. E., & Christenson, S. (1987). Evaluating students' instructional environments. *Remedial and Special Education, 8,* 17–24.

Zins, J. E., Curtis, M. J., Graden, J. L., & Ponti, C. R. (1988). *Helping students succeed in the regular classroom*. San Francisco, Jossey-Bass.

Chapter 7

Adamson, D. R., Cox, J., & Schuller, J. (1989). Collaboration/consultation: Bridging the gap from resource room to regular classroom. *Teacher Education and Special Education, 12,* 52–55.

Alberto, P. A., & Troutman, A. C. (1990). *Applied behavior analysis for teachers*. 3d. ed. Columbus, OH: Merrill.

Allen, J. B., Clark, F., Gallagher, F., & Scofield, F. (1982). Classroom strategies for accommodating exceptional learners. Materials developed under Grant No. OEGOO7902045, Division of Personnel Preparation, Office of Special Education and Rehabilitative Services, U.S. Department of Education.

Alley, G., & Deshler, D. (1979). *Teaching learning disabled adolescents: Strategies and methods*. Denver: Love.

Archambault, F. X. (1989). Instructional setting and other design features of compensatory education programs. In R. E. Slavin, N. L. Karweit, & N. A. Madden (Eds.), *Effective programs for students at risk* (pp. 220–263). Boston: Allyn & Bacon.

Archbald, D. A., & Newman, F. M. (1988). *Beyond standardized testing: Assessing authentic academic achievement in the secondary school.* Reston, VA: National Association of Secondary School Principals.

Black, A., & Ammon, P. (1992). A developmental-constructivist approach to teacher education. *Journal of Teacher Education, 43* (5), 323–335.

Becker, W. C., & Carnine, D. (1980). Direct instruction: An effective approach for educational intervention with the disadvantaged and low performers. In B. J. Lahey & A. E. Kazkin (Eds.), *Advances in child clinical psychology* (pp. 429–473). New York: Plenum.

Bickel, W. E., & Bickel, D. D. (1986). Effective schools, classrooms, and instruction: Implications for special education. *Exceptional Children, 52,* 489–500.

Bos, C. S. (1988). Process-oriented writing: Instructional implications for mildly handicapped students. *Exceptional Children, 54,* 521–527.

Brookover, W. B., Beamer, L., Efthim, H., Hathaway, D., Lezotte, L., Miller, S., Passalacqua, J., & Tornatzky, L. (1982). *Creating effective schools.* Holmes Beach, FL: Learning Publications, Inc.

Brophy, J., & Good, T. L. (1986). Teacher behavior and student achievement. In M. C. Wittorkc (Ed.), *Handbook of research on teacherin.* 3d ed. (pp. 328–275). New York: Macmillan.

Carroll, J. B. (1985). The model of school learning: Progress of an idea. In C. W. Fisher & D. Berliner (Eds.), *Perspectives on instructional time* (pp. 29–58). New York: Longman.

Cohen, L. G., & Spruill, J. A. (1990). *A practical guide to curriculum-based assessment for special educators.* Springfield, IL: Charles C. Thomas.

Cohen, P. A., Kulik, J. A., & Kulik, C. C. (1982). Educational outcomes of tutoring: A meta-analysis of findings. *American Educational Research Journal, 19,* 137–148.

Cohen, S. B. (1982). Assigning report card grades to the mainstreamed child. *Teaching Exceptional Children,* 86–89.

Cole, C. L. (1987). Self-management. In C. R. Reynolds & L. Mann (Eds.), *Encyclopedia of special education* (pp. 1404–1405). New York: John Wiley & Sons.

Crawford, J. (1989). Instructional activities related achievement gain in Chapter I classes. In R. E. Slavin, N. L. Karweit, & N. A. Madden (Eds.), *Effective programs for students at risk* (pp. 264–290). Boston: Allyn & Bacon.

Dawson, M. M. (1987). Beyond ability grouping: A review of the effectiveness of ability grouping and its alternatives. *School Psychology Review, 16,* 348–369.

Denham, C., & Lieberman, A. (Eds.). (1980) *Time to learn.* Washington, DC: National Institute of Education.

Deshler, D., & Schumaker, J. B. (1986). Learning strategies: An instructional alternative for low-achieving adolescents. *Exceptional Children, 52,* 583–590.

Englert, C. S., & Raphael, T. E. (1988). Constructing well-formed prose: Process, structure, and metacognitive knowledge. *Exceptional Children, 54,* 513–520.

Fisher, C. W., Filby, N. N., Marliave, R. S., Cahen, L. S., Dishaw, M. M., Moore, J. E., & Bcrlincr, D. (1978). *Teaching behaviors, academic learning time and student achievement* (Final report of Phase III-B, Beginner Teacher Evaluation Study). San Francisco, CA: Far West Regional Laboratory.

Frisby, C. (1987). Alternative assessment committee report: Curriculum-based assessment. *CASP Today, 36,* 15–26.

Fuchs, L. S. (1989). Evaluating solutions, monitoring progress, and revising intervention plans. In M.R. Shinn (Ed.), *Curriculum-based measurement: Assessing special children* (pp.153–181). New York: Guilford.

Gartner, A. & Lipsky, D. K. (1990). Students as instructional agents. In W. Stainback & S. Stainback (Eds.), *Support networks for inclusive schooling: Interdependent integrated education* (pp. 81–94). Baltimore: Paul H. Brookes.

Gettinger, M. (1988). Methods of proactive classroom mangement. *School Psychology Review, 17,* 227–242.

Gersten, R., Woodward, J., & Darch, C. (1986). Direct instruction: A research-based approach to curriculum design and teaching. *Exceptional Children, 53,* 17–31.

Gloeckler, T., & Simpson, C. (1988). *Exceptional students in regular classrooms.* Mountain View, CA: Mayfield.

Goldman, S. R., & Rueda, R. (1988). Developing writing skills in bilingual exceptional children. *Exceptional Children, 54,* 543–551.

Goldstein, A. P. (1988). *The prepare curriculum: Teaching prosocial competencies.* Champaign, IL: Research.

Graves, D. H. (1983). *Writing: Teachers and children at work.* Exeter, NH: Heinemann.

Greenwood, C. R. (1991). Longitudinal analysis of time, engagement, and achievement in at risk versus non-risk students. *Exceptional Children, 57,* 512–534.

Haring, T. G., Breen, C., Pitts-Conway, V., Lee, M., & Gaylord-Ross, R. (1987). Adolescent peer tutoring and special friend experience. *Journal of the Association for Persons with Severe Handicaps, 12*(4), 280–286.

Idol, L., Paolucci-Whitcomb, P., & Nevin, A. (1986). *Collaborative consultation.* Austin, TX: PRO-ED.

Jarolimek, J., & Foster, C. D. (1981). *Teaching and learning in the elementary school.* 2d ed. New York: Macmillan.

Jenkins, J. R., & Jenkins, L. M. (1987). Making peer tutoring work. *Educational Leadership, 44*(6), 64–68.

Johnson, D. W., & Johnson, R. T. (1986). Mainstreaming and cooperative learning strategies. *Exceptional Children, 52,* 553–561.

Jones, J. A. (1975). Teacher-made lesson tapes. *Teacher, 92*(5), 108–109.

Kinnison, L. R., Hayes, C., & Accord, J. (1981). Evaluating student progress in mainstreamed classes. *Teaching Exceptional Children, 13*(3), 97–99.

Kiraly, J., & Bedell, J. J. (1984). Grading the mainstreamed handicapped student. *NASSP Bulletin, 68,* 111–115.

Larrivee, B. (1989). Effective strategies for academically handicapped students in the regular classroom. In R. E. Slavin, N. L. Karweit, & N. A. Madden (Eds.), *Effective programs for students at risk* (pp. 291–319). Boston: Allyn & Bacon.

Lenz, B. K., & Deshler, D. D. (1990). Principles of strategies instruction as the basis of effective preservice teacher education. *Teacher Education and Special Education, 13,* 82–95.

Lynn, D. R. (1986). Peer helpers: Increasing positive student involvement in school. *School Counselor, 34,* 62–66.

Lloyd, J. W., Crowley, E. P., Kohler, F. W., & Strain, P. S. (1988). Reaching the applied research agenda: Cooperative learning, prereferral, teacher consultation, and peer-mediated interventions. *Journal of Learning Disabilities, 21,* 43–51.

Long, N. J., & Newman, R. G. (1980). Managing surface behavior of children in school. In N. J. Long, W.C. Morse, & R. G. Newman (Eds.), *Conflict in the classroom.* Belmont, CA: Wadsworth.

Morse, W. C. & R. G. Newman (Eds.), *Conflict in the classroom: The education of emotionally disturbed children.* 4th ed. Belmont, CA: Wadsworth.

Lovitt, T. (1989). Constructing graphic organizers. *Graphic organizer interactive video packet.* Salt Lake City, UT: Utah Learning Resource Center.

Macarthur, C. A. (1988). The impact of computers on the writing process. *Exceptional Children, 54,* 536–542.

Maheady, L., Sacca, M. K., & Harper, G. F. (1988). Classwide peer tutoring with mildly handicapped high school students. *Exceptional Children, 55,* 52–59.

Marston, D. B. (1989). A curriculum-based measurement approach to assessing academic performance: What it is and why do it. In M. R. Shinn (Ed.), *Curriculum-based measurement: Assessing special children* (pp.18–78). New York: Guilford.

Mayle, J., & Riegel, R. H. (1979). *Maladies and remedies: Guidelines for modifications of materials and methods for mainstreamed adolescents with academic difficulties.* Plymouth, MI: Plymouth-Canton Community School District.

McDonnell, J., Wilcox, B., & Hardman, M. L. (1991). *Secondary programs for students with developmental disabilities.* Boston: Allyn & Bacon.

Meier, F. E. (1992). *Competency-based instruction for teachers of students with special learning needs.* Boston: Allyn & Bacon.

Moncur, J. (1991). *The A.B.C.'s of peer tutoring.* Unpublished manuscript.

Morgan, D. P., & Jenson, W. R. (1988). *Teaching behaviorally disorderded students: Preferred practices.* Columbus, OH: Merrill.

Moyer, J. C., Sowder, L., Threadgill-Sowder, J., & Moyer, M. B. (1984). Story problem formats: Drawn versus telegraphic. *Journal for Research in Mathematics Education, 15,* 342–351.

Nattiv, A. (1988). Cooperative learning: An overview. *Journal of Humanistic Education, 12*(1), 2–7.

Nattiv, A. (1990). Enhancing cooperative skill development in the classroom. *Utah Association for Supervision and Curriculum Development Journal, 1*(1), 7–9.

Newman, J. (1981). *Television in the classroom: What the research says.* Olympia, WA: Washington Office of the State Superintendent of Public Instruction, Division of Instructional and Professional Studies, ERIC Document (ED 206 263).

Olson, J., & Platt, J. (1992). *Teaching children and adolescents with special needs.* Columbus, OH: Merrill.

Payne, J., Polloway, E., Smith, J., & Payne, R. (1981). *Strategies for teaching the mentally retarded.* 2d ed. Columbus, OH: Merrill.

Reynolds, M. C., & Lakin, K. C. (1987). Noncategorical special education: Models for research and practice. In M. C. Wang, M. C. Reynolds, & H. J. Walberg (Eds.), *Handbook for special education: Research and practice, Vol. 1: Learner characteristics and adaptive education* (pp. 331–356). New York: Pergamon.

Rhode, G., Jenson, W. R., & Reavis, H. K. (1992). *The tough kid book: Practical classroom management strategies.* Longmont, CO: Sopris West.

Rockwell, S. (1993). *Tough to reach/tough to teach: Students with behavior problems.* Reston, VA: Council for Exceptional Children.

Roehler, L., & Duffy, G. G. (1984). Direct explanation of comprehension processes. In G. Duffy, L. Roehler, & J. Mason (Eds.), *Comprehension instruction: Perspectives and suggestions* (pp. 265–280). New York: Longman.

Rosenshine, B., & Stevens, R. (1986). Teaching functions. In M. C. Wittrock (Ed.), *Handbook of research on teaching* (pp. 376–391). New York: Macmillan.

Rosenshine, B. V., & Berliner, D. C. (1978). Academic engaged time. *British Journal of Teacher Education, 4,* 3–16.

Rotholz, D. A. (1987). Currrent considerations on the use of one-to-one instruction with autistic students: Review and recommendations. *Education and Treatment of Children, 10* (3), 271–278.

Russell, S. J., Corwin, R., Mokros, J. R., & Kapisovksy, P. M. (1989). *Beyond drill and practice: Expanding the computer mainstream.* Reston, VA: Council for Exceptional Children.

Salend, S. J., & Washin, B. (1988). Team-assisted individualization with handicapped adjudicated youth. *Exceptional Children, 55,* 174–180.

Sasso, G. M., & Rude, H. A. (1988). The social effects of integration on nonhandicapped children. *Education and Training in Mental Retardation, 23,* 18–23.

Sheingold, K., & Hadley, M. (1990). *Accomplished teachers: Integrating computers into classroom practice.* New York: Bank Street College of Education.

Shanks, R. D. (1986). Grading mainstreamed handicapped students: A position paper. ERIC Document Reproduction No. 278 204. Grand Island School District, Grand Island, NE.

Shapiro, E. S. (1988). Preventing academic failure. *School Psychology Review, 17,* 601–613.

Slavin, R. (1990). *Cooperative learning: Theory, research and practice.* Englewood Cliffs, NJ: Prentice-Hall.

Slavin, R. E., Madden, N. A., & Leavey, M. B. (1984). Effects of cooperative learning and individualized instruction on mainstreamed students. *Exceptional Children, 50,* 434–443.

Slavin, R. E., & Stevens, R. J. (1991). Cooperative learning and mainstreaming. In J. W. Lloyd, N. N. Singh, & A. C. Repp (Eds.), *The regular education initiative: Alternative perspectives on concepts, issues, and models* (pp. 177–192). Sycamore, IL: Sycamore.

Sprague, J., & McDonnell, J. (1984). *Effective use of secondary-age peer tutors: A resource manual for classroom teachers.* Eugene, OR: Specialized Training Program, University of Oregon.

Stainback, W., & Stainback, S. (1990). Facilitating peeer supports and friendships. In W. Stainback & S. Stainback (Eds.), *Support networks for inclusive schooling: Interdependent integrated education* (pp. 51–64). Baltimore: Paul H. Brookes.

Stallings, J. A. (1980). Allocated academic learning time revisited. *Educational researcher, 9* (1), 11–16.

Stephens, T. M. (1977). *Teaching skills to children with learning and behavior disorders.* Columbus, OH: Merrill.

Stevens, R., & Rosenshine, B. (1981). Advances in research on teaching. *Exceptional Education Quarterly, 2* (1), 1–9.

Strain, P. S., & Odom, S. L. (1986). Peer social initiations: Effective intervention for social skills development of exceptional children. *Exceptional Children, 52,* 543–551.

Voeltz, L. M. (1982). Effects of structured interactions with severely handicapped peers on children's attitudes. *American Journal of Mental Deficiency, 86* (4), 380–390.

Welch, M., & Link, D. P. (1992). Informal assessment of paragraph composition. *Intervention in School and Clinic, 27* (3), 145–149.

Wilson, R., & Wesson, C. (1986). Making every minute count: Academic learning time in LD classrooms. *Learning Disabilities Focus, 2* (1), 13–19.

Wolf, D. P. (1989). Portfolio assessment: Sampling student work. *Educational Leadership, 46* (7), 35–39.

Zirpoli, T. J., & Melloy, K. J. (1993). *Behavior management: Applications for teachers and parents,* Table 7–1. Columbus, OH: Merrill.

Chapter 8

Ackland, R. (1991). A review of the peer coaching literature. *Journal of Staff Development, 12* (1), 22–27.

Adamson, D. R., Matthews, P., & Schuller, J. (1990). Five ways to bridge the resource room-to-regular classroom gap. *Teaching Exceptional Children, 22,* 74–77.

Adamson, D. R., Cox, J., & Schuller, J. (1989). Collaboration/consultation: Bridging the gap from the resource room to regular classroom. *Teacher Education and Special Education, 12,* 52–55.

Archer, A. L., & Isaacson, S. L. (1990). Teaching others how to teach strategies. *Teacher Education and Special Education, 13* (2), 63–72.

Bauwens, J., Hourcade, J. J., & Friend, M. (1989). Cooperative teaching: A model for general and special education integration. *Remedial and Special Education, 10,* 17–22.

Brann, P., Loughlin, S., & Kimball, W. H. (1991). Guidelines for cooperative teaching between general and special education teachers. *Journal of Educational and Psychological Consultation, 2,* 197–200.

Chalfant, J. C., & Van Dusen Pysh, M. (1989). Teacher assistance teams: Five descriptive studies on 96 teams. *Remedial and Special Education, 10,* 49–58.

Cline, D. (1984). Achieving quality and relevance in in-service teacher education: Where are we? *Teacher Education and Special Education, 7,* 199–208.

Daresh, J. C. (1985). Research trends in staff development and in-service education. (ERIC Document No. ED 292180).

Dillon, E. A. (1979). Staff development content delivery. *Journal of Teacher Education, 30,* 42–43.

Dugoff, S. K., Ives, R. K., & Shotel, J. R. (1985). Public school and university staff perceptions of the role of the resource teacher. *Teacher Education and Special Education, 8,* 75–82.

Elliott, S. N., & Sheridan, S. M. (1992). Consulting and teaming: Problem solving among educators, parents, and support personnel. *Elementary School Journal, 92* (3), 261–284.

Epstein, J. L., Lockard, B. L., & Dauber, S. L. (1991). Staff development for middle school education. *Journal of Staff Development, 12,* 36–41.

Erchul, W. P. (1987). A relational communication analysis of control in school consultation. *Professional School Psychology, 2,* 111–122.

Fiedler, J. F., & Knight, R. R. (1986). Congruence between assessed needs and IEP goals of identified behaviorally disabled students. *Behavioral Disorders, 12,* 22–27.

Friend, M., & McNutt, G. (1987). A comparative study of resource teacher job descriptions and administrators' perceptions of resource teacher responsibilities. *Journal of Learning Disabilities, 20,* 224–228.

Fuchs, D., Fuchs, L. S., Dulan, J., Roberts, H., & Fernstrom, P. (1992). Where is the research on consultation effectiveness? *Journal of Educational and Psychological Consultation, 3,* 151–174.

Fullan, M. G. (1990). Staff development, innovation, and institutional development. In B. Joyce (Ed.), *Changing school culture through staff development* (pp. 3–25). Alexander, VA: Association for Supervision and Curriculum Development.

Gall, M. D., Haisley, F. G., Baker, R. G., & Perez, M. (1984, April). The current status of staff development activities for teachers: A loose coupling interpretation. Paper presented at the annual meeting of American Educational Research Association, New Orleans, LA.

Gelzheiser, L. M., & Meyers, J. (1990). Special and remedial education in the classroom: Theme and variations. *Reading, Writing, and Learning Disabilities, 6,* 419–436.

Gersten, R., Woodward, J., & Darch, C. (1986). Direct instruction: A research-based approach to curriculum design and teaching. *Exceptional Children, 53,* 17–31.

Gettinger, M. (1988). Methods of proactive classroom management. *School Psychology Review, 17,* 227–242.

Goodwin, D. L., & Coates, T. J. (1973). Increasing teacher effectiveness through social systems change: Training school psychologists as change agents. *California Journal of Educational Research, 25,* 147–156.

Graden, J. L., Casey, A., & Christenson, S. L. (1985). Implementing a prereferral intervention system: Part I—The model. *Exceptional Children, 51,* 377–384.

Gutkin, T. B., & Curtis, M. J. (1990). School-based consultation: Theory, techniques, and research. In T. B. Gutkin and C. R. Reynolds (Eds.), *The handbook of school psychology.* 2d ed. (pp. 577–611). New York: Wiley. Harrington, & Gibson, 1986.

Heron, T. E., Drevno, G., & Harris, K. C. (1992). Working effectively with teams to develop, implement, and evaluate instructional programs for students with learning disabilities. Paper presented at the 14th International Conference of the Council for Learning Disabilities, Kansas City, MO.

Huefner, D. S. (1991). Judicial review of the special education program requirements under the Education For All Handicapped Children Act: Where have we been and where should we be going? *Harvard Journal of Law and Public Policy, 14,* 483–516.

Idol, L. (1989). The resource/consulting teacher: An integrated model of service delivery. *Remedial and Special Education, 10,* 38–48.

Idol, L. (1988). A rationale and guidelines for establishing special education consultation programs. *Remedial and Special Education, 9,* 48–58.

Idol-Maestas, L., & Ritter, S. (1985). A follow-up study of resource/consulting teachers: Factors that facilitate and inhibit teacher consultation. *Teacher Education and Special Education, 8,* 121–131.

Johnson, L. J., & Pugach, M. C. (1991). Peer collaboration: Accommodating students with mild learning and behavior problems. *Exceptional Children, 57,* 454–461.

Jones, E. V., & Lowe, J. (1990). Changing teacher behavior: Effective staff development. *Adult Learning, 1* (7), 8–10.

Kratochwill, T. R., & Bergan, J. R. (1990). *Behavioral consultation in applied settings: An individual guide.* New York: Plenum.

Kuh, G. D., Hutson, H., Orbaugh, T., & Byers, K. (1980). Needs assessment in regular education in-service training: A problem-focused approach. *Teacher Education and Special Education, 3,* 15–21.

Lloyd, J. W., Crowley, E. P., Kohler, F. W., & Strain, P. S. (1988). Redefining the applied research agenda: Cooperative learning, prereferral, teacher consultation, and peer-mediated interventions. *Journal of Learning Disabilities, 21,* 43–51.

Maher, C. A., & Bennett, R. E. (1984). *Planning and evaluating special education services.* Englewood Cliffs, NJ: Prentice-Hall.

McDonnell, J., B., Wilcox, & Hardman, M. L. (1991). *Secondary programs for students with developmental disabilities.* Boston: Allyn & Bacon.

McDonnell, L. M. (1985). Implementing low-cost school improvement strategies. *Elementary School Journal, 85,* 423–438.

McKellar, N. A. (1991). Enhancing the IEP process through consultation. *Journal of Educational and Psychological Consultation, 2,* 175–187.

Meyers, J., Gelzheiser, L. M., & Yelich, G. (1991). Do pull-in programs foster teacher collaboration? *Remedial and Special Education, 12,* 7–15.

Morsink, C. V., Thomas, C. C., & Correa, V. I. (1991). *Interactive teaming: Consultation and collaboration in special programs.* Columbus, OH: Merrill.

Nevin, A., & Thousand, J. (1986). What the research says about limiting or avoiding referrals to special education. *Teacher Education and Special Education, 9,* 149–161.

Nowacek, E. J. (1992). Professionals talk about teaching together: Interviews with five collaborating teachers. *Intervention In School and Clinic, 27* (5), 262–276.

Pfeiffer, S. I., & Hefferman, L. (1984). Improving multidisciplinary team functions. In C. A. Maher, R. J. Illback, & J. E. Zins (Eds.), *Organizational psychology in the schools: A handbook for professionals* (pp. 282–301). Springfield, IL: Charles C. Thomas.

Poland, S. F., Thurlow, M. L., Ysseldyke, J. E., & Mirkin, P. K. (1982). Current psychoeducational assessment and decision-making practices as reported by directors of special education. *Journal of School Psychology, 20,* 171–179.

Powers, D. A. (1983). Mainstreaming and the in-service education of teachers. *Exceptional Children, 49,* 432–439.

Pugach, M. & Johnson, L. (1988). Peer collaboration. *Teaching Exceptional Children, 20* (1), 75–77.

Reynolds, M. C., & Birch, J. W. (1988). *Adaptive mainstreaming.* New York: Longman.

Schumaker, J. B., & Clark, F. L. (1990). Achieving implementation of strategy instruction through effective in-service education. *Teacher Education and Special Education, 13,* 105–116.

Self, H., Benning, A., Marston, D., & Magnusson, D. (1991). Cooperative teaching project: A model for students at risk. *Exceptional Children, 58,* 26–34.

Schulte, A. C., Osborne, S. S., & McKinney, J. D. (1990). Academic outcomes for students with learning disabilities in consultation and resource programs. *Exceptional Children, 57,* 162–172.

Sharp, P. A. (1992). The 'never-evers' of workshop facilitation. *Journal of Staff Development, 13* (2), 38–40.

Sheridan, S. M., & Kratochwill, T. R. (1991). Behavioral consultation in educational settings. In J. W. Lloyd, N. N. Singh, & A. C. Repp (Eds.), *The regular education initiative: Alternative perspectives on concepts, issues, and models* (pp. 193–210). Sycamore, IL: Sycamore.

Showers, B. (1984). *Peer coaching: A strategy for facilitating transfer of training.* Eugene: Center for Educational Policy and Management, University of Oregon.

Showers, B., Joyce, B., & Bennett, B. (1987). Synthesis of research on staff development: A framework for future study and a state-of-the-art analysis. *Educational Leadership, 45* (3), 72–75.

Smylie, M. A., & Conyers, J. G. (1991). Changing conceptions of teaching influence: The future of staff development. *Journal of Staff Development, 12,* 12–16.

Strickland, B. B., & Turnbull, A. P. (1990). *Developing and Implementing Individualized Education Programs.* Columbus, OH: Merrill.

Van Reusen, A. K., & Bos, C. S. (1990). I PLAN: Helping students communicate in planning conferences. *Teaching Exceptional Children, 22* (4), 30–32.

Van Reusen, A. K., Bos, C. S., Schumaker, J. B., & Deshler, D. D. (1987). *The educational planning strategy.* Lawrence, KS: EXCELLENTerprises.

VonBrock, M. B., & Elliott, S. N. (1987). Influence of treatment effectiveness information on the acceptability of classroom interventions. *Journal of School Psychology, 25,* 131–144.

Weil, M., Karls, J., & Associates (1985). *Case management in human service practice.* San Francisco, Jossey-Bass.

Welch, M., Judge, T., Anderson, J., Bray, J., Child, B., & Franke, L. (1990). The collaborative options-outcome planner: A tool for implementing prereferral consultation. *Teaching Exceptional Children, 22,* 30–31.

Welch, M., & Williams, A. B. (1991, October). The collaborative strategies systems project: A field-based teacher education program to empower teachers and students with strategies. Paper presented at the 69th Annual Council for Exceptional Children Conference, Atlanta.

Wesson, C. L., & Keefe, M. (1989). Teaching library skills to special education students. *School Library Media Quarterly, 17,* 71–77.

West, J. F., & Idol, L. (1990). Collaborative consultation in the education of mildly handicapped and at risk students. *Remedial and Special Education, 11,* 22–32.

Wilcox, B., & Bellamy, G. T. (1987a). *The Activities Catalog: An alternative curriculum for youth and adults with severe disabilities.* Baltimore: Paul H. Brookes.

Wilcox, B., & Bellamy, G. T. (1987b). *A comprehensive guide to The Activities Catalog: An alternative curriculum for youth and adults with severe disabilities.* Baltimore: Paul H. Brookes.

Ysseldyke, J. E. (1991). Classification of handicapped students. In M. C. Wang, M. C. Reynolds, & H. J. Walberg (Eds.), *Handbook of special education: Research and practice—Vol.1: Learner characteristics and adaptive education* (pp. 253–272). New York: Pergamon.

Ysseldyke, J. E. (1983). Current practices in making psychoeducational decisions about learning-disabled students. *Journal of Learning Disabilities, 16,* 226–233.

Zins, J. E., & Curtis, M. J. (1984). Building consultation into the education service delivery system. In C. A. Maher, R. J. Illback, & J. E. Zins (Eds.), *Organizational psychology in the schools* (pp. 213–242). Springfield, IL: Charles C. Thomas.

Chapter 9

Baker, D. P., & Stevenson, D. L. (1986). Mothers' strategies for children's school achievement: Managing the transition to high school. *Sociology of Education, 59,* 156–166.

Batsche, G. M. (1992). Introductory statement. In S. L. Christenson & J. C. Conoley (Eds.), *Home-school collaboration: Enhancing children's academic and social competence* (p. xv). Silver Spring, MD: National Association of School Psychologists.

Bauch, P. A. (1988). Is parent involvement different in private schools? *Educational Horizons, 66,* 78–82.

Becher, R. M. (1986). Parent involvement: A review of research and principles of successful practice. In L. G. Katz (Ed.). *Current topics in early childhood education.* Vol. VI (pp. 85–122). Norwood, NJ: Ablex.

Becker, H. J., & Epstein, J. L. (1982). Parent involvement: A survey of teacher practices. *The Elementary School Journal, 83,* 85–102.

Berger, E. H. (1991). Parent involvement: Yesterday and today. *The Elementary School Journal, 3,* 209–219.

Braun, L., & Swap, S. (1987). *Building home-school partnerships with Amrica's changing families.* Boston: Wheelock College.

Bronfenbrenner, U. (1979). *The ecology of human development.* Cambridge, MA: Harvard University Press.

Carlson, C. I. & Sincavage, J. M. (1987). Family-oriented school psychology practice: Results of a national survey of NASP members. *School Psychology Review, 16,* 519–526.

Carnegie Foundation for the Advancement of Teaching. (1988). *The condition of teaching.* Princeton, NJ: Author.

Children's Defense Fund (1989). *A vision for America's future.* Washington, DC: Author.

Christenson, S. L., & Cleary, M. (1990). Consultation and the parent-educator partnership: A perspective. *Journal of Educational and Psychological Consultation, 1,* 219–241.

Christenson, S. L., Rounds, T., and Gorney, D. (1992). Family factors and student achievement: An avenue to increase students' success. *School Psychology Quarterly, 7,* 178–206.

Coleman, J. S., Campbell, E., Mood, A., Weinfeld, E., Hobson, C., York, R., & McPartland, J. (1966). *Equality of educational opportunity.* Washington, DC: U.S. Government Printing Office.

Comer, J. P. (1984). Home-school relationships as they affect the academic success of children. *Education and Urban Society, 16,* 323–337.

Comer, J. P. (1980). *School power.* New York: Free Press.

Comer, J. P. (1988). Educating poor minority children. *Scientific American, 259* (5), 42–48.

Comer, J. P. & Haynes, N. M. (1991). Parent involvement in schools: An ecological approach. *The Elementary School Journal, 91,* 271–278.

Conoley, J. C. (1987). Schools and families: Theoretical and practical bridges. *Professional School Psychology, 2,* 191–203.

Conoley, J. C. (1989). Cognitive-behavioral approaches and prevention in the schools. In J. N. Hughes & R. J. Hall (Eds.), *Cognitive behavioral psychology in the schools* (pp. 535–568). New York: Guilford.

Dauber, S. L., & Epstein, J. L. (1989). Parents' attitudes and practices of involvement in inner-city elementary and middle schools (CREMS Report 38). Baltimore: Johns Hopkins University, Center for Research on Elementary and Middle Schools.

Davidson, J., & Koppenhaver, D. (1988). *Adolescent literacy: What works and why.* New York: Garland.

Davies, D. (1987). Looking for an ecological solution. *Equity and Choice, 4,* 3–7.

Davis, W. E. (1991, August). Promoting effective communication between schools and parents of disadvantaged students. Paper presented at the 99th Annual Convention of the American Psychological Association, San Francisco, CA.

Davis, W. E., & McCaul, E. J. (1991). *The emerging crisis: Current and projected status of children in the United States.* Orono, ME: College of Education, University of Maine.

Dornbusch, S. M., & Ritter, P. L. (1988). Parents of high school students: A neglected resource. *Educational Horizons, 66,* 75–77.

Dunst, C. J., Johanson, C., Rounds, T., Trivette, C. M., & Hamby, D. (1992). Characteristics of parent-professional partnerships. In S. L. Christenson & J. C. Conoley (Eds.), *Home-school collaboration: Enhancing children's academic and social competence* (pp. 157–174). Silver Spring, MD: National Association of School Psychologists.

Epstein, J. L. (1982, March). *Student reactions to teachers' practices of parent involvement.* Paper presented at the annual meeting of the American Educational Research Association, New York.

Epstein, J. L. (1984, Winter). School policy and parent involvement: Research results. *Educational Horizons,* pp. 70–72.

Epstein, J. L. (1985). Home and school connections in schools of the future: Implications of research on parent involvement. *Peabody Journal of Education, 62,* 18–41.

Epstein, J. L. (1986). Parents' reactions to teacher practices of parent involvement. *The Elementary School Journal, 86,* 277–294.

Epstein, J. L. (1987). Toward a theory of family-school connections: Teacher practices and parent involvement. In K. Hurrelmenn, F. Kaufmann, & F. Losel (Eds)., *Social intervention: Potential and constraints* (pp. 121–136). New York: deGruyter.

Epstein, J. L. (1990a). School and family connections: Theory, research, and implications for integrating sociologies of education and family. In D. Unger & M. Sussman (Eds.), *Families in community settings: Interdisciplinary perspectives* (pp. 99–126). New York: Haworth.

Epstein, J. L. (1990b). Single parents and the schools: Effects of marital status on parent and teacher interactions. In M. T. Hallinan, D. M. Klein, & J. Glass (Eds.), *Change in societal institutions* (pp. 91–121). New York: Plenum.

Epstein, J. L. (1991). Effects on student achievement of teachers' practices of parent involvement. In S. B. Silvern (Ed.), *Advances in reading/language research: Vol. 5. Literacy through family, community, and school interaction* (pp. 261–276). Greenwich, CT: JAI.

Epstein, J. L. (1992). School and family partnerships: Leadership roles for school psychologists. In S. L. Christenson & J. C. Conoley (Eds.), *Home-school collaboration: Enhancing children's academic and social competence* (pp. 499–515). Silver Spring, MD: National Association of School Psychologists.

Epstein, J. L. (in press). Single parents and the schools: Effects of marital status on parent and teacher interactions. In M. Hallanan (Ed.), *Changing societal institutions*. New York: Plenum.

Epstein, J. L., & Casner-Lotto, J. (1988). Building effective parent involvement programs: The role of business. Paper prepared for Work in America Institute.

Epstein, J. L., & Scott-Jones, D. (in press). School-family-community connections for accelerating student progress in the elementary and middle grades. In H. Levin (Ed.), *Accelerating the education of at risk students*. Philadelphia: Falmer.

Educational Testing Service (1992). *America's smallest school: The family*. Princeton, NJ: Author.

Fehrmann, P. G., Keith, T. Z., & Reimers, T. M. (1987). Home influences on school learning: Direct and indirect effects of parent involvement on high school grades. *Journal of Educational Research, 80,* 330–337.

Fine, M. J. (1984). Parent involvement. In J. E. Ysseldyke (Ed.), *School psychology: The state of the art* (pp. 195–224). Minneapolis: National School Psychology Training Network.

Goldenberg, C. (1987). Low-income Hispanic parents' contributions to their first grade children's word-recognition skills. *Anthropology and Education Quarterly, 18,* 149–179.

Gordon, I. J. (1977). Parent education and parent involvement: Retrospect and prospect. *Childhood Education, 54,* 71–77.

Henderson, A. (1987). *The evidence continues to grow*. Columbia, MD: National Committee for Citizens in Education.

Hoover-Dempsey, K. V., Bassler, O. C., & Brissie, J. S. (1987). Parent involvement: Contributions of teacher efficacy, school socioeconomic status, and other school characteristics. *American Educational Research Journal, 24,* 417–435.

Inger, M. (1992, August). Increasing the school involvement of hispanic parents. *ERIC Digest, 80.*

Kagan, S. L., & Holdeman, A. L. (1989). Family support and the schools. *Family Resource Coalition Report, 8* (2), 1–2, 26.

Leitch, M., & Tangri, S. (1988). Barriers to home-school collaboration. *Educational Horizons, 66,* 70–74.

Levin, H. (1987). Accelerated school for disadvantaged students. *Educational Leadership, 44* (6), 19–21.

Lightfoot, S. (1978). *Worlds apart: Relationships between families and schools*. New York: Basic Books.

Milne, A. M., Myers, D. E., Rosenthal, A. S., & Ginsburg, A. (1986). Single parents, working mothers, and the educational achievement of school children. *Sociology of Education, 59,* 125–139.

Mosteller, F., & Moynihan, D. P. (1972). *On equality of educational opportunity*. New York: Random House.

Mullen, B. L. (1989). Implementation of parent involvement in math program in Creve Couer schools, Creve Couer Illinois. Paper presented at the annual meeting of the American Educational Research Assoication, San Francisco.

National Center for Health Statistics. (1991). Advance report of final natality statistics, 1989. *Monthly Vital Statistics Report, 40* (8). Hyattsville, MD: Public Health Service.

National Dissemination Study Groups (1989). *Educational programs that work*. Longmont, CO: Sopris West.

National School Boards Association (1986). Day care in the public schools. *Leadership Reports, 1,* Alexandria, VA: Author.

Natriello, G., McDill, E. L., Pallas, A. M. (1990). *Schooling disadvantaged children: Racing against catastrophe*. New York: Teachers College Press, Columbia University.

Nickse, R. S., Speicher, A. M., & Buchek, P. C. (in press). An intergenerational adult literacy project: A family intervention/prevention model. *The Journal of Reading*.

Nye, B. A. (1989). Effective parent education and involvement models and programs: Contemporary strategies for school implementation. In M. J. Fine (Ed.), *The second handbook on parent education: Contemporary perspectives* (pp. 325–345). New York: Academic.

Peterson, N. L., & Cooper, C. S. (1989). Parent education and involvement in early intervention programs for handicapped children: A different perspective on parent needs and parent-professional relationships. In M. J. Fine (Ed.), *The second handbook on parent education* (pp. 197–234). New York: Academic.

Public Law 99-457 (1986). Education of the Handicapped Act Amendments of 1986. United States Department of Education.

Power, T. J. (1985). Perceptions of competence: How parents and teachers view each other. *Psychology in the Schools, 22,* 68–78.

Rodman, H., Pratto, D., & Nelson, R. (1985). Child care arrangements and children's functioning: A comparison of self-care and adult-care children. *Developmental Psychology, 21,* 413–418.

Searls, E. F., Lewis, M. B., & Morrow, Y. B. (1982). Parents as tutors—it works!. *Reading Psychology, 3,* 117–129.

Seeley, D. (1989). A new paradigm for parent involvement. *Educational Leadership, 47* (2), 46–48.

Steinberg, L. (1986). Latchkey children and susceptibility to peer pressure: An ecological analysis. *Developmental Psychology, 22,* 433–439.

Stevenson, D. L., & Baker, D. P. (1987). The family-school relation and the child's school performance. *Child Development, 58,* 1348–1357.

Swap, S. M. (1992). Parent involvement and success for all children: What we know now. In S. L. Christenson & J. C. Conoley (Eds.), *Home-school collaboration: Enhancing children's academic and social competence* (pp. 53–80). Silver Spring, MD: National Association of School Psychologists.

Swap, S. M. (1993). *Developing home-school partnerships: From concepts to practice*. New York: Teachers College Press.

Tizard, J., Schofied, W., & Hewison, J. (1982). Collaboration between teachers and parents in assisting children's reading. *British Journal of Education, 52,* 1–15.

U.S. Department of Education (1986). *What works: Research about teaching and learning.* Washington, DC: U. S. Government Printing Office.

U.S. Department of Education (1987). *What works: Schools that work: Educating disadvantaged children.* Washington, DC: U. S. Government Printing Office.

Wang, M. C., Gennari, P., & Waxman, H. C. (1985). The Adaptive Learning Environment Model: Design, implementation, and effects. In M. C. Wang & H. J. Walberg (Eds.), *Adapting instruction to individual differences* (pp. 121–235). Berkeley, CA: McCutchen.

Chapter 10

Anderson, B. (1986). *Homework: What do national assessment results tell us?* Princeton, NJ: National Assessment of Educational Progress, Educational Testing Service (ERIC Document Reproduction Service No. 276 980).

Anesko, K. M., & Levine, F. M. (1987). *Winning the homework war.* New York: Simon and Schuster.

Brinckerhoff, J., & Vincent, L. (1986). Increasing parental decision-making at the Individualized Educational Program meeting. *Journal of the Division for Early Childhood, 11,* 46–58.

Canter, L., & Hausner, D. (1987). *Homework without tears: A parent guide for motivating children to do homework and succeed in school.* New York: Harper & Row.

Chadwick, B. A., & Day, R. C. (1971). Systematic reinforcement: Academic performance of underachieving students. *Journal of Applied Behavioral Analysis, 4,* 311–319.

Comer, J. P. & Haynes, N. M. (1991). Parent involvement in schools: An ecological approach. *The Elementary School Journal, 91,* 271–278.

Cooper, H. (1989). *Homework.* White Plains, NY: Longman.

Davies, D. (1990). *Schools Reaching Out: What have we learned? A final report: Part I.* Boston: Institute for Responsive Education.

DiPrete, T. A. (1981). *Discipline, order, and student behavior in American high schools.* Chicago: National Opinion Research Center.

Epstein, J. L. (1983). *Homework practices, achievements, and behaviors of elementary school students.* Baltimore, MD: Johns Hopkins University, Center for the Social Organization of Schools (ERIC Document Reproduction Service No. 250 351).

Epstein, J. L. (1984, Winter). School policy and parent involvement: Research results. *Educational Horizons,* pp. 70–72.

Epstein, J. L. (1986). Parents' reactions to teacher practices of parent involvement. *The Elementary School Journal, 86,* 277–294.

Epstein, J. L. (1987a). Parent involvement: What research says to administrators. *Education and Urban Society, 19,* 119–136.

Epstein, J. L. (1987b). What principals should know about parent involvement. *Principal, 66,* 6–9.

Epstein, J. L. (in press). Parent-teacher conferences. In *Encyclopedia of School Administration and Supervision.* Phoenix, AZ: Oryx.

Epstein, J. L., & Becker, H. J. (1982). Teachers' reported practices of parent involvement: Problems and possibilities. *The Elementary School Journal, 83,* 103–111.

Epstein, J. L., & Dauber, S. L. (1991). School programs and teacher practices of parent involvement in inner-city elementary and middle schools. *The Elementary School Journal, 91,* 289–305.

Epstein, J. L., Jackson, V. E., & Salinas, K. C. (1992). *Manual for teachers: Teachers Involve Parents in Schoolwork (TIPS) language arts and science/health interactive homework in the middle grades.* Center on Families, Communities, Schools, and Children's Learning. Baltimore, MD: Johns Hopkins University.

Epstein, J. L., & Salinas, K. C. (1991). *Teachers Involve Parents in Schoolwork (TIPS): Social studies and art manual.* Baltimore, MD: Johns Hopkins University, Center on Families, Communities, Schools, and Children's Learning.

Epstein, J. L., & Salinas, K. C. (1992). *Manual for teachers: Teachers Involve Parents in Schoolwork (TIPS) math and science interactive homework in the elementary grades.* Baltimore, MD: Johns Hopkins University, Center on Families, Communities, Schools, and Children's Learning.

Fine, M. J. (1980). The parent education movement: An introduction. In M. J. Fine (Ed.), *Handbook on parent education* (pp. 3–26). New York: Academic.

Fredrick, W. C., & Walberg, H. J. (1980). Learning as a function of time. *Journal of Educational Research, 73,* 183–194.

Galloway, J., & Sheridan, S. M. (in press). Implementing scientific practices through case studies: Examples using home-school interventions and consultation. *Journal of School Psychology.*

Galloway, J., & Sheridan, S. M. (1992, March). Parent-teacher consultation: Forging home-school partnerships in treating academic underachievement. Paper presented at the annual meeting of the National Association of School Psychologists, Nashville.

Graue, M. E., Weinstein, T., & Walberg, H. J. (1983, April). School-based home instructino and learning: A quantitative synthesis. Paper presented at the annual meeting of the American Educational Research Association, Montreal, Canada.

Harris, V. W., & Sherman, J. A. (1974). Homework assignments, consequences, and class performance in social studies and mathematics. *Journal of Applied Behavior Analysis, 7,* 505–519.

Hart, D., & Rechif, M. (1986). *Mind movers: Creative homework assignments—Grades 3–12.* New York: Addison-Wesley.

Hauser-Cram, J. (1983). *A question of balance: Relationships between teachers and parents.* Doctoral dissertation, Harvard Graduate School of Education.

Henderson, A. T., Marburger, C. L., & Ooms, T. (1986). *Beyond the bake sale: An educator's guide to working with parents.* Columbia, MD: National Committee for Citizens in Education.

Huang, L. N. (1992, March). *Elements of cultural competence.* Paper presented at the 24th Annual Convention of the National Association of School Psychologists, Nashville, TN.

Jenson, W. R., Sheridan, S. M., Olympia, D., & Andrews, D. (in press). Homework and disabled students: A practical parent-based approach. *Journal of Learning Disabilities.*

Keith, T. Z. (1982). Time spent on homework: A large sample path analysis. *Journal of Educational Research, 74,* 248–253.

Keith, T. Z. (1987). Children and homework. In A. Thomas & J. Grimes (Eds.) *Children's needs: Psychological perspectives* (pp. 275–282). Washington DC: NASP Publications.

Kelley, M. L. (1990). *School-home notes: Promoting children's classroom success*. New York: Guilford.

Kelley, M. L., & Carper, L. B. (1988). Home-based reinforcement procedures. In J. C. Witt, S. N. Elliott, & F. M. Gresham (Eds.), *Handbook of behavior therapy in education* (pp. 419–438). New York: Plenum.

Kuepper, J. E. (1987). *Homework helpers: A guide for parents offering assistance*. Minneapolis, MN: Educational Media Corporation.

Kramer, J. J. (1990). Training parents as behavior change agents: Successes, failures, and suggestions for school psychologists. In T. B. Gutkin & C. R. Reynolds (Eds.), *Handbook of school psychology*. 2d ed. (pp. 683–702). New York: Wiley.

Leler, H. (1983). Parent education and involvement in relation to the schools and to parents of school-aged children. In R. Haskins & D. Adams (Eds.), *Parent education and public policy* (pp. 141–180). Norwood, NJ: Ablex.

Malen, B., & Ogawa, R. (1988). Professional-patron influence on site-based governance councils: A confounding case study. *Educational Evaluation adn Policy Analysis, 10,* 251–270.

Neville, M. H., & Jenson, W. R. (in press). *What, me worry? Practical solutions to everyday parenting problems*. Longmont, CO: Sopris-West.

Olympia, D. E., Jenson, W. R., & Neville, M. R. (1990). *Do-it-yourself homework manual: A sanity saver for parents*. Unpublished manuscript. Department of Educational Psychology, University of Utah.

Olympia, D., Sheridan, S. M., & Jenson, W. R. (1994). Homework: A natural means of home-school collaboration. *School Psychology Quarterly, 9,* 60–80.

Olympia, D., Sheridan, S. M., Jenson, W. R., & Andrews, D. (1994). Using student managed interventions to increase homework completion and accuracy. *Journal of Applied Behavioral Analysis, 27,* 85–100.

Paschal, R. A., Weinstein, T. & Walberg, H. J. (1984). The effects of homework on learning: A quantitative synthesis. *Journal of Educational Research, 78,* 97–104.

Polachek, S. W., Kniesner, T. J., & Harwood, H. J. (1978). Educational production functions. *Educational Researcher, 10,* 7–17.

Rousseau, M. A., Poulson, C. L., & Salzberg, C. L. (1984). Naturalistic procedures for homework participation by inner-city middle school students. *Education and Treatment of Children, 7,* 1–15.

Rutter, M., Maughn, B., Mortimore, P., Ouston, J., & Smith, A. (1979). *Fifteen thousand hours: Secondary schools and their effects on children*. Cambridge, MA: Harvard University Press.

Searls, E. F., Lewis, M. B., & Morrow, Y. B. (1982). Parents as tutors—it works!. *Reading Psychology, 3,* 117–129.

Sheridan, S. M. (1993). Models for working with parents. In J. E. Zins, T. R. Kratochwill, & S. N. Elliott (Eds.), *Handbook of consultation services for children: Applications in educational and clinical settings* (pp. 110–133). San Francisco: Jossey Bass.

Sheridan, S. M. (1992). Consultant and client outcomes of competency-based behavioral consultation training. *School Psychology Quarterly, 7,* 245–270.

Sheridan, S. M., & Colton, D. L. (in press). Conjoint behavioral consultation: A review and case study. *Journal of Educational and Psychological Consultation*.

Sheridan, S. M., & Kratochwill, T. R. (1992). Behavioral parent-teacher consultation: Conceptual and research considerations. *Journal of School Psychology, 30,* 117–139.

Sheridan, S. M., Kratochwill, T. R., & Elliott, S. N. (1990). Behavioral consultation with parents and teachers: Delivering treatment for socially withdrawn children. *School Psychology Review, 19,* 33–52.

Sheridan, S. M., Kratochwill, T. R., & Bergan, J. R. (in press). *Conjoint behavioral consultation: A procedural manual.* New York: Plenum.

Sheridan, S. M., & Steck, M. (1993, April). Acceptability of conjoint behavioral consultation: A national survey of school psychologists. Paper presented at the annual meeting of the National Association of School Psychologists, Washington, D.C.

Swap, S. (1990). *Schools Reaching Out and success for all children: Two case studies.* Boston: Institute for Responsive Education.

Swap, S. M. (1992). Parent involvement and success for all children: What we know now. In S. L. Christenson & J. C. Conoley (Eds.), *Home-school collaboration: Enhancing children's academic and social competence* (pp. 53–80). Silver Spring, MD: National Association of School Psychologists.

Swap, S. (1993). *Developing home-school partnerships: From concepts to practice.* New York: Teachers College Press.

Tangri, S., & Moles, O. (1987). Parents and the community. In V. Richardson-Koehler (Ed.), *Educator's handbook: A research perspective* (pp. 519–550). New York: Longman.

Taverne, A., & Sheridan, S. M. (in press). Parent training in interactive book reading: An investigation of its effects with families at risk. *School Psychology Quarterly.*

Tizard, J., Schofied, W., & Hewison, J. (1982). Collaboration between teachers and parents in assisting children's reading. *British Journal of Education, 52,* 1–15.

Williams, M. (1989). *Neighborhood organizing for urban school reform.* New York: Teachers College Press.

Zeldin, S. (1990). *Organizational structures and interpersonal relations: Policy implications for Schools Reaching Out.* Boston: Institute for Responsive Education.

Chapter 11

Charney, H. (1993). Project achievement: A six-year study of a dropout prevention program in bilingual schools. *Social Work in Education, 15* (2), 113–117.

Chaskin, R. J., & Richman, H. A. (1993). Concerns about school-linked services: Institution-based versus community-based models. *Education and Urban Society, 25,* 201–211.

Clark T. A. (1992). Collaboration to build competence: The urban superintendents' perspective. *The ERIC Review, 21* (2), 2–6.

Gajar, A., Goodman, L., & McAfee, J. (1993). *Secondary schools and beyond: Transition of individuals with mild disabilities.* Columbus, OH: Merrill.

Gonder, P. O. (1981). Exchanging school and community resources. In D. Davies (Ed.), *Communities and their schools* (pp. 297–329). New York: McGraw-Hill.

Hart, T. E. (1988). *Building Coalitions for Support of Schools.* Eugene, OR: OSSC, University of Oregon. (Eric Document Reproduction Service No. ED 297482).

Kirst, M. W. (1993). Financing school-linked services. *Education and Urban Society, 25,* 166–174.

Kuhn, S. E. (Spring, 1990). How business helps schools. *Fortune, 121* (12), 91–94.

Jehl, J., & Kirst, M. (1993). Getting ready to provide school-linked services: What schools must do. *Education and Urban Society, 25,* 153–165.

McDonnell, J., Wilcox, B., & Hardman, M. L. (1991). *Secondary programs for students with developmental disabilities.* Boston: Allyn & Bacon.

Mulak, G., Cohen, S. T., & Teets-Grimm, K. (1992). Hospitals and school districts: Creating a partnerships for child protection services. *Social Work in Health Care, 17* (1), 39–51.

National Association of State Boards of Education (1992). *Partners in education improvement: Schools, parents, and the community.* Alexandria, VA: Author.

National School Boards Association (1991). *LINK-UP: A resource directory for interagency collaborations to help children achieve.* Alexandria, VA: Author.

Neubert, D. A., Tilson, G. P., Jr., & Ianacone, R. N. (1989). Postsecondary transition needs and employment patterns of individuals with mild disabilities. *Exceptional Children, 55,* 494–500.

Peterson, N. L. (1991). Interagency collaboration under Part H: The key to comprehensive, multidisciplinary, coordinated infant/toddler intervention services. *Journal of Early Intervention, 15,* 89–105.

Santa Ana Unified School District (1993). End of year report: 1992–1993. Santa Ana, CA.

Sheridan, S. M. (in press). Fostering school/community relationships. In A. Thomas & J. Grimes (Eds.), *Best practices in school psychology—III.* Silver Springs, MD: National Association of School Psychologists.

Soler, M., & Shauffer, C. (1993). Fighting fragmentation: Coordination of services for children and families. *Education and Urban Society, 25* (2), 129–140.

Tangri, S., & Moles, O. (1987). Parents and the community. In V. Richardson-Koehler (Ed.), *Educator's handbook: A research perspective* (pp. 519–545). New York: Longman.

Wimmer, D. (1981). Functional learning curricula in the secondary schools. *Exceptional Children, 47,* 610–616.

Chapter 12

Allen-Meares, P., Pugach, M. (1982). Facilitating interdisciplinary collaboration on behalf of handicapped children and youth. *Teacher Education and Special Education, 5* (1), 30–36.

Bergan, J. R. & Kratochwill, T. R. (1990). Behavioral consultation. New York: Plenum.

Blaine, R., & Sobsy, R. (1983). Implementing transdisciplinary services for severely handicapped persons. *Special Education in Canada, 58,* 12–14.

Carr, W., & Kemmis, S. (1983). *Becoming critical: Knowing through action research.* Geelong, Victoria: Deakin University Press.

Dowhower, S. L., Melvin, M. P., & Sizemore, P. (1990). Improving writing instruction through teacher action research. *Journal of Staff Development, 11* (3), 22–27.

Epstein, J. L., Lockard, B. L., & Dauber, S. L. (1991). Staff development for middle school education. *Journal of Staff Development, 12* (1), 36–41.

Family Education Rights and Privacy Act of 1974. 20 U.S.C.A. Section 123g, with accompanying regulations set down in 45 C.F.R. Part 99.

Fuchs, D., Fuchs, L. S., Dulan, J., Roberts, H., & Fernstrom, P. (1992). Where is the research on consultation effectiveness? *Journal of Educational and Psychological Consultation, 3,* 151–174.

Golightly, C. J. (1987). Transdisciplinary training: A step forward in special education teacher preparation. *Teacher Education and Special Education, 10,* (3), 126–130.

Gove, M. K., & Kennedy-Calloway, C. (1992). Action research: Empowering teachers to work with at risk students. *Journal of Reading, 35,* 526–534.

Graden, J. L., Casey, A., & Bonstrom, O. (1985). Implementing a prereferral intervention system: Part II. The data. *Exceptional Children, 51,* 487–496.

Gutkin, T. B., & Curtis, M. J. (1990). School-based consultation: Theory, techniques, and research. In T. B. Gutkin & C. R. Reynolds (Eds.) The handbook of school psychology. 2d ed. (pp. 577–611). New York: Wiley.

Holmes Group (1986). *Tomorrow's teachers.* East Lansing, MI: Author.

Holmes Group (1990). *Tomorrow's schools.* East Lansing, MI: Author.

Howey, K. R. (1985). Six major functions of staff development: An expanded imperative. *Journal of Teacher Education, 36,* 58–64.

Hughes, J. N. (1986). Ethical issues in school consultation. *School Psychology Review, 15,* 489–499.

Humes, C. W., & Hohenshil, T. H. (1987). Elementary counselors, school psychologists, school social workers: Who does what? *Elementary School Guidance and Counseling,* 37–45.

Johnson, D. W., & Johnson, F. P. (1991). *Joining together: Group therapy and group skills.* 4th ed. Englewood Cliffs, NJ: Prentice-Hall.

Jones, E. V., & Lowe, J. (1990). Changing teacher behavior: Effective staff development. *Adult Learning, 1* (7), 8–10.

Jones, K. H., & Bender, W. N. (1993). Utilization of paraprofessionals in special education: A review of the literature. *Remedial and Special Education, 14,* 7–14.

Kratochwill, T. R., & Bergan, J. R. (1990). *Behavioral consultation in applied settings: An individual guide.* New York: Plenum.

Kratochwill, T. R., Elliott, S. N., & Rotto, P. J. (1990). Best practices in behavioral consultation. In A. Thomas & J. Grimes (Eds.), *Best practices in school psychology–II* (pp. 147–169). Washington, DC: NASP.

Kosmidou, C., & Usher, R. (1991). Facilitation in action research. *Interchange, 22* (4), 24–40.

Kyle, D. W., & Hovda, R. A. (1987). Action research: Comments on current trends and future possibilities. *Peabody Journal of Education, 64,* 170–175.

Liston, D. P., & Zeichner, K. M. (1990). Reflective teaching and action research in preservice teacher education. *Journal of Education for Teaching, 16,* 235–254.

Merenbloom, E. Y. (1984). Staff development: The key to effective middle schools. *NASSP Bulletin, 68,* 24–33.

Miller, D. M., & Pine, G. J. (1990). Advancing professional inquiry for educational improvement through action research. *Journal of Staff Development, 11* (3), 56–61.

Natriello, G., McDill, E. L., & Pallas, A. M. (1990). *Schooling disadvantaged children: Racing against catastrophe.* New York: Teachers College Press.

Oja, S. N. & Pine G. J. (1987). Collaborative action research: Teachers' stages of development and school contexts. *Peabody Journal of Education, 64,* 96–115.

Piersel, W. (1985). Behavioral consultation: An approach to problem solving in educational settings. In J. R. Bergan (Ed.), *School psychology in contemporary society: An introduction* (pp. 252–280). Columbus, OH: Merrill.

Prasse, D. P., & Fafard, M. (1982). Interdisciplinary training and professional interaction: A training challenge. *Teacher Education and Special Education, 5,* 26–29.

Pugach, M. & Allen-Meares, P. (1985). Collaboration at the preservice level: Instructional and evaluation activities. *Teacher Education and Special Education, 8,* 3–11.

Roach, V. (1991). Special education: New questions in an era of reform. *Issues in Brief: National Association of State Boards of Education, 11* (6), 1–7.

Ross, D. D. (1987). Action research for preservice teachers: A description of why and how. *Peabody Journal of Education, 64,* 131–150.

Sapon-Shevin, M. (1987). The national education reports and special education: Implications for students. *Exceptional Children, 53,* 300–307.

Smylie, M. A., & Conyers, J. G. (1991). Changing conceptions of teaching influence the future of staff development. *Journal of Staff Development, 12* (1), 12–16.

Wallace (1987).

Welch, M. (1989). A cultural perspective and the second wave of educational reform. *Journal of Learning Disabilities, 22,* 537–540.

Welch, M., & Sheridan, S. M. (1993). Educational partnerships in teacher education: Reconceptualizing how teacher candidates are prepared for teaching students with disabilities. *Teacher-in-Action Education, 15,* (3) 35–46.

Welch, M., Sheridan, S. M., Hart, A. W., Fuhriman, A., Connell, M., & Stoddart, T. (1992). An interdisciplinary approach in preparing professionals for educational partnerships. *Journal of Educational and Psychological Consultation, 3,* 1–23.

Credits

Table 3-4 *Criteria for Judging the Adequacy of an Action Plan*

From *Collaboration in the Schools: An Inservice and Preservice Curriculum for Teachers, Support Staff, and Administrators. Instructor's Manual* (p. 218) by J. F. West, L. Idol, and G. Cannon, 1989, Austin, TX: Pro Ed. Copyright 1989 by Pro-Ed, Inc. Adapted by permission.

Table 3-5 *Decision-making Rules for Analyzing Data Trends*

From *Collaboration in the Schools: An Inservice and Preservice Curriculum for Teachers, Support Staff, and Administrators. Instructor's Manual* (p. 233) by J. F. West, L. Idol, and G. Cannon, 1989, Austin, TX: Pro Ed. Copyright 1989 by Pro-Ed, Inc. Adapted by permission.

Table 4-2 *Suggestions for Sending Messages*

From *Joining Together: Group Theory and Group Skills* 4th ed. (p. 110) by D. W. Johnson and F. P. Johnson, 1991, Englewood Cliffs: Prentice Hall. Copyright 1991 by Allyn & Bacon. Adapted by permission.

Figure 6-2 *An Advanced Organizer for an Ecological Assessment Interview*

From "Ecological assessment: A collaborative approach to planning instructional interventions" by M. Welch, 1994, *Intervention in School and Clinic, 29,* pp. 160-164. Copyright (1994) by Pro-Ed, Inc. Reprinted by permission.

Figure 9-1 *Epstein's Overlapping Spheres of Influence Model*

From *Social Intervention: Potential and Constraints* (p. 127) by K. Hurrelmann, F. X. Kaufmann, and F. Losel (Eds.), 1987, New York, de Gruyter. Copyright 1987 by de Gruyter. Reprinted by permission.

Table 10-2 *Killer Phrases*

From *Beyond the Bake Sale: An Educator's Guide to Working with Parents* (p. 67) by A. T. Henderson, C. L. Marburger, and T. Ooms, 1986, Columbia, Maryland, National Committee for Citizens in Education. Copyright 1986 by National Committee for Citizens in Education. Adapted with permission.

Table 10-4 *Procedures for Establishing Home-School Programs*

From *Beyond the Bake Sale: An Educator's Guide to Working with Parents* (pp. 46-49) by A. T. Henderson, C. L. Marburger, and T. Ooms, 1986, Columbia, Maryland, National Committee for Citizens in Education. Copyright 1986 by National Committee for Citizens in Education. Adapted with permission.

Table 10-7* *Process and Outcome Goals of Conjoint Behavioral Consultation

From "Behavioral parent-teacher consultation: Conceptual and research considerations" by S. M. Sheridan and T. R. Kratochwill, 1992, *Journal of School Psychology, 30*, p. 124. Copyright 1992 by Pergamon Press. Reprinted by permission.

Figure 10-1* *Structural Model for Conjoint Behavioral Consultation

From *The Regular Education Initiative* (p. 206) by J. W. Lloyd, N. N. Singh, and A. C. Repp, 1991, Pacific Grove, CA: Brooks/Cole Publishing Company. Copyright 1991 by Brooks/Cole Publishing Company. Reprinted by permission.

Figure 10-2* *Sample Home-School Note for Primary Students

From *What, Me Worry? Practical Solutions to Everyday Parenting Problems* (p. 45) by M. H. Neville and W. R. Jenson, 1994, Longmont, CO: Sopris West. Copyright 1994 by W. R. Jenson, Reprinted by permission.

Index